Six Sigma DMAIC and Markov Chain Monte Carlo Applications to Financial Risk Management

Vojo Bubevski
Vojo Bubevski Consulting, UK

A volume in the Advances in Finance, Accounting, and Economics (AFAE) Book Series

Published in the United States of America by
IGI Global
Business Science Reference (an imprint of IGI Global)
701 E. Chocolate Avenue
Hershey PA, USA 17033
Tel: 717-533-8845
Fax: 717-533-8661
E-mail: cust@igi-global.com
Web site: http://www.igi-global.com

Library of Congress Cataloging-in-Publication Data

CIP Data Pending
ISBN: 979-8-3693-3787-5
eISBN: 979-8-3693-3788-2

This book is published in the IGI Global book series Advances in Finance, Accounting, and Economics (AFAE) (ISSN: 2327-5677; eISSN: 2327-5685)

British Cataloguing in Publication Data
A Cataloguing in Publication record for this book is available from the British Library.

For electronic access to this publication, please contact: eresources@igi-global.com.

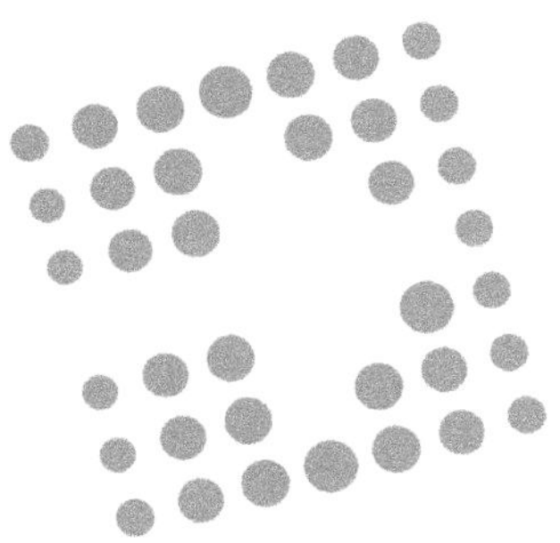

Advances in Finance, Accounting, and Economics (AFAE) Book Series

Ahmed Driouchi
Al Akhawayn University, Morocco

ISSN:2327-5677
EISSN:2327-5685

Mission

In our changing economic and business environment, it is important to consider the financial changes occurring internationally as well as within individual organizations and business environments. Understanding these changes as well as the factors that influence them is crucial in preparing for our financial future and ensuring economic sustainability and growth.

The **Advances in Finance, Accounting, and Economics (AFAE)** book series aims to publish comprehensive and informative titles in all areas of economics and economic theory, finance, and accounting to assist in advancing the available knowledge and providing for further research development in these dynamic fields.

Coverage

- Investments and Derivatives
- Wages and Employment
- Managerial Accounting
- E-Finance
- Economics Geography
- Microeconomics
- Public Finance
- Evidence-Based Studies
- E-Accounting
- Environmental And Social Accounting

IGI Global is currently accepting manuscripts for publication within this series. To submit a proposal for a volume in this series, please contact our Acquisition Editors at Acquisitions@igi-global.com or visit: http://www.igi-global.com/publish/.

The Advances in Finance, Accounting, and Economics (AFAE) Book Series (ISSN 2327-5677) is published by IGI Global, 701 E. Chocolate Avenue, Hershey, PA 17033-1240, USA, www.igi-global.com. This series is composed of titles available for purchase individually; each title is edited to be contextually exclusive from any other title within the series. For pricing and ordering information please visit http://www.igi-global.com/book-series/advances-finance-accounting-economics/73685. Postmaster: Send all address changes to above address.

Titles in this Series

For a list of additional titles in this series, please visit: http://www.igi-global.com/book-series/advances-finance-accounting-economics/73685

Financial Inclusion, Sustainability, and the Influence of Religion and Technology
Awais Ur Rehman (Faculty of Management Sciences, University of Central Punjab, Pakistan) and Arsalan Haneef Malik (College of Business Management, Department of Accounting and Finance, Institute of Business Management (IoBM), Karachi, Pakistan)
Business Science Reference • © 2024 • 324pp • H/C (ISBN: 9798369314753) • US $270.00

Recent Developments in Financial Management and Economics
Abdelkader Mohamed Sghaier Derbali (Taibah University, Saudi Arabia)
Business Science Reference • © 2024 • 436pp • H/C (ISBN: 9798369326831) • US $325.00

Issues of Sustainability in AI and New-Age Thematic Investing
Mohammad Irfan (NSB Academy, India) Khaled Hussainey (University of Portsmouth, UK) Syed Ahmad Chan Bukhari (St. John's University, USA) and Yunyoung Nam (Department of Computer Science and Engineering, Soonchunhyang University, South Korea)
Business Science Reference • © 2024 • 295pp • H/C (ISBN: 9798369332825) • US $325.00

Exploring Central Bank Digital Currencies Concepts, Frameworks, Models, and Challenges
Guneet Kaur (University of Stirling, UK) Pooja Lekhi (University Canada West, Canada) and Simriti Popli (Kaplan International College, UK)
Business Science Reference • © 2024 • 359pp • H/C (ISBN: 9798369318829) • US $325.00

Harnessing Blockchain-Digital Twin Fusion for Sustainable Investments
Syed Hasan Jafar (Woxsen University, India) Raul Villamarin Rodriguez (Woxsen University, India) Hemachandran Kannan (Woxsen University, India) Shakeb Akhtar (Woxsen University, India) and Philipp Plugmann (SRH Hochschule für Gesundheit Gera, Germany)
Business Science Reference • © 2024 • 441pp • H/C (ISBN: 9798369318782) • US $290.00

Harnessing Technology for Knowledge Transfer in Accountancy, Auditing, and Finance
Samuel Kwok (Xi'an Jiaotong-Liverpool University, China) Mohamed Omran (Xi'an Jiaotong-Liverpool University, China) and Poshan Yu (Xi'an Jiaotong-Liverpool University, China & European Business University of Luxembourg, Luxembourg)
Business Science Reference • © 2024 • 279pp • H/C (ISBN: 9798369313312) • US $275.00

701 East Chocolate Avenue, Hershey, PA 17033, USA
Tel: 717-533-8845 x100 • Fax: 717-533-8661
E-Mail: cust@igi-global.com • www.igi-global.com

Dedication

This book is dedicated to the author for achieving a substantial career, publishing many written works in eminent international conferences and journals, being featured as a guest speaker at several prominent conferences internationally. He published many written works in eminent international conferences and journals and was featured as a guest speaker at several prominent conferences internationally. The author published one chapter in an editor's book. He also published 72 books in multiple languages: 12 in English; eight in French, Italian, Portuguese, Russian, and Spanish; seven in German; five in Dutch and Polish; and one in Macedonian. Also, he created his website "Bubevski Consulting™", which is available on the Internet (Link: https://bubevski-consulting.website/).

The author's distinguished book "Six Sigma Improvements for Basel III and Solvency II in Financial Risk Management" published by IGI Global was recognised by the "BookAuthority" in the "100 Best Financial Risk Management Books of All Time" and currently ranked with 3.93 stars (Ref. https://bookauthority.org/author/Vojo-Bubevski).

Bernstein stated, "The risk will always be there, so we must explore many interesting tools that can help us to control risks we cannot avoid taking" (Bernstein & Damodaran 1998). The author's Six Sigma DMAIC Methods are one such tool.

Table of Contents

Preface

Most industries today recognise Six Sigma as a standard means to accomplish process and quality improvements and increase their customers' satisfaction. The financial industry has accepted and successfully applied Six Sigma, but only to improve its operations and provide higher-quality services to its customers. Six Sigma introductory topics for financial professionals were published in September 2003 (Stamatis 2003). Hayler and Nichols (2006) showed how American Express, Bank of America, and Wachovia have applied Six Sigma, Lean, and Process Management to their service-based operations by providing specific, real-world examples and offering step-by-step solutions. Also, Tarantino and Cernauskas (2009) provided an operational risk framework by using proven quality control methods such as Six Sigma and Total Quality Management (TQM) in financial risk management to forestall major risk management failures.

In the author's book, *Novel Six Sigma Approaches to Risk Assessment and Management,* published by IGI Global (Bubevski 2017), a new Six Sigma DMAIC (Define, Measure, Analyse, Improve, and Control) generic method for improving Risk Management was presented. Elaboration on applications of this new method to Risk Management was presented in the following fields: Finance, Oil and Gas, Research and Development, Software Engineering, Project Management, Agriculture, Production, and Retail.

Subsequently, the author published his original work, *Six Sigma Improvements for Basel III and Solvency II in Financial Risk Management* (Bubevski 2018). The significant recognition of the original work (Bubevski 2018), encouraged the author to work on another book, which is the book presented herein. The book is enhanced with Sensitivity and What-If Analysis, and Markov Chain Monte Carlo.

The book elaborates on comprehensive applications of Six Sigma DMAIC, as well as advanced novel concepts and tools for Financial Risk Management. The concepts and tools include Stochastic Models, Simulation, Optimisation, Six Sigma DMAIC, Markov Chain Monte Carlo, Sensitivity Analysis, and What-If Analysis.

The book is practical and it only provides advanced methods and tools to improve the financial risk management process. That is, the book does not teach financial risk management concepts.

Mostly, the book is purposed for experienced financial managers in general, and specifically financial risk analysts and financial risk managers. In addition, the book will be very beneficial to academics in teaching and practicing Financial Risk Management. In addition, the other stakeholders would derive benefit from the book as it is self-explanatory. The operations in the book can be also performed by average manager-level financial industry employee of a company. Also, it will be useful to the degree students studying the topics of Finance in general, and specifically, Financial Risk Management, Risk and Decision Analysis, and Operations Research providing simple examples for practicing on their subjects of study.

The book assumes a working knowledge of the subject. By applying the proposed approach, readers will substantially improve and facilitate the financial risk measurement and assessment, which will ultimately and systematically enhance the financial risk management in their financial institutions. This is an important objective, which if achieved, will gain significant benefits.

Financial risk managers and regulators of financial institutions define risk as the uncertainty of outcomes and the negative consequences that it may have on an institution, and both aim at enhancing the resiliency of institutions to adverse situations. As a result of their efforts, risks became better identified, assessed, and monitored, risk practices improved and risk models became more widespread.

Financial risks are defined according to the sources of uncertainty. The major classes of financial risks are credit risk, market risk, liquidity risk, interest rate risk, and foreign exchange risk.

Today, risk management has become a core central function for financial firms, banks, funds, and insurance companies. Financial risk management is a process of identification, assessment, and prioritisation of risk followed by the coordination of actions and deployment of resources to minimise, monitor, and control the impact of undesired events. The objective of financial risk management is to ensure that uncertainty does not affect or has a minimal impact on, the achievement of the goals of a financial institution.

Financial crises can expose underlying faults in the financial institution's systems and processes. The 2008 financial crisis exposed the failure of a prevalent laissez-faire economic and regulatory philosophy that financial institutions could and should manage their own risk with little outside interference. Now, many see the danger of fragile financial service networks bringing systemic risk to the real economy. So, financial organisations face increasing regulations such as Basel III for banks, and Solvency II for insurance. To meet the requirements of the increased and rigorous regulation, financial organisations are striving to improve their formal risk assessment and management processes, which is their ultimate objective. The major focus of Basel III and Solvency II is the solvency risk.

Solvency risk is the risk of being unable to absorb losses with the available capital. According to the principle of "capital adequacy" promoted by regulators, a minimum capital base is required to absorb unexpected losses potentially arising from the current risks of the firm. Solvency issues arise when the unexpected losses exceed the capital level, as they did during the 2008 financial crisis for several firms. This capital buffer sets the default probability of the bank/insurer, i.e., the probability that potential losses exceed the capital base.

To help financial organisations to achieve their ultimate objective and meet the Basel III and Solvency II requirements, this book broadly presents applications of advanced tools and methods for improving Risk Management in Finance specifically elaborating on different aspects of financial risk analysis and management.

Bernstein stated, *"The risk will always be there, so we must explore many interesting tools that can help us to control risks we cannot avoid taking"* (Bernstein and Damodaran 1998). As inspired by Bernstein, the Six Sigma DMAIC structured framework, as well as new risk analysis concepts, was applied to Financial Risk Management to improve the process and help control financial risks.

In addition to conventional stochastic optimisation (Lee, C.F., Lee, A.C., and J. Lee 2010) and Monte Carlo simulation (Bratley et al 1983, Rubinstein & Kroese 2008), the approach tactically applies the DMAIC framework to Financial Risk Management. DMAIC and Financial Risk Management are generic, compatible, and complementary processes. The DMAIC structured framework tactically merges the two processes resulting in a powerful synergetic tool. Also, the risk analysis concepts such as Neural Networks, Sensitivity Analysis, What-If Analysis, and Markov Chain Monte Carlo, significantly enhanced the controlling of financial risks.

The methods apply to internal models for Solvency II and Basel III. By using it, financial institutions can reduce the solvency risk, capital requirements, and Value at Risk (VAR), thus achieving higher business capabilities and competitiveness, which is their ultimate objective.

It should be noted that this book will demonstrate the application of the approach based on real-world published financial projects including projects' data. However, for elaboration, hypothetical scenarios are used to emulate real-world published projects. In the research and demonstration experiments, Microsoft™ Excel® was used for modelling; and Palisade™ @RISK® and RISKOptimizer® were used for Monte Carlo simulation and stochastic optimisation respectively. The terms simulation and Monte Carlo simulation are interchangeably used in the book.

This book elaborates on Six Sigma DMAIC and Markov Chain Monte Carlo applications to Financial Risk Management. The Financial Risk Management with Six Sigma DMAIC is improved with Sensitivity Analysis and What-If Analysis. In addition, the book is enhanced with Markov Chain Monte Carlo for Price Evolution.

The book elaborates on the following 14 chapters i) Six Sigma Quotation Process; ii) Six Sigma DMAIC Yield Analysis; iii) Six Sigma DMAIC Failure Rate; iv) Six Sigma DMAIC Failure Rate with RiskTheo Functions; v) Financial Statements Predictions; vi) New Products Profitability Analysis; vii) Banks' Credit Losses Analysis; viii) Discounted Cash Flow Projections; ix) Comprehensive Investment Risk Assessment; x) Risk Assessment in Investment Portfolio; xi) Estimating Loan Interest rates and Payments; xii) Bank Loan Portfolio Credit Risk Analysis; xiii) Price Evolution with Markov Chain Monte Carlo; and xiv) Financial Risk Management Future Directions.

Vojo Bubevski
Vojo Bubevski Consulting, UK

REFERENCES

Bernstein, P. L., & Damodaran, A. (1998). *Investment Management*. John Wiley & Sons.

Bratley, P. F., & Bennett, L. (1983). *A Guide to Simulation*. Springer-Verlag. doi:10.1007/978-1-4684-0167-7

Bubevski, V. (2016). Risk Management: A Novel Six Sigma Approach. In B. Darnel (Ed.), *Risk Management: Past Present and Future*. Nova Science Publishers.

Bubevski, V. (2017). *Novel Six Sigma Approaches to Risk Assessment and Management*. IGI Global.

Bubevski, V. (2018). *Six Sigma Improvements for Basel III and Solvency II in Financial Risk Management*. IGI Global.

Hayler, R., & Nichols, M. D. (2006). Six Sigma for Financial Services: How Leading Companies Are Driving Results Using Lean, Six Sigma, and Process Management. McGraw-Hill.

Lee, C. F., Lee, A. C., & Lee, J. (Eds.). (2010). Handbook of Quantitative Finance and Risk Management. Springer. doi:10.1007/978-0-387-77117-5

Rubinstein, R. Y., & Kroese, D. P. (2008). *Simulation and the Monte Carlo Method*. John Wiley & Sons.

Stamatis, D. H. (2003). *Six Sigma for Financial Professionals*. Wiley.

Tarantino, A., & Cernauskas, D. (2009). Risk Management in Finance: Six Sigma and Other Next-Generation Techniques. Wiley.

Acknowledgment

I would like to thank you very much my daughter for reviewing the manuscript and suggesting very relevant improvements. She has also substantially helped with the editing and formatting of the manuscript. Her contribution has been essential for the successful publication of the book.

Also, acknowledgements to Palisade Corporation for publishing the data of the real project for Risk Analysis. I have used these data for the experiments demonstrated in this book, which proved the concept of the applied approach. This substantially increased my confidence and allowed me to publish this book.

Introduction

FINANCIAL RISK MANAGEMENT

Generally, the risk is considered as a probability or threat of damage, injury, liability, loss, or any other negative occurrence that is caused by external or internal vulnerabilities, and that may be avoided through pre-emptive action. In Finance specifically, risk is defined as the randomness of the return of investments, including both positive and negative outcomes. From this perspective, a greater expected return is associated with greater variability of outcomes. However, from the aspect of financial regulators and risk managers, risk is defined as the uncertainty that has adverse consequences on earnings or wealth or the uncertainty associated with negative outcomes only. Regulations (i.e., Basel III for banking and Solvency II for insurance) aim at enhancing the resiliency of financial firms and the financial system in stressed conditions. Risk managers are generally accountable for identifying, assessing, and controlling the likelihood and the consequences of adverse events for financial organisations.

The broad classes of financial risks are credit risk, market risk, liquidity risk, and interest rate risk, which are further divided into subclasses relative to the specific events that trigger losses.

Risk management is a process that necessitates that the risks of a financial institution are identified, assessed, and controlled. Nowadays, risk management has become a core central function for financial corporations including banks, funds, and insurance companies.

Risk processes include the identification, monitoring, and control of risks. Risk models serve for measuring and quantifying risk and provide the inputs for the management processes and decisions. To be effective, they should be implemented within a dedicated organisational framework that should be enterprise-wide.

All risk processes imply that risk policies are properly defined and that the risk appetite of the firm is well defined. Within this framework, the common process for controlling risks is based on risk limits and risk delegations. Limits impose upper bounds on the potential loss of transactions, or of portfolios of transactions.

Limits aim at avoiding those adverse events, that affect a transaction or a portfolio of transactions, and impair the credit standing of the firm. Financial institutions need to segment their activities into meaningful portfolios, for example by business unit, product, or type of clients. Limits of exposure are set for each segment and down to transactions, forming a hierarchy of limits and sub-limits. For example, credit risk limits are set by segment, then by a counterparty, and then by an individual transaction. For market risk, limits can be set for specific books of trades, then desks, and then trades.

Delegations serve for decentralisation of the risk decisions, within limits. Delegations are authorisations to act and take risks on behalf of the organisation. Delegations decentralise and simplify the risk process by allowing local managers to make decisions without referring to the upper levels of the organisation, within the scope of their delegations. For example, they simplify the risk process for transactions that are small enough to be dealt with by local procedures.

Any limit system requires one or several measures of risk used for determining whether or not a transaction, or a portfolio of transactions, complies with limits. Various risk metrics are used for setting limits for credit risk. The amount at risk, or exposure, is a simple measure of the amount that could be lost in the event of a default of the borrower. Other metrics capture other dimensions of credit risk. For example, trades might be allowed only for eligible borrowers based on their credit quality. Or limits can apply to regulatory capital for credit risk, which combines various components of credit risk, exposure, loss after recoveries, and credit quality.

Credit limit systems are based on common criteria, for example, i) Diversify the commitments across various dimensions such as customers, industries, and regions; ii) Avoid lending to any borrower an amount that would increase its debt beyond its borrowing capacity; iii) The equity of the borrower sets up some reasonable limit to its debt given acceptable levels of debt/equity ratios and repayment ability; iv) Set up a maximum risk level, for example, defined by the credit standing of borrowers, above which lending is prohibited; and v) Ensure a minimum diversification across counterparties and avoid concentrations of risk on a single borrower, an industry or a region.

To be comprehensive and consistent, the limit system has to be financial institution-wide. Global limit systems aggregate all risks on any single counterparty, no matter which business unit initiates the risk, across all transactions with the financial organisation.

Generally, the financial risk assessment requires defining the risk and understanding how to measure it. Different risk models are used for risk assessment, e.g., the Capital Asset Pricing Model (CAPM), Arbitrage Pricing Model (APM), and other multifactor risk models (Damodaran 1998). Alternative measures of risk can also be used for risk assessment, e.g., Standard Deviation, Variance, Value at Risk (VAR), Conditional Value at Risk (CVAR), etc. (Clark 1998). Also, absolute risk measures are used for risk assessment such as Standard Deviation and Variance, as well as the risk measures relative to a market index (i.e., a benchmark), for example, Beta. Moreover, risk-adjusted measures can be used such as the Sharpe Ratio and Treynor Ratio (Jacob 1998). Moreover, Plantinga (2007) discussed methodologies for measuring and evaluating the performance of financial institutions for management purposes. He elaborated methods for i) Measuring returns on investment; and ii) Evaluating performance considering the Sharpe Ratio, Jensen's Alpha, Treynor Ratio, and Information Ratio, as well as the downside risk measures, i.e., Sortino Ratio and Fouse Index.

Miller (1992) argues that treatments of risk in the international management literature largely focus on particular uncertainties to the exclusion of other interrelated uncertainties. His paper develops a framework for categorizing the uncertainties faced by firms operating internationally and outlines both financial and strategic corporate risk management responses.

A paper by Hsieh (1993) demonstrates that when log price changes are not independent and identically distributed (IID), their conditional density may be more accurate than their unconditional density for describing short-term behaviour. Using the BDS test (i.e., Brock, Dechert, and Scheinkman test which detects nonlinear serial dependence in time series) of independence and identical distribution, daily log price changes in four currency futures contracts are found to be not IID. While there appear to be no predictable conditional mean changes, conditional variances are predictable and can be described by an autoregressive volatility model that seems to capture all the departures from independence and identical distribution. Based on this model, daily log price changes are decomposed into a predictable part, which is described parametrically by the autoregressive volatility model, and an unpredictable part, which can be modelled by an empirical density, either parametrically or non-parametrically. This two-step semi-nonparametric method yields a conditional density for daily log price changes, which has many uses in financial risk management.

Froot, Scharfstein, and Stein (1993) in their paper presented a general framework for analysing corporate risk management policies. By observing that if external sources of finance are costlier to corporations than internally generated funds, there will typically be a benefit to hedging. Hedging adds value to the extent that it helps ensure that a corporation has sufficient internal funds available to take advantage of attractive investment opportunities. The authors argue that this simple observation has wide-ranging implications for the design of risk management strategies. They delineate how these strategies should depend on such factors as shocks to investment and financing opportunities. They also discuss exchange rate hedging strategies for multinationals, as well as strategies involving "nonlinear" instruments like options.

Stulz (1996) in his paper presents a theory of corporate risk management that attempts to go beyond the "variance-minimisation" model that dominates most academic discussions on the subject. It argues that the primary goal of risk management is not to dampen swings in corporate cash flows or value but rather to protect against the possibility of costly lower-tail outcomes–situations that would cause financial distress or make a company unable to carry out its investment strategy. By eliminating downside risk and reducing the expected costs of financial trouble, risk management can also help a company achieve both its optimal capital structure and its optimal ownership structure. For, besides increasing corporate debt capacity, the reduction of downside risk also encourages larger equity stakes for managers by shielding their investments from "uncontrollable-s."

The paper also departs from standard finance theory in suggesting that some companies may have a comparative advantage in bearing certain financial market risks–an advantage that derives from information acquired through their normal business activities. Although such specialised information may lead some companies to take speculative positions in commodities or currencies, it is more likely to encourage "selective" hedging, a practice in which the risk manager's "view" of future price movements influences the percentage of the exposure that is hedged. To the extent that such view-taking becomes an accepted part of a company's risk management program, it is important to evaluate managers' bets on a risk-adjusted basis and relative to the market. If risk managers want to behave like money managers, they should be evaluated like money managers.

Alexander (1996) published a book discussing the mathematical applications in finance. During the past 20 years or so, and especially since the last financial crisis, the advances in mathematical applications to financial analysis and forecasting have been enormous. Mathematical methods are not only being used in forecasting but also the vitally important area of risk management. This book is the definitive source for professionals seeking an introduction to the very latest thinking on risk analysis and risk management strategies. Each chapter contains an introductory survey of the area, followed by a technical exposition of the main ideas that are at the forefront of current research.

Froot and Stein (1998) developed a framework for analysing the capital allocation and capital structure decisions facing financial institutions. The model incorporates two key features: i) value-maximising banks have a well-founded concern with risk management, and ii) not all the risks they face can be frictionlessly hedged in the capital market. This approach allows showing how bank-level risk management considerations should factor into the pricing of those risks that cannot be easily hedged. The authors examine several applications, including the evaluation of proprietary trading operations, and the pricing of non-hedgeable derivatives positions. They also compare the approach to the Risk-Adjusted Return on Capital (RAROC) methodology that has been adopted by many banks.

Christoffersen, Diebold, and Schuermann (1998) in their paper consider the question: "Is volatility forecast-ability important for long-horizon risk management, or is a traditional constant volatility assumption adequate?" The authors elaborate on this question, exploring the interface between long-horizon financial risk management and long-horizon volatility forecast-ability and, in particular, whether long-horizon volatility is forecastable enough such that volatility models are useful for long-horizon risk management.

A paper published by Diebold, Hahn, and Tay (1999) provides a framework for evaluating and improving multivariate density forecasts. Among other things, the multivariate framework is used to evaluate the adequacy of density forecasts involving cross-variable interactions, such as time-varying conditional correlations. Also, provided are conditions under which a technique of density forecast "calibration" can be used to improve deficient density forecasts. The authors show how the calibration method can be used to generate good density forecasts from econometric models, even when the conditional density is unknown. Finally, motivated by recent advances in financial risk management, provided is a detailed application to multivariate high-frequency exchange rate density forecasts.

Lawton and Jankowski (2009) edited a collection of works of some of the most prominent industry professionals and academics focussing on investment performance evaluation. Also, Meier (2009) elaborated on how institutional investors evaluate the return on investment. Standard Deviation and risk measures versus the market were utilised including Alpha, Beta Excess Return, Information Ratio, Sharpe Ratio, and Tracking Error. In addition, Busse, Goyal, and Wahal (2010) used to aggregate and average estimates of alphas for performance measurement of institutional investment management considering the return on investment.

A handbook of quantitative finance and risk management edited by Lee, C.F., Lee, A.C., and J. Lee (2010) is a combination of economics, accounting, statistics, econometrics, mathematics, stochastic process, and computer science and technology. Increasingly, the tools of financial analysis are being applied to assess, monitor, and mitigate risk, especially in the context of globalisation, market volatility, and economic crisis. This three-volume handbook is one of the most comprehensive in the field, integrating the most current theory, methodology, policy, and practical applications. Including contributions from an international array of experts, the book is unparalleled in the breadth and depth of its coverage. In Volume 1, the handbook presents an overview of quantitative finance and risk management research, covering the essential theories, policies, and empirical methodologies used in the field. Chapters provide an in-depth discussion of portfolio theory and investment analysis. Volume 2 covers options and option pricing theory and risk management. Volume 3 presents a wide variety of models and analytical tools. Throughout, the handbook extensively offers illustrative case examples and worked equations. It is an essential reference for academics, educators, students, policymakers, and practitioners.

Homaifar (2004) published a comprehensive guide to managing global financial risk. From the balance of payment exposure to foreign exchange and interest rate risk to credit derivatives and other exotic options, futures, and swaps for mitigating and transferring risk, this book provides a simple yet comprehensive analysis of complex derivatives pricing and their application in risk management. The risk posed by foreign exchange transactions stems from the volatility of the exchange rate, the volatility of the interest rates, and factors unique to individual companies which are interrelated. To protect and hedge against adverse currency and interest rate changes, multinational corporations need to take concrete steps to mitigate these risks. This book offers a thorough treatment of the price, foreign currency, and interest rate risk management practices of multinational corporations in a dynamic global economy. It lays out the pros and cons of various hedging instruments, as well as the economic cost-benefit analysis of alternative hedging vehicles. Written in a detailed yet user–friendly manner, this resource provides treasurers and other financial managers with the tools they need to manage their various exposures to credit, price, and foreign exchange risk.

Hasan, Kapadia, and Siddique (2017) debate that rating downgrades can have adverse consequences on a firm due to the feedback effect, even when ratings lack informational content. In this paper, the authors consider whether the rating agency attempts to mitigate the feedback effect through its rating actions. Using Moody's issuer ratings over 1982–2009, they show that firms with greater external financing constraints are less likely to be downgraded. The issuer bias is robust, and its economic significance increases at times when economy-wide credit spreads are unusually high. The paper documents that severely constrained firms whose ratings are affirmed or upgraded have long-term positive excess equity returns.

Dash et al (2017) established that with the rise of computing power and new analytical techniques, banks can now extract deeper and more valuable insights from their ever-growing mountains of data. And they can do it quickly, as many key processes are now automated (and many more soon will be). For risk departments, which have been using data analytics for decades, these trends present unique opportunities to better identify, measure, and mitigate risk. Critically, they can leverage their vast expertise in data and analytics to help leaders shape the strategic agenda of the bank.

Financial Risk Management is a major aspect of Basel III and Solvency II. Jorion (2011), in his book on financial risk management, presented the utilisation of the Monte Carlo Simulation for options valuation and VAR calculation. He also generally elaborated on Optimal Hedging, applying the Optimal Hedge Ratio, i.e., the minimal variance hedge ratio. In addition, he specifically described the application of Optimal Hedging in two important cases: Duration Hedging and Beta Hedging.

The new regulation requirements introduced by Basel III and Solvency II focus on the solvency risk to impose a required amount of equity value based on the risk associated with the investments of asset portfolios. The banking and insurance industry is responding to these requirements by developing internal models based essentially on the VAR, parametric (GARCH, EGARCH), and simulation (Monte Carlo) models, extended to CVAR and Copulas.

Asset and Liability Management (ALM) originated from the duration analysis proposed by Macaulay (1938) and Redington (1952). Subsequently, ALM has evolved into a powerful and integrated tool for the analysis of assets and liabilities to value not only the interest rate risk but the liquidity risk, solvency risk, firm strategies, and asset allocation as well (Bloomsbury 2012).

The frontier of ALM is based on stochastic optimisation and simulation models that involve an asset allocation approach by considering the liabilities aspect as well. Specifically, an internal Monte Carlo Simulation model for Solvency II (i.e., an ALM-market risk simulation model) was presented by Bourdeau (2009).

In addition, Adam (2007) published a comprehensive guide to ALM from a quantitative aspect with economic explanations. He presented advanced ALM stochastic models for Solvency II and Basel II & III using optimisation and simulation methodologies.

Engelmann & Rauhmeier (2006) edited a book about Basel II. This book compiles articles by various authors addressing the estimation of three key risk parameters: the probability of default (PD), loss-given default (LGD), and exposure at default (EAD). The authors identify their intended audience as risk managers and quantitative risk or rating analysts working on credit risk and regulatory issues. These groups likely will find this book an accessible reference. The exposition related to regulatory issues is quite good and worthwhile for all.

Mitra and Schwaiger (2011) published a book that brings together state-of-the-art quantitative decision models for asset and liability management in respect of pension funds, insurance companies, and banks. It takes into account new regulations and industry risks, covering new accounting standards for pension funds, Solvency II implementation for insurance companies, and Basel II accord for banks.

Editors Christodoulakis and Satchell (2007) collected papers that are beginning to appear by regulators, consultants, and academics, to provide the first collection that focuses on the quantitative side of model validation. Risk model validation is an emerging and important area of research and has arisen because of Basel I and II. These regulatory initiatives require trading institutions and lending institutions to compute their reserve capital in a highly analytic way, based on the use of internal risk models. It is part of the regulatory structure that these risk models be validated both internally and externally, and there is a great shortage of information as to best practices. The book covers the three main areas of risk: Credit Risk and Market and Operational Risk. Risk model validation is a requirement of Basel I and II. In this first collection of papers in this new and developing area of research, international authors cover model validation in credit, market, and operational risk.

Barfield (2011) covered the revised Basel Accord framework Basel III, introduced in the wake of the global financial crisis. The new measures are designed to update and strengthen the resilience of the international banking sector, and this book will cover in-depth what the new measures mean in practice. It could be essential reading for compliance, legal, and other senior management in banks, and their advisers.

Editors Cannata & Quagliariello (2011) presented expert contributions from those deeply and directly involved in the creation of the new global standards. Their book is a must-read for market practitioners and regulators who need to understand the emerging framework of financial regulation, its implications, and its impact. After three of the most tumultuous years in financial markets in living memory, the regulatory die was cast in December 2010. This book provides the reader with a comprehensive discussion of the contents of the regulatory reform, taking advantage of the knowledge of experts who contributed to shaping the new rules. With a foreword from Mario Draghi - an eminent banking official, and written by experts deeply involved in these reforms, this work provides a practical and global perspective on the new standards. The book combines technical rigor with an accessible style to provide the essential primer to the new regulatory blueprint and the rationale behind it. It discusses the technical aspects and disciplines of modern markets and provides summaries of the most important elements, the thinking behind them, how they will be implemented, and the potential repercussions.

This work focuses on the market practices that contributed to the financial turmoil and the subsequent policy response from the G20 and the Financial Stability Board that led to the proposals of the Basel Committee. Also, the book analyses the new definition of regulatory capital, the new framework for the trading book, changes to the counterparty credit risk capital rules, and the new measures for mitigating pro-cyclicality. In addition, it analyses the elements designed to complement the capital rules: the leverage ratio, a global minimum liquidity standard, initiatives regarding credit rating agencies; how to handle systemically important banks, and remuneration. Finally, it surveys the changing regulatory landscape, looking at crisis management and resolution, the impact of the new regulations, and the future architecture of financial supervision and regulation.

Bessis (2015) in his book Risk Management in Banking provided the industry's seminal reference that offers a comprehensive review of all aspects of the field. The text covers a complete range of risk topics in banking including asset-liability management, risk-based capital, value at risk, loan portfolio management, capital allocation, and other fundamental risk factors. All these topics are examined within the new mindset inspired by the financial crisis. This practical guide contains the latest information on topics such as ALM, Basel III, liquidity analysis, market risk, credit risk, derivatives, structured products, securitisations, and more. In this book, professionals will discover an easily navigable resource that is filled with research and practices that reflect the most recent changes in the field.

The Basel III handbook by Ramirez (2017) delves deep into the principles underpinning the capital dimension of Basel III to provide a more advanced understanding of real-world implementation. Going beyond the simple overview or model, this book merges theory with practice to help practitioners work more effectively within the regulatory framework and utilise the complex rules to more effectively allocate and enhance capital. A European perspective covers the CRD IV directive and associated guidance, but practitioners across all jurisdictions will find value in the strategic approach to decisions surrounding business lines and assets; an emphasis on analysis urges banks to shed unattractive positions and channel capital toward opportunities that fit their risk and return profile. Real-world cases demonstrate successful capital initiatives as models for implementation, and in-depth guidance on Basel III rules equips practitioners to more effectively utilise this complex regulatory treatment.

The specifics of Basel III implementation vary, but the underlying principles are effective around the world. This book expands upon existing guidance to provide a deeper working knowledge of Basel III utility, and the insight to use it effectively to i) Improve asset quality and risk and return profiles; ii) Adopt a strategic approach to capital allocation; iii) Compare Basel III implementation varies across jurisdictions; iv) Examine successful capital enhancement initiatives from around the world.

There is a popular misconception about Basel III being extremely conservative and a deterrent to investors seeking attractive returns. In reality, Basel III presents both the opportunity and a framework for banks to improve their assets and enhance overall capital the key factor is a true, comprehensive understanding of the regulatory mechanisms. The Handbook of Basel III Capital Enhancing Bank Capital in Practice provides advanced guidance for advanced practitioners and real-world implementation insight.

BASEL III

Basel III is a comprehensive set of reform measures, developed by the Basel Committee on Banking Supervision (BCBS), to strengthen the regulation, supervision, and risk management of the banking sector. These measures aim to i) improve the banking sector's ability to absorb shocks arising from financial and economic stress, whatever the source; ii) improve risk management and governance; and iii) strengthen banks' transparency and disclosures (Atkinson and Blundell-Wignall 2010; BCBS 2010a, 2010b, 2011; BIS 2011; Cosimano and Hakura 2011).

The evolution of the Basel Accord is presented in Table 1 (Seal 20016).

Currently, the Basel Accord for bank regulation is Basel III. Issued by the Basel Committee on Banking Supervision, the Basel III standards on capital and liquidity, along with measures from July 2009 on the trading book and structured finance, are the centrepiece of the regulatory community's response to the crisis. Even though it was implemented in January 2013, Basel III must be fully phased in by January 2019.

Table 1. Evolution of the Basel Accord

Basel I	**•Minimum risk-based capital, the definition of capital**
MRA	•Market risk treatment in the trading book; standard and internal model approaches
Basel II	•Credit Risk, Operational Risk –standard and internal model approaches •Pillars 2 and 3
Basel 2.5	•Enhanced Market Risk standards •Securitisation enhancements
Basel III	•Definition of capital, Capital buffers: pro-cyclicality and capital conservation; Leverage •Enhanced risk coverage; Liquidity framework
Review of Trading Book	•New Standardised Approach •New Trading Book Boundary •New Standards for Models

The Basel Committee on Banking Supervision (2014) issued the second consultative paper on the fundamental review of trading book capital requirements. The revisions to the capital framework set out in this paper aim to contribute to a more resilient banking sector by strengthening capital standards for market risks. They form part of the Committee's broader agenda to reform regulatory standards for banks in response to the financial crisis. The revisions in this paper also reflect the Committee's increased focus on achieving a regulatory framework that can be implemented consistently by supervisors across jurisdictions. As such, they incorporate the lessons learned from the Committee's recent investigations into the variability of market risk-weighted assets.

The financial crisis exposed material weaknesses in the overall design of the framework for capitalising on trading activities. The level of capital required against trading book exposures proved insufficient to absorb losses. As an important response to the crisis, the Committee introduced a set of revisions to the market risk framework in July 2009 (part of the "Basel 2.5" package of reforms). At the time, the Committee recognised that the Basel 2.5 revisions did not fully address the shortcomings of the framework. In response, the Committee initiated a fundamental review of the trading book regime, beginning with an assessment of "what went wrong". The Committee published the first consultative paper in May 2012. Having reflected on the comments received, this paper sets out more detailed proposals for reforming the trading book regime, including the draft text for the Basel Accord.

The Committee has focused on the following key areas as part of its review:

1. The Basel Committee on Banking Supervision provides a forum for regular cooperation on banking supervisory matters. It seeks to promote and strengthen supervisory and risk management practices globally. The Committee comprises representatives from Argentina, Australia, Belgium, Brazil, Canada, China, France, Germany, Hong Kong SAR, India, Indonesia, Italy, Japan, Korea, Luxembourg, Mexico, the Netherlands, Russia, Saudi Arabia, Singapore, South Africa, Spain, Sweden, Switzerland, Turkey, the United Kingdom, and the United States. Observers on the Basel Committee are the European Banking Authority, the European Central Bank, the European Commission, the Financial Stability Institute, and the International Monetary Fund.
2. To view the first consultative paper, see Basel Committee on Banking Supervision, Fundamental review of the trading book, May 2012 (www.bis.org/publ/bcbs219.pdf). It is intended that this sec-

ond consultative paper can be read as a standalone document, without the need for cross-reference with the first consultative paper.

3. See Basel Committee on Banking Supervision, Regulatory Consistency Assessment Programme (RCAP) – Analysis of risk-weighted assets for market risk, January 2013 (revised February 2013), www.bis.org/publ/bcbs240.pdf.

The Basel Committee on Banking Supervision (2016) provides a forum for regular cooperation on banking supervisory matters. Its objective is to enhance understanding of key supervisory issues and improve the quality of banking supervision worldwide. This document sets out revised standards for minimum capital requirements for Market Risk by the Basel Committee on Banking Supervision ("the Committee"). The text herein is intended to replace the existing minimum capital requirements for market risk in the global regulatory framework, including amendments made after the June 2006 publication of Basel II: International Convergence of Capital Measurement and Capital Standards - Comprehensive Version. Consistent with the policy rationales underpinning the Committee's three consultative papers on the Fundamental Review of the Trading Book,1 the revised market risk framework consists of the following key enhancements:

1. A revised internal models' approach (IMA). The new approach introduces a more rigorous model approval process that enables supervisors to remove internal modelling permission for individual trading desks, more consistent identification and capitalisation of material risk factors across banks, and constraints on the capital-reducing effects of hedging and diversification.
2. A revised standardised approach (SA). The revisions fundamentally overhaul the standardised approach to make it sufficiently risk-sensitive to serve as a credible fall-back for, as well as a floor to, the IMA, while still providing an appropriate standard for banks that do not require a sophisticated treatment for market risk.
3. A shift from Value-at-Risk (VAR) to an Expected Shortfall (ES) measure of risk under stress. The use of ES will help to ensure a more prudent capture of "tail risk" and capital adequacy during periods of significant financial market stress.
4. Incorporation of the risk of market illiquidity. Varying liquidity horizons are incorporated into the revised SA and IMA to mitigate the risk of sudden and severe impairment of market liquidity across asset markets. These replace the static 10-day horizon assumed for all traded instruments under VAR in the current framework.
5. A revised boundary between the trading book and banking book. The establishment of a more objective boundary will serve to reduce incentives to arbitrage between the regulatory banking and trading books, while still being aligned with banks' risk management practices.

The IPOL - EGOV Briefing (2016) describes the evolution of the Basel framework since the first standards were enacted and describes the ongoing revisions of the Basel III framework. The main findings of different impact assessments are reminded, as well as the different positions of various stakeholders. This is regularly updated and was initially prepared in advance of ECON's Open Coordinators and Banking Union Working Group meeting on 12 October 2016 with Mr. Bill Coen, Secretary-General of the Basel Committee on Banking Supervision (BCBS).

Over the last decades, banking regulatory capital requirements have changed substantially. In 1988, the first Basel Accord introduced an international standard to compute banks' regulatory capital. Today, nearly 30 years later, the BCBS is preparing what has already been coined by some as 'Basel IV'.

Over the years, capital standards drafted by the BCBS have shifted from simplicity to risk sensitivity, probably at the expense of transparency and comparability of capital position across banks.

SOLVENCY II

Solvency II is designed to introduce a harmonised insurance regulatory regime across the European Union (EU) that will protect policyholders and minimise market disruption. The regulation sets stronger requirements for capital adequacy, risk management, and disclosure. Primarily this concerns the amount of capital that EU insurance companies must hold to reduce the risk of insolvency. Solvency II is an EU Directive, which is in effect since 1 January 2016 (Cruz 2009; Bourdeau 2009; GDV 2005; SST 2004).

The European Commission launched the Solvency II project in May 2001. The intention was to accomplish a fundamental review of the insurance regulatory framework, not least the Solvency I regime, which would come into force in January 2004 but was already perceived as flawed. The key features of the Solvency II regime – the three-pillar structure and the focus on risk management as a complement to the capital requirements – can be traced back to three reports published between 2002 and 2003.

The second stage of work, which started in 2004, was about the Commission putting flesh on the bones. It relied heavily on the Committee of European Insurance and Occupational Pensions Supervisors (CEIOPS) to provide technical advice and assess the impact of measures.

The financial crisis pushed the European economy into a profound recession and sent banking regulators into a spin. Reform plans for insurers, however, were fairly modest. In early 2009, CEIOPS published a report on the lessons learned from the crisis and its main recommendation was for Solvency II to be adopted. Time – and hard data – would prove it short-sighted.

The industry and regulators experienced an epiphany in March 2011, after the publication of the results of the Solvency II fifth quantitative impact study (QIS). The last of a series of planned QISs intended to inform the design of the technical measures of Solvency II was conducted in the second half of 2010, regarding insurers' position at the end of 2009. This was the height of the crisis, a time when spreads – understood as the difference between yields on assets in insurers' portfolios and the swap-based discount rate – were historically high.

The Solvency II Directive was published on 25 November 2009. Policymakers knew that before the regime would come into force, the text would have to be amended through a second directive – the Omnibus II – to reflect impending changes in the EU institutional supervisory structure, notably the creation of the European Insurance and Occupational Pensions Authority (EIOPA), which replaced CEIOPS. This change was uncontroversial – a similar amendment for banking regulations was swiftly adopted in 2010 – yet the approval process of Omnibus II was going to take three years. The reason was that once the Commission 'reopened' Solvency II, policymakers – and industry lobbyists – would not let it 'close' before a solution for long-term products was found.

The stalemate in political discussions forced the Commission to postpone the application date of Solvency II in September 2012. This was a half-hearted decision, but it was also a minor concession given the growing demands for the capital pillar of Solvency II to be dropped or postponed indefinitely. While Solvency II was not yet applicable, it was published, so, legally speaking, it was "in force" and provided a legal hook, they argued. The final version of the guidelines was adopted in September of that year, to apply from 2014. In recent years, the Commission has adopted and later amended the delegated acts, and EIOPA issued hundreds of guidelines.

Solvency II was made effective on 1 January 2016, after almost 15 years in the making.

THE SIX SIGMA DMAIC APPROACH TO FINANCIAL RISK ASSESSMENT AND MANAGEMENT

Considering that Six Sigma DMAIC methodology and Risk Assessment are generic, and very compatible and complementary processes, the proposed approach merges the two processes resulting in a powerful synergetic tool. This approach tactically applies the DMAIC framework to Financial Risk Assessment to improve the Risk Management process by focusing on the objective achievement and associated risk factors. The approach applies the conventional stochastic methodologies within the DMAIC framework. The synergy of these complementary methodologies provides for an important systematic improvement in Financial Risk Management. In addition to conventional techniques, the new concept involves:

1. Stochastic measurement of Financial Risk Assessment performance by using the Six Sigma process capability metrics considering the objective achievement and major risk factors; and
2. Continuous monitoring and control of process performance by iteratively and recursively applying the DMAIC framework to meet the objective and mitigate risks.

Six Sigma Generic Mathematical Concepts

All the mathematical calculations in the book are problem-specific. So, they are presented in the individual chapters of the book. However, there is only one exception, which is the calculation of the Six Sigma capability metrics, which are presented below.

To measure the process performance, the Six Sigma capability metrics, including *Process Capability* (*Cp*), *Process Capability Index* (*Cpk*), and *Sigma Level* (σ-*L*), are used. For this purpose, the following Six Sigma target parameters are specified for every measured attribute of the process: i) Lower Specified Limit (*LSL*); ii) Target Value (*TV*); iii) Upper Specified Limit (*USL*). The definitions of *Process Capability* (*Cp*), *Process Capability Index* (*Cpk*), and *Sigma Level* (σ-*L*) are as follows (Montgomery 2004, Keller 2011).

Process Capability (Cp): Estimates what the process is capable of producing if the process mean were to be centred between the specification limits. Assumes process output is approximately normally distributed. If the process means is not centred, *Process Capability* (*Cp*) overestimates process capability. *Process Capability* (*Cp*) is calculated by the following formula.

$$Cp = (USL - LSL) / (6 * \sigma) \tag{1}$$

where *USL* is the Upper Specified Limit, *LSL* is the Lower Specified Limit, and σ is the standard deviation of the process output, which is assumed to be approximately normally distributed.

Process Capability Index (Cpk): Estimates what the process is capable of producing, considering that the process means may not be centred between the specification's limits. *Process Capability Index* is negative ($Cpk < 0$) if the process mean falls outside of the specification limits. Assumes process output is approximately normally distributed. *Process Capability Index* (*Cpk*) is calculated by the formula.

$$Cpk = min\ (((USL - \mu) / (3 * \sigma)),\ ((\mu - LSL) / (3 * \sigma))) \qquad (2)$$

where *USL* is the Upper Specified Limit; *LSL* is the Lower Specified Limit; μ is the mean value of the process output distribution; and σ is the standard deviation of the process output, which is assumed to be approximately normally distributed (Keller 2011).

Sigma Level (σ-L): *Sigma Level* (σ-*L*) is a Six Sigma metric that measures the error rate of a process, based on the DPMO (Defects per one Million Opportunities) estimate. The Sigma Level estimate is a long-term estimate of the process, including a potential 1.5 Sigma Shift that could occur over longer periods. This 1.5 Sigma shift is an "industry-standard" estimate of process Sigma Levels. It estimates the process capability in terms of Standard Deviation (σ) of the process output distribution.

For example, the Six Sigma Level refers to having six standard deviations between the mean of the actual performance of a process and the expected performance limits of the process. That translates to a 0.999997 probability (99.9997%) that the process performance is as desired, or to fewer than 3.4 DPMO. *Sigma Level* (σ-*L*) can be calculated in Excel using the formula:

$$\sigma\text{-}L = (NORM.S.INV\ (1 - ErrorRate)) + 1.5 \qquad (3)$$

Where the Excel function *NORM.S.INV* is the inverse of the standard normal cumulative distribution. *(1 - ErrorRate)* is the probability, where *ErrorRate* is a decimal number (for example, 30% Error Rate is equivalent to 300,000 DPMO = 0.3 *ErrorRate*, which would calculate Sigma Level as 2.02); and, the constant 1.5 is the potential Sigma Shift.

Also, there are tables available to convert DPMO to *Sigma Level* (σ-*L*), and *Sigma Level* (σ-*L*) to DPMO (Keller 2011).

The simulation models demonstrated in the book calculate the Six Sigma process capability metrics: *Process Capability* (*Cp*); *Process Capability Index* (*Cpk*); and *Sigma Level* (σ-*L*); by using the following Palisade™ @ RISK® functions:

$$Cp = RiskCp\ (\mu) \qquad (4)$$

$$Cpk = RiskCpk(\mu) \qquad (5)$$

$$\sigma\text{-}L = RiskSigmaLevel(\mu) \qquad (6)$$

where μ is the mean value of the process output distribution.

Sharpe Ratio is a portfolio performance measure compared to the *Free Risk Rate* to the risk associated with it. That is the gain per unit of risk taken. A higher Sharp Ratio indicates a better portfolio performance in response to the risk involved. *Sharpe Ratio* is calculated by using the following formula:

$$\text{Sharpe Ratio} = (\mu - r) / \sigma \qquad (7)$$

Were, μ = *Mean Return* (for example, i.e., calculated by the Monte Carlo Simulation model); σ = *Standard-Deviation* (i.e., calculated by the Monte Carlo Simulation model); and r = *Risk-Free Rate*, which is estimated to be 5.35%.

Generic Six Sigma DMAIC Algorithms for Financial Risk Assessment and Management

The generic algorithms for Six Sigma DMAIC Financial Risk Management determine the techniques and calculations within the five DMAIC phases. These algorithms are presented by the author (Bubevski 2017, Ch. 1). Applications of Six Sigma DMAIC to Risk Management are also elaborated by the author (Bubevski 2017).

More About Six Sigma DMAIC

Six Sigma DMAIC is the central subject of this book. The book is aimed at financial practitioners with adequate financial training, so it will be useful to introduce the concepts and functioning of Six Sigma. A brief description of the Six Sigma methods is presented. In addition, Six Sigma references are provided to the reader which allows them to read more about the subject.

Most industries today recognize Six Sigma as a standard means to accomplish process and quality improvements. The process that led to Six Sigma originated in the 19th Century with the bell curve developed by Carl Friedrich Gauss. In the 1920s, statistician Carl Shewhart, a founding member of the Institute of Mathematical Statistics, showed that a process required correction after it had deviated Three Sigma from the mean. Six Sigma refers to having six standard deviations between the mean of the actual performance of a process and the expected performance limits of the process. That translates to a 0.999997 probability (99.9997%) that the process performance is as desired, or to fewer than 3.4 Defects per one Million Opportunities (DPMO).

The Six Sigma Evolution

The Six Sigma evolution began in the late 1970s when a Japanese firm took over a Motorola factory that manufactured television sets in the United States and the Japanese promptly set about making drastic changes to the way the factory operated. Under Japanese management, the factory was soon producing TV sets with 1/20th the number of defects they had produced under Motorola management. Finally, Motorola recognized its quality was awful. Since then, Motorola management has decided to take quality seriously. I.e., Motorola's CEO in 1981 challenged his company to achieve a tenfold improvement in performance over five years.

Before 1987, Six Sigma was solely a statistical term. Since 1987, it has spread to other companies and advanced from a problem-solving technique to a quality strategy. However, this unique philosophy only became well known after GE made it a central focus of its business strategy in 1995. Today, Six Sigma is the fastest-growing business management system in the industry, which has ultimately become a sophisticated quality philosophy.

Mikel J. Harry is called the "godfather" of Six Sigma and is acknowledged as the leading authority on theory and practice. In 1984, after Harry was awarded a doctorate from Arizona State University, he joined Motorola where he worked with Bill Smith, a veteran engineer who was in Mikel Harry's words, "the father of Six Sigma". In 1985, Smith and Harry together developed a four-stage problem-solving approach: Measure, Analyse, Improve, and Control (MAIC). Later, the MAIC discipline became the road map for achieving Six Sigma quality.

In January 1987, Motorola launched a long-term quality program, called "The Six Sigma Quality Program". The program was a corporate program that established Six Sigma as the required capability level to approach the standard of 3.4 DPMO. This new standard was to be used in everything, that is, in products, processes, services, and administration. Motorola then updated its quality goal to improve product and service quality ten times by 1989, one hundred-fold by 1991, and achieve Six Sigma capability by 1992. With a deep sense of urgency, Motorola spread dedication to quality to every facet of the corporation achieved a culture of continual improvement to assure Total Customer Satisfaction, and established their ultimate goal: zero defects in everything they do. After implementing Six Sigma, in 1988, Motorola was among the first recipients of the Malcolm Baldrige National Quality Award. Since then, Six Sigma has constantly caught the attention of the industry.

At that time, enamoured by Motorola's success, several other companies, such as Unisys Corporation, Asea Brown Boveri (ABB), and Texas Instruments, began a similar pursuit. But it was in late 1993 when Six Sigma began to transform business, i.e., the year that Harry moved to Allied Signal and their CEO decided to adopt Six Sigma. At Allied Signal, an entire system of leadership and support systems began to form around the statistical problem-solving tools of Six Sigma.

Not long after Allied Signal began its pursuit of Six Sigma quality, General Electric (GE) began to get interested in Six Sigma. In 1995, GE conducted a cost-benefit analysis of Six Sigma's implementation. The analysis showed that if GE, then running at three to Four Sigma quality level, were to raise its quality to Six Sigma, the cost-saving opportunity would be somewhere between $7 billion and $10 billion, i.e., 10% to 15% of sales. Then, in January 1996, teaming with Six Sigma Academy, GE announced the launch of Six Sigma.

There are two important contributions from GE's way of implementation to the evolution of Six Sigma. First, they demonstrated the great paradigm of leadership. Second, they backed the Six Sigma program up with a strong rewards system to show their commitment to it. GE changed its incentive compensation plan for the entire company so that 60% of the bonus was based on financials and 40% on Six Sigma results. The new system successfully attracted GE employees' attention to Six Sigma. Moreover, Six Sigma training had become a prerequisite for the advancement of GE's corporate leadership.

In the last two decades, the financial industry also applied Six Sigma to improve their operations and the quality of services thus increasing customers' satisfaction.

Six Sigma Methodologies and Tools

There are three major methodologies used within Six Sigma, according to the book by De Feo and Barnard (2005).

<u>DMAIC:</u> This method is used primarily for improving existing business processes. DMAIC stands for i) Define the problem and the project goals; ii) Measure in detail the various aspects of the current process; iii) Analyse data to, among other things, find the root defects in a process; iv) Improve the process; v) Control how the process is done in the future.

<u>DMADV:</u> This method is typically used to create new processes and new products or services. DMADV stands for i) Define the project goals; ii) Measure critical components of the process and the product capabilities; iii) Analyse the data and develop various designs for the process, eventually picking

the best one; iv) Design and test details of the process; v) Verify the design by running simulations and a pilot program, and then handing over the process to the client.

Lean Six Sigma: A methodology that relies on a collaborative team effort to improve performance by systematically removing waste and reducing variation. It combines lean manufacturing/lean enterprise and Six Sigma to eliminate the seven kinds of waste: i) Overproduction; ii) Waiting time; iii) Transport; iv) Inappropriate Processing; v) Excess Inventory; vi) Unnecessary Motion; vii) Defects.

There are also many different management tools used within Six Sigma. While there are too many to list, here are details on a few of them.

Five Whys: This is a method that uses questions to get to the root cause of a problem. The method is simple: simply state the final problem (the car wouldn't start, I was late to work again today) and then ask the question "why," breaking down the issue to its root cause. In these two cases, it might be: because I didn't maintain the car properly and because I need to leave my house earlier to get to work on time. The process first came to prominence at Toyota.

CTQ Tree: The Critical to Quality Tree diagram breaks down the components of a process that produces the features needed in your product and service if you wish to have satisfied customers.

Root Cause Analysis: Much like the Five Whys, this is a process by which a business attempts to identify the root cause of a defect and then correct it, rather than simply correcting the surface "symptom" of the problem.

Ultimately, all of the tools and methodologies in Six Sigma serve one purpose: to streamline business processes to produce the best products and services possible with the smallest number of defects. Its adoption by corporations around the globe is both an indicator of and a testament to its remarkable success in today's business environment.

Six Sigma DMAIC

Six Sigma DMAIC is one of the principal Six Sigma methodologies. DMAIC comprises i) Define: defining the process, objectives, and quality goals; ii) Measure: establishing the metrics and measuring the current process performance; iii) Analyse: analysing the measurement results and collected data to determine the root causes of the process variability and risk; iv) Improve: considering alternatives to eliminate the root causes and determining and applying the improvement solution to upgrade the process; and v) Control: continuous monitoring and establishing corrective mechanisms to rectify the deviations and control the process performance in the future (Siviy, Penn, and Stoddard 2007).

The proposed approach applies the framework of the principal Six Sigma DMAIC methodology (Siviy, Penn, and Stoddard 2007; Borror 2009). So, let us have a closer look at DMAIC. DMAIC is a data-driven improvement methodology used for improving, optimising, and stabilising business processes and designs. The DMAIC improvement cycle is the core tool used to drive Six Sigma projects. However, DMAIC is not exclusive to Six Sigma and can be used as the framework for other improvement applications.

All of the DMAIC process phases are required and always proceed in the given order as follows.

Define: The Define phase is approximately a 2 to 3-week process based on the project inputs and begins with the selection of the project champion. This phase is all about establishing the project therefore many individual activities to complete. There are multiple tools and concepts available in the Define phase of Six Sigma. The goals of the Define Phase are: i) Understand the project, including its purpose and scope; ii) Determine whether the process is a good candidate for DMAIC; iii) Map the current process; iv) Detail customer expectations; v) Estimate timelines and costs using project management tools.

Measure: The purpose of this stage is to objectively establish current baselines as the basis for improvement. This is a data collection step, the purpose of which is to establish process performance baselines. The performance metric baseline(s) from the Measure phase will be compared to the performance metric after the project to determine objectively whether significant improvement has been made. The team decides on what should be measured and how to measure it. It is usual for teams to invest a lot of effort into assessing the suitability of the proposed measurement systems. Good data is at the heart of the DMAIC process:

Analyse: This stage's objective is to identify, validate, and select the root cause for elimination. A large number of potential root causes (process inputs, X) of the project problem are identified via root cause analysis (for example a fishbone diagram). The top 3-4 potential root causes are selected using multi-voting or other consensus tools for further validation. A data collection plan is created and data are collected to establish the relative contribution of each root cause to the project metric, Y. This process is repeated until "valid" root causes can be identified. Within Six Sigma, often complex analysis tools are used. However, it is acceptable to use basic tools if these are appropriate. Of the "validated" root causes, all or some can be: i) List and prioritise potential causes of the problem; ii) Prioritise the root causes (key process inputs) to pursue in the Improve step; iii) Identify how the process inputs (Xs) affect the process outputs (Ys). Data are analysed to understand the magnitude of the contribution of each root cause, X, to the project metric, Y. Statistical tests using p-Values accompanied by Histograms, Pareto charts, and line plots are often used to do this; iv) Detailed process maps can be created to help pinpoint where in the process the root causes reside, and what might be contributing to the occurrence.

Improve: The purpose of this step is to identify, test, and implement a solution to the problem; in part or whole. This depends on the situation. Identify creative solutions to eliminate the key root causes to fix and prevent process problems. Use brainstorming techniques like Six Thinking Hats and Random Word. Some projects can utilise complex analysis tools like DOE (Design of Experiments) but try to focus on obvious solutions if these are apparent. However, the purpose of this step can also be to find solutions without implementing them. The goals of this phase are: i) Create; ii) Focus on the simplest and easiest solutions; iii) Test solutions using Plan-Do-Check-Act (PDCA) cycle; iv) Based on PDCA results, attempt to anticipate any avoidable risks associated with the "improvement" using the Failure mode and effects analysis (FMEA); v) Create a detailed implementation plan; vi) Deploy improvements.

Control: The purpose of this step is to sustain the gains. Monitor the improvements to ensure continued and sustainable success. Create a control plan and update it as required. A Control chart can be useful during the Control stage to assess the stability of the improvements over time by serving as i) a guide to continue monitoring the process; and ii) provide a response plan for each of the measures being monitored in case the process becomes unstable.

Six Sigma-Related Work

Mostly, Six Sigma is used today for operational risk management. For example, in his book Neef (2003) emphasised three important operational risk management necessities for corporations: i) to mobilise comprehensive knowledge to allow key decision-makers to "sense and respond" quickly and correctly to developing risks; ii) to create an objective, scenario-based guidelines by using knowledge management techniques among key organizational leaders, and providing workable systems for managers to surface potentially dangerous issues; and iii) to adopt standards that enable companies to audit and monitor their performance, e.g., ISO 9000, Six Sigma, etc.

The book by De Feo and Barnard (2005) is the first Six Sigma book to incorporate the full philosophy and methodology of the Juran Institute. This book can help to achieve the same sustainable bottom-line results. The book includes performance-improving applications based on the Juran Trilogy of Planning Processes, Control Processes, and systematically achieving Breakthrough Processes. Practical and bottom-line conscious, these Juran methods and strategies are enhanced by real-world studies from Juran business clients. This is a handbook for change and a friend for business survival and renewal. It can provide: i) Solutions to frequently seen chronic cultural problems that cross multiple functions in an organization; ii) Examples of common bottlenecks and how to remove them; iii) Improvement, implementation, and strategies for all levels of management. The Juran Institute has helped companies around the globe to successfully reshape their management processes.

The book by Siviy, Penn, and Stoddard (2007) about CMMI® and Six Sigma focuses on the synergistic, rather than the competitive, implementation of CMMI and Six Sigma——with synergy translating to "faster, better, cheaper" achievement of mission success. Topics range from the formation of the value proposition to specific implementation tactics. The authors illustrate how not taking advantage of what both initiatives have to offer puts an organization at risk of sinking time, energy, and money into "invent-ing" a solution that already exists. Along the way, they debunk a few myths about Six Sigma applications in software. While the authors concentrate on the interoperability of Six Sigma and CMMI, they also recognize that organizations rarely implement these two initiatives. Accordingly, the discussion turns to the emerging realm of "multi-model" process improvement and strategies and tactics that transcend models to help organizations effectively knit together a single unified internal process standard.

Tarantino and Cernauskas (2009) applied an operational risk framework in finance by using proven quality control methods such as Six Sigma and Total Quality Management (TQM) to forestall major operational risk management failures.

Also, Abbott (2012) published a handbook for using Six Sigma for operational risk management at an executive level. In this book, Six Sigma's application in risk management of product manufacturing industries is considered. Lost opportunity costs are explored, as well as the traits of effective operations and their managers, decision-making, and the difference between responsibility and accountability, are comprehensively covered.

Rael (2017) in his book defined the Enterprise Risk Management (ERM) process and costs of preven-tion to manage operational risk, by using quality concepts such as TQM & Six Sigma, while showing how these elements are both necessary and highly desired in an organisation's strategic decision-making. This book provides a best-practice view on the latest developments in ERM, explains how-to guidance on developing ERM processes at the enterprise and department levels, facilitates enterprise-wide ERM participation via practical information and examples, and delivers cross-functional management and implementation of ERM.

REGARDING THE CHAPTER 13: PRICE EVOLUTION WITH MARKOV CHAIN MONTE CARLO

Chapter 13 of the book presents a generic model for Price Evolution with the Markov Chain Monte Carlo (MCMC) method. MCMC is a stochastic simulation process observed through a time where the probability distribution of the next stage of the process, given the current state, is independent of the past states. MCMC simulation model is governed by the initial state at time zero and a one-step transition probability matrix. Each row of this matrix shows the probability distribution of the next state, given the current state for that row. An additional model illustrates the evolution of prices through time. It assumes that there is an underlying process, such as the state of the economy, that follows an MCMC with three states. Then for any given state, the price change is simulated with a probability distribution with parameters that depend on the state. The presented model is generic and applicable to all prices.

Markov Chain Monte Carlo (MCMC): An Abstract

Markov Chain Monte Carlo (MCMC) is a simulation technique that can be used to find the posterior distribution and to sample from it. Thus, it is used to fit a model and to draw samples from the joint posterior distribution of the model parameters. The different MCMC algorithms differ in their performance to speed and convergence depending on the model structure. Gibbs's sampling, Metropolis–Hasting algorithm, and Hamiltonian Monte Carlo are briefly presented in a nontechnical way. The software Open BUGS and Stan are MCMC samplers. Convergence of the chains is assessed graphically using trace plots and diagnostic statistics such as the value or the Monte Carlo error.

An Overview of Markov Chain Monte Carlo

Markov Chain Monte Carlo (MCMC) is a method to approximate a distribution from random samples. It specifically uses a probabilistic model called Markov chains. A Markov chain is a description of how probable it is to transfer from one state into another. The probability of this transfer depends thereby only on the previous state. It may be noted that these transfer probabilities should be known, otherwise a Hidden Markov Model might be the correct choice.

The term Metropolis-Hastings algorithm is a type of MCMC. Another important term in the language of Markov chains is the Equilibrium State. For example, when looking at a Markov chain definition the question is, how high the probability is that a happening will be in one week or even further in the future.

The focus of the Metropolis-Hastings algorithm is the Acceptance Probability. How can be derived such a formula? More importantly, how can be ensured that it converges towards the posterior distribution?

The chain has an equilibrium state. This state is also called the Stationary State. Applying this to a Markov chain from an algorithm should be noted that it converges toward the target distribution as the chain converges to its Stationary State.

Compared to other sampling algorithms, the MCMC algorithm is used to sample from a 1D Distribution, its main use lies in the distribution analysis of multi-dimensional problems. Its core disadvantage in the 1D case lies in the fact that its samples are correlated. It, therefore, results in a lower sampling resolution. This can be solved by other types of sampling algorithms such as adaptive rejection sampling.

Another challenge that arises with the MCMC algorithm is how fast the Markov chain converges towards the target distribution. This property is highly dependent on the number of parameters and the configuration of the MCMC algorithm. The Hamiltonian Monte Carlo algorithm solves this challenge by generating larger steps between the samples furthermore resulting in a smaller correlation between them.

To conclude, the discussion above was regarding the MCMC algorithm, specifically the Metropolis-Hastings variant. Also, the creation of a Markov chain by selecting samples from a distribution above was mentioned. Finally, it was stated that this chain then converges towards a posterior distribution.

Markov Chain Monte Carlo Literature

Gamerman & Lopes (2006): While there have been few theoretical contributions to the Markov Chain Monte Carlo (MCMC) methods in the past decade, the current understanding and application of MCMC to the solution of inference problems has increased by leaps and bounds. Incorporating changes in theory and highlighting new applications, Markov Chain Monte Carlo: Stochastic Simulation for Bayesian Inference, Second Edition presents a concise, accessible, and comprehensive introduction to the methods of this valuable simulation technique. The second edition includes access to an internet site that provides the code, written in R and WinBUGS, used in many of the previously existing and new examples and exercises. More importantly, the self-explanatory nature of the codes will enable modification of the inputs to the codes and variation on many directions will be available for further exploration.

Major changes from the previous edition: i) More examples with discussion of computational details in chapters on Gibbs sampling and Metropolis-Hastings algorithms; ii) Recent developments in MCMC, including reversible jump, slice sampling, bridge sampling, path sampling, multiple-try, and delayed rejection; iii) Discussion of computation using both R and WinBUGS; iv) Additional exercises and selected solutions within the text, with all data sets and software available for download from the Web; and v) Sections on spatial models and model adequacy

The self-contained text units make MCMC accessible to scientists in other disciplines as well as statisticians. The book will appeal to everyone working with MCMC techniques, especially research and graduate statisticians and biostatisticians, and scientists handling data and formulating models. The book has been substantially reinforced as a first reading of material on MCMC and, consequently, as a textbook for modern Bayesian computation and Bayesian inference courses.

Gelman (2013): The winner book of the 2016 De Groot Prize from the International Society for Bayesian Analysis. Now in its third edition, this classic book is widely considered the leading text on Bayesian methods, lauded for its accessible, practical approach to analysing data and solving research problems. Bayesian Data Analysis, Third Edition continues to take an applied approach to analysis using up-to-date Bayesian methods. The authors——all leaders in the statistics community——introduce basic concepts from a data-analytic perspective before presenting advanced methods. Throughout the text, numerous worked examples drawn from real applications and research emphasize the use of Bayesian inference in practice.

New to the Third Edition: i) Four new chapters on nonparametric modelling; ii) Coverage of weakly informative priors and boundary-avoiding priors; iii) Updated discussion of cross-validation and predictive information criteria; iv) Improved convergence monitoring and effective sample size calculations for iterative simulation; v) Presentations of Hamiltonian Monte Carlo, variational Bayes, and expectation propagation; and vi) New and revised software code.

The book can be used in three different ways. For undergraduate students, it introduces Bayesian inference starting from first principles. For graduate students, the text presents effective current approaches to Bayesian modeling and computation in statistics and related fields. For researchers, it provides an assortment of Bayesian methods in applied statistics. Additional materials, including data sets used in the examples, solutions to selected exercises, and software instructions, are available on the book's web page.

Gilks (1996): In a family study of breast cancer, epidemiologists in Southern California increase the power for detecting a gene-environment interaction. In Gambia, a study helps a vaccination program reduce the incidence of Hepatitis B carriage. Archaeologists in Austria place a Bronze Age site in its true temporal location on the calendar scale. And in France, researchers map a rare disease with relatively little variation.

Each of these studies applied Markov chain Monte Carlo methods to produce more accurate and inclusive results. General state-space Markov chain theory has seen several developments that have made it both more accessible and more powerful to the general statistician. Markov Chain Monte Carlo in Practice introduces MCMC methods and their applications, providing some theoretical background as well. The authors are researchers who have made key contributions to the recent development of MCMC methodology and its application.

Considering the broad audience, the editors emphasize practice rather than theory, keeping the technical content to a minimum. The examples range from the simplest application, Gibbs's sampling, to more complex applications. The first chapter contains enough information to allow the reader to start applying MCMC in a basic way. The following chapters cover the main issues, important concepts and results, techniques for implementing MCMC, improving its performance, assessing model adequacy, choosing between models, and applications and their domains.

Markov Chain Monte Carlo in Practice is a thorough, clear introduction to the methodology and applications of this simple idea with enormous potential. It shows the importance of MCMC in real applications, such as archaeology, astronomy, biostatistics, genetics, epidemiology, and image analysis, and provides an excellent base for MCMC to be applied to other fields as well.

MODELLING TOOLS

Any appropriate modelling tools for Monte Carlo simulation and stochastic optimisation can be used to implement the approach. Specifically, in the research and demonstration experiments for this book, Microsoft™ Excel® was used for modelling; and Palisade™ @RISK® and RISKOptimizer® were used for Monte Carlo simulation and stochastic optimisation respectively.

It is important and should be emphasised that the approach is independent of the choice of tools. If the readers want to use the Palisade™ tolls, they should visit the Palisade™ website and download the free trial version of the tools, which lasts for 15 days. So, they can experiment and subsequently buy the tools if found useful (Winston 2000, 2001).

ABOUT THE FUTURE OF FINANCIAL RISK MANAGEMENT

The financial risk landscape is changing fast. Every day's headlines bring new reminders that the future is on its way as the financial risk evolves. New trends and new challenges are around every corner and new financial risk strategies, techniques, and regulations are required. The outlines of new trends, challenges, strategies, techniques, and regulations of financial risk management are presented below.

In an early paper by Li (2003), the future trends and challenges of financial risk management were considered at the beginning of the millennium. First, the historical developments and the early 2000s status of financial risk management were assessed. Then, key features of the financial industry in the digital economy were discussed. It is argued that technological innovations, particularly in computing and telecommunication, will continue to have an important influence on the then-future development of financial risk management. Based on past and then-present financial risk management as well as the general trends in the financial industry, some then-future trends and challenges of financial risk management in the digital economy were discussed. Finally, some implications for financial institutions, corporations, and emerging economies were given.

Alexander (2005) established that in 2005, the research on financial risk management applications of econometrics focused on the accurate assessment of individual market and credit risks with relatively little theoretical or applied econometric research on other types of risk, aggregation risk, data incompleteness, and optimal risk control. The author debates that consideration of the model risk arising from crude aggregation rules and inadequate data could lead to a new class of reduced-form Bayesian risk assessment models. Logically, these models should be set within a common factor framework that allows proper risk aggregation methods to be developed. The paper explains how such a framework could also provide the essential links between risk control, risk assessments, and the optimal allocation of resources.

The Institute of Risk Management (IRM) in their report Risk Agenda 2025 (IRM 2015) explores the future direction the profession of risk management is likely to take. In this report, they have gathered the wisdom of some of our key stakeholders and members on the opportunities and threats the profession faces, as well as how they are likely to impact risk management by 2025.

Härle, Havas & Samandari (2016) discuss the future of risk management for banks. The authors established that risk management in banking has been transformed over the past decade, largely in response to regulations that emerged from the global financial crisis and the fines levied in its wake. But important trends are afoot that suggest risk management will experience even more sweeping change in the next decade. The change expected in the risk function's operating model illustrates the magnitude of what lies ahead. Today, about 50 percent of the function's staff are dedicated to risk-related operational processes such as credit administration, while 15 percent work in analytics. "McKinsey Research" suggests that by 2025, these numbers will be closer to 25 and 40 percent, respectively. No one can draw a blueprint of what a bank's risk function will look like in 2025, or predict all forthcoming disruptions, be they technological advances, macroeconomic shocks, or banking scandals. However, the fundamental trends do permit a broad sketch of what will be required of the risk function of the future.

Koch et al (2017) published a discussion paper on Basel IV. Since Basel III was rolled out, the Basel Committee on Banking Supervision (BCBS) has been reviewing risk-measurement approaches internationally and among banks. One outcome of this review was the new standardised measurement approach (SMA) for operational risk, which was proposed in 2016. The committee also began a discussion on aggregated internal-rating model floors, concerned about the wide variation in the levels of risk-weighted assets (RWA) issued from banks' internal models. The committee finalised standards for minimum capital requirements for market risk—the fundamental review of the trading book (FRTB) in January 2016. The committee plans to make technical revisions to this framework in 2017–18, however, and the country-level implementation is still under discussion.

A structured review of Six Sigma and implications for future research were presented by Aboelmaged (2010). This study systematically analysed the published work on Six Sigma from 417 referred journal articles in business and management disciplines, information systems and computer science, engineering, healthcare, etc. Conclusions from the analysis were that: i) Six Sigma research was rapidly growing, covering various disciplines and domains with a great focus on Six Sigma tools and techniques; ii) empirical research was dominant with more emphasis on a case study approach; and iii) the growing gap between manufacturing and service focused works confirmed the return of Six Sigma to manufacturing, i.e., its initial origin. Although a large volume of applications was published, Six Sigma is still under development and offers potential opportunities for future research and applications.

To date, however, Six Sigma DMAIC has not been broadly applied to financial risk management specifically on an ongoing basis. This book proposed a generic Six Sigma DMAIC structured approach to financial risk management, which is a recent concept (Bubevski 2017) and certainly has potential prospects for future research and applications.

RISK MANAGEMENT FUTURE DIRECTIONS

Eminent Risk Management scholars and practitioners are referenced considering the future direction for Risk Management in general across industries. Also, references to the future directions for specific industries, disciplines, and corporate businesses are provided including 1) Financial Risk Management; 2) Information Systems Security; 3) Energy Sector; 4) Project Management; 5) Construction Industry; 6) Supply Chain; 7) Agriculture; and 8) Six Sigma.

Continuous change is a universal principle. The universe is endlessly changing, so is our world and everything in it. What was yesterday is not today, and what is today, won't be tomorrow. Consequently, the scenery of risk and risk management is rapidly changing as well. So, new strategies are constantly required to assess and control risk.

Albinson, Blau, and Chu (2016) published a generic report across industries about future risk management tendencies. They argue that organisations would respond to risk change by using cognitive technologies to supplement and, at times, even replace human decision-making. Also, they would deploy widespread controls as part of their operations to monitor and manage risk in real-time. In addition, improvements in behavioural sciences would help to comprehend risk insights, influence risk behaviours, and improve risk decision-making. Moreover, organisations would realise that 100% risk prevention is impossible, so investment in detecting risk events as they happen as well as containing and reducing the impact of risk events would increase. Finally, risk transfer instruments would progressively be used to protect organisations from a wider range of risks, e.g., cyber-attacks, climate change, geopolitical risks, terrorism, business disruptions, etc.

The report also claims that risk change would influence changes within organisations. For example, the marketplace would reward organisations that take on strategic, high-risk inventions. Or, as risks become more measurable and tangible, organisations would be more able to determine an accurate upside value of risk.

Lastly, as businesses engage more deeply with a large number of external stakeholders, they rely more heavily on them to identify, manage, and reduce risks together. The constant threat of disruption resulting from emerging technologies, business model transformations, and ecosystem changes, will force executives to make significant strategic choices to drive organisational success. To survive in a hyper-connected world, organisation leaders would proactively address the accelerated and amplified risks to their reputations.

Another generic study addressing future research directions in management control systems (MCS) was published by Chenhall (2003). This article presented a critical review of findings from contingency-based studies over the past 20 years, resulting in proposals for applying MCS to organisational frameworks. The author argues that recent developments, including strategic risk management, are only just beginning to be understood by researchers. Likewise, product life cycles place demands for new product initiatives and alter cost structures. So, decreasing life cycles increases operating risk and requires increased capital investment. Understanding how MCS innovations can assist management from these perspectives will probably become more and more important. Also, recent MCS research has recognized that managers have a 'strategic choice' to position their organizations in particular environments. For example, if the current product range is too uncertain, they may need to reformulate the product strategy in a more predictable market. This may limit potential opportunities and may require the organisation to study its approaches to the trade-off between potential returns and acceptable risk.

Alexander (2005) discussed the future aspects of Financial Risk Management. The author claimed that current research on financial risk management focuses on the truthful assessment of individual market and credit risks. So, there is comparatively little theoretical or applied econometric research on other types of risk, aggregation risk, data incompleteness, and optimal risk control. The paper discussed that the model risk originating from crude aggregation rules and insufficient data could lead to a new class of reduced-form Bayesian risk assessment models. Logically, these models should be set within a common factor framework that allows proper risk aggregation methods to be developed. The paper explained how such a framework could also provide the essential links between risk control, risk assessments, and the optimal allocation of resources.

A study of future directions in information systems security was published by Crossler et al (2013). This study claimed that although the major weaknesses of information security are the system users within an organisation, the emphasis of present security research is on technical matters. The study emphasised the future directions for "Behavioral InfoSec" research, arguing that this is a novel developing area. It presented the challenges currently faced, as well as the future directions that researchers should explore, for example, separating insider divergent behaviour from insider misbehaviour, approaches to understanding hackers, improving information security compliance, security cross-cultural research, and security data gathering and measurement matters.

Future directions in the energy sector were discussed by Edwards (2008). The article reviewed examples of Knowledge Management (KM) in the energy sector and identified key current issues. Important conclusions were made and future directions for research and implementation were identified. For example, in an uncertain future, enough diversity is required to successfully continue innovation, and organisations should retain the learning and knowledge. More specifically for the energy sector in the future, new sources of energy will require new processes as well as new technology, and perhaps differently trained and educated personnel. The theory should be further applied such as knowledge-based systems and the associated techniques of knowledge elicitation. Also, studying the wider theory of knowledge sharing and organisational learning would be required. For example, the movement of complexity theories into the mainstream and knowledge-based view of the organisation should be utilised.

Lyneis and Ford (2007) studied the application of system dynamics on projects, assessed project progress, and proposed directions for future development. Regarding future routes for risk management and project controls, the authors focus on several aspects of project management including i) project conditions required for project control decisions; ii) actions to take when a project is forecasted to miss performance targets; iii) amounts, durations, combinations, and order of application of measures to be applied to improve performance as much as is possible; iv) heuristics for managing project dynamics to improve performance; and v) qualitative and quantitative models required for these heuristics. They concluded that all these aspects should rigorously be studied using simulation models.

A study by Edwards and Bowen (1998) reviewed and analysed the works on construction and project risk management published from 1960 to 1997, to find practical and research tendencies and associated emphases. The objective was to identify variations in the knowledge and conduct of construction and project risk. The paper suggested that research on the categories of construction risk deserves greater attention. It also deemed that chronological aspects of risk and risk communication are key fields for investigation.

Packendorff (1995) published a theoretical paper discussing new research directions in project management (PM). This study identified three key limitations of PM theoretical research: i) PM is understood as a general theory in its own right; ii) research on PM is not adequately experiential, and iii) projects are perceived as utensils. It claimed that a diversity of theoretical perspectives should be employed in future research on "temporary organizations" aiming to create mid-range theories on different kinds of projects.

Future directions of Supply Chain Risk Management (SCRM) were studied by Singhal, Agarwal, and Mittal (20011). They claimed that organisations have implemented outsourcing, global partnerships, and lean strategies to improve their efficiency; however, these strategies made them vulnerable to market uncertainties, dependencies, and disruptions. Additionally, natural disasters and manufactured crises have negatively affected the strategic, operational, and tactical performance of organisations. These issues have initiated academic and corporate interest to consider risk as a major problem. The authors employ a multi-layered top-town taxonomy to classify and codify the literature and put forward probable dimensions for future research to capture the basic elements of diversified risk issues related to the supply chain. They also studied the SCRM literature concentrating on coordination and decision-making.

Idrees (2009) discussed the future research directions in agriculture considering the agribusiness supply chain. The author proposed a Total Risk Management Process model arguing that an agriculture sector-specific framework can be developed by implementing this model. Also, future research in this area can address food or country-specific issues. This approach can be applied to the non-organic food industry as well. Although only the crop sector of agriculture was covered, other agriculture areas can be explored to further gain the benefits of this research.

A structured review of Six Sigma and implications for future research were presented by Aboelmaged (2010). This study systematically analyzed the published work on Six Sigma from 417 referred journal articles in business and management disciplines, information systems and computer science, engineering, healthcare, etc. Conclusions from the analysis were that: i) Six Sigma research was rapidly growing, covering various disciplines and domains with a great focus on Six Sigma tools and techniques; ii) empirical research was dominant with more emphasis on a case study approach; and iii) the growing gap between manufacturing and service focused works confirmed the return of Six Sigma to manufacturing, i.e., its initial origin. Although a large volume of applications was published, Six Sigma is still under development and offers potential opportunities for future research and applications.

To date, however, Six Sigma has not been specifically applied to risk management on an ongoing basis. This book proposed a generic Six Sigma DMAIC structured approach to risk management. In conclusion, considering that Six Sigma is in expansion today and offers future opportunities for implementations (Aboelmaged 2010), the proposed approach has not only contemporary but prospects for utilisation across industries as well.

REFERENCES

Abbott, J. C. (2012). The Executive Guide to Six Sigma. Robert Houston Smith Publishers.

Aboelmaged, M. G. (2010). Six Sigma quality: A structured review and implications for future research. *International Journal of Quality & Reliability Management*, *27*(3), 268–317. doi:10.1108/02656711011023294

Albinson, N., Blau, A. & Chu, Y. (2016). *The future of risk: New game, new rules*. Deloitte.

Alexander, C. (1996). *The handbook of risk management and analysis*. John Wiley & Sons.

Alexander, C. (2005). The Present and Future of Financial Risk Management. *Journal of Financial Econometrics*, *3*(1), 3–25. doi:10.1093/jjfinec/nbi003

Atkinson P., & Blundell-Wignall A. (2010). Thinking beyond Basel III –Necessary solutions for capital and liquidity. *OECD Market Trends*, *98*(1).

Barfield, R. (2011). *2011. A Practitioners Guide to Basel III and Beyond*. Sweet & Maxwell.

Basel Committee on Banking Supervision. (2014). *Consultative Document: Fundamental review of the trading book: A revised market risk framework*. Bank for International Settlements, Basel Committee on Banking.

Basel Committee on Banking Supervision. (2016). *Standards: Minimum capital requirements for market risk*. Bank for International Settlements, Basel Committee on Banking Supervision.

BIS. (2011). *Basel III: Long-term impact on economic performance and fluctuations*. Working paper No 338, February 2011.

Bloomsbury. (2012). *Asset Liability Management for Financial Institutions: Balancing Financial Stability with Strategic Objectives*. Bloomsbury.

Borror, C. M. (2009). *The Certified Quality Engineer Handbook* (3rd ed.). ASQ Quality Press.

Bourdeau, M. (2009). Market Risk Measurement Under Solvency II. In M. Cruz (Ed.), *The Solvency II Handbook* (pp. 193–226). Risk Books – Incisive Media.

Bubevski, V. (2017). *Novel Six Sigma Approaches to Risk Assessment and Management*. IGI Global.

Busse, J. A., Goyal, A., & Wahal, S. (2010). Performance and Persistence in Institutional Investment Management. *The Journal of Finance*.

Cannata, F., & Quagliariello, M. (2011). *Basel III and Beyond*. Risk Books.

Chenhall, R.H. (2003). Management control systems design within its organizational context: findings from contingency-based research and directions for the future. *Accounting, Organizations and Society*, *28*, 127–168.

Christodoulakis, G. A., & Satchell, S. (Eds.). (2007). *The Analytics of Risk Model Validation, Elsevier Science & Technology*. Academic Press Inc. Ltd.

Christoffersen, P., Diebold, F. X., & Schuermann, T. (1998). Horizon Problems and Extreme Events in Financial Risk Management. Economic Policy Review, 4(3).

Clark, R. G. (1998). Alternative Measures of Risk. In P. L. Bernstein & A. Damodaran (Eds.), *Investment Management* (pp. 81–98). John Wiley & Sons.

Crossler, R. E. (2013). *Future directions for behavioral information security research. In Computers & Security* (Vol. 32). Elsevier Ltd.

Cruz, M. (2009). *The Solvency II Handbook*. Risk Books – Incisive Media.

Damodaran, A. (1998). Models of Risk. In P. L. Bernstein & A. Damodaran (Eds.), *Investment Management* (pp. 58–80). John Wiley & Sons.

Dash, R., Kremer, A., Nario, L., & Waldron, D. (2017). Risk analytics enters its prime. *McKinsey Working Papers on Risk*, 3.

De Feo, J.A. & Barnard, W.W. (2005). *JURAN Institute's Six Sigma Breakthrough and Beyond*. McGraw-Hill Education.

Diebold, F. X., Hahn, J., & Tay, A. S. (1999, November). Multivariate Density Forecast Evaluation and Calibration in Financial Risk Management: High-Frequency Returns on Foreign Exchange. *The Review of Economics and Statistics*, *81*(4), 661–673. doi:10.1162/003465399558526

Edwards, J. S. (2008). Knowledge management in the energy sector: Review and future directions. *International Journal of Energy Sector Management*, *2*(2), 197–217. doi:10.1108/17506220810883216

Edwards, P.J., & Bowen, P.A. (1998). Risk and risk management in construction: a review and future directions for research. *Engineering, Construction and Architectural Management*, *5*(4), 339 –349.

Engelmann, B., & Rauhmeier, R. (Eds.). (2006). *The Basel II Risk Parameters: Estimation, Validation, and Stress Testing*. Springer. doi:10.1007/3-540-33087-9

Froot, K.A., Scharfstein, D.S., & Stein, J.C. (1993). Risk Management: Coordinating Corporate Investment and Financing Policies. *The Journal of Finance*, *48*(5), 1629-1658.

Froot, K.A., & Stein, J. (1998). Risk management, capital budgeting, and capital structure policy for financial institutions: An integrated approach. *Journal of Financial Economics*, *47*(1), 55–82.

Gamerman, D., & Lopes, H. F. (2006). Markov Chain Monte Carlo: Stochastic Simulation for Bayesian Inference. Chapman and Hall/CRC. doi:10.1201/9781482296426

GDV. (2005). *Discussion Paper for a Solvency II Compatible Standard Approach*. Gesamtverband der Deutschen Versicherungswirtschaft.

Gelman, A. (2013). Bayesian Data Analysis. Chapman and Hall/CRC. doi:10.1201/b16018

Gilks, A. (1996). Markov Chain Monte Carlo in Practice. Chapman and Hall/CRC.

Härle, P., Havas, A., & Samandari, H. (2016). The future of bank risk management. *McKinsey Working Papers on Risk*, 3.

Hasan, M. N., Kapadia, N., & Siddique, A. (2017, December). Issuer bias in corporate ratings toward financially constrained firms. *The Journal of Credit Risk*, *13*(4), 1–35. doi:10.21314/JCR.2017.226

Homaifar, G. A. (2004). Managing Global Financial and Foreign Exchange Rate Risk. Wiley.

Hsieh, D. A. (1993). Implications of Nonlinear Dynamics for Financial Risk Management. Journal of Financial and Quantitative Analysis.

Idrees, F. (2009). *Total Risk Management Process in Agrifood Supply Chain*. Academic Press.

IPOL - EGOV Briefing. (2016). *Upgrading the Basel standards: from Basel III to Basel IV.* European Parliament.

IRM. (2015). *Perspectives on the future of risk.* The Institute of Risk Management (IRM).

Jacob, N. L. (1998). Evaluating Investment Performance. In P. L. Bernstein & A. Damodaran (Eds.), *Investment Management* (pp. 329–371). John Wiley & Sons.

Jorion, P. (2011). *Financial Risk Manager Handbook*. John Wiley & Sons.

Keller, P. (2011). *Six Sigma Demystified* (2nd ed.). McGraw-Hill Education.

Koch, S., Schneider, R., Schneider, S., & Schröck, G. (2017). Bringing Basel IV into focus. *McKinsey Working Papers on Risk*, 4.

Lawton, P., & Jankowski, T. (2009). Investment Performance Measurement: Evaluating and Presenting Results. CFA Institute.

Li, S. (2003). Future trends and challenges of financial risk management in the digital economy. *Managerial Finance*, *29*(5/6), 111–125. doi:10.1108/03074350310768797

Lyneis, J. M., & Ford, D. N. (2007). System Dynamics Applied to Project Management. System Dynamics Review, 23(2-3), 157–189.

Macaulay, F. R. (1938). *Some Theoretical Problems Suggested by the Movements of Interest Rates*. National Bureau of Economic Research.

Meier, J. P. (2009). Investment Performance Appraisal. In Investment Performance Measurement: Evaluating and Presenting Results. CFA Institute.

Miller, K.D. (1992). A Framework for Integrated Risk Management in International Business. *Journal of International Business Studies*, *23*(2), 311–331.

Mitra, G., & Schwaiger, K. (2011). *Asset and Liability Management Handbook*. Palgrave Macmillan.

Montgomery, D. C. (2004). *Introduction to Statistical Quality Control*. John Wiley & Sons, Inc.

Neef, D. (2003). Strategy and Risk Management: An Integrated Practical Approach. Taylor & Francis Ltd.

Packendorff, J. (1995). Inquiring into the temporary organization: New directions for project management research. *Scandinavian Journal of Management*, *11*(4), 319–333.

Personal RePEc Archive (MPRA). (2007). MPRA Paper No 5048.

Plantinga, A. (2007). Performance Measurement and Evaluation. Academic Press.

Rael, R. (2017). Managing Corporation Reputation and Risk: A Strategic Approach Using Knowledge Management. John Wiley & Sons.

Ramirez, J. (2017). *Liquidity Management: Handbook of Basel III Capital: Enhancing Bank Capital in Practice*. John Wiley & Sons.

Redington, F. M. (1952). Review of the Principles of Life Office Valuations. *Journal of the Institute of Actuaries, 78*(3), 286-340.

Sigma and Other Next-Generation Techniques. (2009). Wiley.

Singhal, P., Agarwal, G., & Mittal, M. L. (2011). Supply chain risk management: Review, classification, and future research directions. *International Journal of Business Science and Applied Management, 6*(3), 15–42.

Siviy, J. M., Penn, L. M., & Stoddard, R. W. (2007). *CMMI® and Six Sigma: Partners in Process Improvement*. Addison-Wesley Professional.

SST. (2004). *White Paper of the Swiss Solvency Test*. Swiss Federal Office of Private Insurance.

Stulz, R. M. (1996). Rethinking Risk Management. Journal of Applied Corporate Finance.

Winston, W. L. (2001). *Decision Models Using Simulation and Optimization II*. Palisade Corporation.

Chapter 1
Six Sigma Quotation Process

ABSTRACT

This chapter represents the Six Sigma quotation process flow of a company's internal sales quotation process. The process is taken from an actual company and has over 36 individual steps involving 10 individuals or departments. It took up to four weeks to get a quote through the system, yet for critical issues, quotes could be expedited through the system in less than one week. Long quote cycle times prevented the company from bidding in often lucrative emergency orders for their products and services. Management suspected that the problems lay with personnel, not the process, but engineers suspected the process and needed a tool to prove it.

INTRODUCTION

This simulation model presents the process flow of a company's internal sales quotation process. The process is taken from an actual company and has over 36 individual steps involving 10 individuals or departments.

First, the engineering team asked the question: How long does it take to process a quotation from the receipt of the request from the customer to the release of the quote to the Engineering department? To answer this, the team broke the process down into four steps. First, the data is collected and entered (Step 1 in the model). Next, it goes into a queue for customer service review (Step 2). During review (Step 3), corrections and additional data are entered into the form and a tracking number is assigned. Finally, the packet is put into a queue for the Engineering department to perform the quotation activity (Step 4).

The team captured the amount of time each quote spent in each step of the process. Data from many quotations appear on the Data sheet, and @RISK's distribution fitting tool was used to create distribution functions that describe the amount of time each step takes. (You can see these distributions in the blue cells on the next sheet.) The output is the total time or the sum of steps 1-4. Built into the output is a RiskSixSigma function defining the USL, LSL, and Target that are used to calculate the Six Sigma statistics Cp, Cpk Lower, Cpk Upper, and Cpk on the output total time after the simulation is run. (LSL, USL, and Target are marked on the output graph shown on the next sheet.) In addition, the mean, min, max, and standard deviation of the total time output are calculated with @RISK statistical functions.

DOI: 10.4018/979-8-3693-3787-5.ch001

@RISK simulation shows that the mean time to process a quote was around 1800 minutes, or more than 28 hours, and can take anywhere from about 900 minutes to well over 2 calendar days. The team knew that the only value-added step of the process was the review step (Step 3), which takes an average of about 35 minutes to complete. When management saw that it took over 24 hours to complete 35 minutes of value-added work, they saw the need for process improvement.

Literature

George's (2005) book "The Lean Six Sigma Pocket Toolbook" is today's most complete and results-based reference to the tools and concepts needed to understand, implement, and leverage Lean Six Sigma. The only guide that groups tools by purpose and use, this hands-on reference provides: Analyses of nearly 100 tools and methodologies--from DMAIC and Pull Systems to Control Charts and Pareto Charts Detailed explanations of each tool to help you know how, when, and why to use it for maximum efficacy Sections for each tool explaining how to create it, how to interpret what you find, and expert tips Lean Six Sigma is today's leading technique to maximize production efficiency and maintain control over each step in the managerial process.

Gygi & Williams (2012) argue that Six Sigma is revealed to everyone. The reader might be in a company that's already implemented Six Sigma, or they may be considering it. They may be a student who wants to learn how it works, or you might be a seasoned business professional who needs to get up to speed. In any case, this updated book edition of Six Sigma is the most straightforward, non-intimidating guide on the market. The book has new and updated material, including real-world examples: i) What Six Sigma is all about and how it works; ii) The benefits of Six Sigma in organizations and businesses; iii) The powerful "DMAIC" problem-solving roadmap; iv) Yellow, Green and Black show how the Six Sigma "belt" system works; v) How to select and utilise the right tools and technologies; vi) Speaking the language of Six Sigma, knowing the roles and responsibilities, and mastering the statistics skills and analytical methods.

Kubiak & Benbow. (2017) published the third edition of the Six Sigma black belt handbook which has been fully revised, updated, and expanded. This edition has been updated to reflect the most recent ASQ Six Sigma Black Belt Body of Knowledge (BOK), released in 2015. Among the many additions are: more exercises, particularly to address the more difficult concepts; new tables and figures to clarify concepts; new content between the DMAIC parts of the book to help smooth the transition between phases and to better relate the underlying concepts of the DMAIC methodology; and more content that ensures that the black belt is fully trained in concepts taught to the green belt. The primary audience for this work is the individual who plans to prepare to sit for the Six Sigma black belt certification examination. A secondary audience for the handbook is the quality and Six Sigma professional who would like a relevant Six Sigma reference book.

Elaboration

Simulation's Data (Six Sigma DMAIC Define)

The simulation model considers the known parameters of Specification Limits and Target for Total Time, which are shown in Table 1.

Table 1. Specification limits and target for total time

LSL	USL	Target
0	1440	720

Simulation's Calculations (Six Sigma DMAIC Define)

The Simulation of Time to Complete Process is shown in Table 2:

Table 2. Simulation of time to complete process

Variable Name	Formula
Step 1	=@RiskTriang (0.025297,5.3,24.147, RiskName("Step 1"))
Step 2	=@RiskTriang (263.65,1204.1,3074.4, RiskName("Step 2"))
Step 3	=@RiskTriang (15.155,32.2,62.938, RiskName("Step 3"))
Step 4	=@RiskNormal (241.142,10.731,24.147, RiskName("Step 4"))
Total	= @RiskOutput ("Total Time",,, RiskSixSigma(H4, I4,J4,0,6))+ SUM(B4:E4)

The Statistical Summary Measures for Total Time are presented in Table 3:

Table 3. Statistical summary measures for total time

Variable Name	Formula
Mean	=@RiskMean(F4)
Min	=@RiskMin(F4)
Max	=@RiskMax(F4)
Std Dev	=@RiskStdDev(F4)
Cp	= @RiskCp(F4)
Cpk Lower	= @RiskCpkLower(F4)
Cpk Upper	= @RiskCpkUpper(F4)
Cpk	= @RiskCpk(F4)

Simulation Analysis, Evaluation, and Risk Attribution (Six Sigma DMAIC Analyse)

The Total Time aspects are analysed below.

Total Time Analysis, Evaluation, and Risk Attribution

Figure 1 displays the Total Time distribution. The Total Time *Mean* is 1,801.78 and the *Standard Deviation* is 584.16. The Six Sigma target parameters are Target Value, i.e., $TV = 720$; $LSL = 0$; and $USL = 1{,}440$. The Six Sigma process capability metrics are $Cp = 0.4108$; $Cpk = -0.2064$; and Sigma Level, i.e., $\sigma\text{-}L = 0.3839$. There is a 5% probability that the *Mean* will be below 913; a 90% probability that it will be in the range of 913 – 2,852; and a 5% probability that it will be above 2,852.

Figure 1. Total time distribution

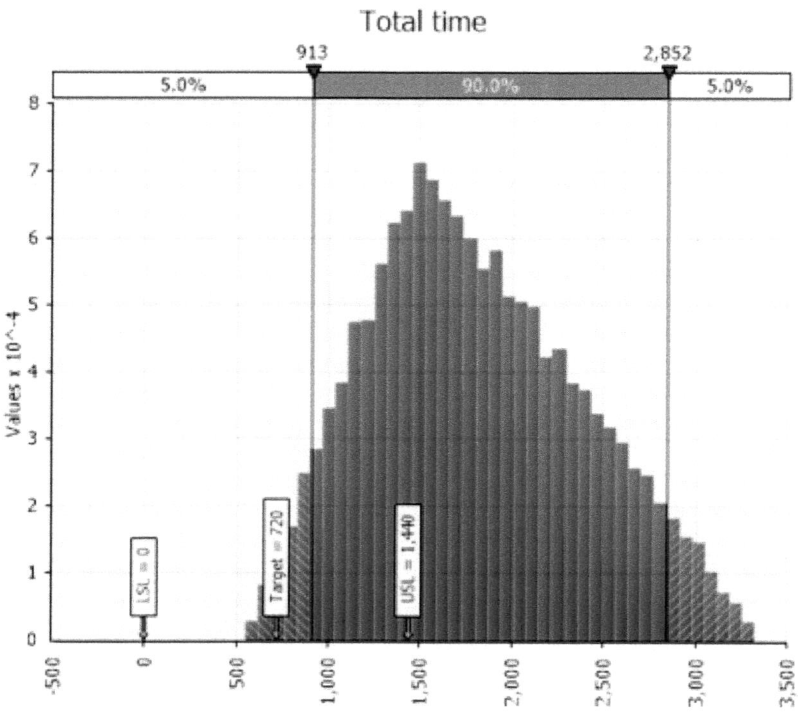

Statistics	Total time
Cell	F4
Minimum	554.20
Maximum	3,328.95
Mean	1,801.78
90% CI	± 9.61
Mode	1,549.37
Median	1,741.46
Std Dev	584.16
Skewness	0.3023
Kurtosis	2.3998
Values	10000
Errors	0
Filtered	0
LSL	0
USL	1,440
Target	720
Cp	0.4108
Cpk	-0.2064
Sigma Level	0.3838
DPM	701,100

Sensitivity Analysis

Sensitivity analysis provides for identifying and quantifying the main contributors to variability and risk based on the probability distribution.

The Inputs Ranked by Effect on Output Mean are given in Figure 2.

Figure 2. Total time inputs ranked by effect on output mean

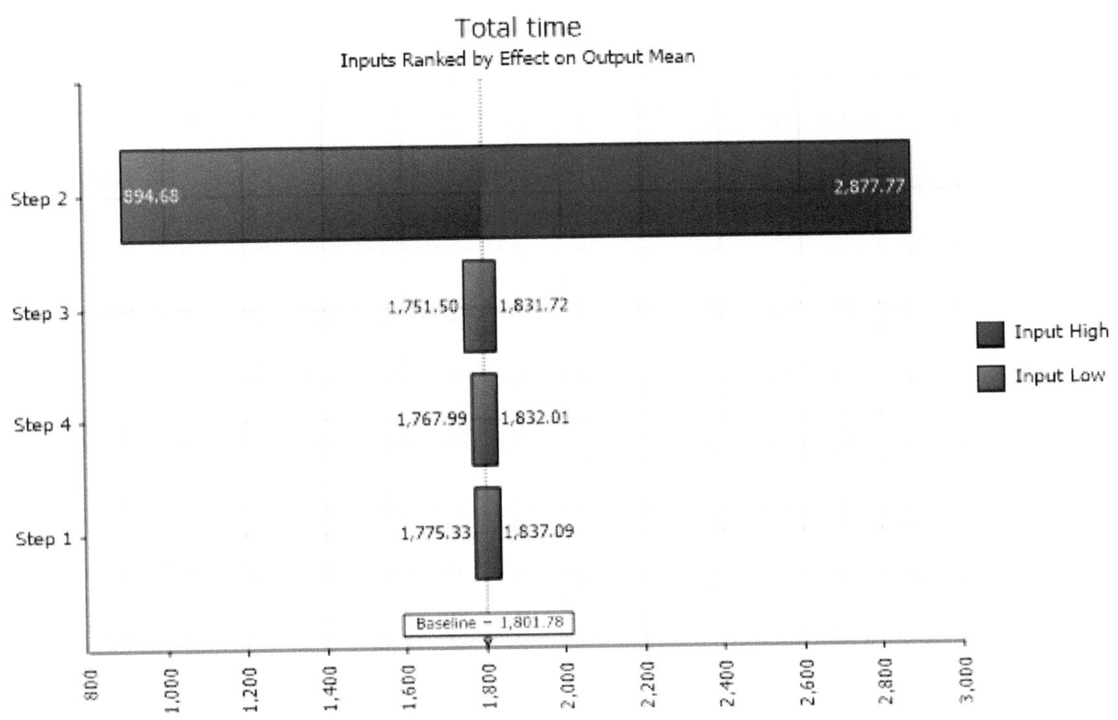

The graph illustrates that the effect of the top variable Step 2, on the Total Time, is a change in the range of 894.68 to 2,877.77, which are respectively left and right from the Baseline of 1,801.78, which is marked on the graph. Other variables are less influential as their associated effects have smaller arrays.

The Regression Coefficients graph is shown in Figure 3.

Figure 3. Total time regression coefficients

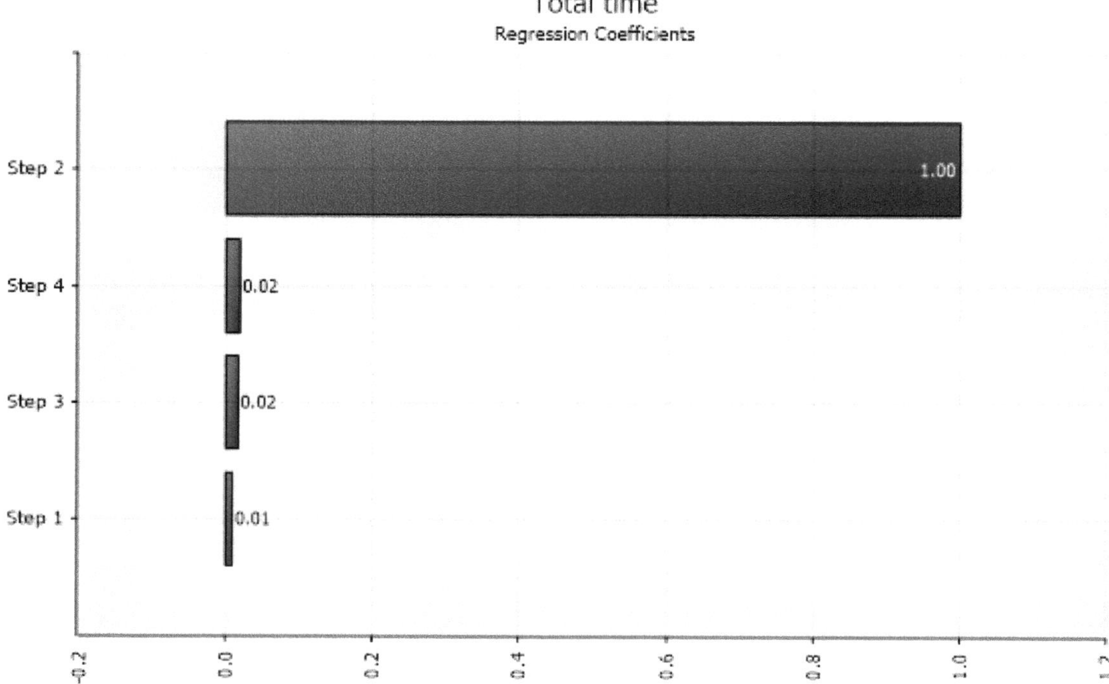

This graph illustrates the top variable with a positive coefficient of 1.00. Therefore, if Step 2 increases by one Standard Deviation, the Total Time will increase by 1.00 Standard Deviations. The other variables Steps 4, 3, and 1 are very much less influential with regression coefficients in the range of 0.02 to 0.01 from top to bottom.

The Correlation Coefficients are presented in Figure 4.

Figure 4. Total time correlation coefficients

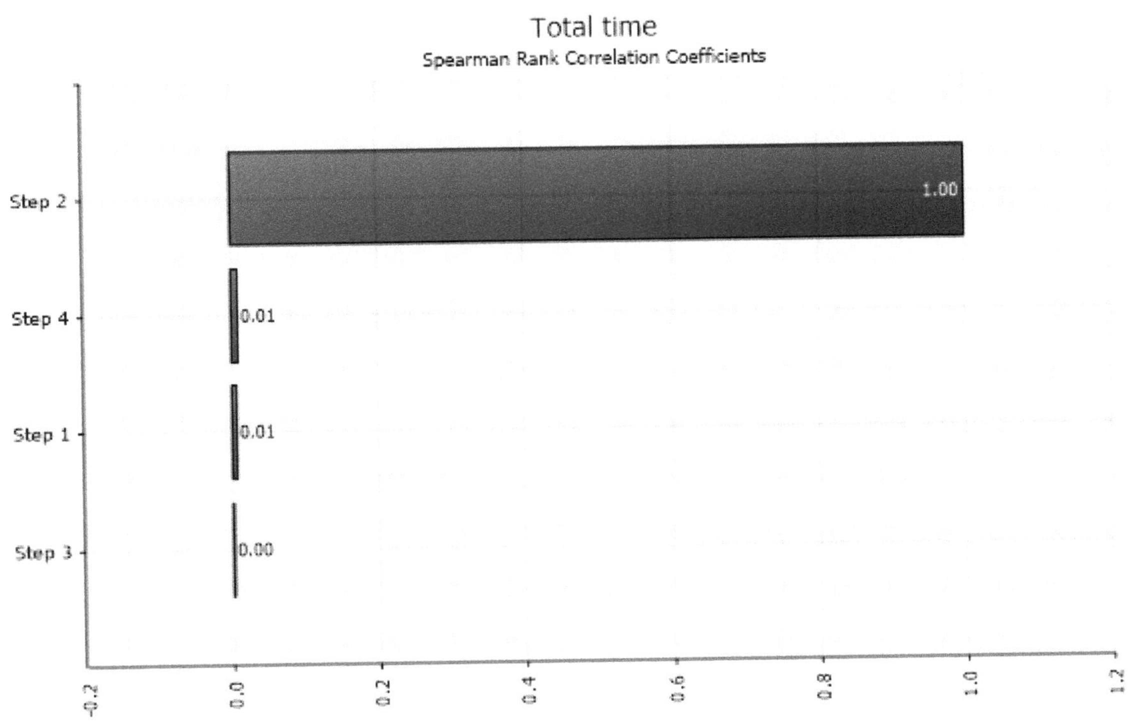

The graph shows the top variable Step 2. If Step 2, with a correlation coefficient of 1.00, increases by one unit, the Total Time will decrease by 1.00 units. Other variables are less influential as their correlation coefficients are in the range of 0.01 to 0.00 from top to bottom.

The Contribution to Variance graph presented in Figure 5 illustrates that the top variable, Step 2, has a contribution of 99.9% to the variance of Total Time. Other variables are less influential as their contribution to variance are all zeros from top to bottom.

Figure 5. Total profit contribution to variance

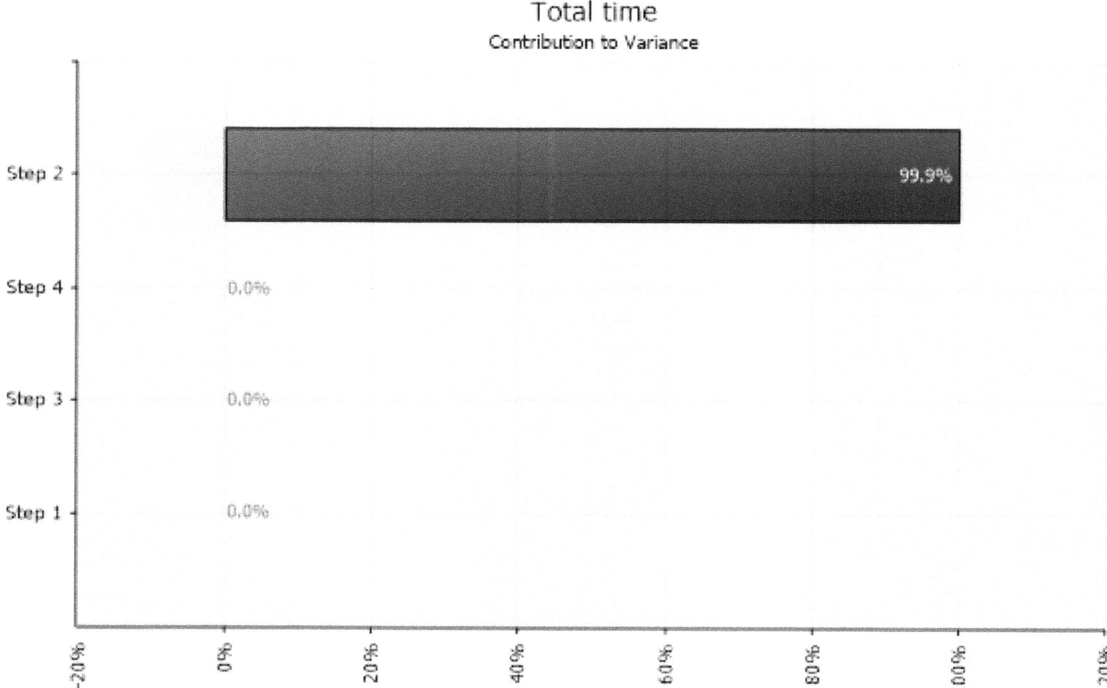

The Change in Output Mean Across the Range of Input Values graph presented in Figure 6 illustrates that the top variable, Step 2, has a contribution of change approximately from 900 to 2,900 minutes to the variance of Total Time. Other variables are very less influential as their contribution to variance is all around 1,800 minutes.

Figure 6. Total time change in output mean across range of input values

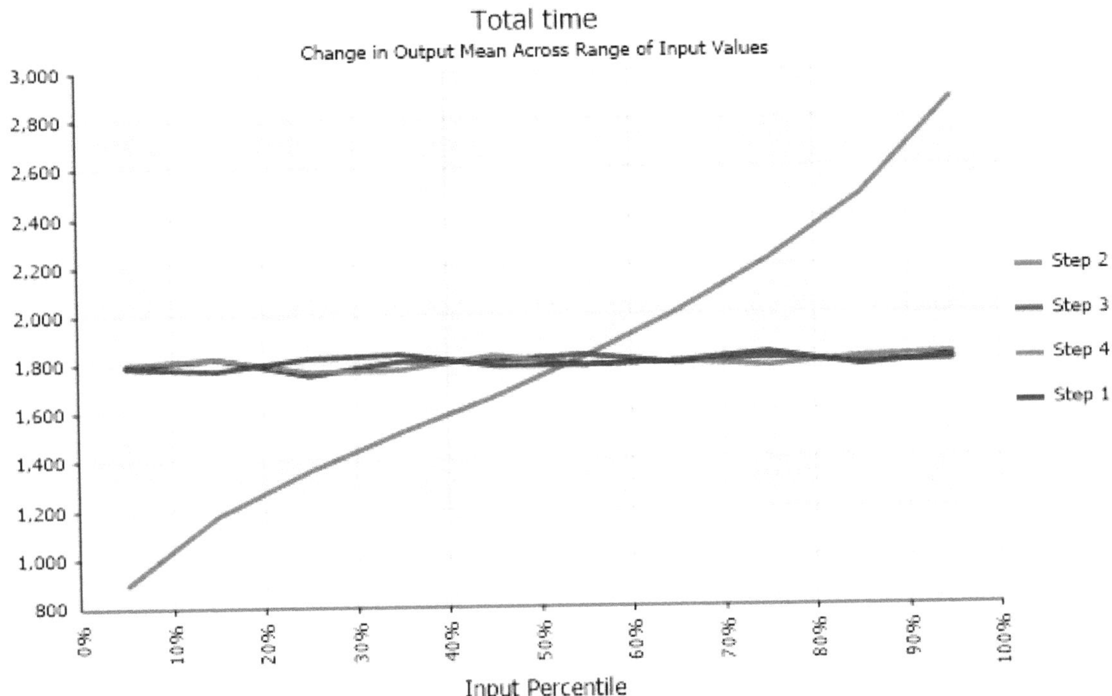

CONCLUSION

This simulation model presented the process flow of a company's internal sales quotation process. The process was taken from an actual company and has over 36 individual steps involving 10 individuals or departments.

First, the engineering team asked the question: How long does it take to process a quotation from the receipt of the request from the customer to the release of the quote to the Engineering department? To answer this, the team broke the process down into four steps. First, the data is collected and entered (Step 1 in the model). Next, it goes into a queue for customer service review (Step 2). During review (Step 3), corrections and additional data are entered into the form and a tracking number is assigned. Finally, the packet is put into a queue for the Engineering department to perform the quotation activity (Step 4).

The team captured the amount of time each quote spent in each step of the process. Data from many quotations appear on the Data sheet, and @RISK's distribution fitting tool was used to create distribution functions that describe the amount of time each step takes. (You can see these distributions in the blue cells on the next sheet.) The output is the total time or the sum of steps 1-4. Built into the output is a RiskSixSigma function defining the USL, LSL, and Target that are used to calculate the Six Sigma statistics Cp, Cpk Lower, Cpk Upper, and Cpk on the output total time after the simulation is run. (LSL, USL, and Target are marked on the output graph shown on the next sheet.) In addition, the mean, min, max, and standard deviation of the total time output are calculated with @RISK statistical functions.

@RISK simulation showed that the mean time to process a quote was around 1800 minutes, or more than 28 hours, and can take anywhere from about 900 minutes to well over 2 calendar days. The team knew that the only value-added step of the process was the review step (Step 3), which takes an average of about 35 minutes to complete. When management saw that it took over 24 hours to complete 35 minutes of value-added work, they saw the need for process improvement.

REFERENCES

George, M. L. (2005). The Lean Six Sigma Pocket Tool-book: A Quick Reference Guide. McGraw-Hill.

Gygi, C., & Williams, B. (2012). *Six Sigma for Dummies*. For Dummies.

Kubiak, T. M., & Benbow, D. W. (2017). The Certified Six Sigma Black Belt Handbook (3rd ed.). Academic Press.

Chapter 2
Six Sigma DMAIC Yield Analysis

ABSTRACT

The imported materials and components are usually include a small number that are defective, but it isn't known how many or how much it is costing. The gathered data is on the number of defective components that become defective at various points in the manufacturing process. On the surface, it appears that defective parts are not a major problem. Upwards of 99% of components are acceptable at each stage of the process. However, the combined effect of the defective parts leads to 15-20% waste in final products, which can translate into 200,000 defective units per million produced. For example, if materials cost $0.50 per unit, you will lose approximately $100,000 in waste before counting labor, machine time, and other expenses. Therefore, Six Sigma DMAIC is used to improve the existing products and/or processes.

INTRODUCTION

DMAIC (Define, Measure, Analyze, Improve, and Control) is used to improve existing products or processes. Suppose you are a costume jewelry manufacturer, coating inexpensive silver with thin layers of gold. You import materials and components from China. A small number of components are always defective, but you don't know how many or how much it costs. You have gathered the data (in the Data sheet) on the number of components that are defective or become defective at various points in the manufacturing process. On the surface, it appears that defective parts are not a major problem. Upwards of 99% of components are acceptable at each stage of the process. However, the combined effect of the defective parts leads to 15-20% waste in final products, which can translate into 200,000 defective units per million produced. For example, if materials cost $0.50 per unit, you will lose approximately $100,000 in waste, before counting labor, machine time, and other expenses. So, you need to reduce the number of defective units produced. However, the process is long and complicated, and you don't know which stage to begin with. Using @RISK, you can simulate many different outcomes and pinpoint the manufacturing stage that is the worst offender. You can also obtain key process capability metrics for each stage, as well as for the entire process, that will help you improve quality and reduce waste. In this way, @RISK is being used in the Measure and Analyze portions of the DMAIC method. @RISK is

DOI: 10.4018/979-8-3693-3787-5.ch002

used to measure the existing state of the process, with capability metrics, and analyze how it might be improved with sensitivity analysis.

Using the historical data, @RISK's distribution fitting feature was used to define distribution functions describing the number of defective parts at each stage of the process: unpackaging/inspection, cutting, cleaning, and electroplating. The defective parts per million (DPPM) for each stage, and the process as a whole, are designated as @RISK outputs with Six Sigma specifications for the specification limits and target values. After the simulation is run, a variety of Six Sigma metrics are obtained for each stage, and the process as a whole.

Finally, sensitivity analysis and a tornado graph reveal that the cutting stage is the most to blame for overall product defects, even though another stage, cleaning, has a lower yield (more defects) on average. Even though the average yield of cutting is higher, the cutting process is less consistent and has more variation than the other processes.

Literature

A book by Panneman & Stemann (2021) is a Six Sigma DMAIC guide in leading a Green Belt project in manufacturing. Where most books about Six Sigma are just a list of available tools, this book explains the Six Sigma tools using a simple 8-step method overlapping the DMAIC phases. Within each step, this book provides a clear description of the tools that readers can use, and when to apply which one in your project. Over 50 tools are presented in this book, and we provide practical examples for each of them. This will equip the readers with the knowledge to solve major manufacturing problems. After reading this book, the readers will be able to lead a DMAIC project following 8 steps, choose which tools are useful for their specific project, and learn how the tools are linked together and used in combination for successful results.

Johnson's (2023) book offers a treasure trove of 100 essential DMAIC tools. These are meticulously curated to guide you through the Define, Measure, Analyse, Improve, and Control phases. The book empowers the readers with the means to eliminate inefficiencies, reduce defects, and optimise every corner of your operations. The book provides: i) Practical explanations of each tool's purpose and application; ii) Real-world case studies showcasing their successful implementations; iii) Step-by-step guides to implement each tool effectively; iv) Expert tips and best practices to help you master the DMAIC methodology; and v) A blueprint for continuous improvement and securing long-term success. The tools in the book provide for redefining organizations' operations and achieving unparalleled results.

Pyzdek & Keller (2023) show readers how to build dynamic teams and foster effective leadership while maximizing customer satisfaction and boosting profits. This new edition features several important updates such as big data and machine learning techniques, mind mapping, applications to healthcare and health statistics, and modern supply chain challenges. The book also lays out cutting-edge applications for obtaining and analysing social media data, decision trees, remote technology, and web scrapers for capturing and analysing Internet data. The latest edition features the use of the free open-source R statistical package and the BlueSky GUI interface.

Savant (2018) has more than a decade of experience in executing, leading, and mentoring hundreds of Lean Six Sigma improvement projects and brings to the readers a simple, straight forward, no-nonsense handbook that will enable them to execute Lean Six Sigma DMAIC projects quickly, effectively, and efficiently. The author shares his belief: "Keep things simple, crisp, and concise, and then executing Lean Six Sigma projects will be easy and fun for you". With this book, the readers will get to know: i) The core essential components needed to execute a DMAIC project; ii) How to execute a DMAIC project, using the core essential components; and iii) To help the readers to deliver a DMAIC faster. Baxter's (2023) book "Lean Six Sigma DMAIC Workbook" is designed to be used for instructor-led workshops yet may be used as a handy reference guide for all levels of practitioners. The workbook contains many tools, techniques, approaches, and exercises to lead the reader through the DMAIC methodology, i.e., Define, Measure, Analyse, Improve, and Control.

The simulation model considers the known parameters of Specification Limits and Targets, which are shown in Table 1.

Table 1. Specification limits and target

LSL	USL	Target
12,000	15,000	14,000
48,000	56,000	52,000
66,000	71,000	68,500
38,000	42,000	40,000
155,000	215,000	180,000

Simulation's Calculations (Six Sigma DMAIC Define)

The Simulation and Outputs are presented as follows. The Defects are shown in Table 2:

Table 2. Simulation of defects

Process	Formula
Unpackaging Inspection	=@RiskTriang (189.808,231.622,251.771, RiskName("Unpackaging Inspection "))
Cutting	=@RiskTriang (246.82,896.51,1275.8, RiskName("Cutting"))
Cleaning	=@RiskTriang (825.32,1036.18,1229.87, RiskName("Cleaning"))
Electroplating	=@RiskWeibull (5.9217,452.71,RiskShift(142.2), RiskName("Electroplating"))

The DPPM is shown in Table 3:

Table 3. Simulation of DPPM

Process	Formula
Unpackaging Inspection	=@RiskOutput (,,, RiskSixSigma(H4,I4,J4,0,6))+D4*1000000/C4
Cutting	=@RiskOutput (,,, RiskSixSigma(H5,I5,J5,0,6))+D5*1000000/C5
Cleaning	=@RiskOutput (,,, RiskSixSigma(H6,I6,J6,0,6))+D6*1000000/C6
Electroplating	=@RiskOutput (,,, RiskSixSigma(H7,I7,J7,0,6))+D7*1000000/C7

The Volume and Yield are shown in Table 4:

Table 4. Simulation of volume and yield

Process	Volume	Yield
Unpackaging Inspection	16,000	=(C4-D4)/C4
Cutting	=C4-D4	=(C5-D5)/C5
Cleaning	=C5-D5	=(C6-D6)/C6
Electroplating	=C6-D6	=(C7-D7)/C7

The Total Yield and DPPM are shown in Table 5:

Table 5. Simulation of total yield and DPPM

Yield	DPPM
= @RiskOutput ("Total Yield")+ PRODUCT(E4:E7)	= @RiskOutput ("Total DPPM",,, RiskSixSigma(H8, I8,J8,0,1))+ SUM(F4:F7)

The Six Sigma Summary Statistics are shown in Table 6a:

Table 6a. Six Sigma summary statistics

Process	Process Cp	Process Cpk	Cpk Lower	Cpk Upper
Unpackaging Inspection	=@RiskCp(F4)	=@RiskCpk(F4)	=@RiskCpkLower(F4)	=@RiskCpkUpper(F4)
Cutting	=@RiskCp(F5)	=@RiskCpk(F5)	=@RiskCpkLower (F5)	=@RiskCpkUpper (F5)
Cleaning	=@RiskCp(F6)	=@RiskCpk(F6)	=@RiskCpkLower (F6)	=@RiskCpkUpper (F6)
Electroplating	=@RiskCp(F7)	=@RiskCpk(F7)	=@RiskCpkLower (F7)	=@RiskCpkUpper (F7)
Total	=@RiskCp(F8)	=@RiskCpk(F8)	=@RiskCpkLower (F8)	=@RiskCpkUpper (F8)

The Six Sigma Summary Statistics continuation are shown in Table 6b:

Table 6b. Six Sigma summary statistics continuation

Process	Process Sigma	Z Lower	Z Upper	Z min
Unpackaging Inspection	=@RiskSigmaLevel(F4)	=@RiskZlower (F4)	=@RiskZupper (F4)	=@RiskZmin (F4)
Cutting	=@RiskSigmaLevel (F5)	=@RiskZlower (F5)	=@RiskZupper (F5)	=@RiskZmin (F5)
Cleaning	=@RiskSigmaLevel (F6)	=@RiskZlower (F6)	=@RiskZupper (F6)	=@RiskZmin (F6)
Electroplating	=@RiskSigmaLevel (F7)	=@RiskZlower (F7)	=@RiskZupper (F7)	=@RiskZmin (F7)
Total	=@RiskSigmaLevel (F8)	=@RiskZlower (F8)	=@RiskZupper (F8)	=@RiskZmin (F8)

Simulation Analysis, Evaluation, and Risk Attribution (Six Sigma DMAIC Analyse)

The Total Yield aspects are analysed below.

Total Yield Analysis, Evaluation, and Risk Attribution

Figure 1 displays the Total Yield distribution. The Total Yield *Mean* is 83.5493% and the *Standard Deviation* is 1.4934%. There is a 5% probability that the *Mean* will be below 81.21%; a 90% probability that it will be in the range of 81.21% – 86.11%; and a 5% probability that it will be above 86.11%.

Figure 1. Total yield distribution

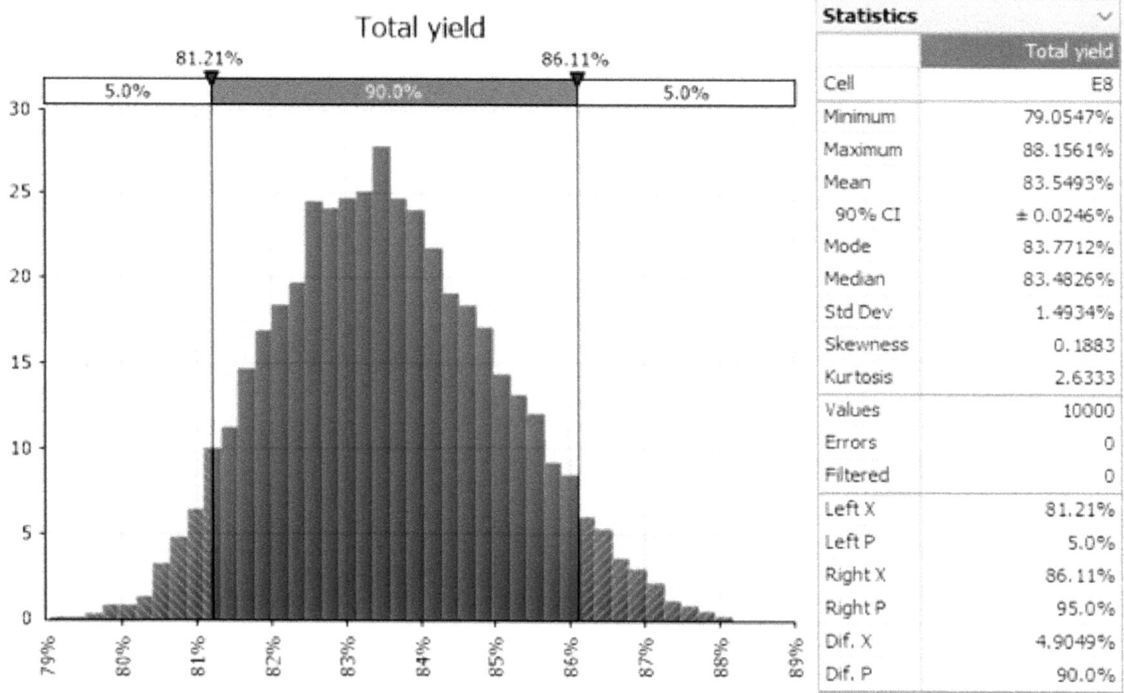

Statistics	Total yield
Cell	E8
Minimum	79.0547%
Maximum	88.1561%
Mean	83.5493%
90% CI	± 0.0246%
Mode	83.7712%
Median	83.4826%
Std Dev	1.4934%
Skewness	0.1883
Kurtosis	2.6333
Values	10000
Errors	0
Filtered	0
Left X	81.21%
Left P	5.0%
Right X	86.11%
Right P	95.0%
Dif. X	4.9049%
Dif. P	90.0%

Sensitivity Analysis

Sensitivity analysis provides for identifying and quantifying the main contributors to variability and risk based on the probability distribution.

The Inputs Ranked by Effect on Output Mean are given in Figure 2.

Figure 2. Total yield inputs ranked by effect on output mean

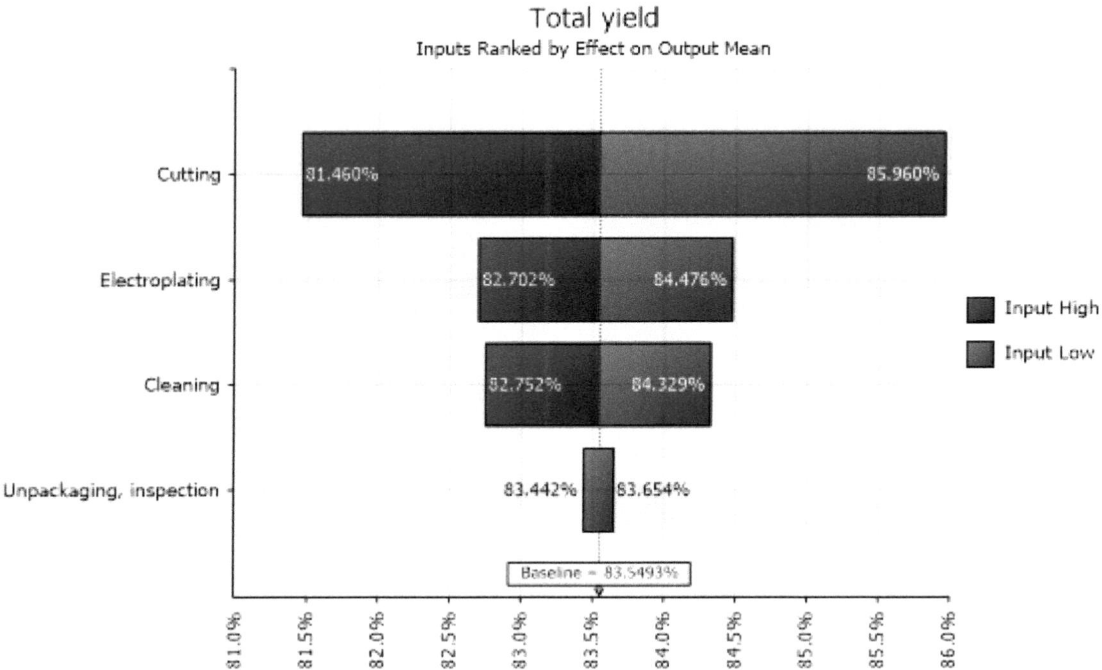

The graph illustrates that the effect of the top variable Cutting, on the Total Yield is a change in the range of 81.460% to 85.960%, which are respectively left and right from the Baseline of 83.5493%, which is marked on the graph. Other variables are less influential as their associated effects have smaller arrays.

The Regression Coefficients graph is shown in Figure 3.

Figure 3. Total yield regression coefficients

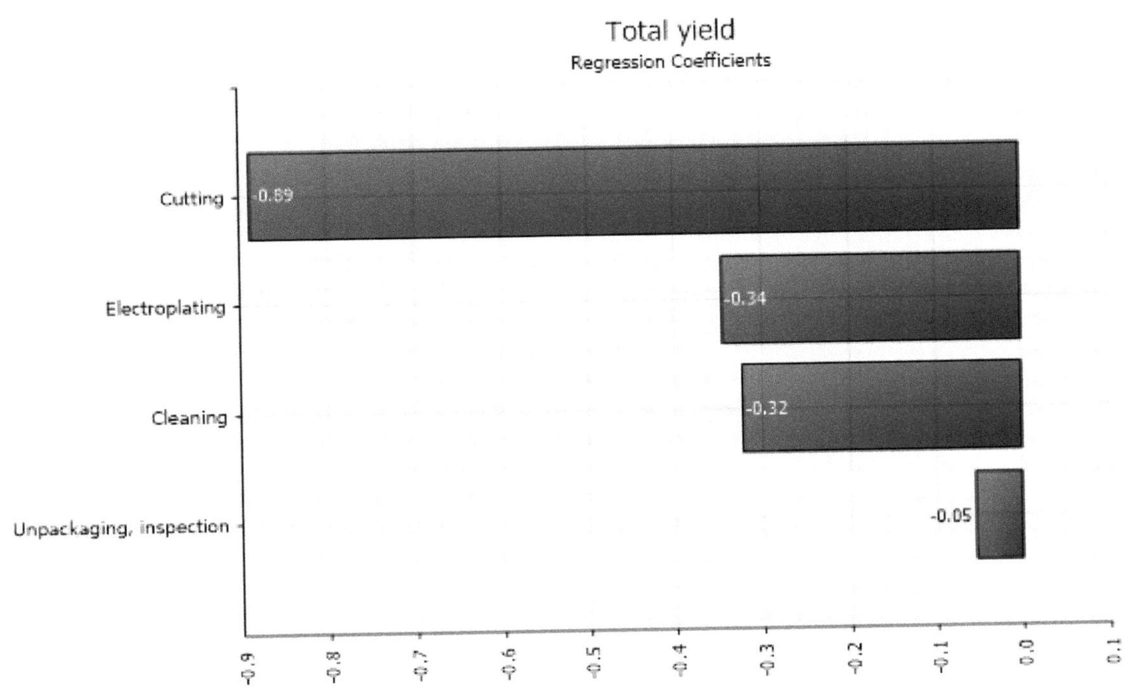

This graph illustrates the top variable Cutting with a negative coefficient of -0.89. Therefore, If Cutting increases by one Standard Deviation, the Total Yield will increase by -0.89 Standard Deviations, i.e., decrease. The other variables are very much less influential with smaller regression coefficients from top to bottom.

The Correlation Coefficients are presented in Figure 4.

Figure 4. Total yield correlation coefficients

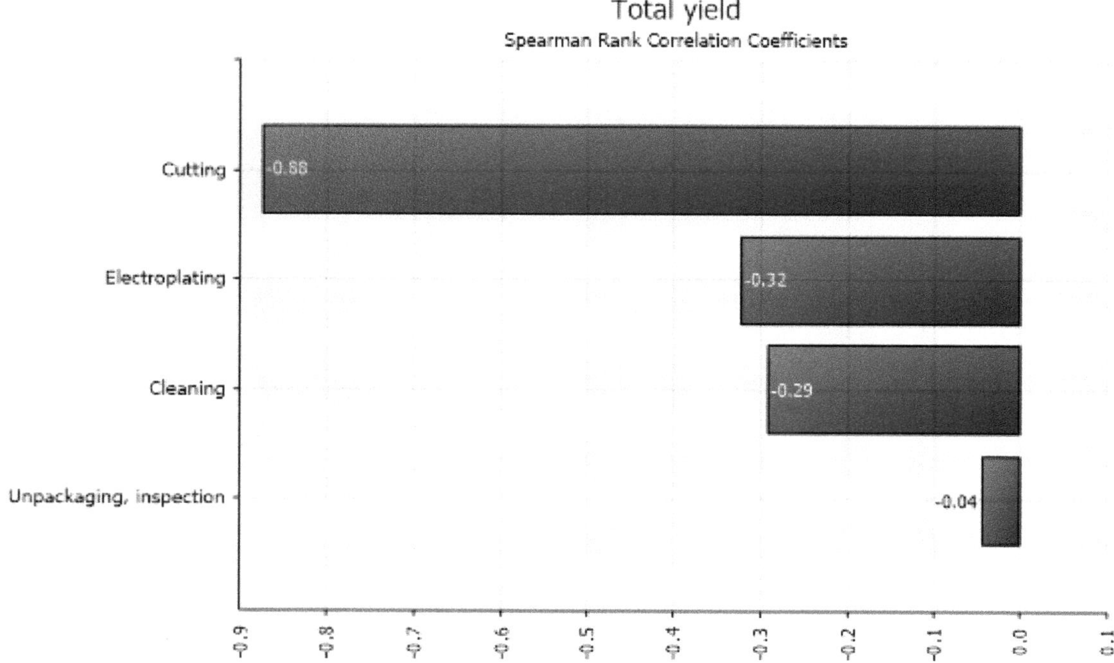

The graph shows that if the top variable Cutting, with a correlation coefficient of -0.88, increases by one unit, the Total Yield will decrease by -0.88 units. Other variables are less influential as their correlation coefficients are significantly smaller from top to bottom.

The Contribution to Variance graph presented in Figure 5 illustrates that the top variable Cutting has a contribution of -77.3% to the variance of Total Yield. Other variables are less influential as their contribution to variance is significantly smaller.

Figure 5. Total yield contribution to variance

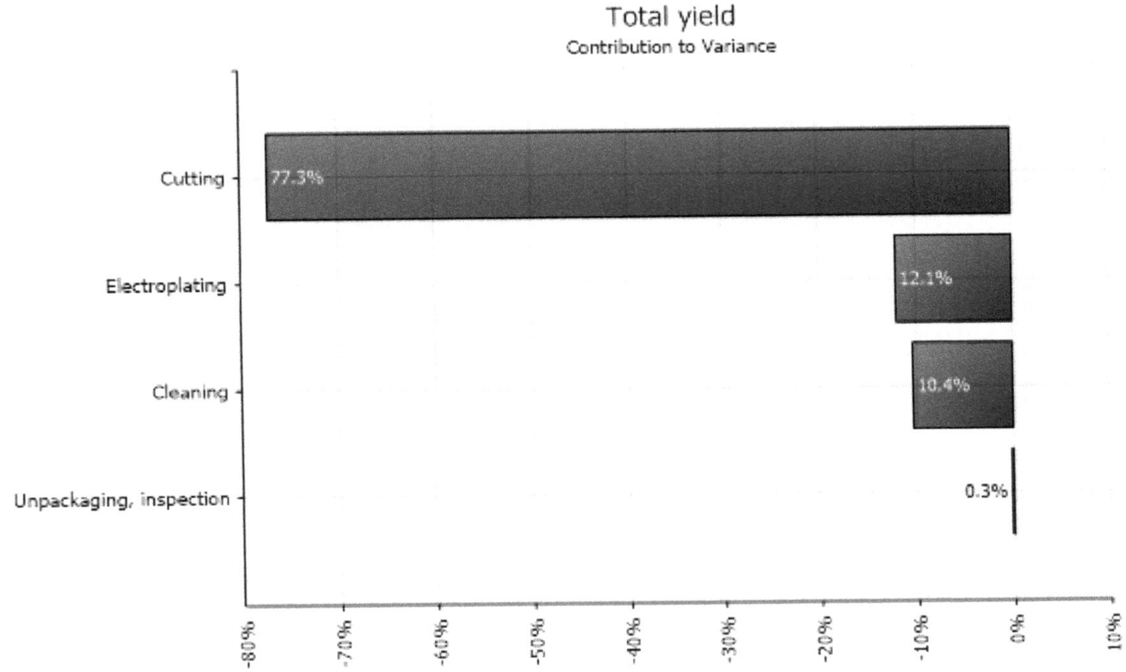

The Change in Output Mean Across the Range of Input Values graph presented in Figure 6 illustrates that the top variable Cutting, has a contribution of change decrease from 86.0% to 81.5% to the variance of Total Yield. Other variables are less influential as their contribution to variance is significantly smaller.

Figure 6. Total yield change in output mean across range of input values

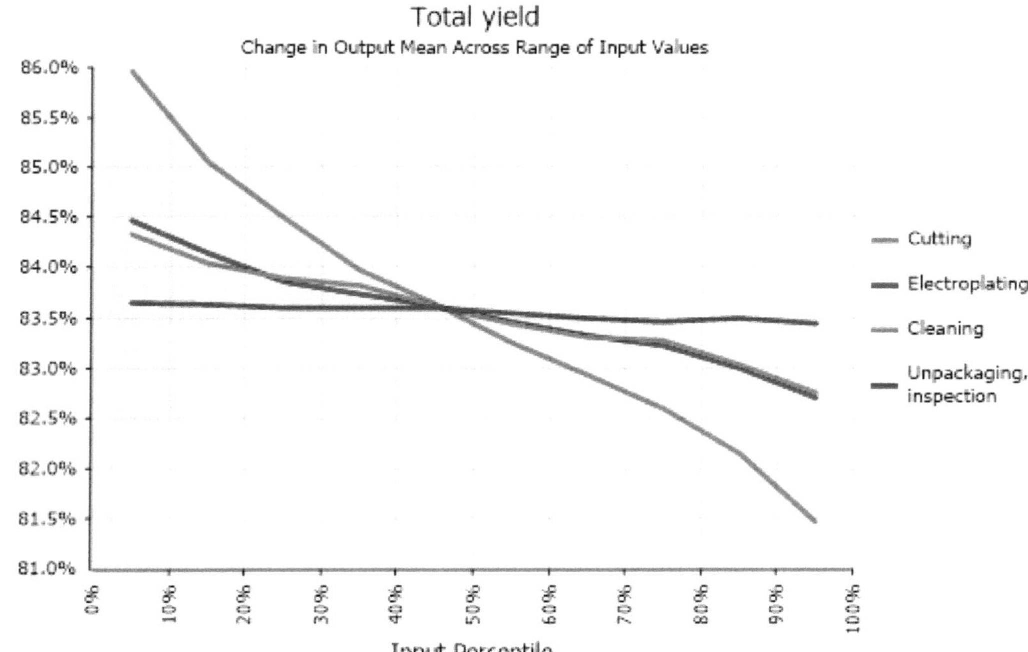

The Total DPPM Aspects Are Analysed Below

Total DPPM Analysis, Evaluation, and Risk Attribution

Figure 7 displays the Total DPPM distribution. The Total DPPM *Mean* is 174,939.11 and the *Standard Deviation* is 16,940.59. The Six Sigma target parameters are Target Value, i.e., $TV = 180{,}000$; $LSL = 155{,}000$; and $USL = 215{,}000$. The Six Sigma process capability metrics are $Cp = 0.5903$; $Cpk = 0.3923$; and Sigma Level, i.e., $\sigma\text{-}L = 1.4829$. There is a 5% probability that the *Mean* will be below 145,989; a 90% probability that it will be in the range of 145,989 – 201,645; and a 5% probability that it will be above 201,645.

Figure 7. Total DPPM distribution

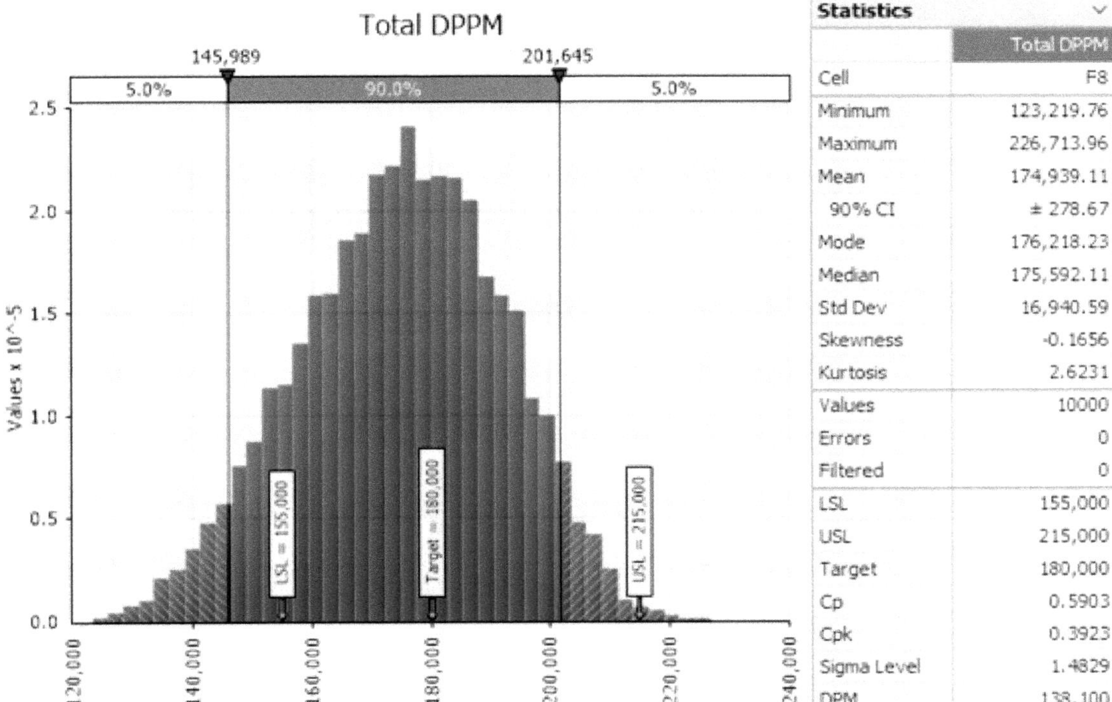

Statistics	Total DPPM
Cell	F8
Minimum	123,219.76
Maximum	226,713.96
Mean	174,939.11
90% CI	± 278.67
Mode	176,218.23
Median	175,592.11
Std Dev	16,940.59
Skewness	-0.1656
Kurtosis	2.6231
Values	10000
Errors	0
Filtered	0
LSL	155,000
USL	215,000
Target	180,000
Cp	0.5903
Cpk	0.3923
Sigma Level	1.4829
DPM	138,100

Sensitivity Analysis

Sensitivity analysis provides for identifying and quantifying the main contributors to variability and risk based on the probability distribution.

The Inputs Ranked by Effect on Output Mean are given in Figure 8.

The graph illustrates that the effect of the top variable Cutting, on the Total DPPM is a change in the range of 147,629.56 to 198,687.33, which are respectively left and right from the Baseline of 174,939.11, which is marked on the graph. Other variables are less influential as their associated effects have smaller arrays.

Figure 8. Total DPPM inputs ranked by effect on output mean

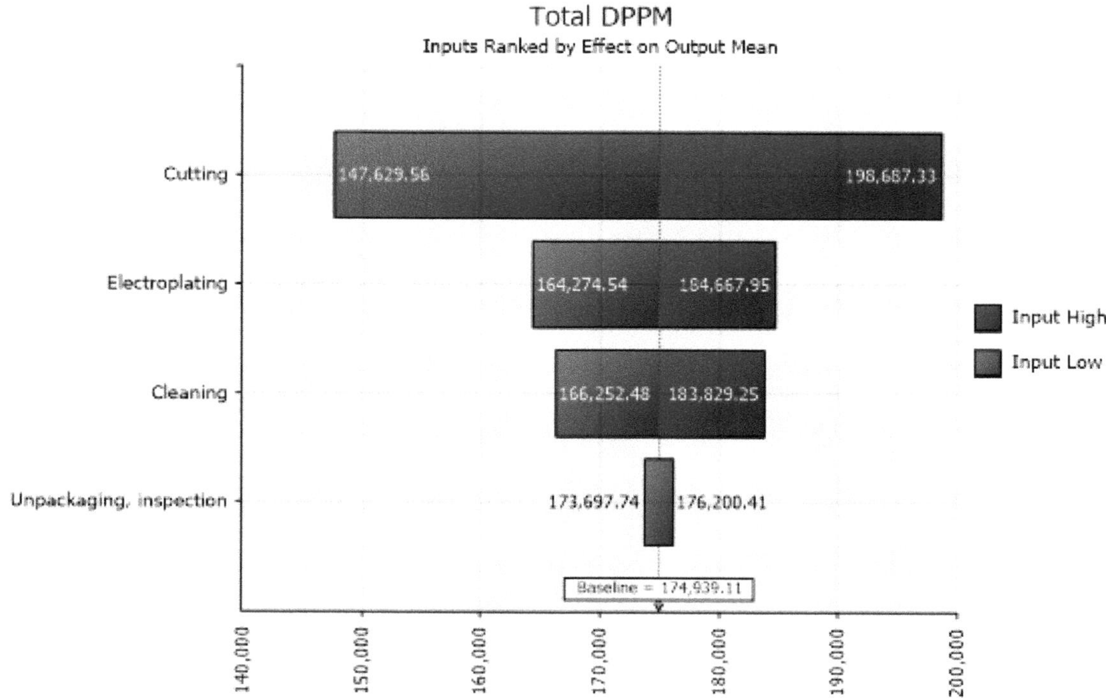

The Regression Coefficients graph is shown in Figure 9.

Figure 9. Total DPPM regression coefficients

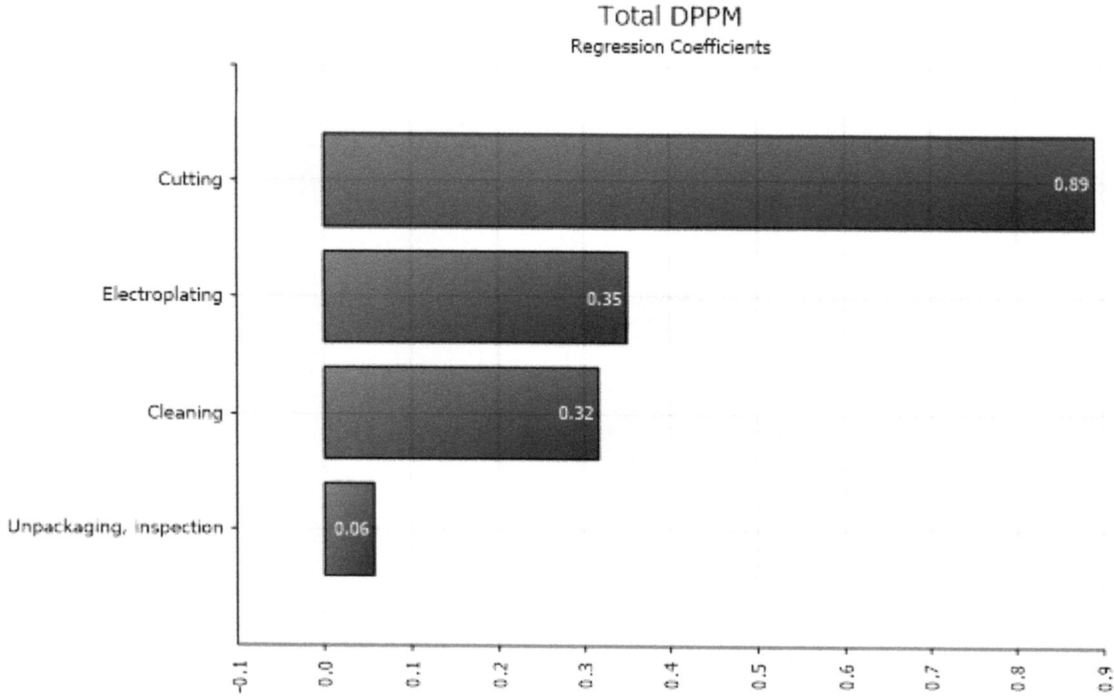

This graph illustrates the top variable Cutting with a coefficient of 0.89. Therefore, If Cutting increases by one Standard Deviation, the Total DPPM will increase by 0.89 Standard Deviations. The other variables are less influential with smaller regression coefficients from top to bottom.

The Correlation Coefficients are presented in Figure 10.

Figure 10. Total DPPM correlation coefficients

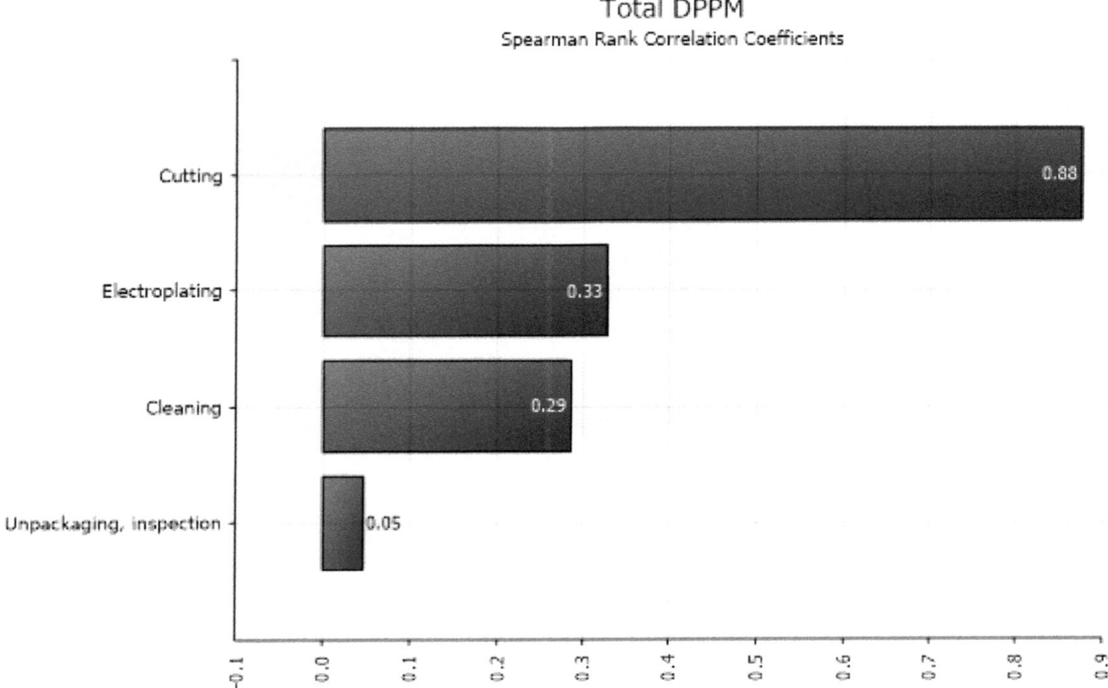

The graph shows that if the top variable Cutting, with a correlation coefficient of 0.88, increases by one unit, the Total DPPM will increase by 0.88 units. Other variables are less influential as their correlation coefficients are smaller from top to bottom.

The Contribution to Variance graph presented in Figure 11 illustrates that the top variable Cutting has a contribution of 77.3% to the variance of Total DPPM. Other variables are less influential as their contribution to variance is significantly smaller.

Figure 11. Total DPPM contribution to variance

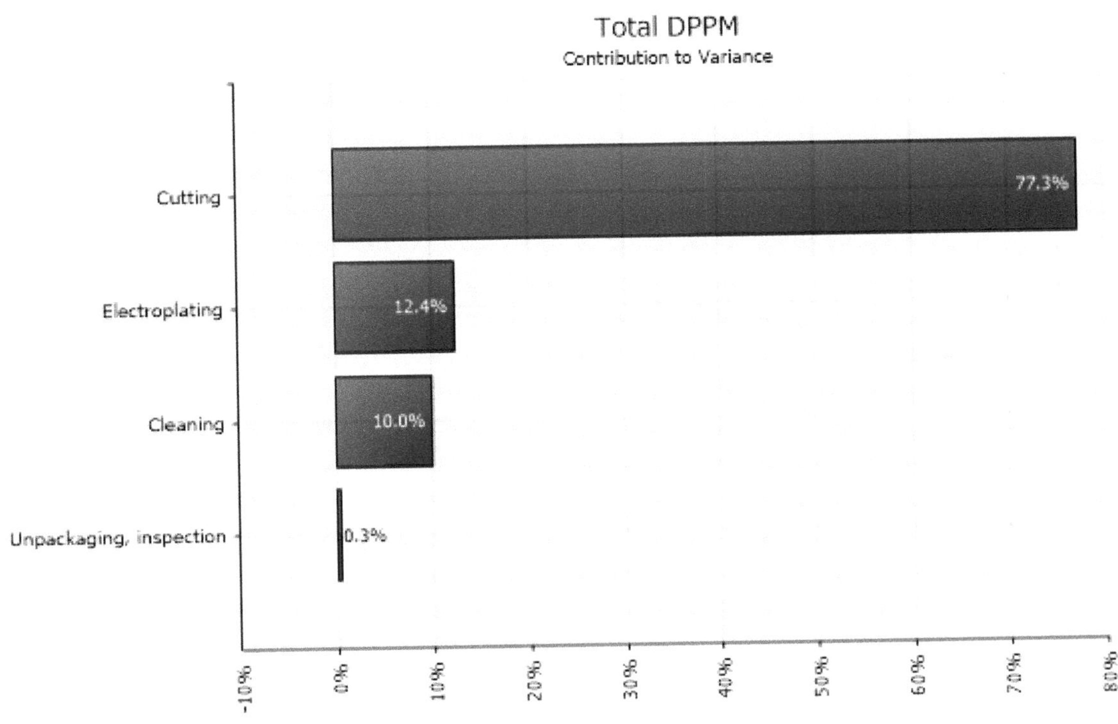

The Change in Output Mean Across the Range of Input Values graph presented in Figure 12 illustrates that the top variable Cutting, has a contribution of change from approximately 147,500 to approximately 198,500 to the variance of Total DPPM. Other variables are less influential as their contribution to variance is significantly smaller.

Figure 12. Total DPPM change in output mean across range of input values

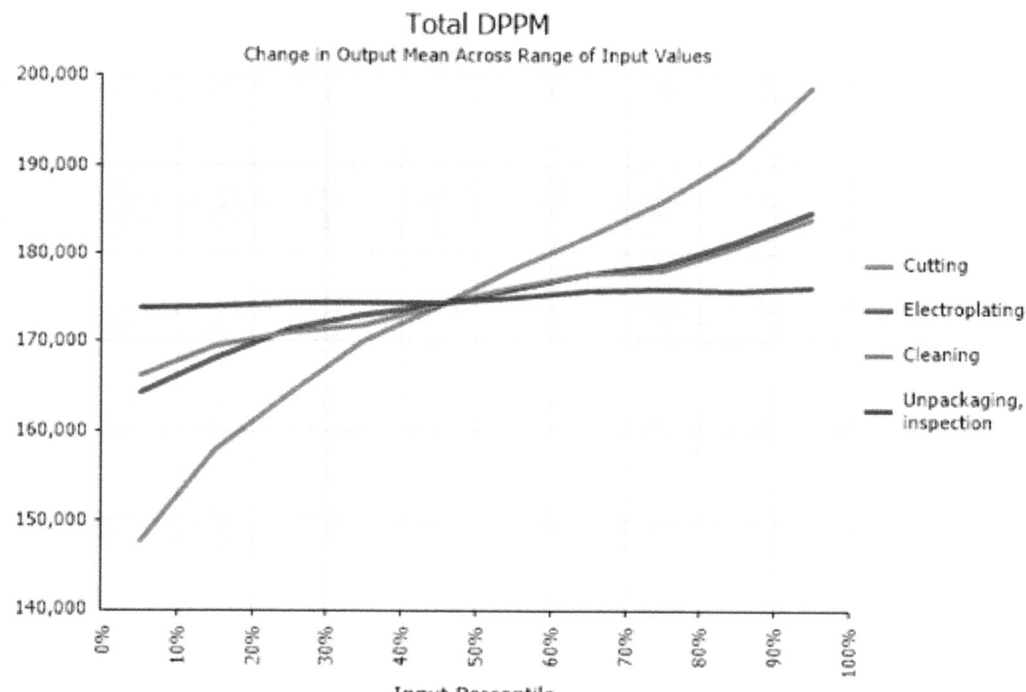

CONCLUSION

DMAIC (Define, Measure, Analyze, Improve, and Control) was used to improve existing products or processes. Suppose you are a costume jewelry manufacturer, coating inexpensive silver with thin layers of gold. You import materials and components from China. A small number of components are always defective, but you don't know how many or how much it is costing. You have gathered the data (in the Datasheet) on the number of components that are defective or become defective at various points in the manufacturing process. On the surface, it appears that defective parts are not a major problem. Upwards of 99% of components are acceptable at each stage of the process. However, the combined effect of the defective parts leads to 15-20% waste in final products, which can translate into 200,000 defective units per million produced. For example, if materials cost $0.50 per unit, you will lose approximately $100,000 in waste, before counting labor, machine time, and other expenses.

You need to reduce the number of defective units produced. However, the process is long and complicated, and you don't know which stage to begin with. Using @RISK, you can simulate many different outcomes and pinpoint the manufacturing stage that is the worst offender. You can also obtain key process capability metrics for each stage, as well as for the entire process, that will help you improve quality and reduce waste. In this way, @RISK is being used in the Measure and Analyze portions of the DMAIC method. @RISK is used to measure the existing state of the process, with capability metrics, and analyze how it might be improved with sensitivity analysis.

Using the historical data, @RISK's distribution fitting feature was used to define distribution functions describing the number of defective parts at each stage of the process: unpackaging/inspection, cutting, cleaning, and electroplating. The defective parts per million (DPPM) for each stage, and the process as a whole, are designated as @RISK outputs with Six Sigma specifications for the specification limits and target values. After the simulation is run, a variety of Six Sigma metrics are obtained for each stage, and the process as a whole.

Finally, sensitivity analysis and a tornado graph revealed that the cutting stage was the most to blame for overall product defects, even though another stage, cleaning, had a lower yield (i.e., more defects) on average. Even though the average yield of cutting was higher, the cutting process was less consistent and had more variation than the other processes.

REFERENCES

Baxter, R. (2023). Lean Six Sigma DMAIC Workbook: for Instructor-Led Workshops, Value Generation Partners.

Johnson, R. (2023). 100 DMAIC Tools: A Comprehensive Guide to Six Sigma Problem Solving. Academic Press.

Panneman, T., & Stemann, D. (2021). Six Sigma DMAIC: 8 Simple Steps for Successful Green Belt Projects. Academic Press.

Pyzdek, T., & Keller, P. A. (2023). The Six Sigma Handbook, Sixth Edition: A Complete Guide for Green Belts, Black Belts, and Managers at All Levels. McGraw Hill.

Savant, S. (2018). DMAIC: Project Execution Essentials Handbook. Independent Publisher.

Chapter 3
Six Sigma DMAIC Failure Rate

ABSTRACT

Six Sigma failure rate model is presented for use in quality control and planning. A manufacturer needs to calculate the percentage of defective products. The DMAIC method (define, measure, analyze, improve, control) comprises the measure and analyze phases, where you wish to measure the current state of quality and analyze the causes of problems or defects. A product is defective when any one of its components does not meet its required tolerance level. Each component is deemed to be satisfactory if some property of its finished state lies within the defined tolerance limits. Properties of each finished component are modeled with a normal distribution in the sample components, which are designated as @RISK outputs with RiskSixSigma property functions defining LSL, USL, and target values for each component. In this way, it's been able to see graphs of the components' quality and calculate Six Sigma statistics on each component.

INTRODUCTION

This chapter represents the Six Sigma Failure Rate model for use in quality control and planning. You are a manufacturer and need to calculate the percentage of defective products. The DMAIC method (Define Measure, Analyze, Improve, Control), comprises the Measure and Analyze phases, where you wish to measure the current state of quality and analyze the causes of problems or defects.

A product is defective when any one of its components does not meet its required tolerance level. Each component is deemed to be satisfactory if some property of its finished state (e.g., its width) lies within the defined tolerance limits. This property of each finished component (e.g., its width) is modeled with a Normal distribution in the Sample column. These cells have also been designated as @RISK outputs with RiskSixSigma property functions defining LSL, USL, and Target values for each component. In this way, you will be able to see graphs of the components' quality and calculate Six Sigma statistics on each component.

After running the simulation, you can see the mean failure rates in column I, as well as other Six Sigma statistics, such as Z score and DPM in columns J and K.

DOI: 10.4018/979-8-3693-3787-5.ch003

Note: Because failures are so uncommon, the simulation should be run for many iterations, such as 10,000, to get accurate results.

Literature

A book by Panneman & Stemann (2021) is a Six Sigma DMAIC guide in leading a Green Belt project in manufacturing. Where most books about Six Sigma are just a list of available tools, this book explains the Six Sigma tools using a simple 8-step method overlapping the DMAIC phases. Within each step, this book provides a clear description of the tools that readers can use, and when to apply which one in your project. Over 50 tools are presented in this book and we provide practical examples for each of them. This will equip the readers with the knowledge to solve major manufacturing problems. After reading this book, the readers will be able to lead a DMAIC project following 8 steps, choose which tools are useful for their specific project, and learn how the tools are linked together and used in combination for successful results.

Johnson's (2023) book offers a treasure trove of 100 essential DMAIC tools. These are meticulously curated to guide you through the Define, Measure, Analyse, Improve, and Control phases. The book empowers the readers with the means to eliminate inefficiencies, reduce defects, and optimise every corner of your operations. The book provides: i) Practical explanations of each tool's purpose and application; ii) Real-world case studies showcasing their successful implementations; iii) Step-by-step guides to implement each tool effectively; iv) Expert tips and best practices to help you master the DMAIC methodology; and v) A blueprint for continuous improvement and securing long-term success. The tools in the book provide for redefining organizations' operations and achieving unparalleled results.

Pyzdek & Keller (2023) show readers how to build dynamic teams and foster effective leadership while maximizing customer satisfaction and boosting profits. This new edition features several important updates such as big data and machine learning techniques, mind mapping, applications to healthcare and health statistics, and modern supply chain challenges. The book also lays out cutting-edge applications for obtaining and analysing social media data, decision trees, remote technology, and web scrapers for capturing and analysing Internet data. The latest edition features the use of the free open-source R statistical package and the BlueSky GUI interface.

Savant (2018) has more than a decade of experience in executing, leading, and mentoring hundreds of Lean Six Sigma improvement projects and brings to the readers a simple, straightforward, no-nonsense handbook that will enable them to execute Lean Six Sigma DMAIC projects quickly, effectively, and efficiently. The author shares his belief: "Keep things simple, crisp, and concise, and then executing Lean Six Sigma projects will be easy and fun for you". With this book, the readers will get to know: i) The core essential components needed to execute a DMAIC project; ii) How to execute a DMAIC project, using the core essential components; and iii) To help the readers to deliver a DMAIC faster. Baxter's (2023) book "Lean Six Sigma DMAIC Workbook" is designed to be used for instructor-led workshops, yet may be used as a handy reference guide for all levels of practitioners. The workbook contains many tools, techniques, approaches, and exercises to lead the reader through the DMAIC methodology, i.e., Define, Measure, Analyse, Improve, and Control. ELABORATION

Simulation's Data (Six Sigma DMAIC Define)

The simulation model considers the known parameters of the Six Sigma Failure Rate, which are shown in Table 1.

Table 1. Six Sigma failure rate parameters

Components	Mean (Target)	Std Dev	Lower (LSL)	Upper (USL)
Component 1	10.00	0.20	9.40	10.60
Component 2	5.00	0.05	4.83	5.15
Component 3	8.00	0.10	7.60	8.30
Component 4	12.00	0.25	11.13	12.88
Component 5	6.00	0.10	5.70	6.50

Simulation's Calculations (Six Sigma DMAIC Define)

The Simulation of the Sample is shown in Table 2:

Table 2. The simulation of sample

Components	Formula
Component 1	=@RiskOutput (,,, RiskSixSigma(F4,G4,C4,0,0))+@RiskNormal(C4,D4)
Component 2	=@RiskOutput (,,, RiskSixSigma(F5,G5,C5,0,0))+@RiskNormal(C5,D5)
Component 3	=@RiskOutput (,,, RiskSixSigma(F6,G6,C6,0,0))+@RiskNormal(C6,D6)
Component 4	=@RiskOutput (,,, RiskSixSigma(F7,G7,C7,0,0))+@RiskNormal(C7,D7)
Component 5	=@RiskOutput (,,, RiskSixSigma(F8,G8,C8,0,0))+@RiskNormal(C8,D8)
Sample Total	=SUM(E4:E8)

The Simulation of "OK?" is shown in Table 3:

Table 3. The simulation of "OK?"

Components	Formula "OK?"
Component 1	=@RiskOutput (,"Components OK",1)+ IF(AND(F4<=E4,E4<=G4),1,0)
Component 2	=@RiskOutput (,"Components OK",2)+ IF(AND(F5<=E5,E5<=G5),1,0)
Component 3	=@RiskOutput (,"Components OK",3)+ IF(AND(F6<=E6,E6<=G6),1,0)
Component 4	=@RiskOutput (,"Components OK",4)+ IF(AND(F7<=E7,E6<=G7),1,0)
Component 5	=@RiskOutput (,"Components OK",5)+ IF(AND(F8<=E8,E5<=G8),1,0)
Product	=@RiskOutput ("Product OK")+ IF(PRODUCT(H4:H8)=1,1,0)

The simulation model presents the Six Sigma DMAIC, which is shown in, Failure Rate, Z Min, and DPM Table 4.

Table 4. Failure rate, Z min, and DPM formulas

Components	Failure Rate	Z Min	DPM
Component 1	=1-@RiskMean(H4)	=@RiskZmin(E4)	=@RiskDPM(E4)
Component 2	=1-@RiskMean(H5)	=@RiskZmin(E5)	=@RiskDPM (E5)
Component 3	=1-@RiskMean(H6)	=@RiskZmin(E6)	=@RiskDPM (E6)
Component 4	=1-@RiskMean(H7)	=@RiskZmin(E7)	=@RiskDPM (E7)
Component 5	=1-@RiskMean(H8)	=@RiskZmin(E8)	=@RiskDPM (E8)
Product	=1-@RiskMean(H9)	None	=SUM(K4:K8)

Simulation Analysis, Evaluation, and Risk Attribution (Six Sigma DMAIC Analyse)

The Six Sigma DMAIC Failure Rate aspects are analysed below.

Component 1 / Sample Analysis, Evaluation, and Risk Attribution

Figure 1 displays the Component 1 / Sample distribution. The *Mean* is 10.00 and the *Standard Deviation* is 0.20. The Six Sigma target parameters are Target Value, i.e., $TV = 10$; $LSL = 9.40$; and $USL = 10.60$. The Six Sigma process capability metrics are $Cp = 0.9998$; $Cpk = 0.9998$; and Sigma Level, i.e., $\sigma\text{-}L = 3.00$. There is a 5% probability that the *Mean* will be below 9.671; a 90% probability that it will be in the range of 9.671 – 10.329; and a 5% probability that it will be above 10.329.

Figure 1. Component 1 / sample distribution

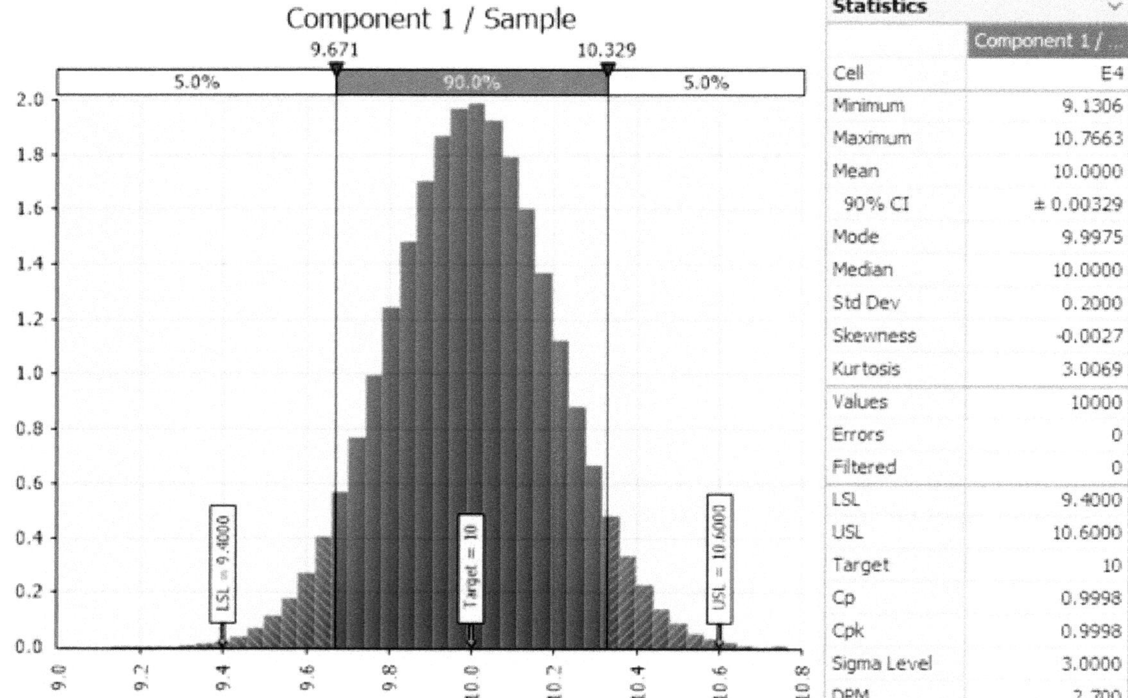

Statistics	Component 1 / ...
Cell	E4
Minimum	9.1306
Maximum	10.7663
Mean	10.0000
90% CI	± 0.00329
Mode	9.9975
Median	10.0000
Std Dev	0.2000
Skewness	-0.0027
Kurtosis	3.0069
Values	10000
Errors	0
Filtered	0
LSL	9.4000
USL	10.6000
Target	10
Cp	0.9998
Cpk	0.9998
Sigma Level	3.0000
DPM	2,700

Sensitivity Analysis

Sensitivity analysis provides for identifying and quantifying the main contributors to variability and risk based on the probability distribution.

The Inputs Ranked by Effect on Output Mean are given in Figure 2.

The graph illustrates that the effect of the variable Component 1 / Sample is a change of the Sample Total in the range of 9.6499 to 10.351, which are respectively left and right from the Baseline of 10.00, which is marked on the graph.

Figure 2. Component 1 / sample inputs ranked by effect on output mean

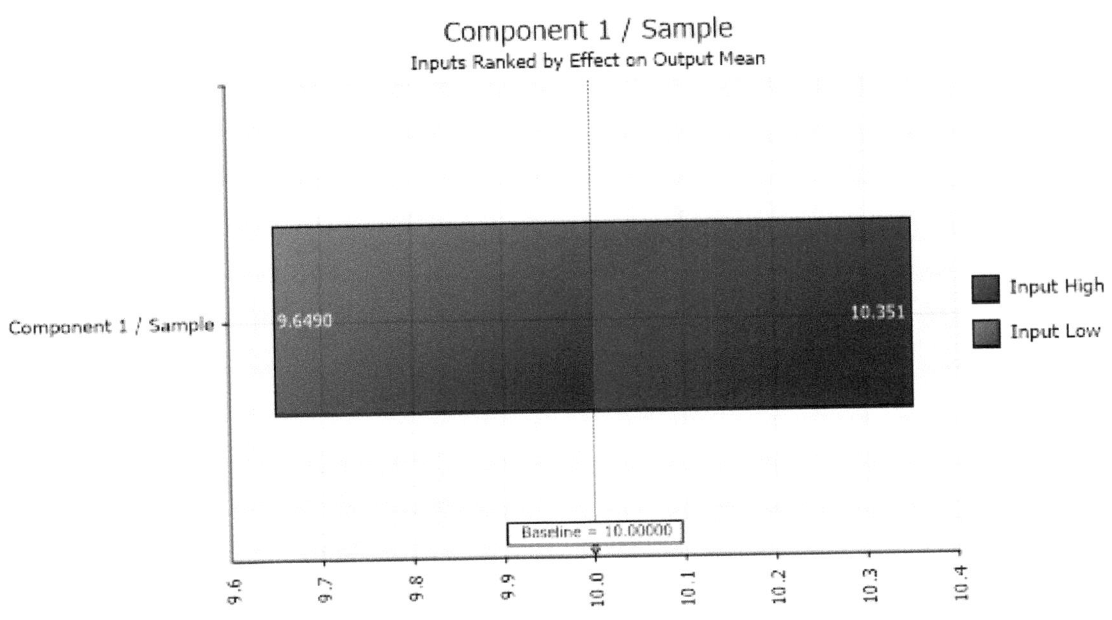

The Regression Coefficients graph is shown in Figure 3.

Figure 3. Component 1 / sample regression coefficients

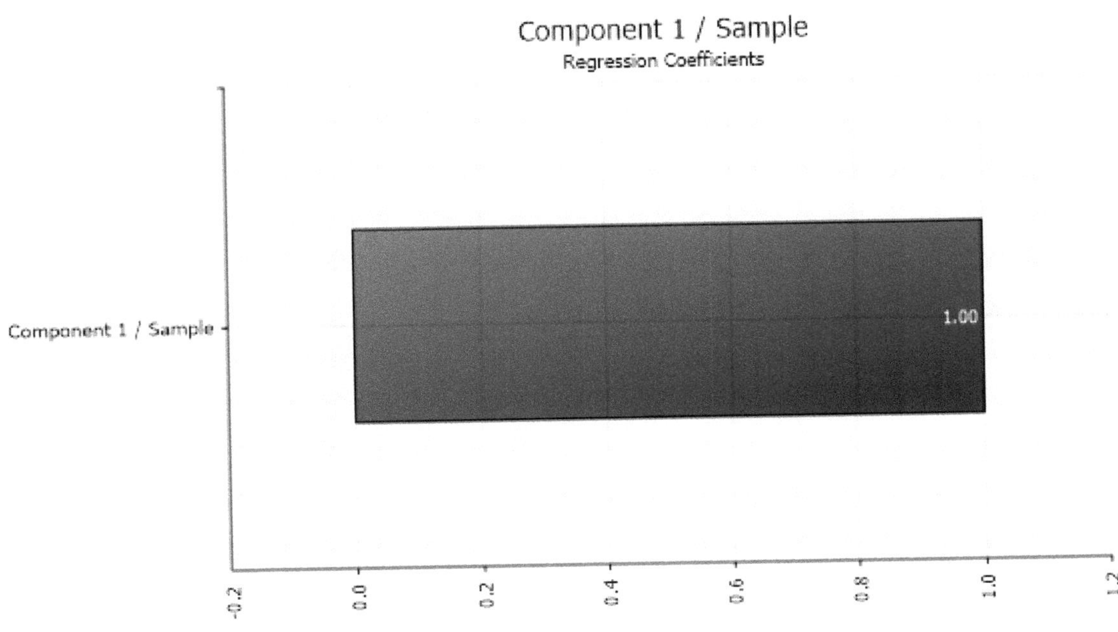

This graph illustrates the Component 1 / Sample variable with a positive coefficient of 1.00. Therefore, if Component 1 / Sample increases by one Standard Deviation, the Sample Total will increase by 1.00 Standard Deviations.

The Correlation Coefficients are presented in Figure 4.

Figure 4. Component 1 / sample correlation coefficients

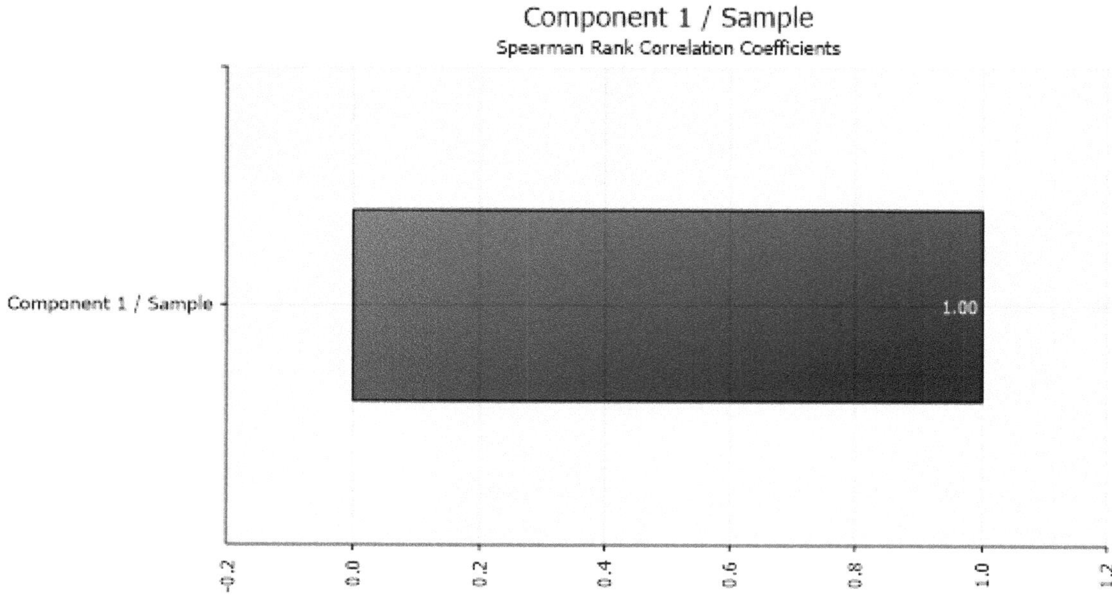

The graph shows that if the variable Component 1 / Sample with a correlation coefficient of 1.00, increases by one unit, the Sample Total will increase by 1.00 units.

The Contribution to Variance graph presented in Figure 5 illustrates that the variable Component 1 / Sample has a contribution of 100.0% to the variance of the Sample Total.

Figure 5. Component 1 / sample contribution to variance

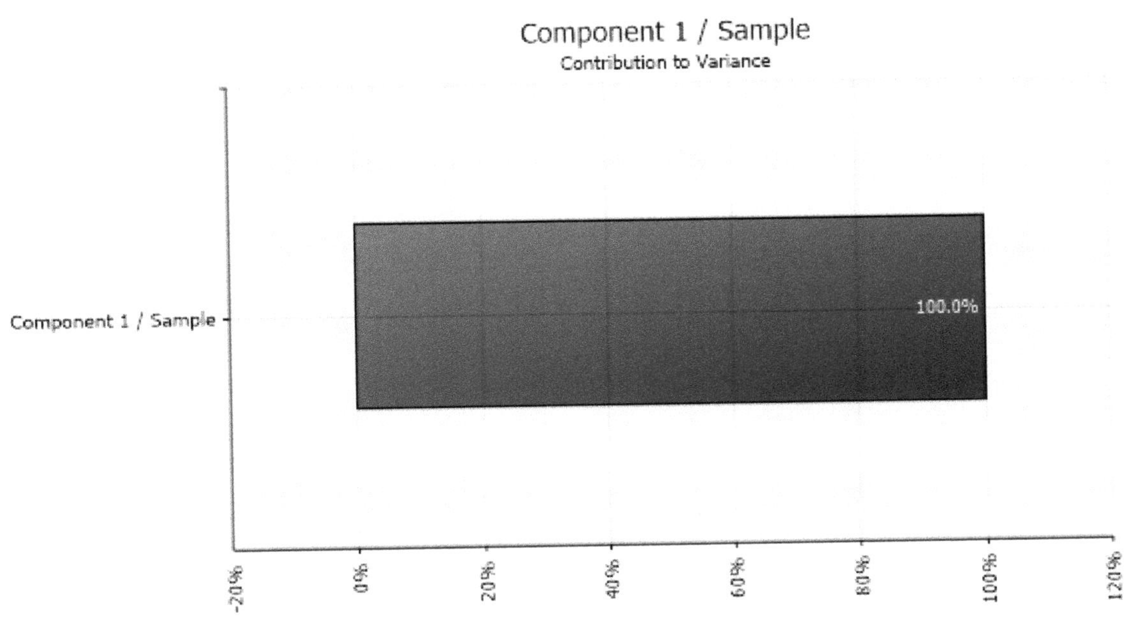

The Change in Output Mean Across a Range of Input Values graph is presented in Figure 6.

Figure 6. Component 1 / sample change in output mean across range of input values

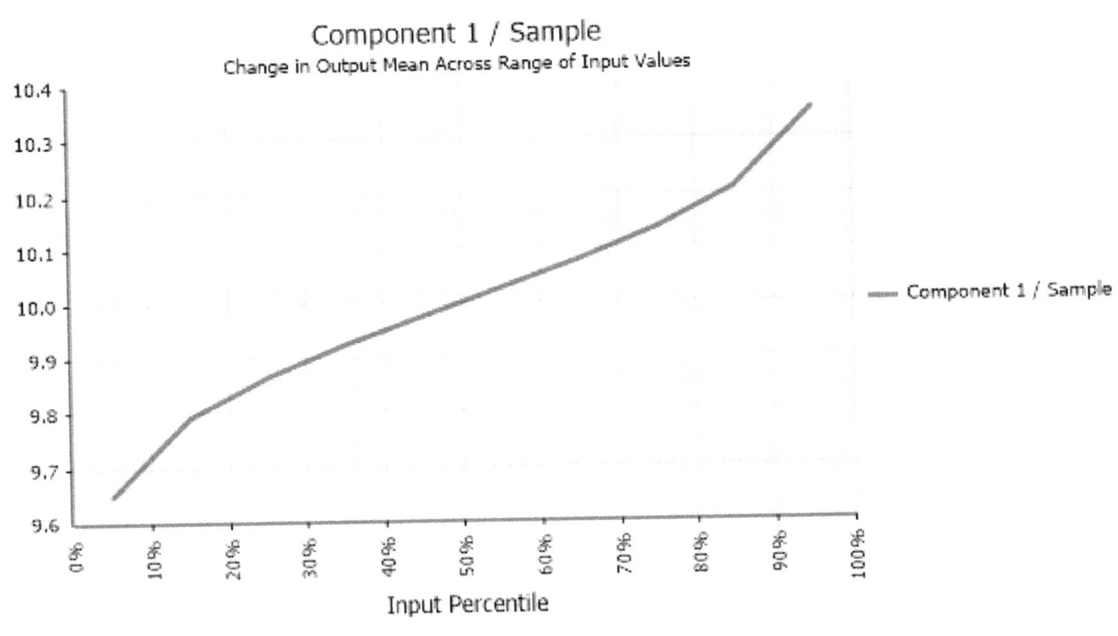

Figure 6 illustrates that the Component 1 / Sample has a contribution of change approximately from 9.65 to 10.35 to the variance of the Sample Total.

Component 2 / Sample Analysis, Evaluation, and Risk Attribution

Figure 7 displays the Component 2 / Sample distribution. The *Mean* is 5.00 and the *Standard Deviation* is 0.0500. The Six Sigma target parameters are Target Value, i.e., $TV = 5$; $LSL = 4.8250$; and $USL = 5.1500$. The Six Sigma process capability metrics are $Cp = 1.0829$; $Cpk = 0.9996$; and Sigma Level, i.e., $\sigma\text{-}L = 3.1559$. There is a 5% probability that the *Mean* will be below 4.9177; a 90% probability that it will be in the range of 4.9177 – 5.0822; and a 5% probability that it will be above 5.0822.

Figure 7. Component 2 / sample distribution

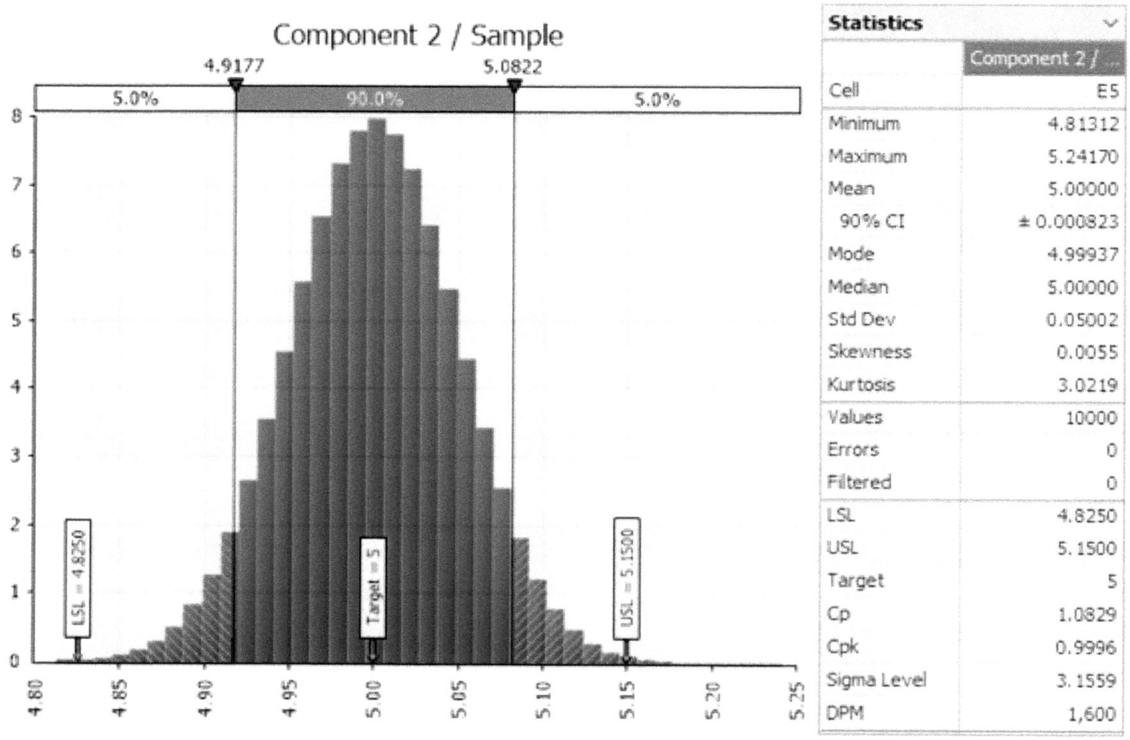
Component 2 / Sample
4.9177
5.0822
5.0%
90.0%
5.0%
LSL = 4.8250
Target = 5
USL = 5.1500
0
1
2
3
4
5
6
7
8
4.80
4.85
4.90
4.95
5.00
5.05
5.10
5.15
5.20
5.25
Statistics
Component 2 / ...
Cell E5
Minimum 4.81312
Maximum 5.24170
Mean 5.00000
90% CI ± 0.000823
Mode 4.99937
Median 5.00000
Std Dev 0.05002
Skewness 0.0055
Kurtosis 3.0219
Values 10000
Errors 0
Filtered 0
LSL 4.8250
USL 5.1500
Target 5
Cp 1.0829
Cpk 0.9996
Sigma Level 3.1559
DPM 1,600

Sensitivity Analysis

Sensitivity analysis provides for identifying and quantifying the main contributors to variability and risk based on the probability distribution.

The Inputs Ranked by Effect on Output Mean are given in Figure 8.

The graph illustrates that the effect of the variable Component 2 / Sample is a change of the Sample Total in the range of 4.9123 to 5.0878, which are respectively left and right from the Baseline of 5.00, which is marked on the graph.

Figure 8. Component 2 / sample inputs ranked by effect on output mean

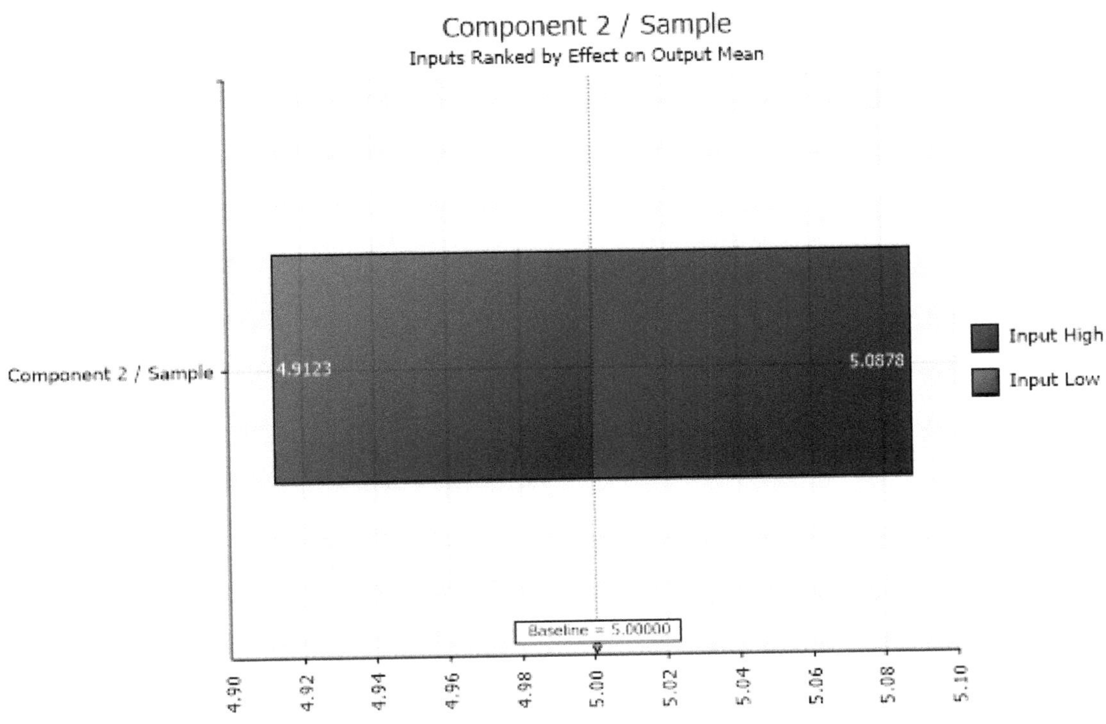

The Regression Coefficients graph is shown in Figure 9.

Figure 9. Component 2 / sample regression coefficients

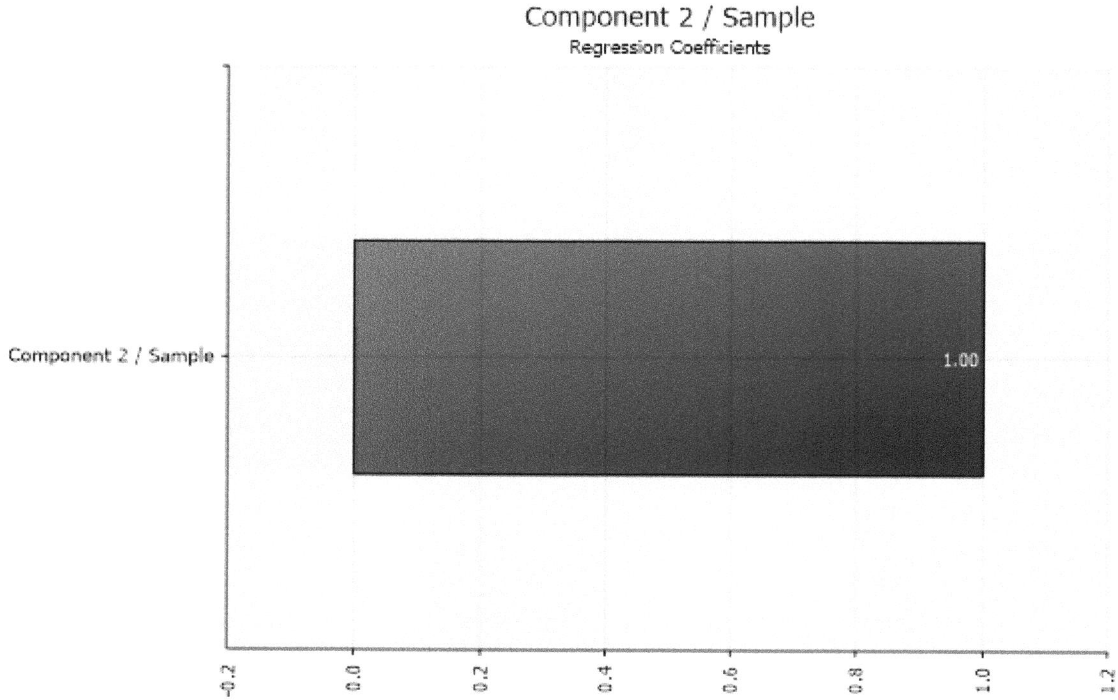

This graph illustrates the Component 2 / Sample variable with a positive coefficient of 1.00. Therefore, if Component 2 / Sample increases by one Standard Deviation, the Sample Total will increase by 1.00 Standard Deviations.

The Correlation Coefficients are presented in Figure 10.

The graph shows that if the variable Component 2 / Sample with a correlation coefficient of 1.00 increases by one unit, the Sample Total will increase by 1.00 units.

Figure 10. Component 2 / sample correlation coefficients

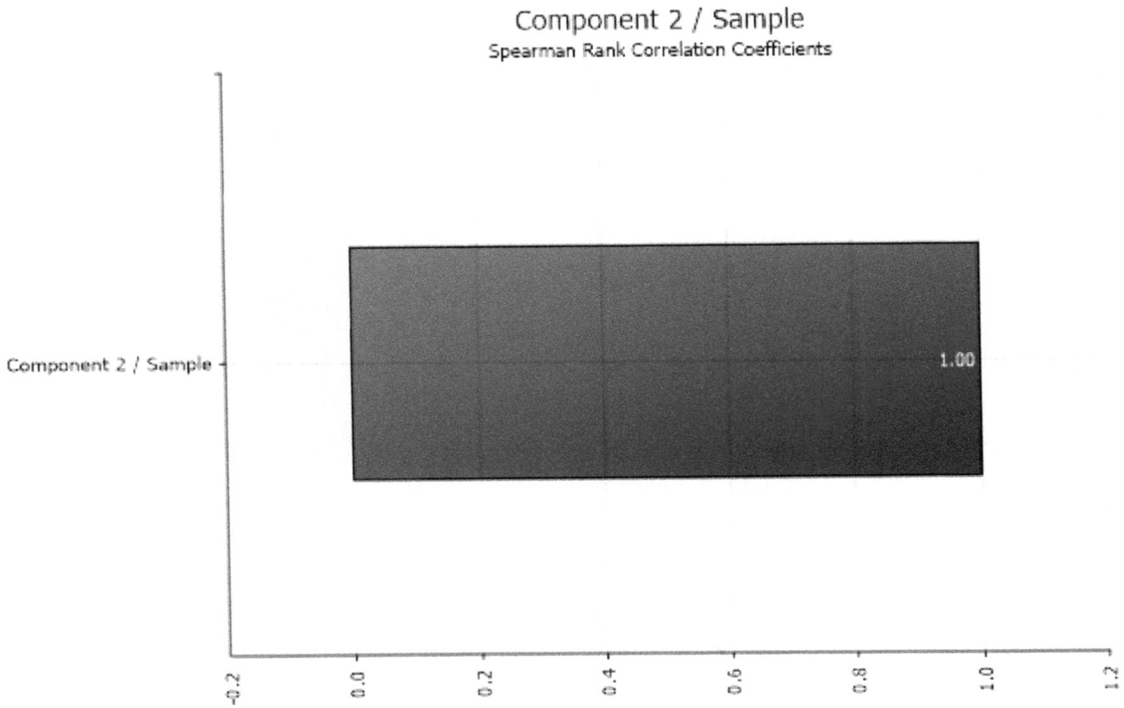

The Contribution to Variance graph is presented in Figure 11.

Figure 11. Component 2 / sample contribution to variance

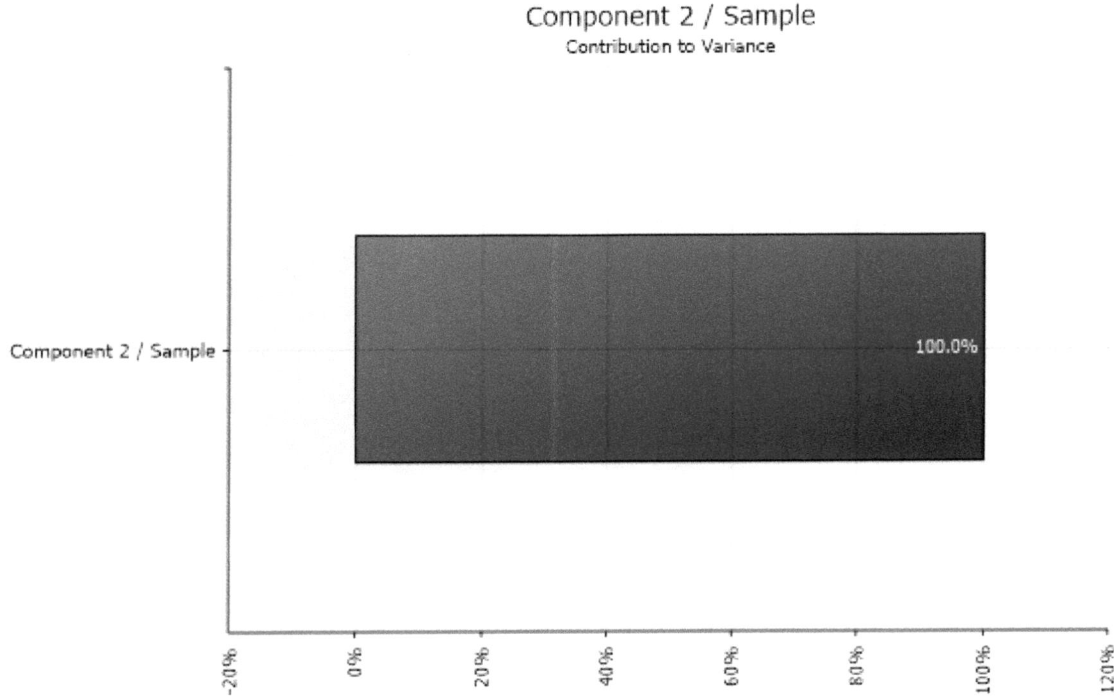

Figure 11 illustrates that the variable Component 2 / Sample has a contribution of 100.0% to the variance of the Sample Total.

The Change in Output Mean Across a Range of Input Values graph is presented in Figure 12.

Figure 12. Component 2 / sample change in output mean across range of input values

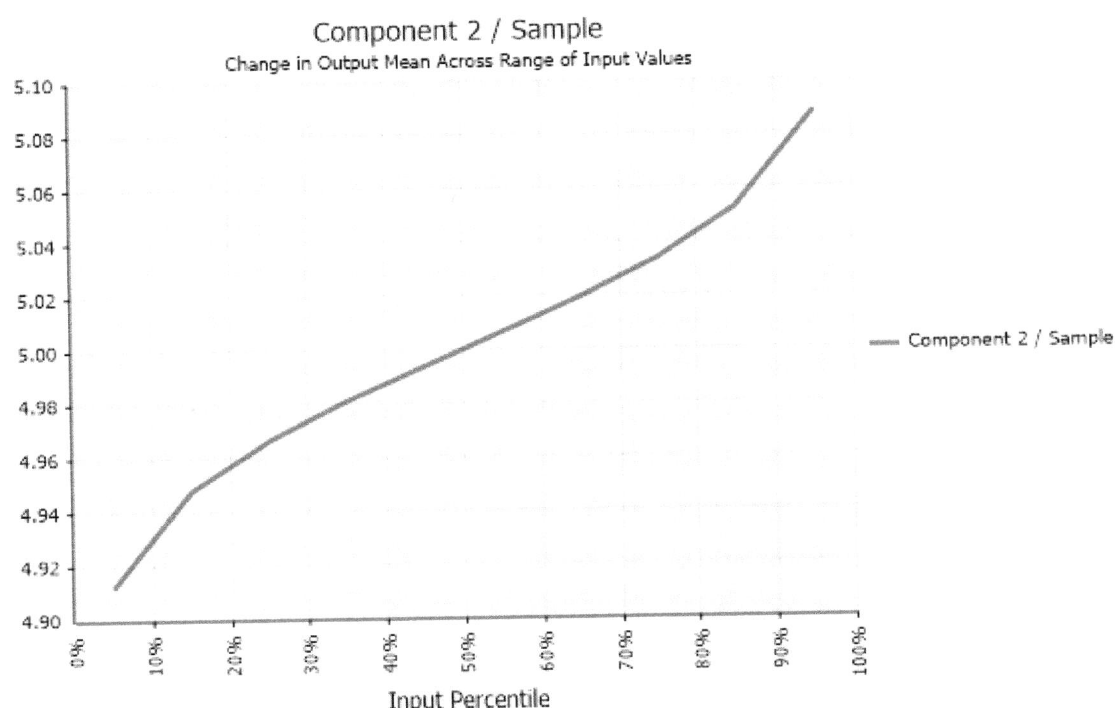

Figure 12 illustrates that Component 2 / Sample has a contribution of change approximately from 4.91 to 5.09 to the variance of the Sample Total.

Component 3 / Sample Analysis, Evaluation, and Risk Attribution

Figure 13 displays the Component 3 / Sample distribution. The *Mean* is 8.00 and the *Standard Deviation* is 0.10. The Six Sigma target parameters are Target Value, i.e., $TV = 8$; $LSL = 7.60$; and $USL = 8.30$. The Six Sigma process capability metrics are $Cp = 1.1667$; $Cpk = 1.00$; and Sigma Level, i.e., $\sigma\text{-}L = 3.1947$. There is a 5% probability that the *Mean* will be below 7.835; a 90% probability that it will be in the range of 7.835 – 8.164; and a 5% probability that it will be above 8.164.

Figure 13. Component 3 / sample distribution

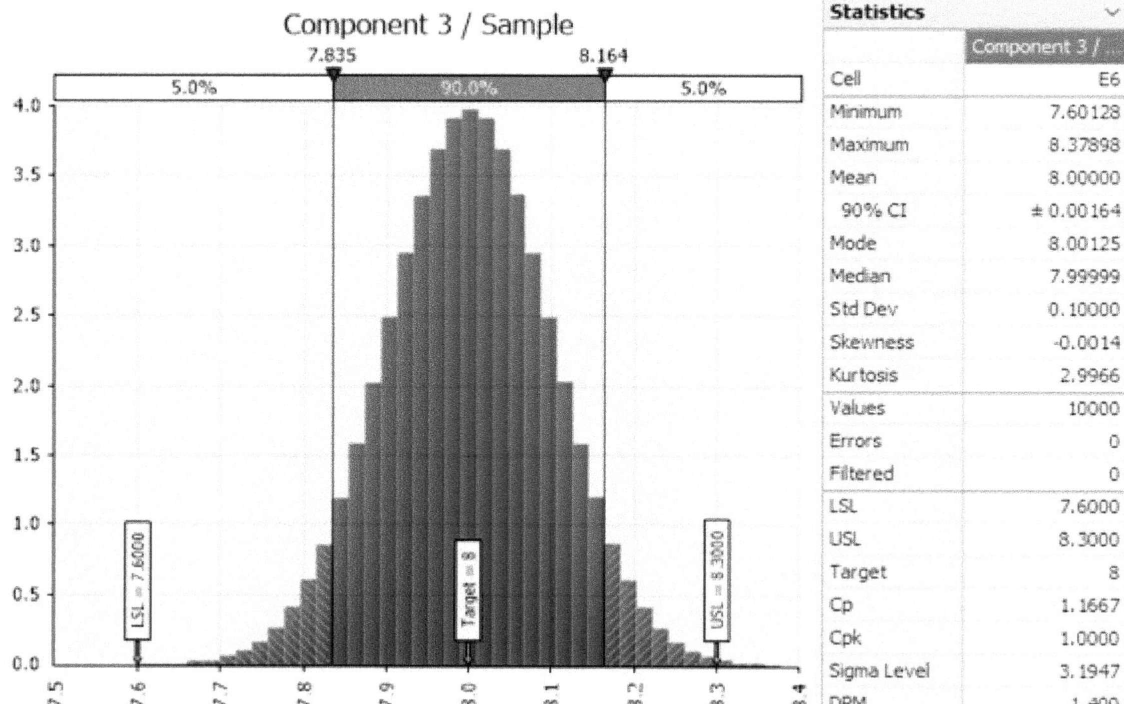

Sensitivity Analysis

Sensitivity analysis provides for identifying and quantifying the main contributors to variability and risk based on the probability distribution.

The Inputs Ranked by Effect on Output Mean are given in Figure 14.

The graph illustrates that the effect of the variable Component 3 / Sample is a change of the Sample Total in the range of 7.8245 to 8.1755, which are respectively left and right from the Baseline of 8.00, which is marked on the graph.

Figure 14. Component 3 / sample inputs ranked by effect on output mean

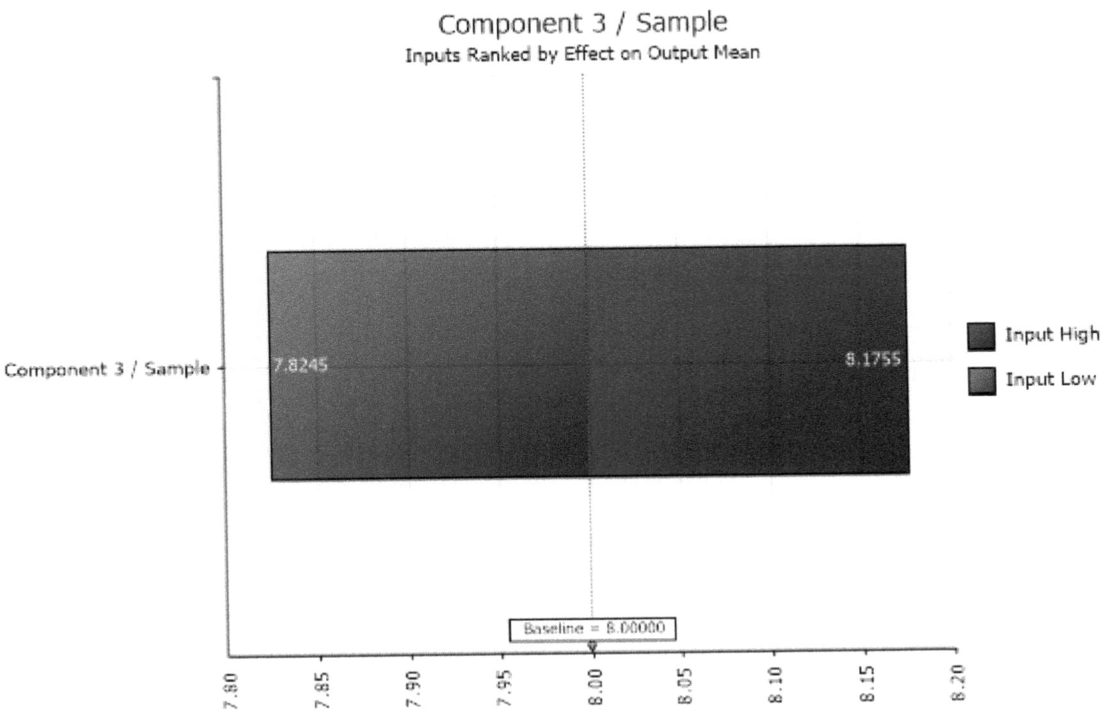

The Regression Coefficients graph is shown in Figure 15.

This graph illustrates the Component 3 / Sample variable with a positive coefficient of 1.00. Therefore, if Component 3 / Sample increases by one Standard Deviation, the Sample Total will increase by 1.00 Standard Deviations.

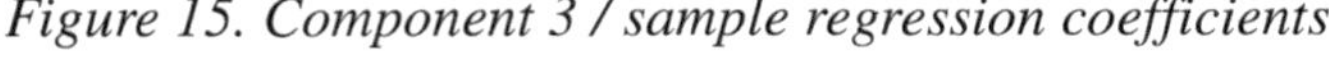

Figure 15. Component 3 / sample regression coefficients

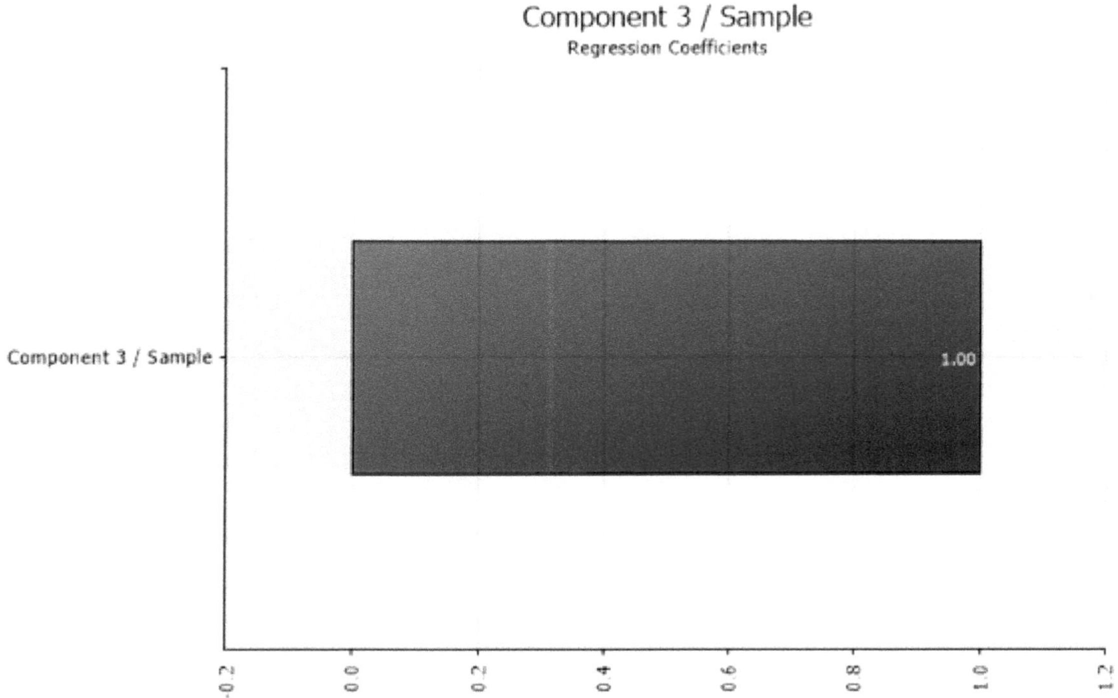

The Correlation Coefficients are presented in Figure 16.

Figure 16. Component 3 / sample correlation coefficients

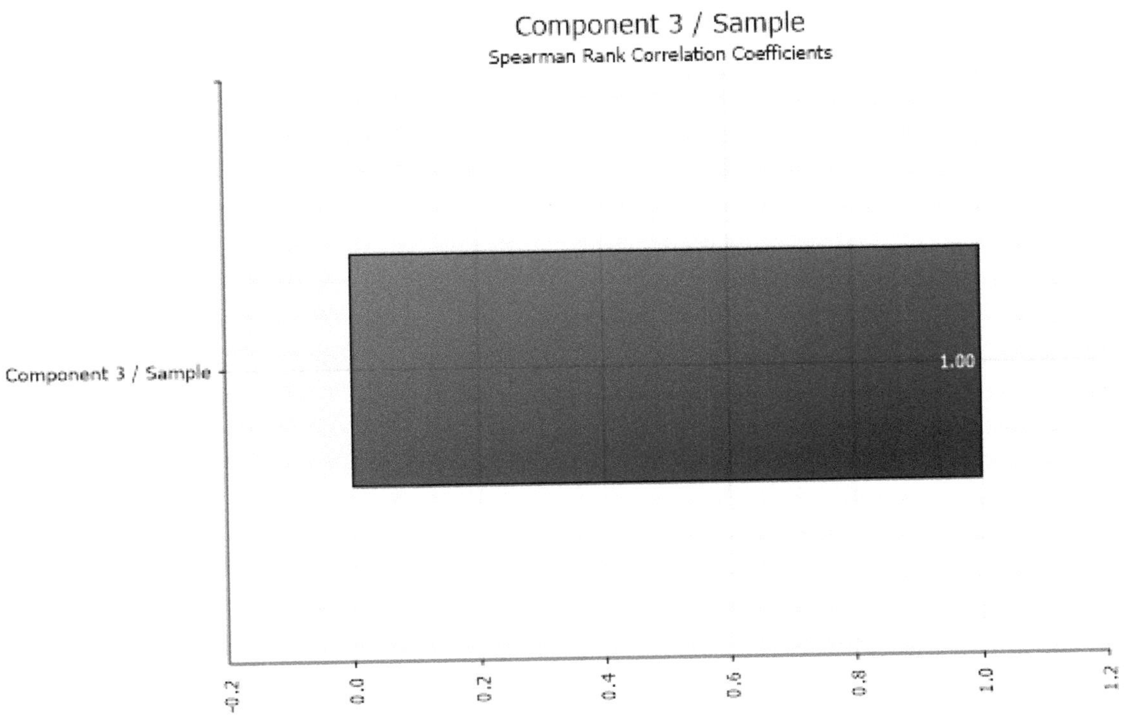

The graph shows that if the variable Component 3 / Sample with a correlation coefficient of 1.00 increases by one unit, the Sample Total will increase by 1.00 units.

The Contribution to Variance graph presented in Figure 17 illustrates that the variable Component 3 / Sample has a contribution of 100.0% to the variance of the Sample Total.

Figure 17. Component 3/ sample contribution to variance

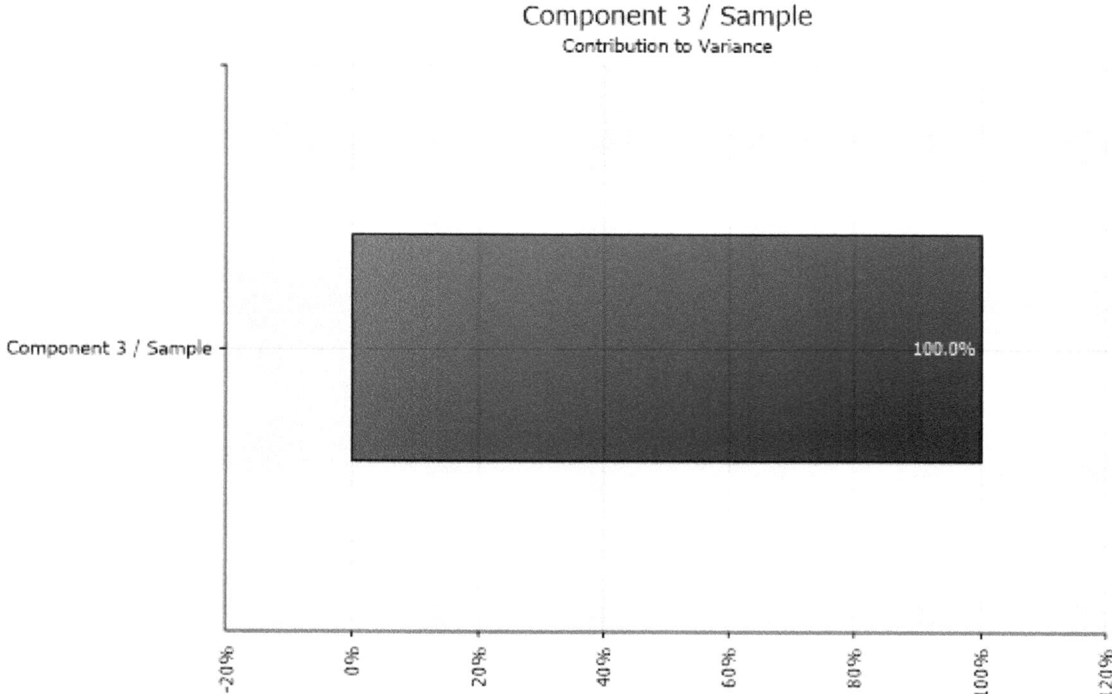

The Change in Output Mean Across a Range of Input Values graph is presented in Figure 18.

Figure 18 illustrates that Component 1 / Sample has a contribution of change approximately from 7.8250 to 8.1750 to the variance of the Sample Total.

Figure 18. Component 3 / sample change in output mean across range of input values

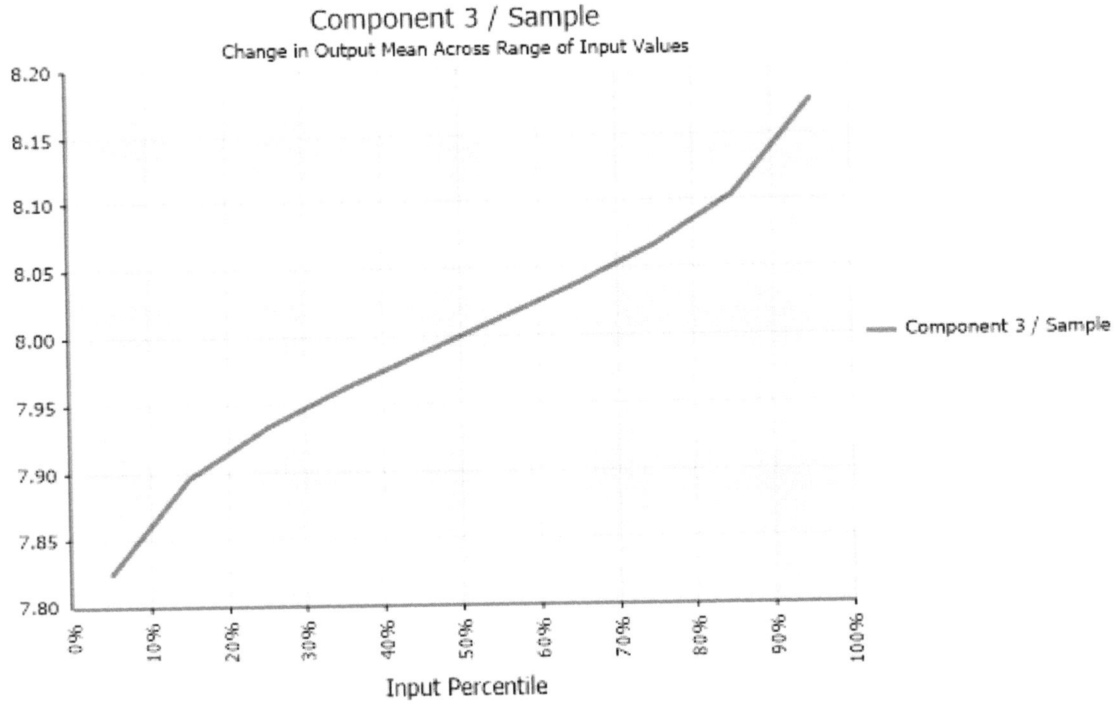

Component 4 / Sample Analysis, Evaluation, and Risk Attribution

Figure 19 displays the Component 4 / Sample distribution. The *Mean* is 12.00 and the *Standard Deviation* is 0.250. The Six Sigma target parameters are Target Value, i.e., $TV = 12$; $LSL = 11.1250$; and $USL = 12.8750$. The Six Sigma process capability metrics are $Cp = 1.1667$; $Cpk = 1.1667$; and Sigma Level, i.e., $\sigma\text{-}L = 3.5401$. There is a 5% probability that the *Mean* will be below 11.589; a 90% probability that it will be in the range of 11.589 – 12.411; and a 5% probability that it will be above 12.411.

Figure 19. Component 4 / sample distribution

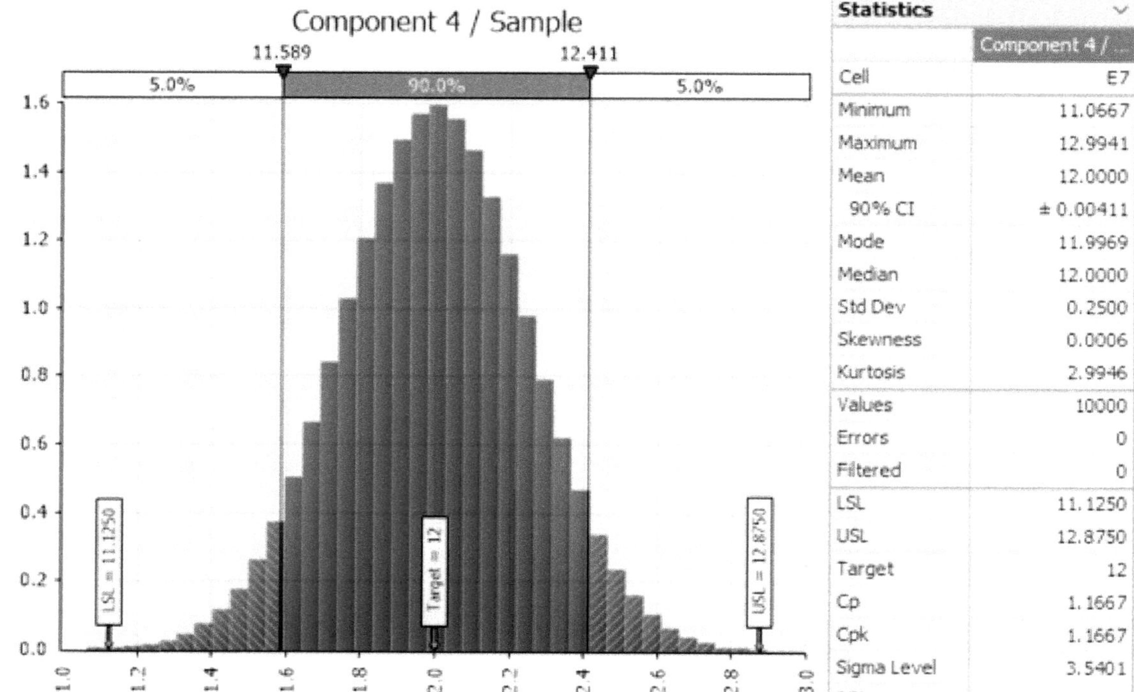

Sensitivity Analysis

Sensitivity analysis provides for identifying and quantifying the main contributors to variability and risk based on the probability distribution.

The Inputs Ranked by Effect on Output Mean are given in Figure 20.

The graph illustrates that the effect of the variable Component 4 / Sample is a change of the Sample Total in the range of 11.561 to 12.439, which are respectively left and right from the Baseline of 12.00, which is marked on the graph.

Figure 20. Component 4 / sample inputs ranked by effect on output

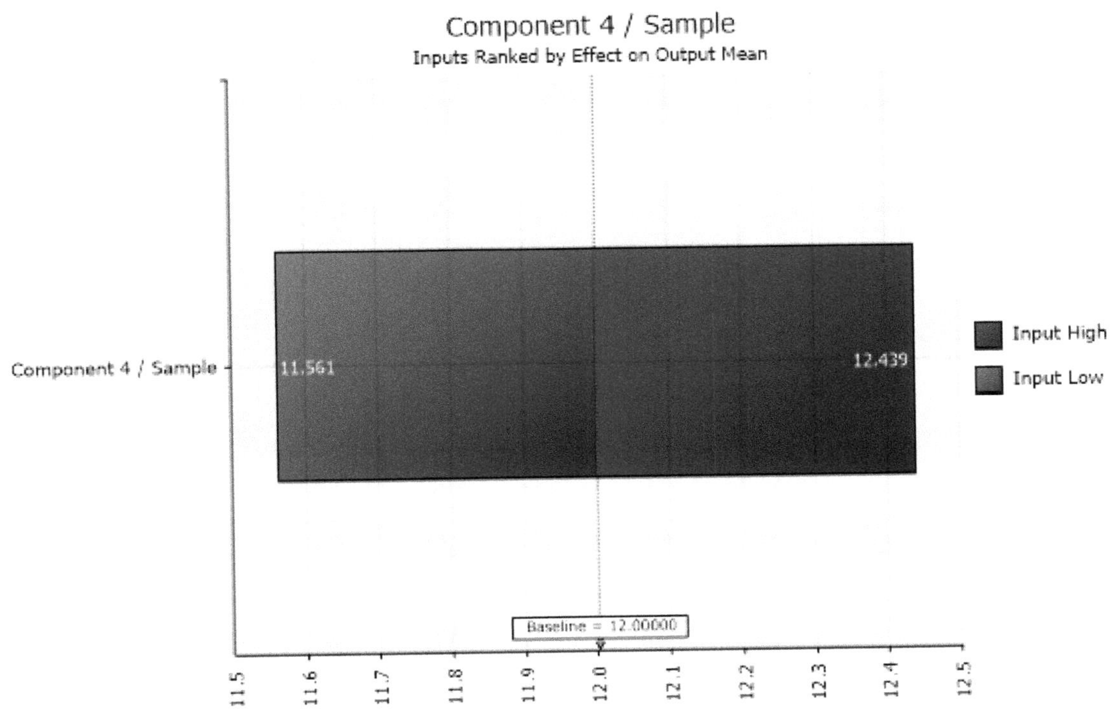

The Regression Coefficients graph is shown in Figure 21.

Figure 21. Component 4 / sample regression coefficients

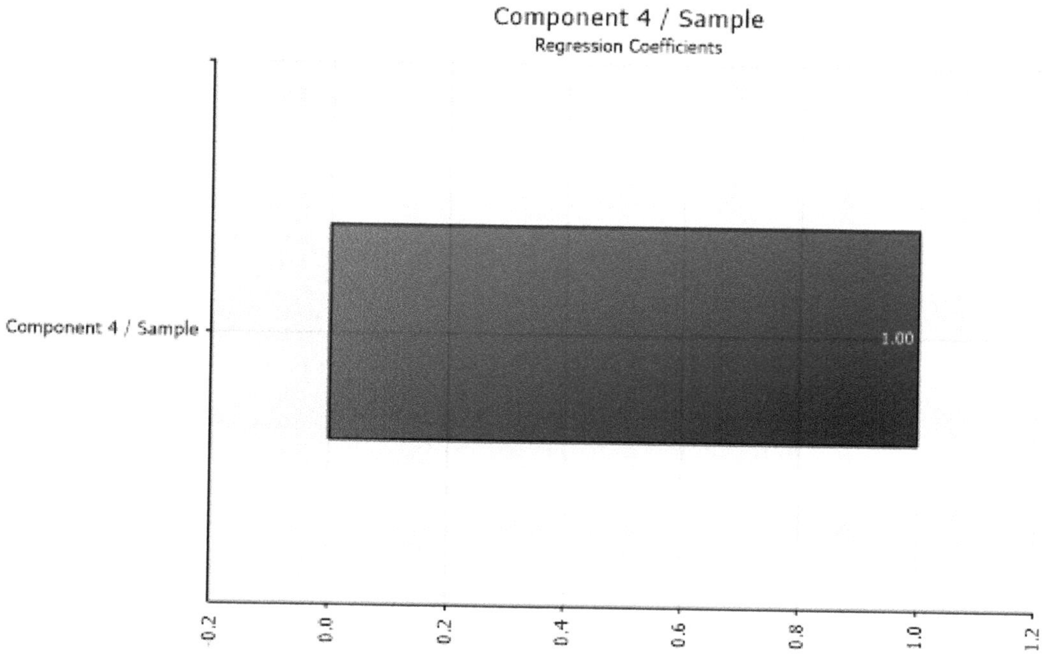

This graph illustrates the Component 4 / Sample variable with a positive coefficient of 1.00. Therefore, if Component 1 / Sample increases by one Standard Deviation, the Sample Total will increase by 1.00 Standard Deviations.

The Correlation Coefficients are presented in Figure 22.

Figure 22. Component 4 / sample correlation coefficients

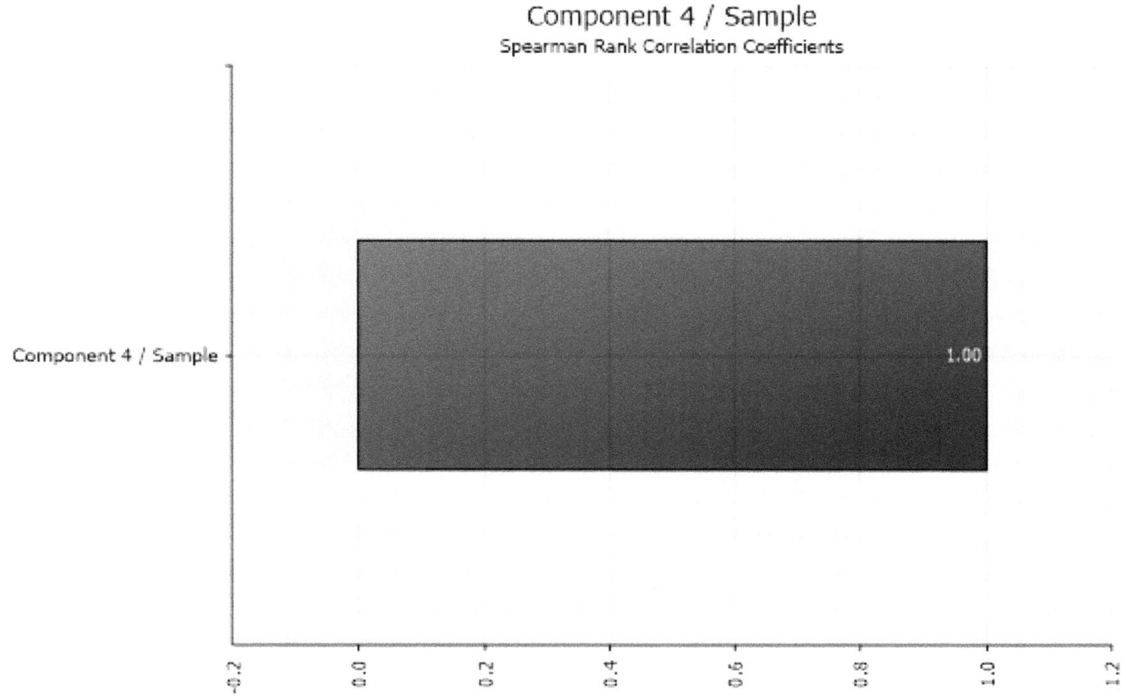

The graph shows that if the variable Component 4 / Sample with a correlation coefficient of 1.00, increases by one unit, the Sample Total will increase by 1.00 units.

The Contribution to Variance graph presented in Figure 23 illustrates that the variable Component 4 / Sample has a contribution of 100.0% to the variance of the Sample Total.

Figure 23. Component 4 / sample contribution to variance

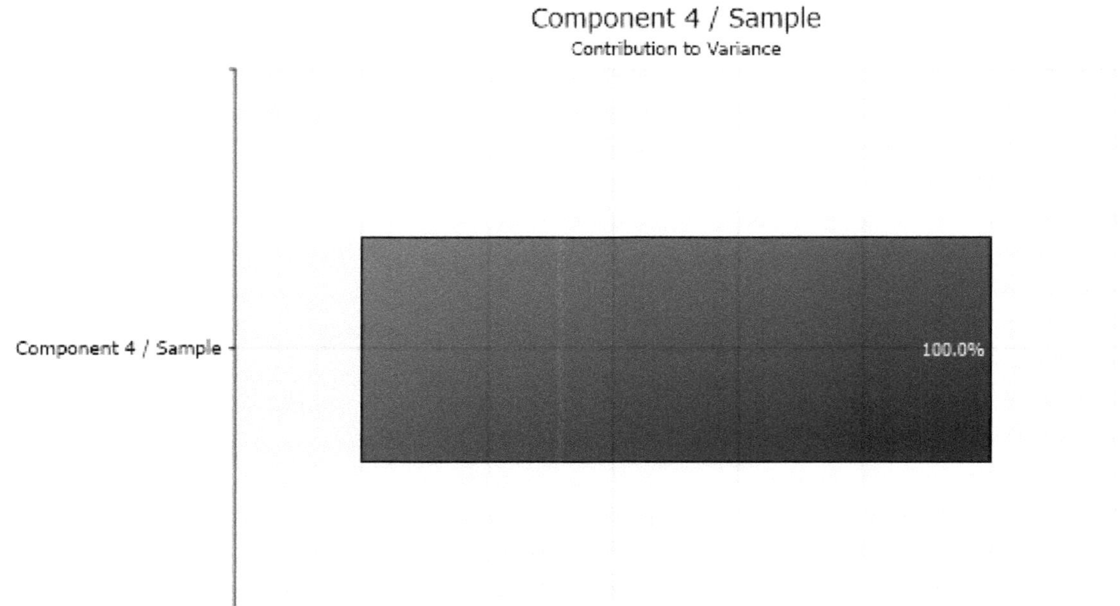

The Change in Output Mean Across a Range of Input Values graph is presented in Figure 24.

Figure 24. Component 4/ sample change in output mean across range of input values

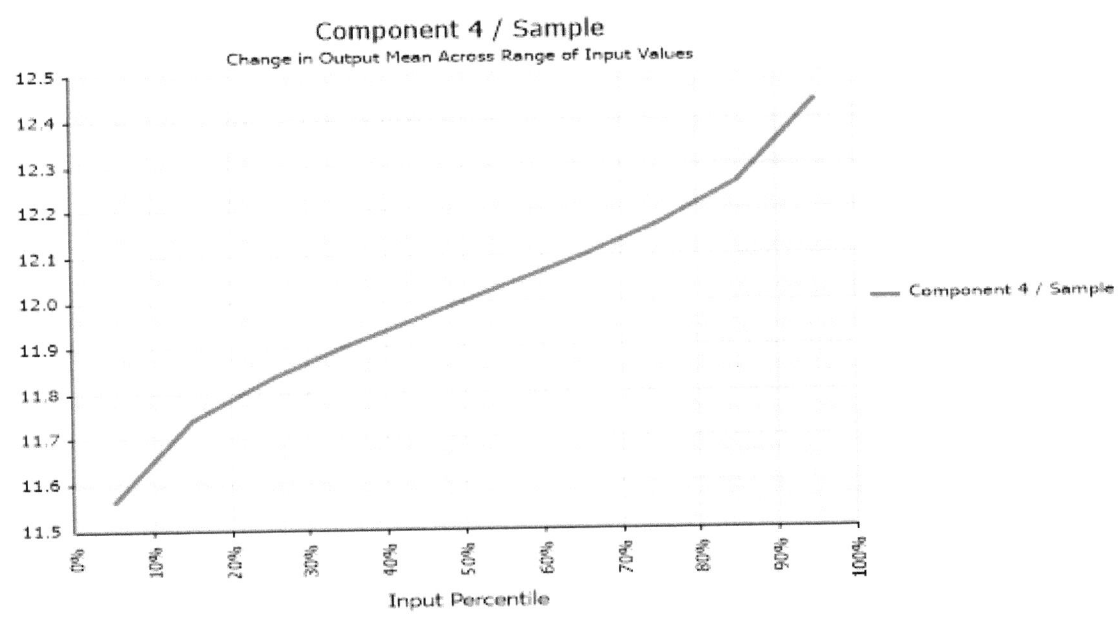

Figure 24 illustrates that Component 41 / Sample (in Red), has a contribution of change approximately from 11.55 to 12.45 to the variance of the Sample Total.

Component 5 / Sample Analysis, Evaluation, and Risk Attribution

Figure 25 displays the Component 5 / Sample distribution. The *Mean* is 6.00 and the *Standard Deviation* is 0.10. The Six Sigma target parameters are Target Value, i.e., $TV = 6$; $LSL = 5.70$; and $USL = 6.50$. The Six Sigma process capability metrics are $Cp = 1.3333$; $Cpk = 1.0000$; and Sigma Level, i.e., $\sigma\text{-}L = 3.1947$. There is a 5% probability that the *Mean* will be below 5.835; a 90% probability that it will be in the range of 5.835 – 6.164; and a 5% probability that it will be above 6.164.

Figure 25. Component 5 / sample distribution

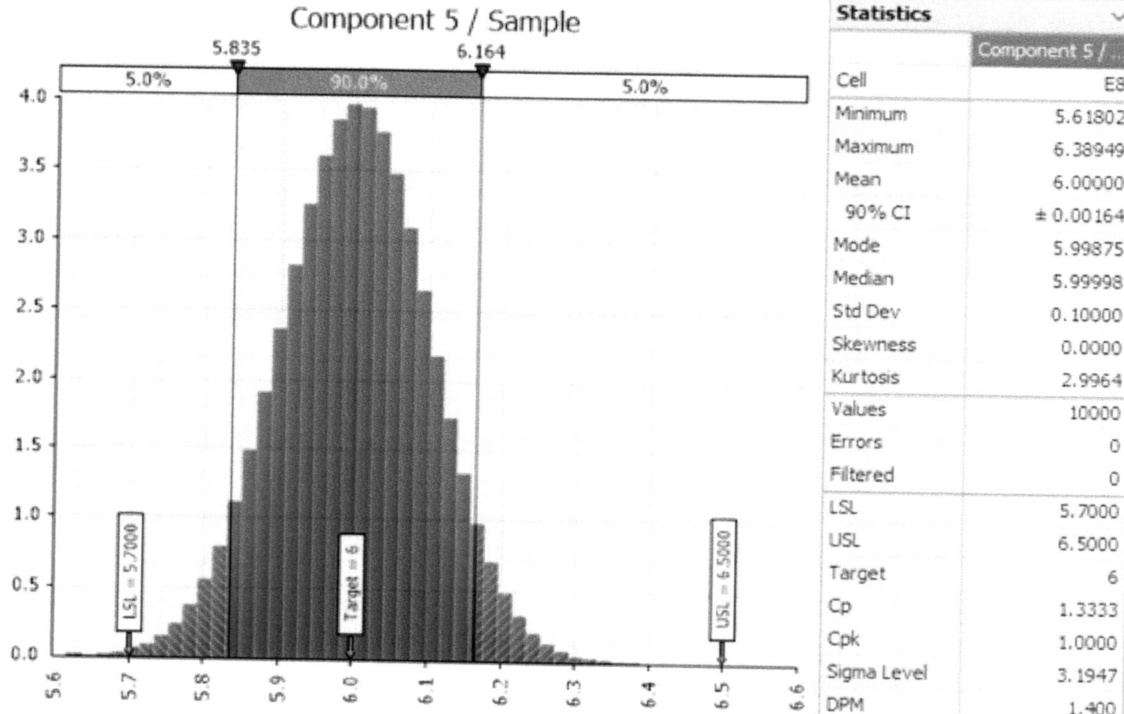

Sensitivity Analysis

Sensitivity analysis provides for identifying and quantifying the main contributors to variability and risk based on the probability distribution.

The Inputs Ranked by Effect on Output Mean are given in Figure 26.

The graph illustrates that the effect of the variable Component 5 / Sample is a change of the Sample Total in the range of 5.8245 to 6.1755, which are respectively left and right from the Baseline of 6.00, which is marked on the graph.

Figure 26. Component 5 / sample inputs ranked by effect on output mean

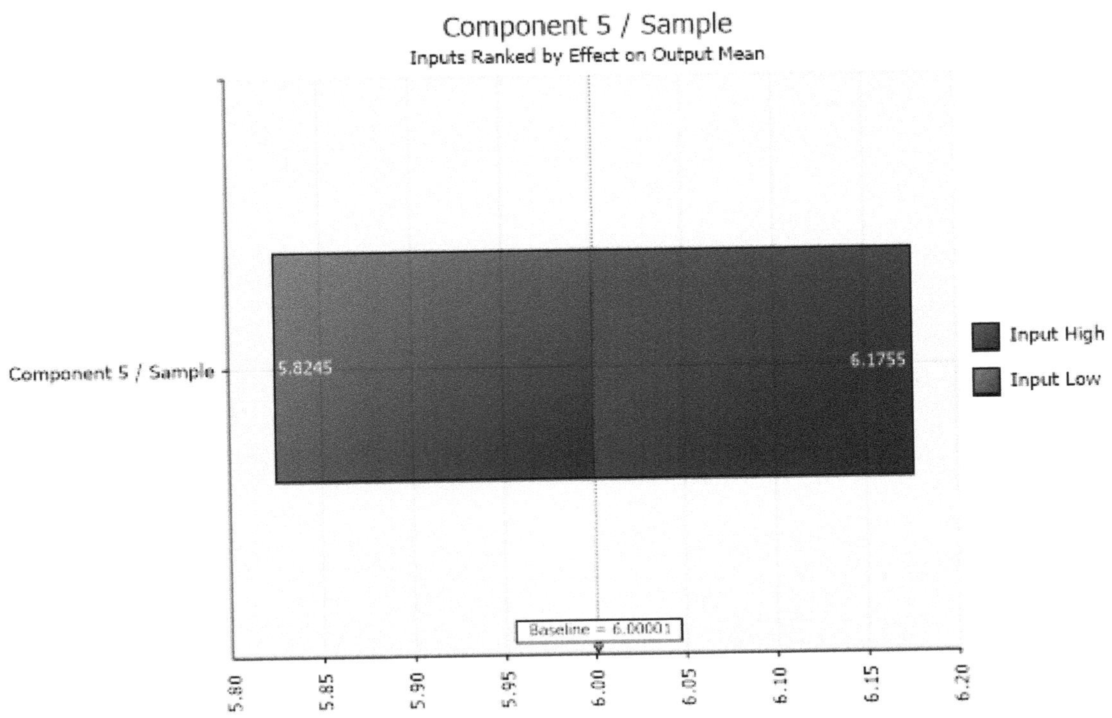

The Regression Coefficients graph is shown in Figure 27.

Figure 27. Component 5 / sample regression coefficients

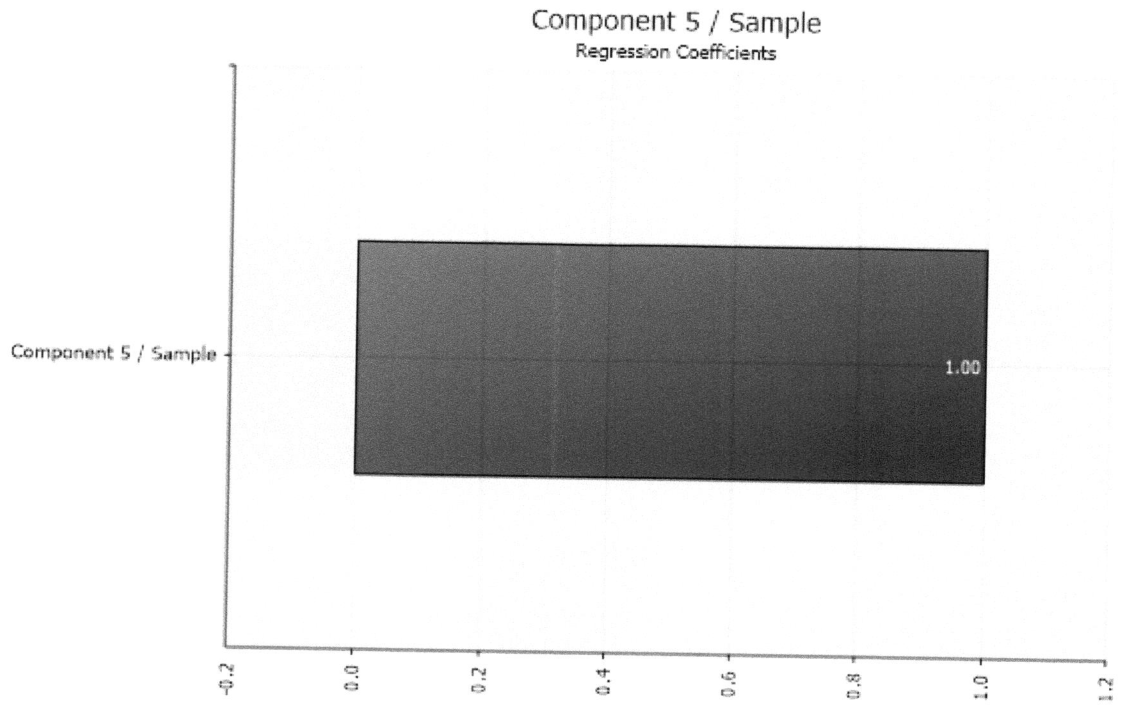

This graph illustrates the Component 5 / Sample variable with a positive coefficient of 1.00. Therefore, if Component 5 / Sample increases by one Standard Deviation, the Sample Total will increase by 1.00 Standard Deviations.

The Correlation Coefficients are presented in Figure 28.

The graph shows that if the variable Component 5 / Sample with a correlation coefficient of 1.00 increases by one unit, the Sample Total will increase by 1.00 units.

Figure 28. Component 5 / sample correlation coefficients

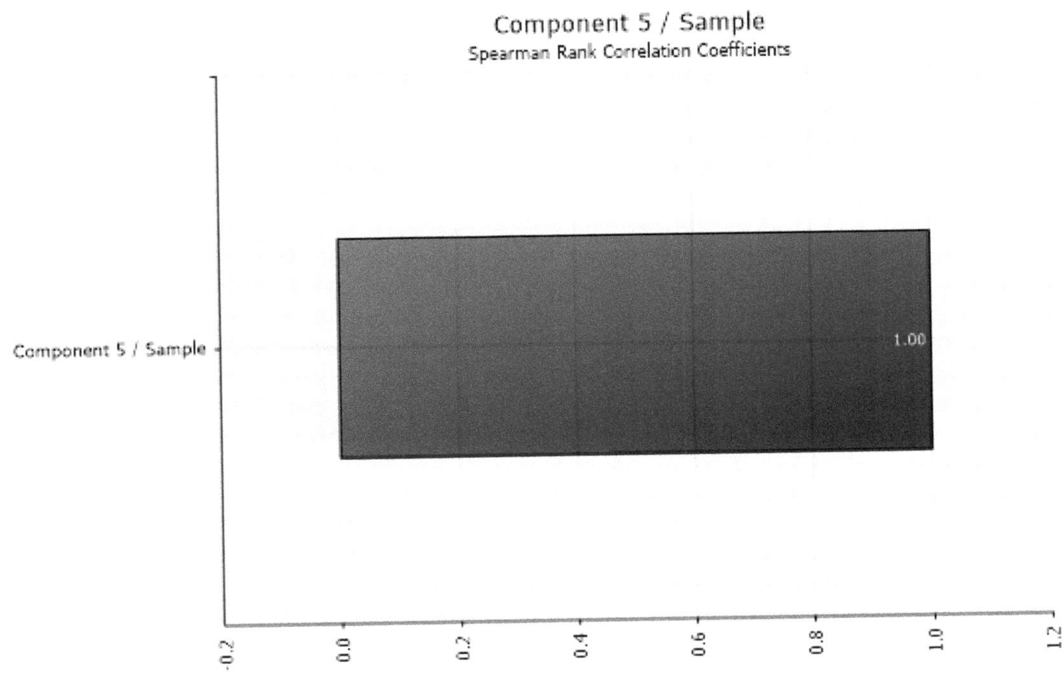

The Contribution to Variance graph presented in Figure 29 illustrates that the variable Component 1 / Sample has a contribution of 100.0% to the variance of the Sample Total.

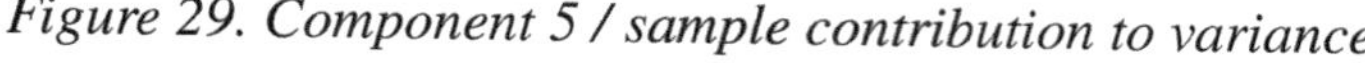

Figure 29. Component 5 / sample contribution to variance

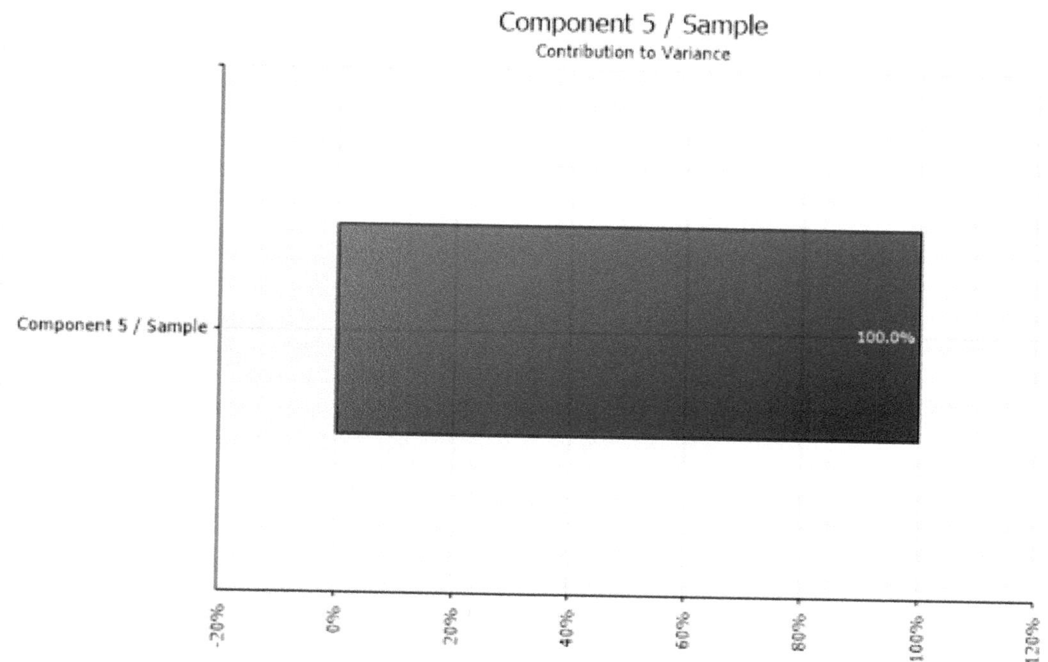

The Change in Output Mean Across a Range of Input Values graph is presented in Figure 30.

Figure 30. Component 5 / sample change in output mean across range of input values

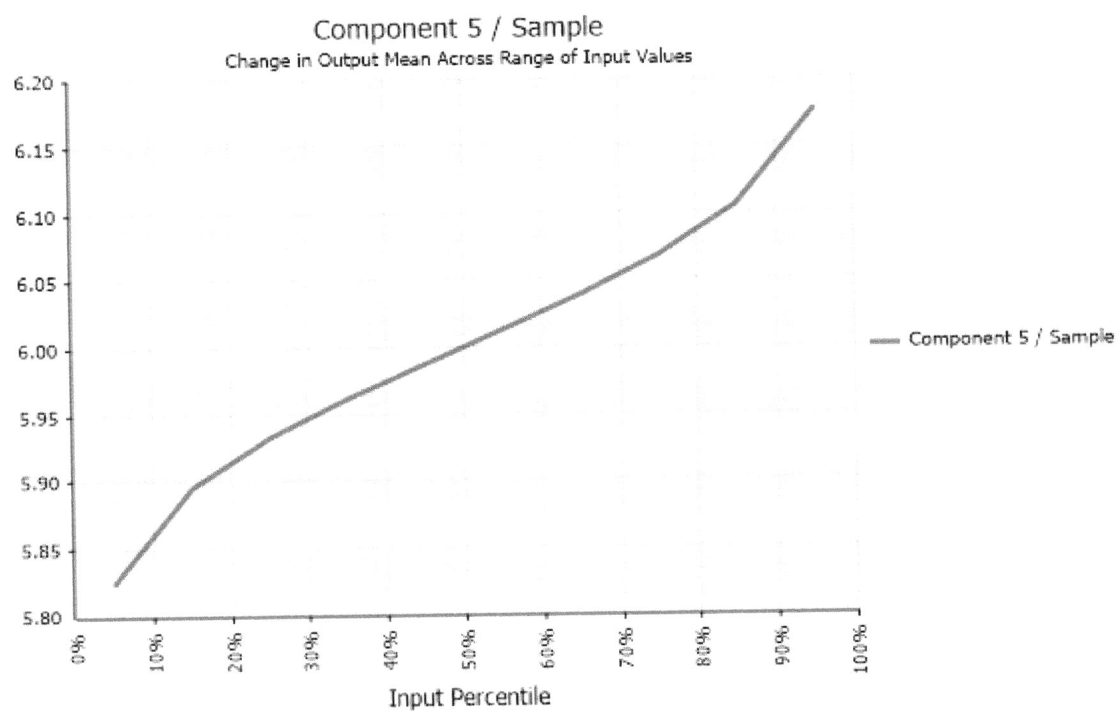

Figure 30 illustrates that Component 5 / Sample has a contribution of change approximately from 5.825 to 6.175 to the variance of the Sample Total.

CONCLUSION

This chapter presented the Six Sigma Failure Rate model for use in quality control and planning. Assume that you are a manufacturer and need to calculate the percentage of defective products. The DMAIC method (Define Measure, Analyze, Improve, Control), comprises the Measure and Analyze phases, where you wish to measure the current state of quality and analyze the causes of problems or defects.

A product is defective when any one of its components does not meet its required tolerance level. Each component is deemed to be satisfactory if some property of its finished state (e.g., its width) lies within the defined tolerance limits. This property of each finished component (e.g., its width) is modeled with a Normal distribution in the Sample column. These cells have also been designated as @RISK outputs with RiskSixSigma property functions defining LSL, USL, and Target values for each component. In this way, you will be able to see graphs of the components' quality and calculate Six Sigma statistics on each component. After running the simulation, it can be seen that the mean Failure Rates, as well as other Six Sigma statistics, such as Z Min score and DPM.

Note: Because failures are so uncommon, the simulation should be run for many iterations, such as 10,000, to get accurate results.

REFERENCES

Baxter, R. (2023). Lean Six Sigma DMAIC Workbook: for Instructor-Led Workshops. Value Generation Partners.

Johnson, R. (2023). 100 DMAIC Tools: A Comprehensive Guide to Six Sigma Problem Solving. Academic Press.

Panneman, T., & Stemann, D. (2021). Six Sigma DMAIC: 8 Simple Steps for Successful Green Belt Projects. Academic Press.

Pyzdek, T., & Keller, P. A. (202)3. The Six Sigma Handbook, Sixth Edition: A Complete Guide for Green Belts, Black Belts, and Managers at All Levels. McGraw Hill.

Savant, S. (2018). DMAIC: Project Execution Essentials Handbook. Independent Publisher.

Chapter 4
Six Sigma DMAIC Failure Rate With RiskTheo Functions

ABSTRACT

The Six Sigma failure rate extension model is presented in quality control and planning. It includes the use of RiskTheo functions (i.e., RiskTheoXtoP) for determining the failure rate without actually running a simulation. RiskTheo functions return theoretical statistics on input distributions rather than returning the statistics on the data from a simulation run. A manufacturer wants to calculate the likely percentage of defective products. A product is defective when any one of its components does not meet its required tolerance level. Each component is deemed to be satisfactory if some property of its finished state lies within the defined tolerance limits. Properties of each finished component are modeled with a normal distribution in RiskTheo failure rate (%). The @RISK outputs with RiskTheo failure rate (%) total values to see graphs of the components' quality and calculate Six Sigma statistics on each component with simulation focusing on the RiskTheoXtoP function.

INTRODUCTION

This chapter represents an extension of the Six Sigma Failure Rate model in quality control and planning. It includes the use of RiskTheo functions (in this case RiskTheoXtoP) for determining the failure rate without actually running a simulation. RiskTheo functions return theoretical statistics on input distributions rather than returning the statistics on the data from a simulation run.

Properties of each finished component are modeled with a Normal Distribution in RiskTheo Failure Rate (%). The @RISK outputs with RiskTheo Failure Rate (%) Total values to see graphs of the components' quality and calculate Six Sigma statistics on each component with simulation focusing on the RiskTheoXtoP function.

You are a manufacturer and want to calculate the likely % of defective products. A product is defective when any one of its components does not meet its required tolerance level. Each component is deemed to be satisfactory if some property of its finished state (e.g., its width) lies within the defined tolerance limits. This property of each finished component (e.g., its width) is modeled with a Normal distribution

DOI: 10.4018/979-8-3693-3787-5.ch004

in the Sample column. In this way, you can see graphs of the components' quality and calculate Six Sigma statistics on each component if you run a simulation.

The component and aggregate failure rate is calculated from the RiskTheoXtoP function, which draws on the Normal distributions in the Sample column. The failure rate from the simulation is also calculated using the RiskMean function if you choose to run a simulation. In this way, you can compare the simulated failure rate with the RiskTheo failure rate. After a simulation, you can also see Six Sigma statistics, such as Z score and DPM.

Note: Because failures are so uncommon, the simulation should be run for many iterations, such as 10,000, to get accurate results. In contrast, the RiskTheo values are exact; they don't depend on the simulation or the number of iterations.

Literature

A book by Panneman & Stemann (2021) is a Six Sigma DMAIC guide in leading a Green Belt project in manufacturing. Where most books about Six Sigma are just a list of available tools, this book explains the Six Sigma tools using a simple 8-step method overlapping the DMAIC phases. Within each step, this book provides a clear description of the tools that readers can use, and when to apply which one in your project. Over 50 tools are presented in this book, and we provide practical examples for each of them. This will equip the readers with the knowledge to solve major manufacturing problems. After reading this book, the readers will be able to lead a DMAIC project following 8 steps, choose which tools are useful for their specific project, and learn how the tools are linked together and used in combination for successful results.

Johnson's (2023) book offers a treasure trove of 100 essential DMAIC tools. These are meticulously curated to guide you through the Define, Measure, Analyse, Improve, and Control phases. The book empowers the readers with the means to eliminate inefficiencies, reduce defects, and optimise every corner of your operations. The book provides: i) Practical explanations of each tool's purpose and application; ii) Real-world case studies showcasing their successful implementations; iii) Step-by-step guides to implement each tool effectively; iv) Expert tips and best practices to help you master the DMAIC methodology; and v) A blueprint for continuous improvement and securing long-term success. The tools in the book provide for redefining organizations' operations and achieving unparalleled results.

Pyzdek & Keller (2023) show readers how to build dynamic teams and foster effective leadership while maximizing customer satisfaction and boosting profits. This new edition features several important updates such as big data and machine learning techniques, mind mapping, applications to healthcare and health statistics, and modern supply chain challenges. The book also lays out cutting-edge applications for obtaining and analysing social media data, decision trees, remote technology, and web scrapers for capturing and analysing Internet data. The latest edition features the use of the free open-source R statistical package and the BlueSky GUI interface.

Savant (2018) has more than a decade of experience in executing, leading, and mentoring hundreds of Lean Six Sigma improvement projects and brings to the readers a simple, straight forward, no-nonsense handbook that will enable them to execute Lean Six Sigma DMAIC projects quickly, effectively, and efficiently. The author shares his belief: "Keep things simple, crisp, and concise, and then executing Lean Six Sigma projects will be easy and fun for you". With this book, the readers will get to know: i) The core essential components needed to execute a DMAIC project; ii) How to execute a DMAIC project, using the core essential components; and iii) To help the readers to deliver a DMAIC faster. Baxter's

(2023) book "Lean Six Sigma DMAIC Workbook" is designed to be used for instructor-led workshops yet may be used as a handy reference guide for all levels of practitioners. The workbook contains many tools, techniques, approaches, and exercises to lead the reader through the DMAIC methodology, i.e., Define, Measure, Analyse, Improve, and Control.

ELABORATION

Simulation's Data (Six Sigma DMAIC Define)

Table 1. Six Sigma failure rate parameters with RiskTheo function

Components	Mean (Target)	Std Dev	Lower (LSL)	Upper (USL)
Component 1	10.00	0.20	9.40	10.60
Component 2	5.00	0.05	4.83	5.15
Component 3	8.00	0.10	7.60	8.30
Component 4	12.00	0.25	11.13	12.88
Component 5	6.00	0.10	5.70	6.50

Simulation's Calculations (Six Sigma DMAIC Define)

The Simulation of the Sample is shown in Table 2:

Table 2. The simulation of sample

Components	Formula
Component 1	=@RiskOutput („, RiskSixSigma(F4,G4,C4,0,0))+@RiskNormal(C4,D4)
Component 2	=@RiskOutput („, RiskSixSigma(F5,G5,C5,0,0))+@RiskNormal(C5,D5)
Component 3	=@RiskOutput („, RiskSixSigma(F6,G6,C6,0,0))+@RiskNormal(C6,D6)
Component 4	=@RiskOutput („, RiskSixSigma(F7,G7,C7,0,0))+@RiskNormal(C7,D7)
Component 5	=@RiskOutput („, RiskSixSigma(F8,G8,C8,0,0))+@RiskNormal(C8,D8)
Sample Total	=SUM(E4:E8)

The Simulation of "OK?" is shown in Table 3:

Table 3. The simulation of "OK?"

Components	Formula "OK?"
Component 1	=@RiskOutput (,"Components OK",1)+ IF(AND(F4<=E4,E4<=G4),1,0)
Component 2	=@RiskOutput (,"Components OK",2)+ IF(AND(F5<=E5,E5<=G5),1,0)
Component 3	=@RiskOutput (,"Components OK",3)+ IF(AND(F6<=E6,E6<=G6),1,0)
Component 4	=@RiskOutput (,"Components OK",4)+ IF(AND(F7<=E7,E6<=G7),1,0)
Component 5	=@RiskOutput (,"Components OK",5)+ IF(AND(F8<=E8,E5<=G8),1,0)
Product	=@RiskOutput ("Product OK")+ IF(PRODUCT(H4:H8)=1,1,0)

The simulation model presents the Six Sigma DMAIC, which is shown in Failure Rate, Z Min, and DPM Table 4.

Table 4. Failure rate from simulation, Z min, and DPM formulas

Components	Failure Rate from Simulation	Z Min	DPM
Component 1	=1-@RiskMean(H4)	=@RiskZmin(E4)	=@RiskDPM(E4)
Component 2	=1-@RiskMean(H5)	=@RiskZmin(E5)	=@RiskDPM (E5)
Component 3	=1-@RiskMean(H6)	=@RiskZmin(E6)	=@RiskDPM (E6)
Component 4	=1-@RiskMean(H7)	=@RiskZmin(E7)	=@RiskDPM (E7)
Component 5	=1-@RiskMean(H8)	=@RiskZmin(E8)	=@RiskDPM (E8)
Product	=1-@RiskMean(H9)	None	=SUM(K4:K8)

The simulation model presents the Six Sigma DMAIC, which is shown in Failure Rate from RiskTheo Table 5.

Table 5. Failure rate from RiskTheo

Components	Failure Rate from RiskTheo
Component 1	=@RiskTheoXtoP(E4,F4)+(-@ RiskTheoXtoP(E4,G4)
Component 2	=@RiskTheoXtoP(E5,F5)+(-@ RiskTheoXtoP(E5,G5)
Component 3	=@RiskTheoXtoP(E6,F6)+(-@ RiskTheoXtoP(E6,G6)
Component 4	=@RiskTheoXtoP(E7,F7)+(-@ RiskTheoXtoP(E7,G7)
Component 5	=@RiskTheoXtoP(E8,F8)+(-@ RiskTheoXtoP(E8,G8)
Product	=1-(1-J4) *(1-J5) *(1-J6) *(1-J7) *(1-J8)

The simulation model presents the calculated Product Values, which are shown in "OK?", Failure Rate form Simulation, Failure Rate form RiskTheo, and DPM Table 4.6.

Table 6. "OK?", failure rate from simulation, failure rate form RiskTheo, and DPM formulas

"OK?"	Failure Rate from Simulation	Failure Rate from RiskTheo	DPM
1	0.730%	0.746%	7,300

The simulation model presents the RiskTheo Failure Rate in Table 7.

Table 7. RiskTheo failure rate (%) formula

RiskTheo Failure Rate (%)
=@RiskOutput (,,,"RiskTheo Failure Rate (%)")+@RiskNormal(C9,D9)

Simulation Analysis, Evaluation, and Risk Attribution (Six Sigma DMAIC Analyse)

The Six Sigma DMAIC RiskTheo Failure Rate (%) aspects are analysed below.

The RiskTheo Failure Rate (%) Analysis, Evaluation, and Risk Attribution

Figure 1 displays the RiskTheo Failure Rate (%) distribution. The *Mean* is 41.00 and the *Standard Deviation* is 0.70. There is a 5% probability that the *Mean* will be below 30.85; a 90% probability that it will be in the range of 30.85 – 42.15; and a 5% probability that it will be above 42.15.

Figure 1. RiskTheo failure rate (%) distribution

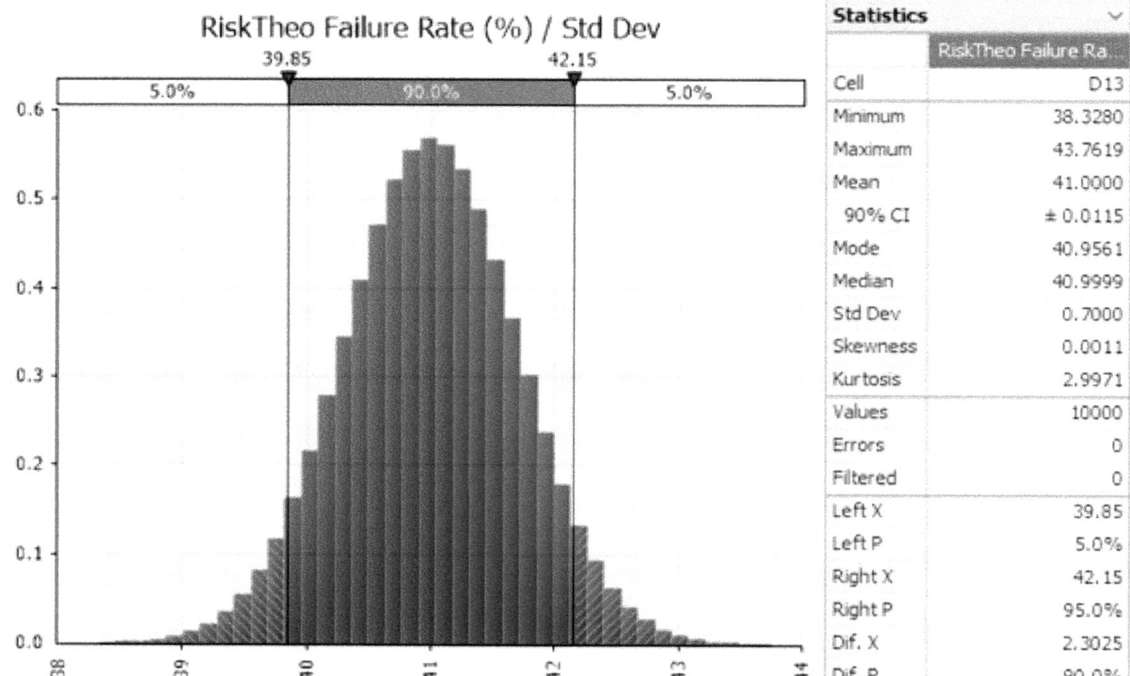

Sensitivity Analysis

Sensitivity analysis provides for identifying and quantifying the main contributors to variability and risk based on the probability distribution.

The Inputs Ranked by Effect on Output Mean are given in Figure 2.

The graph illustrates that the effect of the variable RiskTheo Failure Rate (%) is a change of the RiskTheo Failure Rate (%) Total in the range of 39.772 to 42.229, which are respectively left and right from the Baseline of 41.00, which is marked on the graph.

Figure 2. RiskTheo failure rate (%) inputs ranked by effect on output mean

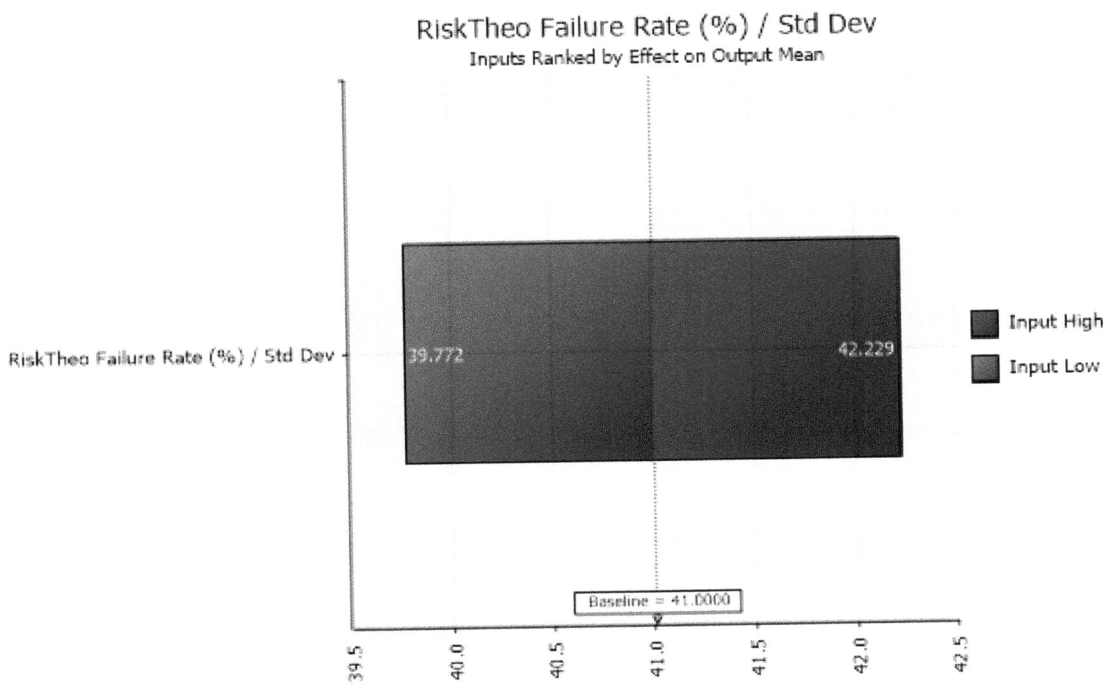

The Regression Coefficients graph is shown in Figure 3.

Figure 3. RiskTheo failure rate (%) regression coefficients

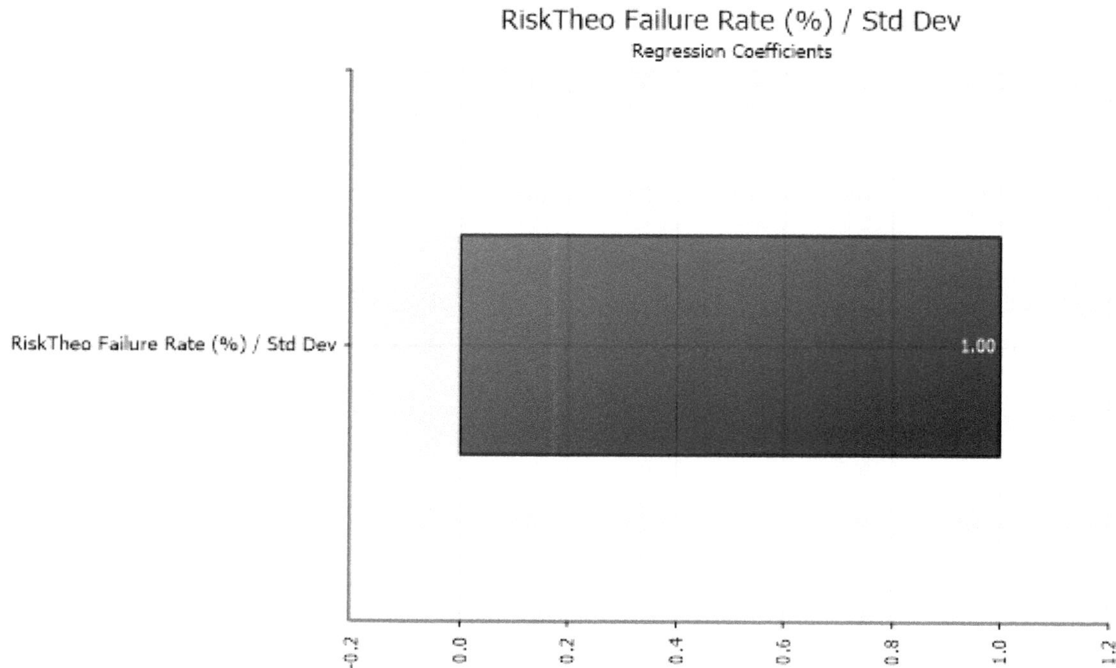

This graph illustrates the RiskTheo Failure Rate (%) variable with a positive coefficient of 1.00. Therefore, if the RiskTheo Failure Rate (%) increases by one Standard Deviation, the RiskTheo Failure Rate (%) Total will increase by 1.00 Standard Deviations.

The Correlation Coefficients are presented in Figure 4.

Figure 4. RiskTheo failure rate (%) correlation coefficients

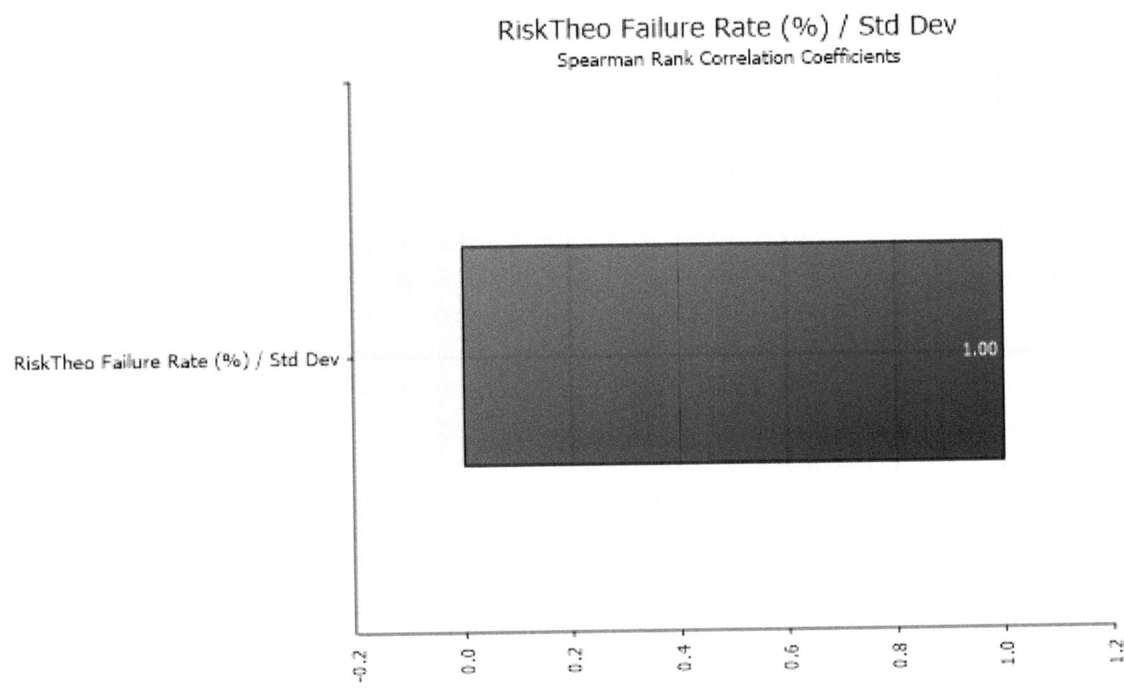

The graph shows that if the variable RiskTheo Failure Rate (%) with a correlation coefficient of 1.00, increases by one unit, the RiskTheo Failure Rate (%) Total will increase by 1.00 units.

The Contribution to Variance graph presented in Figure 5 illustrates that the variable RiskTheo Failure Rate (%) has a contribution of 100.0% to the variance of the RiskTheo Failure Rate (%) Total.

Figure 5. RiskTheo failure rate (%) contribution to variance

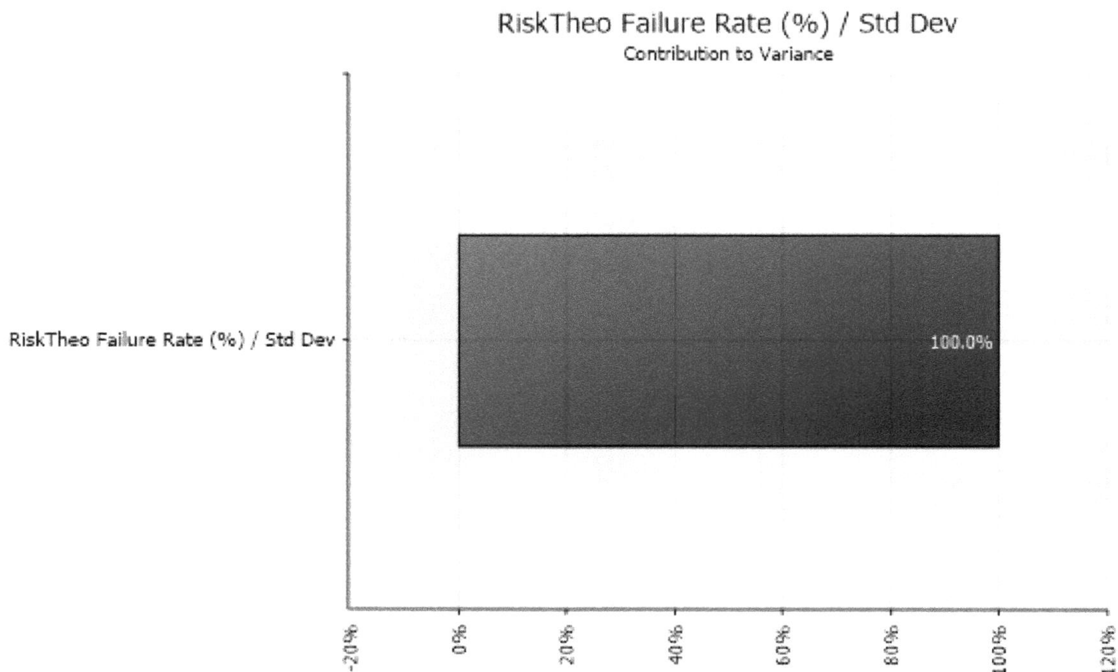

The Change in Output Mean Across a Range of Input Values graph is presented in Figure 6.

Figure 6. RiskTheo failure rate (%) change in output mean across range of input values

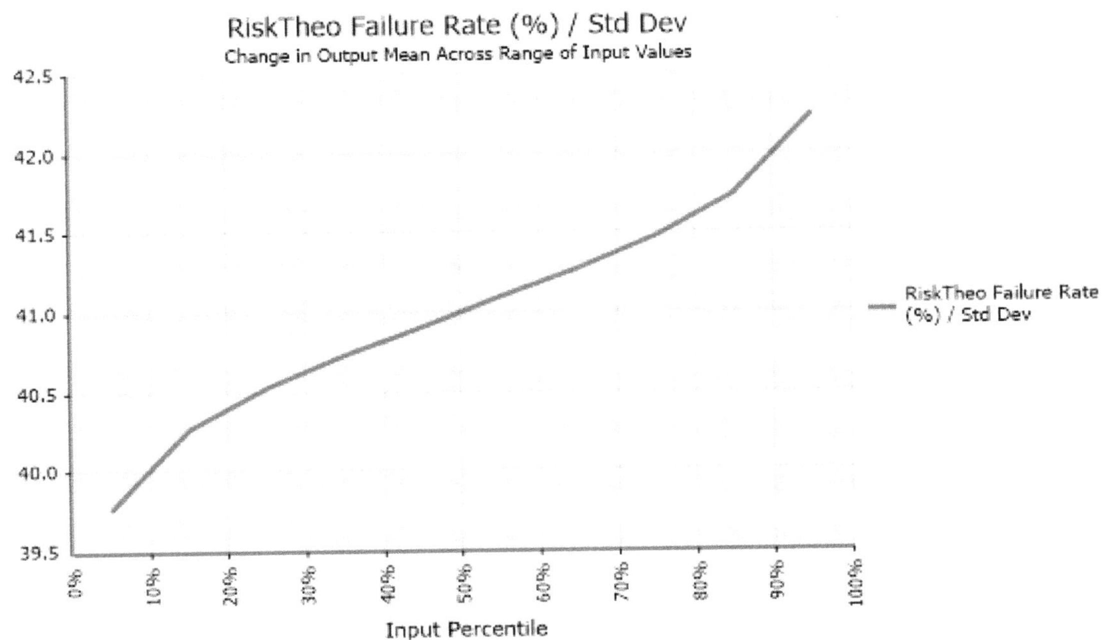

Figure 6 illustrates that the RiskTheo Failure Rate (%)has a contribution of change approximately from 39.75 to 42.25 to the variance of the RiskTheo Failure Rate (%) Total.

CONCLUSION

This chapter represented an extension of the Six Sigma Failure Rate model in quality control and planning. It includes the use of RiskTheo functions (in this case RiskTheoXtoP) for determining the failure rate without actually running a simulation. RiskTheo functions return theoretical statistics on input distributions rather than returning the statistics on the data from a simulation run.

Properties of each finished component were modeled with a Normal Distribution in RiskTheo Failure Rate (%). The @RISK outputs with RiskTheo Failure Rate (%) Total values to see graphs of the components' quality and calculate Six Sigma statistics on each component with simulation focusing on the RiskTheoXtoP function.

You are a manufacturer and want to calculate the likely % of defective products. A product is defective when any one of its components does not meet its required tolerance level. Each component is deemed to be satisfactory if some property of its finished state (e.g., its width) lies within the defined tolerance limits. This property of each finished component (e.g., its width) is modeled with a Normal distribution in the Sample column. In this way, you can see graphs of the components' quality and calculate Six Sigma statistics on each component if you run a simulation.

The component and aggregate failure rates were calculated from the RiskTheoXtoP function, which draws on the Normal distributions in the Sample column. The Failure Rate from the simulation is also calculated using the RiskMean function if you choose to run a simulation. In this way, you can compare the simulated failure rate with the RiskTheo failure rate. After a simulation, you can also see Six Sigma statistics, such as Z score and DPM.

Note: Because failures are so uncommon, the simulation should be run for many iterations, such as 10,000, to get accurate results. In contrast, the RiskTheo values are exact; they don't depend on the simulation or the number of iterations.

REFERENCES

Baxter, R. (202)3. Lean Six Sigma DMAIC Workbook: for Instructor-Led Workshops. Value Generation Partners.

Johnson, R. (2023). 100 DMAIC Tools: A Comprehensive Guide to Six Sigma Problem Solving. Academic Press.

Panneman, T., & Stemann, D. (2021). Six Sigma DMAIC: 8 Simple Steps for Successful Green Belt Projects. Academic Press.

Pyzdek, T., & Keller, P. A. (2023). The Six Sigma Handbook, Sixth Edition: A Complete Guide for Green Belts, Black Belts, and Managers at All Levels. McGraw Hill.

Savant, S. (2018). DMAIC: Project Execution Essentials Handbook. Independent Publisher.

Chapter 5
Financial Statements Prediction

ABSTRACT

This chapter presents an example of modelling financial statements for businesses. The model is created for general forecasting purposes, including financing needs and credit analysis. In this example, a company has a fairly healthy forecasted cash flow for 2020 but also aims to reduce its long-term debt in 2020 to a desired amount from the known debt in 2019. The company is forecasting that, in the base case, its financial position will be sufficient to do this. However, it wishes to analyze the probability that a short-term financing facility will be needed. The short-term debt could be zero; therefore, the probability that it is non-zero is thoroughly analyzed.

INTRODUCTION

The simulation model to forecast the financial statements considers the following aspects: Income Statement, Balance Sheet, Ratios, Checks, Balancing Items, and Cash Flow Statement.

The Income Statement includes the following variables: Sales, Sales Cost, Other Costs, Depreciation, Operating Profit, Net Interest Expense, Taxable Profit, Tax, Net Income, Dividends, and Retained Earnings.

Balance Sheet comprises the following variables: Cash, Short-term Investments, Inventory, Accounts Receivable, Total Current Assets, Net PPE (Property, Plant, and Equipment), Total Assets, Accounts Payable, Taxes Payable, Dividends Payable, Short-term Debt, Current Liabilities, Long-term Debt, Total Liabilities Pre-Equity, Share Common Stock Capital, Accumulated Retained Earnings and Total Liabilities & Equity.

Ratios, Checks, and Balancing Items involve the following variables: Balancing Check Zero, Net Debt, Operating Assets, LHS excl. Balancing s/t Investments, RHS excl. Balancing s/t Debt and Amount Required to Balance.

Cash Flow Statement includes the following variables: Operating Net Income, Operating Depreciation, Operating Increase in Inventory, Operating Increase in Accounts Receivable, Operating Increase Accounts Payable, Operating Increase in Taxes Payable, Operating Sub-Total, Investment in PPE, Investing Sub-Total, Financing Increase in Short-term Investments, Financing Increase in Short-term Debt, Financing

DOI: 10.4018/979-8-3693-3787-5.ch005

Increase in Long-term Debt, Financing Increase in Common Stock, Financing Payment of Dividend, Financing Sub-Total, Net Increase in Cash from CFS, Net Increase in Cash from BS, and Check Zero.

The company has the actual Financial Statements data for 2018 and 2019. Therefore, the forecast for 2020 is based on the actual data for the previous two years. The company had a fairly good cash flow for 2018 and 2019. Thus, the important objectives are to reduce its: i) Long-term debt in 2020 to $70 MM from $97 MM in 2019; and ii) Short-term debt in 2020 to zero from $2 MM in 2019, to avoid the requirement for short-term financing.

A simulation model is created to forecast the Financial Statements. Five simulations are run to provide a comprehensive analysis. The five simulation results are evaluated, including sensitivity analysis, and compared considering the risk factors. The short-term debt objective is achieved by three simulations and the long-term debt is achieved by all simulations.

The comparison of the simulation results concludes that Simulation 1 predicted the maximal Operating Profit and Net Income, with minimal associated risk factors.

Literature

Ittelson's (2020) book is an introduction to financial accounting and explains the accounting and financial reporting concepts. It simply demonstrates how the balance sheet, income statement, and cash flow statement work together. The terms and the concepts are simply explained with basic transaction examples. Buffett & Clark (2011) have written a simple guide for reading financial statements from Buffett's successful perspective. They clearly outline Warren Buffett's strategies in a way that will appeal to novices and Buffett practitioners. Inspired by the seminal work of Buffett's mentor, Benjamin Graham, this book presents Buffett's interpretation of financial statements with anecdotes and quotes from the master investor himself. This book is destined to become a classic in the world of investment books. The book is a perfect companion for financial professionals across businesses.

In their book, Fridson & Alvarez (2011) combine the financial statement academic work with real-life examples to form a good reference for business professionals. The case studies in the book provide samples of the techniques that companies use. Also, the book shows illustrative cases of financial statement analysis for businesses.

Skonieczny's (2012) book helps readers understand the basics of financial statements. The material covered includes step-by-step instructions on how to read and understand the balance sheet, the income statement, and the cash flow statement. It also covers information about how these three statements are interconnected with one another.

The Warren Buffett Accounting Book by Brodersen & Pysh (2014) is the second-volume learning experience of Warren Buffett's three favourite books. This book teaches i) two methods for calculating the intrinsic value of a company; ii) what is a discount rate and how it works; iii) detailed instructions on how to read an income statement, balance sheet, and cash flow statement; and iv) how to calculate important ratios to properly value any business. Higson (2006) explains the logic of financial statements, and how to use them to analyse businesses in economic terms. The book covers several topics including the analysis of growth, business modelling, financial performance, accounting models, cash flow, and financial statement reporting. The book also examines the main problem areas in accounting and reviews the two dominant accounting systems: GAAP (Generally Accepted Accounting Principles), and IFRS (International Financial Reporting Standards).

The Problem Statement Create a simulation model to forecast the Financial Statements. Five simulations should be run to provide a comprehensive analysis. Evaluate the five simulation results, including sensitivity analysis, and compare them considering the risk factors. Consider that short-term debt and long-term debt should be achieved. Compare the simulation results, discuss them, and identify the simulation which predicts the maximal Operating Profit and Net Income, with minimal associated risk factors. ELABORATION

The scenario presented in this chapter is hypothetical, using the data published by Palisade™ Corporation. Project's Data (DMAIC Define)

The simulation model to forecast the financial statements considers the following items: i) Income Statement; ii) Balance Sheet; iii) Ratios, Checks, and Balancing Items; and iv) Cash Flow Statement. The Income Statement includes the variables shown in Table 1:

Table 1. Income statement

Income Statement	2018	2019	2020
Sales	950	1000	#NAME?
Sales Cost	625	645	#NAME?
Other Costs	210	215	#NAME?
Depreciation	47	50	#NAME?
Operating Profit	68	90	#NAME?
Net Interest Expense	5	6	4.32
Taxable Profit	63	84	#NAME?
Tax	19	25	#NAME?
Net Income	44	59	#NAME?
Dividends	13	17	#NAME?
Retained Earnings	31	42	#NAME?

The Balance Sheet comprises the variables shown in Table 2:

Table 2. Balance sheet

Balance Sheet	2018	2019	2020
Cash	20	25	#NAME?
Short-term Investments	10	20	#NAME?
Inventory	100	110	#NAME?
Accounts Receivable	70	75	#NAME?
Total Current Assets	200	230	#NAME?
Net PPE	290	310	#NAME?
Total Assets	490	540	#NAME?
Accounts Payable	80	84	#NAME?
Taxes Payable	19	25	#NAME?
Dividends Payable	13	17	#NAME?
Short-term Debt	10	2	#NAME?
Current Liabilities	122	128	#NAME?
Long-term Debt	95	97	70
Total pre-Equity Liabilities	217	225	#NAME?
Share Common Stock Capital	125	125	125
Accumulated Retained Earnings	148	190	#NAME?
Total Liability & Equity	490	540	#NAME?

The BS (Balance Sheet) Ratios, Checks, and Balancing Items contain the variables shown in Table 3:

Table 3. BS ratios, checks, and balancing items

BS Ratios, Checks & Balancing Items	2018	2019	2020
Balancing Check Zero	0	0	#NAME?
Net Debt	75	54	#NAME?
Operating Assets	400	436	#NAME?
LHS excl. Balancing s/t Investments			#NAME?
RHS excl. Balancing s/t Debt			#NAME?
Amount Required to Balance			#NAME?
Total Liability & Equity	490	540	#NAME?

Cash Flow Statement includes the variables shown in Table 4:

Table 4. Cash flow statement

Cash Flow Statement	2018	2019	2020
Operating Net Income	-	-	#NAME?
Operating Depreciation	-	-	#NAME?
Operating Increase in Inventory	-	-	#NAME?
Operating Increase in Accounts Receivable	-	-	#NAME?
Operating Increase in Accounts Payable	-	-	#NAME?
Operating Increase in Taxes Payable	-	-	#NAME?
Operating sub Total	-	-	#NAME?
Investment in PPE	-	-	#NAME?
Investing sub Total	-	-	#NAME?
Financing Increase in Short-term Investments	-	-	#NAME?
Financing Increase in Short-term Debt	-	-	#NAME?
Financing Increase in Long-term Debt	-	-	-27.000
Financing Increase in Common Stock	-	-	0.000
Financing Payment of Dividend	-	-	17.000
Financing sub Total	-	-	#NAME?
Net Increase in Cash CFS	-	-	#NAME?
Net Increase in Cash BS	-	-	#NAME?
Check Zero	-	-	#NAME?

The company has the actual Financial Statements data for 2018 and 2019 as presented in Tables 1, 2, and 3 above. Therefore, the forecast for 2020 (i.e., the calculated data) is based on the actual data for the previous two years. The company had a fairly good cash flow for 2018 and 2019.

Calculations (DMAIC Define)

The Microsoft™ Excel® and Palisade™ @RISK® formulae are used for the calculations presented in this section.

PERT Parameters and Six Sigma Targets

The PERT Most Likely (*MostLikely*) parameters are given in Table 5. The Minimum (*Min*) and Maximum (*Max*) PERT parameters are calculated from the Most Likely parameter with the following formulae for all five simulations:

$$\text{Min} = \text{MostLikely} * 0.9 \tag{1}$$

$$\text{Max} = \text{MostLikely} * 1.1 \tag{2}$$

Table 5. PERT most likely parameters

Statements Data	Sim 1	Sim 2	Sim 3	Sim 4	Sim 5
Sales	4.74%	5.00%	5.26%	5.53%	5.79%
Sales Cost	58.63%	61.89%	65.14%	68.40%	71.66%
Other Costs	19.62%	20.71%	21.80%	22.89%	23.98%
Depreciation	15.52%	16.38%	17.24%	18.11%	18.97%
Cash	2.07%	2.19%	2.30%	2.42%	2.53%
Inventory	9.69%	10.23%	10.76%	11.30%	11.84%
Accounts Receivable	6.69%	7.06%	7.43%	7.81%	8.18%
Net PPE	27.69%	29.23%	30.76%	32.30%	33.84%
Accounts Payable	7.57%	7.99%	8.41%	8.83%	9.25%

Note: In the Calculations section below, the variables in Table 5 are calculated by using the PERT distribution, which is specified as "*RiskPert(Min, MostLikely, Max)*" (an @RISK function). The variables for the respective PERT parameters are detailed above. This generic reference is not specified in the Calculations section.

The Six Sigma Target Value (*TV*) parameters are given in Table 56. The Lower Specified Limit (*LSL*) and Upper Specified Limit (*USL*) parameters are calculated from the Target Value (*TV*) parameter with the following formulae for all five simulations:

$$LSL = TV * 0.9 \tag{3}$$

$$USL = TV * 1.1 \tag{4}$$

Table 6. Six Sigma target value parameters

Statements Data	Sim 1	Sim 2	Sim 3	Sim 4	Sim 5
Operating Profit	179.7	131.97	83.95	35.79	-12.68
Net Income	122.83	89.41	55.77	22.04	-11.91
Total Assets	639.67	596.55	553.16	567.94	596.55
Short-term Debt	0.00	0.00	0.00	58.29	130.70
Total Liability & Equity	639.67	596.55	553.16	567.94	596.55
Operating sub Total	207.214	156.835	106.1	55.165	3.869
Investing sub Total	28.137	47.641	67.3	86.971	106.8
Financing sub Total	-182.395	-111.252	-39.5	32.29	104.697
Net Increase in Cash CFS	-3.319	-2.057	-0.762	0.484	1.765

Note: In the Calculations section below, the variables in Table 6 are calculated by using the @RISK function, which is specified as "*RiskSixSigma(USL, LSL, TV)*". The variables for the respective Six Sigma parameters are detailed above. This generic reference is not specified in the Calculations section.

Income Statement Calculations

Income Statement variables are in Table 1. The calculations are given below.

Sales (*Sales*):

Sales=(1+RiskPert(Min,MostLikely,Max))*_Sales(2019) (5)

where *Sales(2019)* is a constant given in Table 1.

Sales Cost (*SalesCost*):

SalesCost = RiskPert(Min,MostLikely,Max))*Sales (6)

Other Cost (*OtherCost*):

OtherCost = RiskPert(Min,MostLikely,Max))*_Sales (7)

Depreciation (*Depreciation*):

Depreciation = RiskPert(Min,MostLikely,Max))*_NetPPE(2019) (8)

where *NetPPE(2019)* is a constant given in Table 1.

Operating Profit (*OpertProfit*):

OpertProfit=RiskOutput("OperatingProfit",, RiskSixSigma(LSL,USL,TV,0,3))+Sales-(SalesCost+ OtherCost+Depreciation) (9)

Net Interest Expense (*NetInterstExpense*):

NetInterstExpense=(NetInterstExpense(2019)/NetDebt(2018))* NetDebt(2019) (10)

where *NetInterstExpense(2019)* is a constant given in Table 1 and *NetDebt(2018)* & *NetDebt(2019)* are constants given in Table 3.

Taxable Profit (*TaxblProfit*):

TaxblProfit= OperatingProfit – NetInterstExpense (11)

Tax (*Tax*):

Tax= AVERAGE(Tax(2018)/TaxblProfit(2018), Tax(2019)/TaxblProfit(2019))* TaxblProfit (12)

where *TaxblProfit* is the Taxable Profit and *Tax(2018)*, *TaxblProfit(2018)*, *Tax(2019)* & *TaxblProfit(2019)* are constants given in Table 1.

Net Income (*NetIncome*):

NetIncome=RiskOutput("Net-Income",, RiskSixSigma(LSL,USL,TV,0,3))+ TaxblProfit -Tax (13)

Dividends (*Dividends*):

Dividends= AVERAGE(Dividends(2018)/NetIncome(2018), Dividends(2019)/NetIncome(2019))* NetIncome (14)

where *Dividends(2018)*, *NetIncome(2018)*, *Dividends(2019)* & *NetIncome(2019)* are constants given in Table 1.

Retained Earnings (*RetainEarnings*):

RetainEarnings= NetIncome - Dividends (15)

Balance Sheet Calculations

The Balance Sheet variables are in Table 2. The calculations are given below.

Cash (*Cash*):

Cash=RiskPert(Min,MostLikely,Max))*_Sales (16)

Short-term Investments (*ShortInvest*):

ShortInvest = MAX(AmountRequirdToBalance,0) (17)

Inventory (*Inventory*):

Inventory = RiskPert(Min,MostLikely,Max))*_Sales (18)

Accounts Receivable (*AccountsReceivbl*):

AccountsReceivbl=RiskPert(Min,MostLikely,Max))*Sales (19)

Total Current Assets (*TotalCurrntAsset*):

TotalCurrntAsset=Cash+ShortInvest+Inventory+AccountsReceivbl (20)

Net PPE (*NetPPE*):

NetPPE= RiskPert(Min,MostLikely,Max))*Sales (21)

Total Assets (*TotalAssets*):

TotalAssets=RiskOutput("TotalAssets",, RiskSixSigma(LSL,USL,TV,0,3))+TotalCurrntAsset+NetPPE (22)

Accounts Payable (*AccountsPaybl*):

AccountsPaybl= RiskPert(Min,MostLikely,Max))*Sales (23)

Taxes Payable (*TaxPayable*):

TaxPayable= Tax (24)

Dividends Payable (*DividendsPaybl*):

DividendsPaybl= Dividends (25)

Short-term Debt (*ShortTermDebt*):

ShortTermDebt=RiskOutput("Short-termDebt",, RiskSixSigma(LSL,USL,TV,0,3))-MIN(AmountRequirdToBalance,0) (26)

Current Liabilities (*CurrntLiabilts*):

CurrntLiabilts=AccountsPaybl+TaxPayable+DividendsPaybl+ ShortTermDebt (27)

Long-term Debt (*LongTermDebt*):

LongTermDebt is a constant as given in Table 2.

Total pre-Equity Liabilities (*TotalPreEqtyLiabilts*):

TotalPreEqtyLiabilts= CurrntLiabilts+LongTermDebt (28)

Share Common Stock Capital (*ShareComStckCapital*):

ShareComStckCapital is a constant as given in Table 2.

Accumulated Retained Earnings (*AccumltdRetainEarnings*):

AccumltdRetainEarnings= AccumltdRetainEarnings(2019)+ RetainEarnings (29)

where *RetainEarnings* is the Retained Earnings.

Total Liabilities & Equity (*TotalLiablts&Equity*):

TotalLiablts&Equity=RiskOutput("Total-Liabilities&Equity",, RiskSixSigma(LSL,USL,TV,0,3))+TotalPreEqtyLiabilts+ ShareComStckCapital+AccumltdRetainEarnings (30)

BS Ratios, Checks & Balancing Items Calculations

The BS (Balance Sheet) ratios, checks, and balancing items are presented in Table 3. The calculations are given below.

Balancing Check Zero (*BalancCheckZero*):

BalancCheckZero = TotalAssets - TotalLiablts&Equity (31)

Net Debt (*NetDebt*):
NetDebt=(ShortTermDebt+LongTermDebt)-(Cash+ShortInvest) (32)
Operating Assets (*OpertngAsset*):
OpertngAsset=NetPPE+Inventory+AccountsReceivbl- AccountsPaybl+Cash (33)
LHS excl. Balancing s/t Investments (*LHSexclBalancStInvest*):
LHSexclBalancStInvest=Inventory+AccountsReceivbl+NetPPE+Cash (34)
RHS excl. Balancing s/t Debt (*RHSexclStBalancDebt*):
RHSexclStBalancDebt=AccountsPaybl+TaxPayable+DividendsPaybl+ LongTtermDebt+ShareCo mStckCapital+AccumltdRetainEarnings
(35)
Amount Required to Balance (*AmountRequirdToBalance*):
AmountRequirdToBalance=RHSexclStBalancDebt- LHSexclBalancStInvest (36)

Cash Flow Statement Calculations

The Cash Flow Statement items are presented in Table 5.4. The calculations are given below.
Operating Net Income (*OpertngNetIncome*):
OpertngNetIncome = NetIncome (37)
Operating Depreciation (*OpertngDepreciation*):
OpertngDepreciation = Depreciation (38)
Operating Increase in Inventory (*OpertngIncrInventory*):
OpertngIncrInventory = Inventory – Inventory(2019) (39)
where *Inventory(2019)* is a constant given in Table 5.2.
Operating Increase in Accounts Receivable (*OpertngIncrAccntsReceivbl*):
OpertngIncrAccntsReceivbl=AccountsReceivbl– AccountsReceivbl(2019) (40)
where *AccountsReceivbl(2019)* is a constant given in Table 5.2.
Operating Increase in Accounts Payable (*OpertngIncrAccntsPaybl*):
OpertngIncrAccntsPaybl= AccountsPaybl – AccountsPaybl(2019) (41)
where *AccountsPaybl(2019)* is a constant given in Table 5.2.
Operating Increase in Taxes Payable (*OpertngIncrTaxPaybl*):
OpertngIncrTaxPaybl= TaxPaybl – TaxPaybl(2019) (42)
where *TaxPaybl(2019)* is a constant given in Table 5.2.
Operating Sub-Total (*OpertngSubTotal*):
OpertngSubTotal=RiskOutput("OperatingSubTotal",, RiskSixSigma(LSL,USL,TV,0,3))+Opertng NetIncome+ OpertngDepreciation-OpertngIncrInventory - OpertngIncrAccntsReceivbl+OpertngIncr AccntsPaybl+ OpertngIncrTaxPaybl (43)
Investment in PPE (*InvstmntInPPE*):
InvstmntInPPE = NetPPE – NetPPE(2019) + Depreciation (44)
where *NetPPE(2019)* is a constant given in Table 5.2.
Investing Sub-Total (*InvestingSubTotal*):
InvestingSubTotal=RiskOutput("InvestingSubTotal",, RiskSixSigma(LSL,USL,TV,0,3))+ Invst-mntInPPE (45)
Financing Increase in Short-term Investments (*FinancIncreasShortTermInvest*):
FinancIncreasShortTermInvest = ShortInvest – ShortInvest(2019) (46)

where *ShortInvest(2019)* is a constant given in Table 5.2.

Financing Increase in Short-term Debt (*FinancIncreasShortTermDebt*):

FinancIncreasShortTermDebt = ShortTermDebt – ShortTermDebt(2019) (47)

where *ShortTermDebt(2019)* is a constant given in Table 5.2.

Financing Increase in Long-term Debt (*FinancIncreasLongTermDebt*):

FinancIncreasLongTermDebt=LongTermDebt–LongTermDebt(2019) (48)

where *LongTermDebt(2019)* is a constant given in Table 5.2.

Financing Increase in Common Stock (*FinancIncreasCommnStock*):

FinancIncreasCommnStock=ShareComStckCapital– ShareComStckCapital(2019) (49)

where *ShareComStckCapital(2019)* is a constant given in Table 5.2.

Financing Payment of Dividend (*FinancPaymntDividend*):

FinancPaymntDividend= DividendsPaybl(2019) (50)

where *DividendsPaybl(2019)* is a constant given in Table 5.2.

Financing Sub-Total (*FinancSubTotal*):

FinancSubTotal=RiskOutput("FinancSubTotal",, RiskSixSigma(LSL,USL,TV,0,3))+(-FinancIncreasShortTermInvest+ FinancIncreasShortTermDebt+FinancIncreasLongTermDebt+ FinancIncreasCommnStock-FinancPaymntDividend) (51)

Net Increase in Cash from CFS (*NetIncrsCashCFS*):

NetIncrsCashCFS=RiskOutput("NetIncrsCashCFS",, RiskSixSigma(LSL,USL,TV,0,3))+OpertngSubTotal- InvestingSubTotal+FinancSubTotal (52)

Net Increase in Cash from BS (*NetIncrsCashBS*):

NetIncrsCashBS=Cash – Cash(2019) (53)

where *Cash(2019)* is a constant in Table 5.2.

Check Zero (*CheckZero*):

CheckZero= NetIncrsCashBS – NetIncrsCashCFS (54)

Measure Financial Statements Results (DMAIC Measure)

The results of the five simulations are presented in Table 5.7 below.

Table 7. Financial statement key aspects prediction ($MM)

Statements Data	Sim 1	Sim 2	Sim 3	Sim 4	Sim 5
Operating Profit	179.6975	131.9745	83.9478	35.7868	-12.6826
Net Income	122.8338	89.4089	55.7711	22.0392	-11.9085
Total Assets	639.6657	596.5495	553.1597	567.9356	596.5498
Short-term Debt	0	0	0	58.2902	130.6966
Total Liability & Equity	639.6657	596.5495	553.1597	567.9356	596.5498
Operating sub-Total	207.2136	156.8350	106.0567	55.1653	3.8686
Investing sub-Total	28.1371	47.6405	67.2710	86.9713	106.8004
Financing sub-Total	-182.3953	-111.2520	-39.5475	32.2902	104.6966
Net Increase in Cash CFS	-3.3188	-2.0575	-0.7619	0.4843	1.7649

The Operating Profit, Net Income, and Operating Total predictions start with $179.6975 MM, $122.8338 MM, and $207.2136 MM respectively in Simulation 1. Then they continuously decline to -$12.6826 MM, -$11.9085 MM, and $3.8686 MM in Simulation 5.

The Total Assets and Total Liability and Equity both start at $639.6657 MM in Simulation 1 and continuously decline to a minimum of $553.1597 MM in Simulation 3. Then they both increase again to $596.5498 MM in Simulation 5. It should be noted that they overlay in the graph (Figure 1).

The Short-term Debt is predicted to be zero in Simulations 1, 2 & 3. Then it increases to $58.2902 MM and $130.6966 MM in Simulation 4 & 5 respectively.

The Investing Total, Financing Total, and Net Increase in Cash predictions start with $28.1371 MM, -$182.3953 MM, and -$3.3188 MM respectively in Simulation 1. Then they continuously increase to $106.8004 MM, $104.6966 MM, and $1.7649 MM in Simulation 5.

The prediction is visually presented in Figure 1.

Figure 1. Financial statement key aspects trend

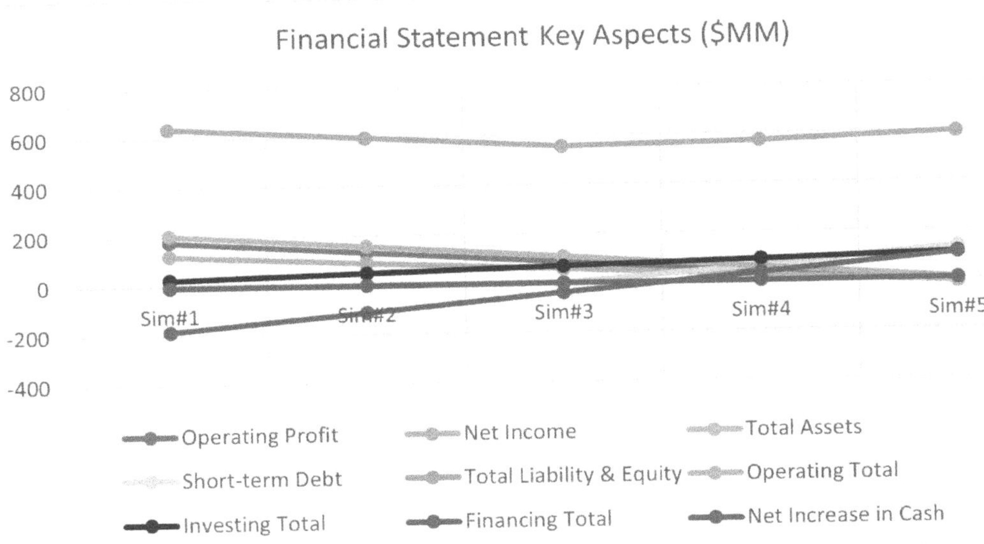

Compare Financial Statements Results (DMAIC Analyse)

The results of the five simulations in Table 7 are compared considering the Operating Profit and associated Standard Deviation. The comparison is shown in Table 8.

Table 8. Compare operating profit & standard deviation ($MM)

Statements Data	Sim 1	Sim 2	Sim 3	Sim 4	Sim 5
Operating Profit	179.6975	131.9745	83.9478	35.7868	-12.6826
Standard Deviation	24.49	25.95	27.42	28.81	30.36

The comparison is graphically presented in Figure 2. It is shown that the Operating Profit reduces, which is a linear approximation. Conversely, the associated Standard Deviation (i.e., the major risk factor), increases, which is also a linear approximation.

The conclusion is that compared with the other simulations, Simulation 1 predicted a maximal Operating profit of $179.6975 MM with minimal Standard Deviation of $24.49 MM, which is the major risk factor. Therefore, Simulation 1 is superior and it will be analysed in detail below.

Figure 2. Financial statement key aspects trend

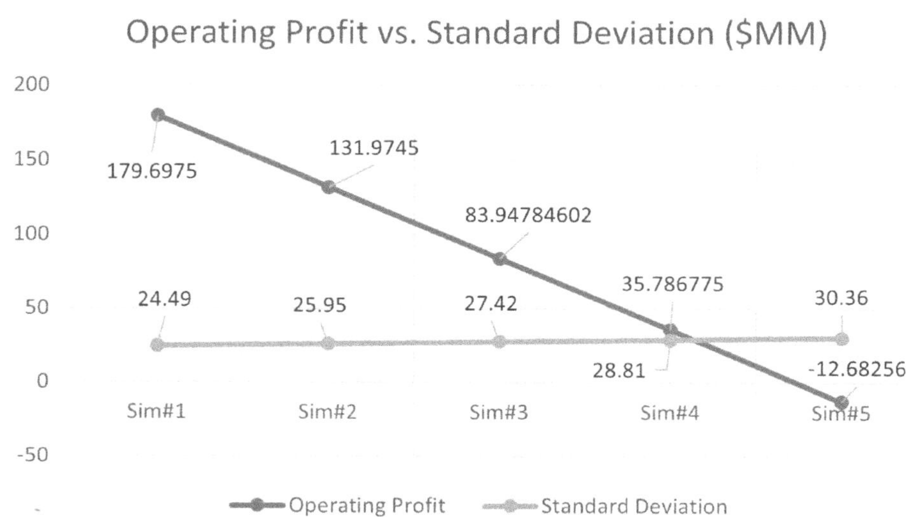

It is important to note that Simulation 1 is superior taking into account only two important aspects, which are only for demonstration purposes. However, in a real-life situation, key aspects of a Financial Statement should be considered to make a decision.

Simulation 1 Prediction Analysis, Evaluation, and Risk Attribution (DMAIC Analyse)

Financial Statement Key Aspects are analysed below.

Operating Profit Analysis, Evaluation, and Risk Attribution

Figure 3 displays the Operating Profit distribution. The Operating Profit *Mean* is $179.70 MM and the *Standard Deviation* is $24.49 MM, i.e., 13.628%. The Six Sigma target parameters are TV = $179.70 MM; LSL = $161.73 MM; and USL = $197.67 MM. The Six Sigma process capability metrics are $Cp = 0.2446$; $Cpk = 0.2446$; and $\sigma\text{-}L = 0.6764$. There is a 5% probability that the *Mean* will be below $139.3 MM; a 90% probability that it will be in the range of $139.3 MM – $219.70 MM; and a 5% probability that it will be above $219.70 MM.

Figure 3. Operating profit distribution

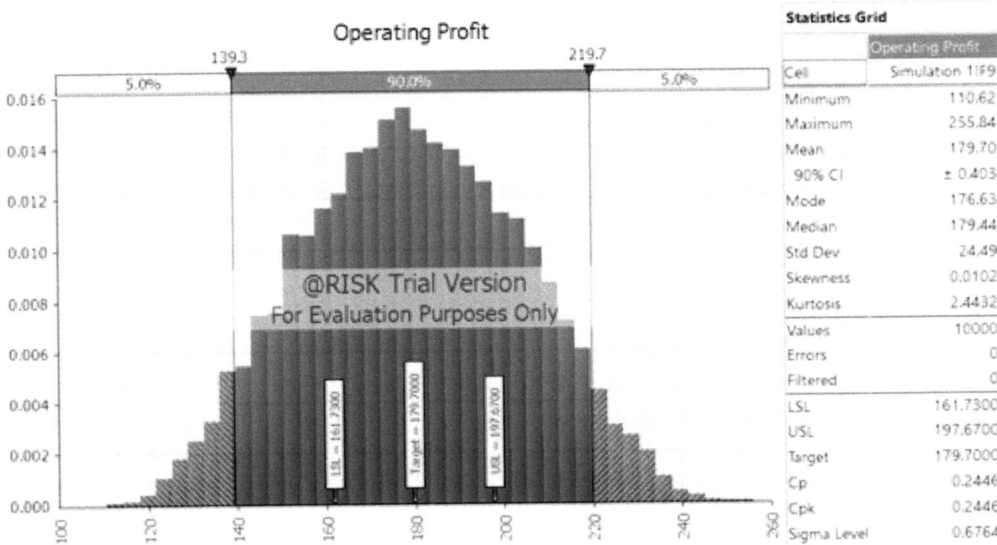

Sensitivity analysis provides for identifying and quantifying the main contributors to variability and risk. The regression coefficients graph (Figure 4) illustrates that if the top variable, Sales Cost (F6) increases by one Standard Deviation, the Operating Profit will change by -0.94 Standard Deviations (i.e., it will decrease, as the regression coefficient is negative), which is the most influential variable. The other variables are less influential, e.g., the second top variable Other Cost ((F7) with a correlation coefficient of -0.32), as their regression coefficients are in the range of -0.32 to 0.02 from top to bottom, which are much smaller than the Sales Cost coefficient.

Figure 4. Operating profit regression coefficients

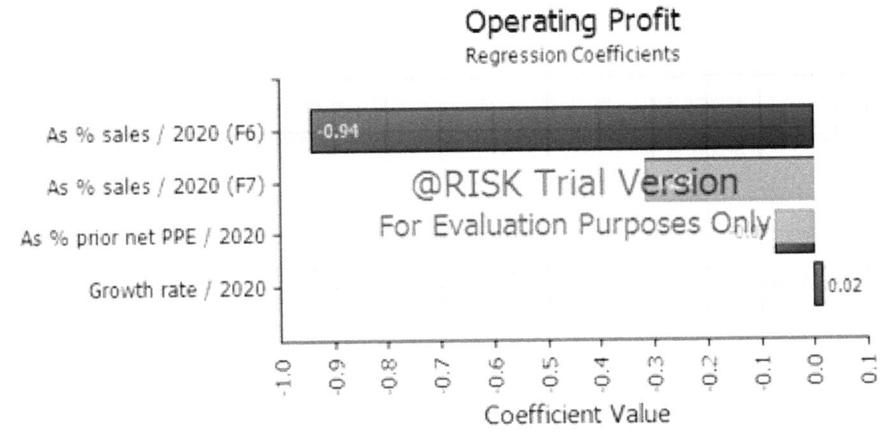

Net Income Analysis, Evaluation, and Risk Attribution

Figure 5 displays the Net Income distribution. The Net Income *Mean* is \$122.83 MM and the *Standard Deviation* is \$17.15 MM, i.e., 13.962%. The Six Sigma target parameters are TV = \$122.83 MM; LSL = \$110.547 MM; and USL = \$135.113 MM. The Six Sigma process capability metrics are Cp = 0.2387; Cpk = 0.2386; and σ-L = 0.6595. There is a 5% probability that the *Mean* will be below \$94.5 MM; a 90% probability that it will be in the range of \$94.5 MM – \$150.9 MM; and a 5% probability that it will be above \$150.9 MM.

Figure 5. Net income distribution

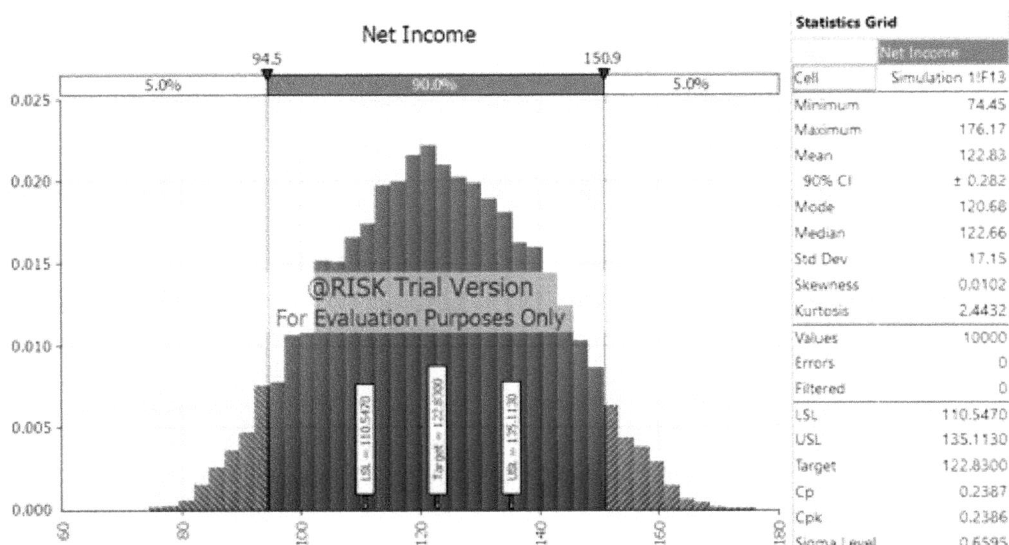

The regression coefficients graph (Figure 6) illustrates that if the top variable Sales Cost (F6) increases by one Standard Deviation, the Net Income will change by -0.94 Standard Deviations, which is the most influential variable. The other variables are less influential, e.g., the second top variable Other Cost ((F7) with a correlation coefficient of -0.32), as their regression coefficients are -0.32, -0.07, and circa 0.02 from top to bottom, i.e., they are much smaller than the Sales Cost coefficient.

Figure 6. Net income regression coefficients

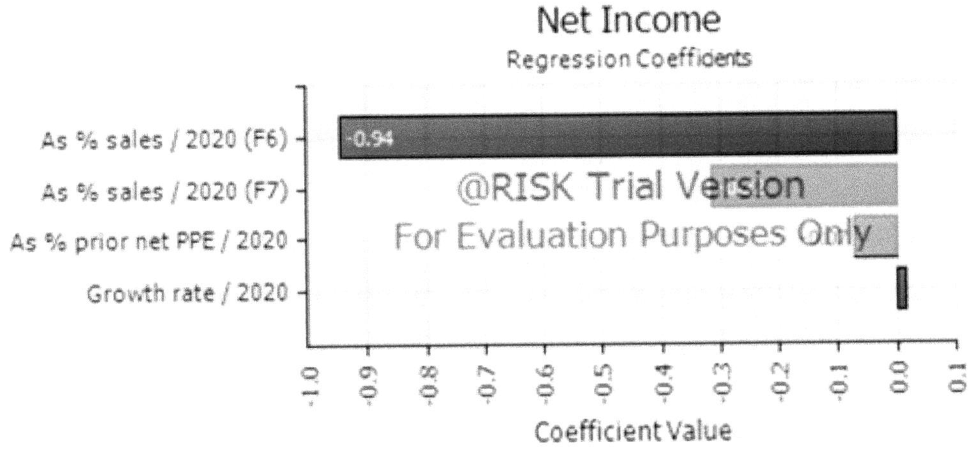

Total Assets Analysis, Evaluation, and Risk Attribution

Figure 7 displays the Total Assets distribution. The Total Assets *Mean* is $639.67 MM and the *Standard Deviation* is $24.66 MM, i.e., 3.855%. The Six Sigma target parameters are TV = $639.67 MM; LSL = $623.678 MM; and USL = $655.662 MM. The Six Sigma process capability metrics are Cp = 0.22161; Cpk = 0.2161; and σ-L = 0.6033. There is a 5% probability that the *Mean* will be below $599.1 MM; a 90% probability that it will be in the range of $599.1 MM – $680.3 MM; and a 5% probability that it will be above $680.3 MM.

Figure 7. Total assets distribution

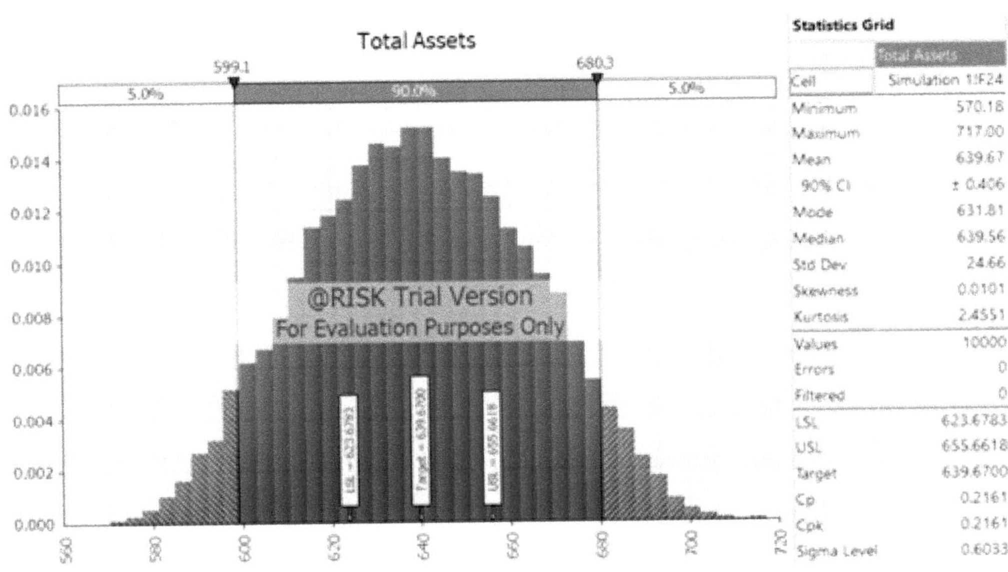

Sensitivity analysis in Figure 8 provides for identifying and quantifying the main contributors to variability and risk.

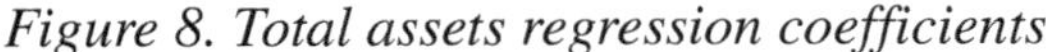

Figure 8. Total assets regression coefficients

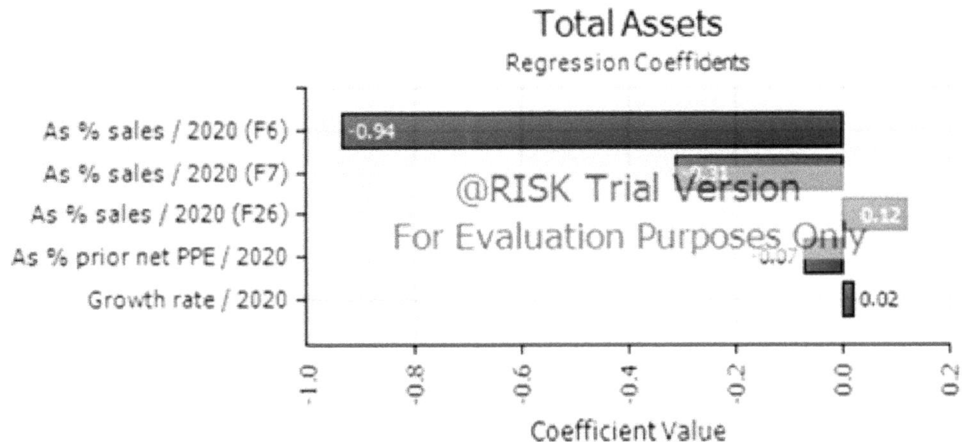

The regression coefficients graph (Figure 8) illustrates that if the top variable Sales Cost (F6) increases by one Standard Deviation, the Total Assets will change by -0.94 Standard Deviations, which is the most influential variable. For example, the variables Other Cost (F7) and Accounts Payable (F26), with respective correlation coefficients of -0.31 and 0.12, are the next most influential. The two least influential variables have regression coefficients of -0.07 and 0.02, which are much smaller than the other coefficients.

Total Liability & Equity Analysis, Evaluation and Risk Attribution

Figure 9 displays the Total Liability and Equity distribution. The Total Liability and Equity *Mean* are \$639.67 MM and the Standard *Deviation* is \$24.66 MM, i.e., 3.855%. The Six Sigma target parameters are *TV* = \$639.67 MM; *LSL* = \$623.678 MM; and *USL* = \$655.662 MM. The Six Sigma process capability metrics are *Cp* = 0.22161; *Cpk* = 0.2161; and σ-*L* = 0.6033. There is a 5% probability that the *Mean* will be below \$599.1 MM; a 90% probability that it will be in the range of \$599.1 MM – \$680.3 MM; and a 5% probability that it will be above \$680.3 MM.

Figure 9. Total liability and equity debt distribution

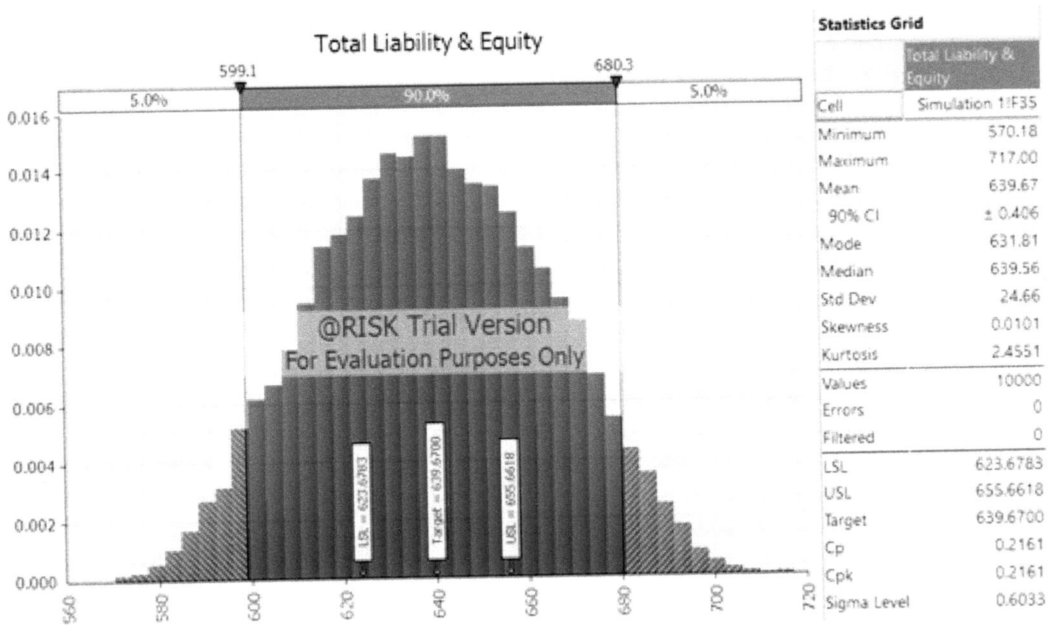

Sensitivity analysis in Figure 10 provides for identifying and quantifying the main contributors to variability and risk.

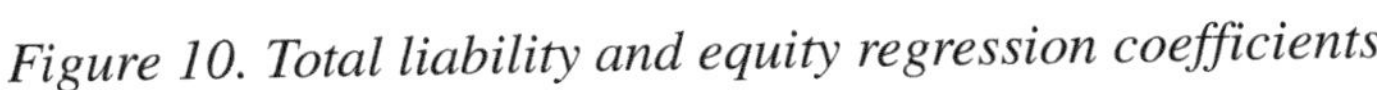

Figure 10. Total liability and equity regression coefficients

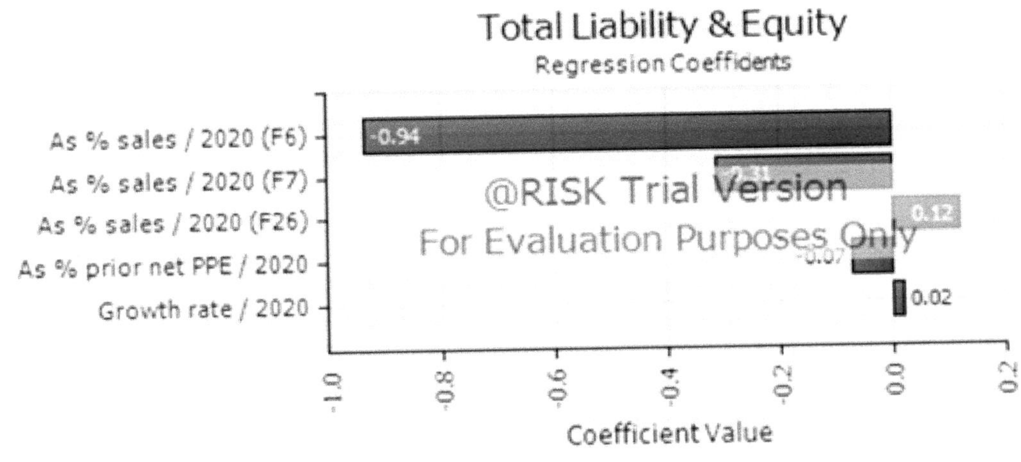

The regression coefficients graph (Figure 10) illustrates that if the top variable Sales Cost (F6) increases by one Standard Deviation, the Total Liability and Equity will change by -0.94 Standard Deviations, which is the most influential variable. The variables Other Cost (F7) and Accounts Payable (F26), with respective correlation coefficients of -0.31 and 0.12, are the next most influential. The two least influential variables have regression coefficients of -0.07 and 0.02, which are much smaller than the other coefficients.

It should be noted that the results for Total Liability & Equity and Total Assets are the same as those established in Table 5.7 and Figure 10 above.

Operating Total Analysis, Evaluation, and Risk Attribution

Figure 11 displays the Operating Total distribution.

Figure 11. Operating total distribution

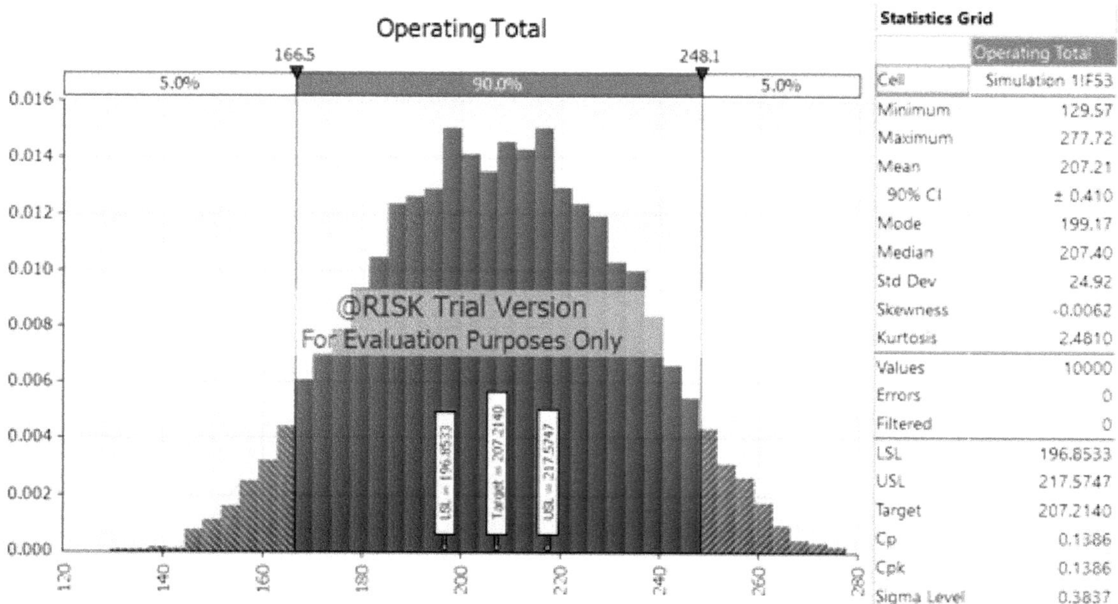

The Operating Total *Mean* is \$207.21 MM and the *Standard Deviation* is \$24.92 MM, i.e., 12.026%. The Six Sigma target parameters are TV = \$207.214 MM; LSL = \$196.853 MM; and USL = \$217.575 MM. The Six Sigma process capability metrics are Cp = 0.1386; Cpk = 0.1386; and σ-L = 0.3837. There is a 5% probability that the *Mean* will be below \$166.5 MM; a 90% probability that it will be in the range of \$166.5 MM – \$248.1 MM; and a 5% probability that it will be above \$248.1 MM.

Sensitivity analysis in Figure 12 provides for identifying and quantifying the main contributors to variability and risk.

Figure 12. Operating total regression coefficients

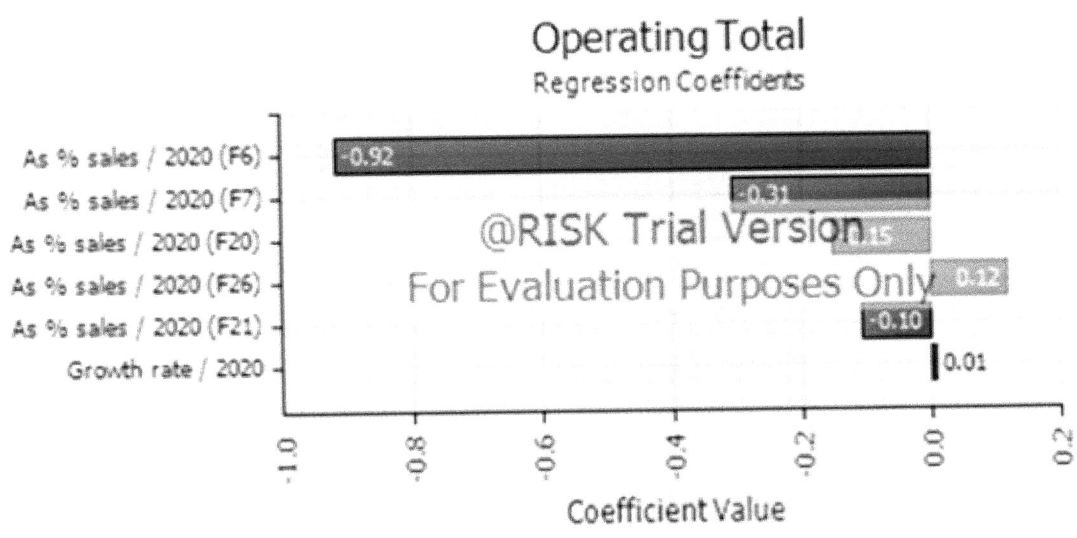

The regression coefficients graph (Figure 12) illustrates that if the top variable, Sales Cost (F6), increases by one Standard Deviation, the Operating Total will change by -0.92 Standard Deviations, which is the most influential variable. The variable Other Cost (F7) with a correlation coefficient of -0.31 is the next most influential. The three least influential variables have regression coefficients of -0.15, 0.12, -0.1, and 0.01, which are much smaller than the other coefficients.

Investing in Total Analysis, Evaluation, and Risk Attribution

Figure 13 displays the Investing Total distribution. The Investing Total *Mean* is $28.137 MM and the *Standard Deviation* is $11.136 MM, i.e., 39.578%. The Six Sigma target parameters are *TV* = $28.137 MM; *LSL* = $14.069 MM; and *USL* = $42.206 MM. The Six Sigma process capability metrics are *Cp* = 0.4211; *Cpk* = 0.4211; and *σ-L* = 1.2073. There is a 5% probability that the *Mean* will be below $9.8 MM; a 90% probability that it will be in the range of $9.8 MM – $46.4 MM; and a 5% probability that it will be above $46.4 MM

Figure 13. Investing total distribution

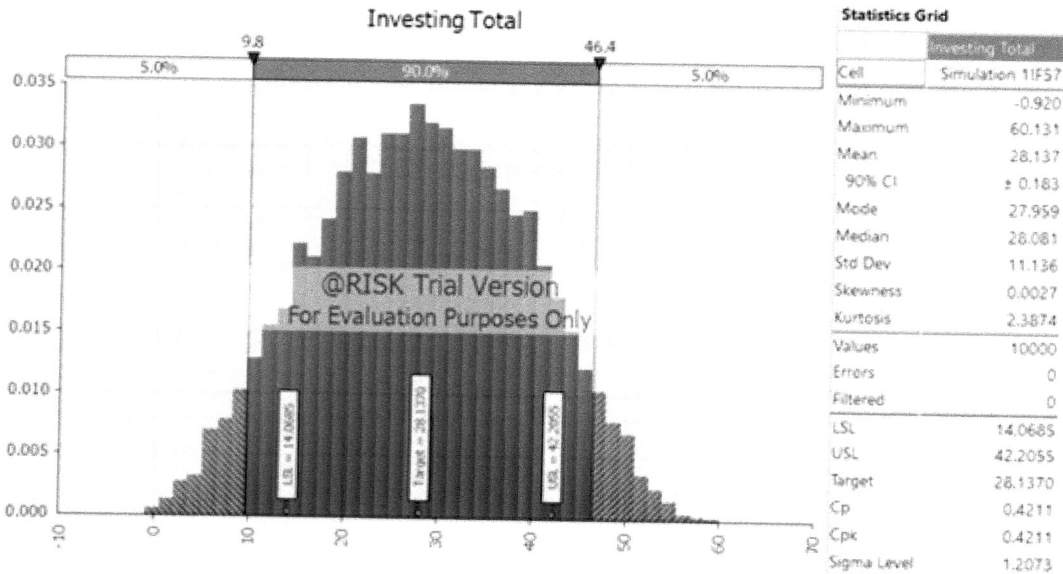

Sensitivity analysis is shown in Figure 14.

Figure 14. Investing total regression coefficients

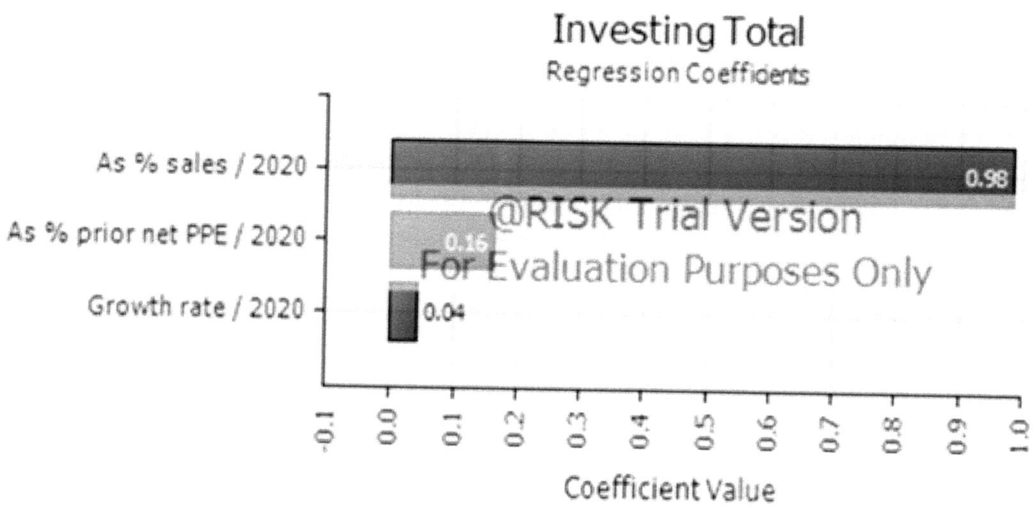

The regression coefficients graph (Figure 14) illustrates that if the top variable, Net PPE (labelled as "As % sales") increases by one Standard Deviation, the Investing Total will increase by 0.98 Standard Deviations, which is the most influential variable. The variables, Depreciation (labelled as "As % prior net PPE") and Sales (labelled as "Grow rate"), with respective correlation coefficients of 0.16 and 0.04, are much less influential.

Financing Total Analysis, Evaluation, and Risk Attribution

Figure 15 displays the Financing Total distribution.

Figure 15. Financing total distribution

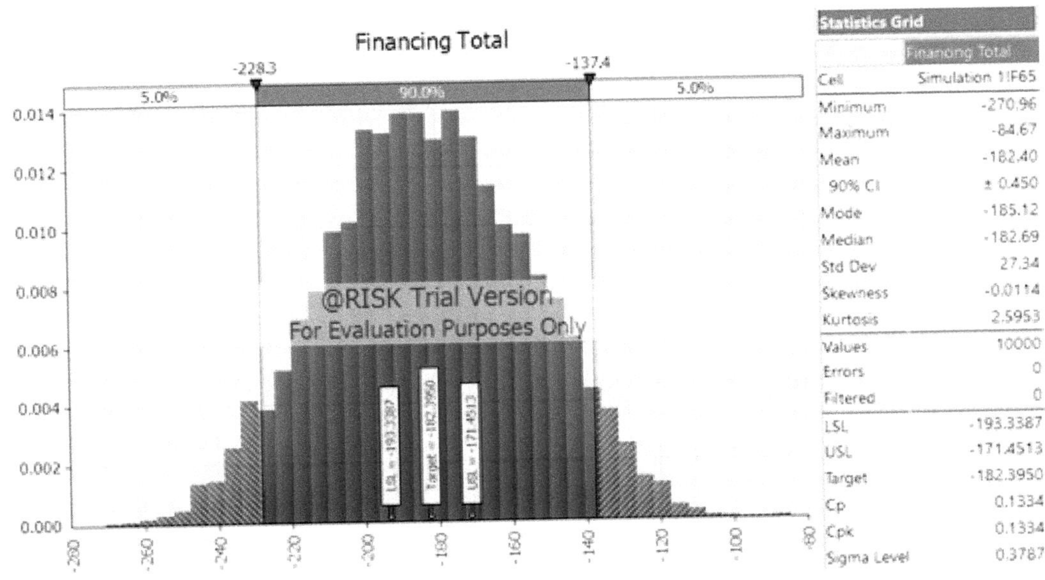

The Financing Total *Mean* is -\$182.40 MM and the *Standard Deviation* is \$27.34 MM, i.e., 14.989%. The Six Sigma target parameters are: *TV* = -\$182.395 MM; *LSL* = -\$193.339 MM; and *USL* = -\$171.451 MM. The Six Sigma process capability metrics are *Cp* = 0.1334; *Cpk* = 0.1334; and σ-*L* = 0.3787. There is a 5% probability that the *Mean* will be below -\$228.3 MM; a 90% probability that it will be in the range -\$228.3 MM to -\$137.4 MM; and a 5% probability that it will be above -\$137.4 MM.

Sensitivity analysis provides for identifying and quantifying the main contributors to variability and risk. The regression coefficients graph (Figure 16) illustrates that if the top variable, Sales Cost (F6) increases by one Standard Deviation, the Financing Total will increase by 0.84 Standard Deviations, which is the most influential variable. The variables, Net PPE (F23) and Other Cost (F7), with respective correlation coefficients of 0.40 and 0.28, are less influential. The bottom six variables are much less influential.

Figure 16. Financing total regression coefficients

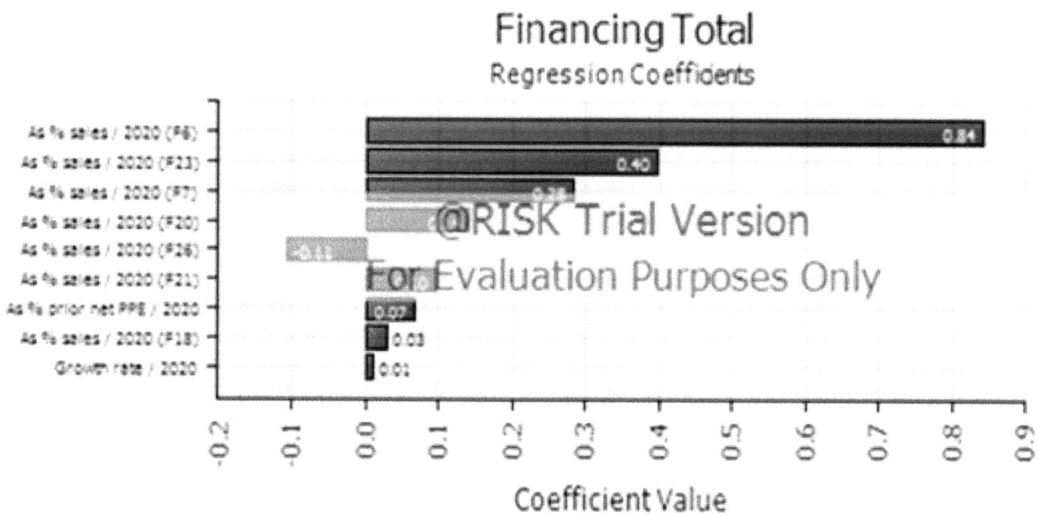

Net Increase in Cash Analysis, Evaluation, and Risk Attribution

Figure 17 displays the Net Cash Increase distribution. The Net Cash Increase *Mean* is -\$3.319 MM and the *Standard Deviation* is \$0.821 MM, i.e., 24.736%. The Six Sigma target parameters are: *TV* = -\$3.319MM; *LSL* = -\$3.651 MM; and *USL* = -\$2.987 MM. The Six Sigma process capability metrics are *Cp* = 0.1348; *Cpk* = 0.1347; and *σ-L* = 0.3623. There is a 5% probability that the *Mean* will be below -\$4.671 MM; a 90% probability that it will be in the range -\$4.671 MM to -\$1.969 MM; and a 5% probability that it will be above -\$1.969 MM.

Figure 17. Net cash increase distribution

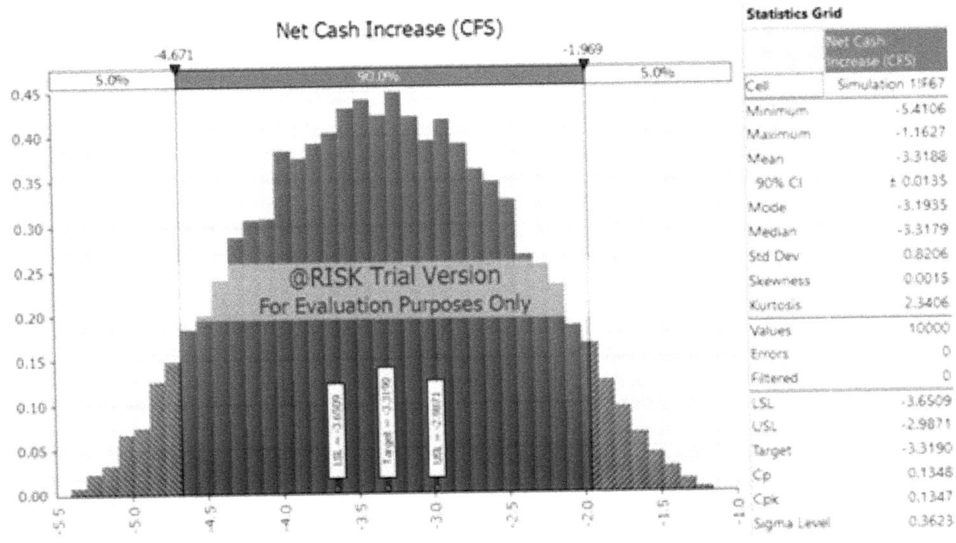

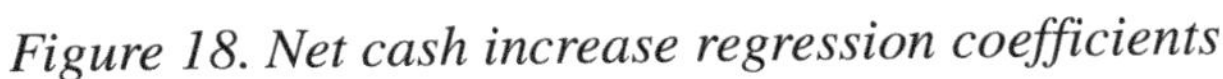

The regression coefficients graph is presented in Figure 18.

Figure 18. Net cash increase regression coefficients

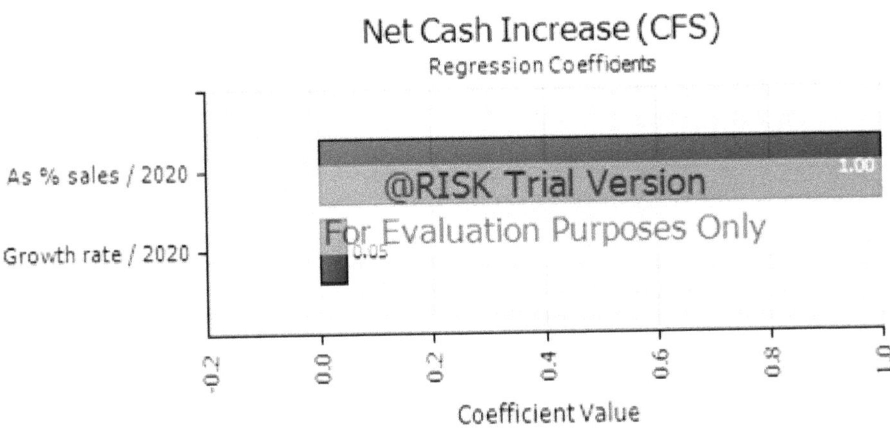

Figure 18 illustrates that if the top variable Cash (labelled as "As % sales") increase by one Standard Deviation, the Net Cash Increase will increase by 1.00 (i.e., per the associated correlation coefficient) Standard Deviations, which is the most influential variable. The variable, Sales (labelled as "Grow rate"), with a correlation coefficient of 0.05, is much less influential.

Short-term Debt Analysis, Evaluation and Risk Attribution

The Short-term Debt is a constant value of zero (i.e., a hypothetical *Mean* with a hypothetical *Standard Deviation* of zero) as shown in Figure 19. It should be noted that a distribution does not apply to this case, so correlation is not applicable.

Figure 19. Short-term debt distribution

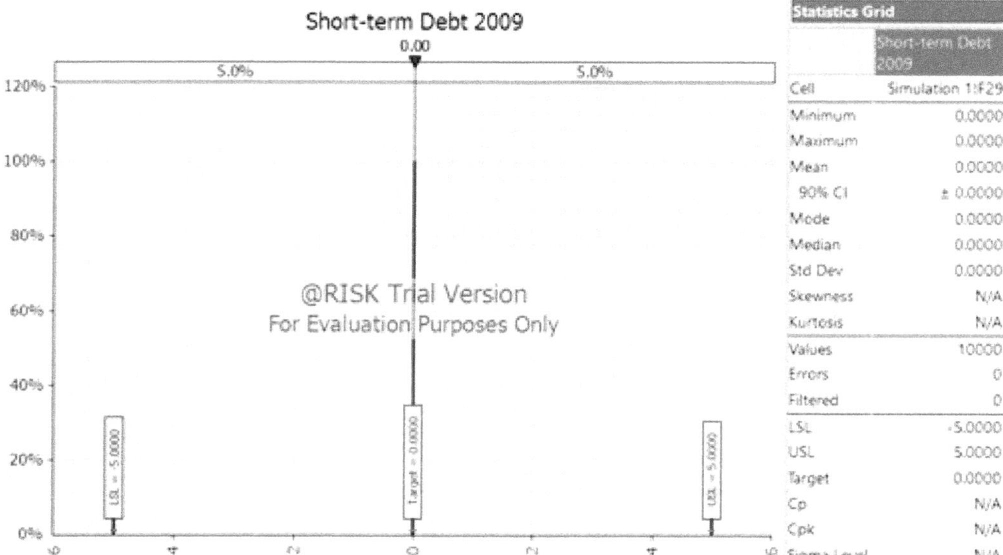

Verification of Results

Referring to Table 8 and Figure 2 above, the conclusion is that compared with the other simulations, the Simulation 1 is superior because it predicted a maximal Operating Profit of $179.6975 MM with minimal Standard Deviation of $24.49 MM, which is the major risk factor. This recognises that Simulation 1 maximises the Operating Profit with minimal risk, which is the ultimate goal. Therefore, the results are satisfactorily verified.

CONCLUSION

This chapter presents an example of financial statements modelling for businesses. The model is created for general forecasting purposes, including financing needs and credit analysis.

The company has the actual Financial Statements data for 2018 and 2019. Therefore, the forecast for 2020 is based on the actual data of the previous two years. The company had fairly good cash flows in 2018 and 2019. Thus, important objectives are to reduce its: i) long-term debt in 2020 to $70 MM from $97 MM in 2019; and ii) short-term debt in 2020 to zero from $2 MM in 2019, to avoid the requirement for short-term financing.

A simulation model is created to forecast the Financial Statements. Five simulations are run to provide a comprehensive analysis. The five simulation results are evaluated, including sensitivity analysis, and compared taking into account the risk factors.

The short-term debt objective is achieved by three simulations and the long-term debt is achieved by all simulations.

The comparison of simulation results concludes that Simulation 1 predicted the maximal Operating Profit with minimal risk, which is the objective of this demonstration.

REFERENCES

Brodersen, S., & Pysh, P. (2014). *Warren Buffett Accounting Book: Reading Financial Statements for Value*. Pylon Publishing.

Buffett, M., & Clark, D. (2011). Warren Buffett and the Interpretation of Financial Statements: The Search for the Company with a Durable Competitive Advantage. Simon & Schuster.

Fridson, M. S., & Alvarez, F. (2011). Financial Statement Analysis: A Practitioner's Guide. John Wiley & Sons.

Higson, C. (2006). Financial Statements: Economic Analysis and Interpretation. Rivington Publishing Ltd.

Ittelson, T. R. (2020). *Financial Statements: A Step-by-step Guide to Understanding and Creating Financial Reports*. New Page Books.

Skonieczny, M. (2012). The Basics of Understanding Financial Statements: Learn how to Read Financial Statements by Understanding the Balance Sheet, the Income Statement, and the Cash Flow Statement. Investment Publishing.

Chapter 6
New Products Profitability Analysis

ABSTRACT

This chapter elaborates on how to estimate the average profitability of new products for businesses. The chapter considers the financial risk and applies the DMAIC stochastic method. The scenario is that a company wants to launch a new product to the market. When a company develops a new product, the profitability of the product is highly uncertain. A stochastic model is used to evaluate the variables involved in marketing the new product, such as market size, use of the product, competition, etc. Simulation is utilized to calculate the net present value (NPV) of profits for five years to assess the associated risks. The analysis of the simulation results helps the company's management to decide whether to introduce the new product or not.

INTRODUCTION

This scenario is that a company wants to launch a new product to the market. The profitability of the product is very uncertain when a company develops a new product. Thus, a comprehensive analysis is necessary to evaluate the profitability for a future period of five years. A stochastic model is used for the analysis.

The model considers the following uncertain inputs: Price, Unit Variable Cost, Interest Rate, Entrant Probability, Competition Percentage, Year 1 Market Size, Year 1 Worst Share, Year 1 Most Likely Share, and Year 1 Best Share.

The simulation model evaluates the variables involved in the marketing of the new product for five years including Market Size, Product Use per Customer, Competitors Enter Market, Market Entrants, Unit Sales, Revenues, Costs, and Profits.

The simulation also calculates the Net Present Value (NPV) of profits over the five years and assesses the associated risks. The analysis of the simulation results helps the company's management to decide whether to introduce the new product or not.

DOI: 10.4018/979-8-3693-3787-5.ch006

Five simulations are run with different values of the uncertain inputs to complete the analysis. The simulation results are analysed for evaluation and sensitivity analysis is performed to identify and quantify the main contributors to variability and risk.

Finally, the simulation results are compared and discussed for conclusions.

Literature

Some references for the profitability of new products are given below.

Slywotzky (2003) presents a general discussion on profitability in 23 compact lessons. The book features an ongoing tutorial between two fictitious individuals: the old and wise teacher, David Shao, the business master, and his pupil, Steve Gardner, a young and ambitious manager. Along the way, Zhao goes through several business models and pushes his students to examine how a variety of businesses go about making money. Through Zhao's teachings, Steve begins to see how profits can be improved simply by taking a step back and gaining a new perspective. Daly (2001) introduces activity-based pricing, a new paradigm for improving profitability by reducing the occurrence of pricing mistakes and placing less emphasis on increasing revenue and more on improving profits. Activity-based pricing will help any company set prices that are attractive to buyers and profitable for the company. This book teaches activity-based pricing to help you make better pricing decisions based on customer demand and a better understanding of what attains profits. It will help to prevent under pricing and allow them to generate a healthier financial return. Simply organised and nontechnical, this in-depth treatment covers the ten vital topics of activity-based pricing. A wealth of examples that illustrate the points made in the text include activity-based pricing models used in real industries. Axson & Rosander (2014) argue that in today's highly competitive and volatile global marketplace, business leaders need rich and relevant information on the true profitability of the products and services they offer to customers. Yet for many, the simple task of measuring the profitability of offerings is buried in a morass of confusing and often arbitrary cost allocations. The solution is to adopt a structured, methodical approach to calculating profitability. Most companies today struggle with identifying which of their offerings and which of their customers are the most profitable. They can measure revenue but not the profit associated with the product or client group — which means they make decisions about what to sell, in which markets, to which customers, and at what price based on partial or inaccurate information. They operate without a single version of the truth. Methods used to allocate large buckets of costs such as sales, advertising, and customer service can be arbitrary and potentially inaccurate. Cokins (2017) in his chapter discusses the design and architecture of activity-based cost management. A cost assignment network provides the solution to calculate relatively more accurate costs and profit margins. In complex, support-intensive organisations there can be a substantial chain of indirect and shared activities supporting the direct work activities that eventually trace into the final cost objects. The work demands are communicated via activity drivers and their driver cost rates. Activity costs are usually traced to a sustaining cost object group popularly called business (or organisational) sustaining costs. This modelling technique separates the business sustaining costs as not being involved with making or delivering a product or serving a customer. It prevents unfairly over-costing products or customers yet allows for all expenses to be traced. Because the product costs will be different from the existing broadly averaged and non-causal relationship method costs, product profits will also be different. Meehan et al. (2011) in their book offer a comprehensive reference for any business professional looking to understand the capabilities and competencies required for effectively managing pricing and profitability, Pricing and Profitability Management explains how to determine the right approach, tools, and techniques for each of the six key categories (pricing strategy, price execution, advanced analytics and optimisation, organisational alignment and governance, pricing technology and data management, and tax and regulatory effectiveness). Exploring each category in detail, the book addresses how an integrated approach to pricing improvement can give a sustainable, competitive advantage to any organisation. The ultimate "how to" manual for any executive or manager interested in price management, the book presents a holistic, comprehensive framework that shows how integrating these pricing categories into a cohesive program leads to impressive gains that cannot be achieved through a single-pronged approach.

The Problem Statement: Perform a comprehensive analysis as necessary to evaluate the profitability of a new product for five years. A stochastic model should be applied to provide for the analysis. Five simulations should be run with different values of the uncertain inputs. Analyse the simulation results for evaluation and utilise sensitivity analysis to identify and quantify the main contributors to variability and risk. Compare the simulation results and discuss them for conclusions. ELABORATION

The scenario presented in this chapter is hypothetical, using published data by Palisade™ Corporation. Project's Data (DMAIC Define) The model considers the following data.

Uncertain Inputs (Table 1): i) Unit Price (*UP*); ii) Unit Cost (*UC*); iii) Interest Rate (*IR*); iv) Entrant Probability (*EP*); v) Competition Percentage (*CP*); vi) Year 1 Market Size (*Y1MS*); vii) Year 1 Worst Share (*Y1WS*); viii) Year 1 Most Likely Share (*Y1MLS*); and ix) Year 1 Best Share (*Y1BS*).

Note: All the inputs presented here have five values each. Thus, "#NAME?" indicates that the actual values for all inputs are defined by formulae given in the Calculations below.

Table 1. Uncertain inputs data

Uncertain Inputs	Value
Unit Price ($)	#Name?
Unit Cost ($)	#Name?
Interest Rate	#Name?
Entrant Probability	#Name?
Competition Percentage	#Name?
Year 1 Market Size	#Name?
Year 1 Worst Share	#Name?
Year 1 Most Likely Share	#Name?
Year 1 Best Share	#Name?

Output Variables per Year Vectors (Table 2): i) Year Vector (*YV(i)*); ii) Market Size Vector (*MSV(i)*); iii) Product Use per Customer Vector (*PUperCV(i)*); iv) Competitors Enter Market Vector (*CEMV(i)*); v) Entrants Vector (*EV(i)*); vi) Unit Sales Vector (*USV(i)*); vii) Revenues Vector (*RV(i)*); viii) Costs Vector (*CV(i)*); and ix) Profits Vector (*PV(i)*). These vectors are for five years, so $i = 1, 2, \ldots, 5$.

Table 2. Output variables per year vectors

Output Variables per Year Vectors					
Year	**1**	**2**	**3**	**4**	**5**
Market Size	#Name?	#Name?	#Name?	#Name?	#Name?
Product Use per Customer	#Name?	#Name?	#Name?	#Name?	#Name?
Competitors Enter Market	#Name?	#Name?	#Name?	#Name?	#Name?
Entrants	#Name?	#Name?	#Name?	#Name?	#Name?
Unit Sales	#Name?	#Name?	#Name?	#Name?	#Name?
Revenues	#Name?	#Name?	#Name?	#Name?	#Name?
Costs	#Name?	#Name?	#Name?	#Name?	#Name?
Profits	#Name?	#Name?	#Name?	#Name?	#Name?

Note: All the values are variables. Thus, "#NAME?" indicates that the actual values are calculated by formulae given in the Calculations below.

Net Present Value (NPV) Variables (Table 3): i) NPV (*NPV*); ii) NPV VAR (*NpvVar*); iii) NPV Percentile 5% (*NpvPercentile5%*); and iv) NPV Percentile 95% (*NpvPercentile95%*).

Note: All the values are variables. Thus, "#NAME?" indicates that the actual values are calculated by formulae given in the Calculations below.

Table 3. Net present value variables

Net Present Value Variables	
Net Present Value (NPV)	**#Name?**
NPV Value at Risk (VAR)	#Name?
NPV Percentile 5%	#Name?
NPV Percentile 95%	#Name?

Calculations (DMAIC Define)

Microsoft™ Excel® and Palisade™ @RISK® formulae are used for the calculations presented in this section.

Uncertain Inputs (Given Data)

Uncertain Inputs are as per Table 1. The data are constant, but to consider the uncertainty, five values are applied for each input. The formulae for the inputs are given below.

Unit Price (*UP*):

UP = RiskSimtable({1.98,2.09,2.2,2.31,2.42}) (1)

Unit Cost (*UC*):

UC = RiskSimtable({0.36,0.38,0.4,0.42,0.44}) (2)

Interest Rate (*IR*):
IR = RiskSimtable({0.09,0.095,0.1,0.105,0.11}) (3)
Entrant Probability (*EP*):
EP = RiskSimtable({0.36,0.38,0.4,0.42,0.44}) (4)
Competition Percentage (*CP*):
CP = RiskSimtable({0.18,0.19,0.2,0.21,0.22}) (5)
Year 1 Market Size (*Y1MS*):
Y1MS=RiskSimtable({900000,950000,1000000,1050000,1100000}) (6)
Year 1 Worst Share (*Y1WS*):
Y1WS = RiskSimtable({0.18,0.19,0.2,0.21,0.22}) (7)
Year 1 Most Likely Share (*Y1MLS*):
Y1MLS = RiskSimtable({0.36,0.38,0.4,0.42,0.44}) (8)
Year 1 Best Share (*Y1BS*):
Y1BS = RiskSimtable({0.63,0.665,0.7,0.735,0.77}) (9)

where, *RiskSimtable* is the @RISK function, which runs five simulations one-by-one with the respective values specified in the formula.

Output Variables per Year Vectors

Output Variables per Year Vectors are given in Table 2. These vectors are for five years, so $i = 1, 2, \ldots, 5$.
Year Vector (*YV(i)*):
YV (i)= i (10)
Market Size Vector (*MSV(i)*):
MSV(1) = Y1MS (11)
where *Y1MS* is the Year 1 Market Size and $i = 1$.
MSV(i)= MSV(i-1) * RiskNormal(1.05,0.01) (12)
where, $i = 2, 3, \ldots,$ 5 and *RiskNormal* is the @RISK distribution with constant parameters.
Product Use per Customer Vector (*PUperCV(i)*):
PUperCV(1) = RiskTriang(Y1WS,Y1MLS,Y1BS) (13)
where $i = 1$ and *RiskTriang* is the @RISK distribution with the parameters *Y1WS*, *Y1MLS*, and *Y1BS*.
PUperCV(i)= PUperCV(i-1)*(1- EV(i-1)* CP) (14)
where, $i = 2, 3, \ldots, 5$, *CP* is the Competition Percentage and *EV(i)* is the Entrants Vector.
Competitors Enter Market Vector (*CEMV(i)*):
CEMV(1) = 0 (15)
where $i = 1$.
CEMV(i)= CEMV(i-1)+EV(i-1) (16)
where, $i = 2, 3, \ldots, 5$ and *EV(i)* is the Entrants Vector.
Entrants Vector (*EV(i)*):
EV(i)= IF(CEMV(i)<3,RiskBinomial(3- CEMV(i),EP),0) (17)
where, $i = 1, 2, \ldots, 5$, *RiskBinomial* is @RISK distribution, *CEMV(i)* is the Competitors Enter Market Vector, and *EP* is the Entrant Probability.
Unit Sales Vector (*USV(i)*):
USV(i) = MSV(i) * PUperCV(i) (18)

where, $i = 1, 2, \ldots, 5$, *MSV(i)* is the Market Size Vector and *PUperCV(i)* is the Product Use per Customer Vector.

Revenues Vector (*RV(i)*):

RV(i) = USV(i)* UP (19)

where, $i = 1, 2, \ldots, 5$, *USV(i)* is the Unit Sales Vector and *UP* is the Unit Price.

Costs Vector (*CV(i)*):

CV(i) = USV(i) * UC (20)

where, $i = 1, 2, \ldots, 5$, *USV(i)* is the Unit Sales Vector and *UC* is the Unit Cost.

Profits Vector (*PV(i)*):

PV(i)= RiskOutput(Concatenate("Profit Year ",YV(i)))+RV(i)-CV(i)

(21)

where, $i = 1, 2, \ldots, 5$, *YV(i)* is the Year Vector, *RV(i)* is the Revenues Vector and *CV(i)* is the Costs Vector.

Net Present Value (NPV) Variables

Net Present Value (NPV) Variables are shown in Table 3.

Net Present Value (*NPV*)):

NPV= NPV(IR, SUM(PV(i)) +

RiskOutput("NPV",,RiskSixSigma(2081136,2543610,2312373,0,3))

(22)

where, $i = 1, 2, \ldots, 5$, *IR* is the Interest Rate, *PV(i)* is the Profits Vector and *RiskSixSigma* is the @ RISK function for Six Sigma limits parameters.

Net Present Value VAR (*NpvVar*):

NpvVar = RiskPercentile(NPV,0.01) (23)

NPV Percentile 5% (*NpvPercentile5%*):

NpvVar = RiskPercentile(NPV,0.05) (24)

NPV Percentile 95% (*NpvPercentile95%*):

NpvVar = RiskPercentile(NPV,0.95) (25)

where, $i = 1, 2, \ldots, 5$, *RiskPercentile* is the @RISK function with two parameters and *NPV* is the Net Present Value.

Simulation #1: Measuring Results (DMAIC Measure)

Simulation #1 is run and the results are presented below.

The Profits Vector results for five years are presented in Table 4.

Table 4. Profits vector results

Profits Vector for Five Years					
Year	**1**	**2**	**3**	**4**	**5**
Profits ($)	568,620.00	480,855.00	436,330.00	416,655.00	411,611.00

The Profits Vector results are graphically presented in Figure 1.

Figure 1. Summary trend of profits vector

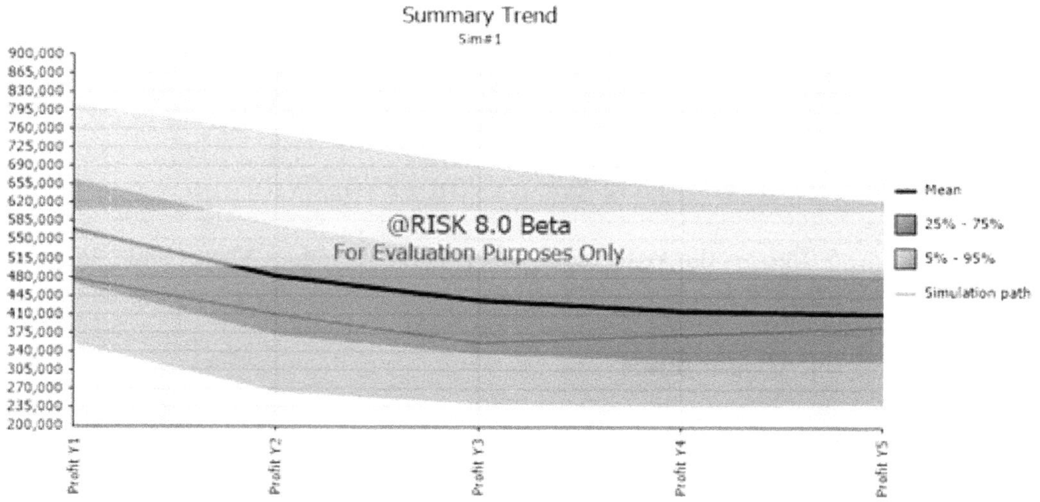

The results for the NPV Variables (Table 6.5) include i) NPV (*NPV*); and ii) NPV VAR (*NpvVar*).

Table 5. NPV variables results

Net Present Value Variables	
Net Present Value ($)	**1,826,007.00**
NPV Value at Risk ($)	917,462.00

Simulation #1: Results Analysis, Evaluation, and Risk Attribution (DMAIC Analyse)

The results for NPV are presented below.

NPV Analysis and Evaluation

The NPV results are shown in Figure 2.

Figure 2. NPV distribution

Statistics Grid	
	NPV (Sim#1)
Cell	The Model!B25
Minimum	$685,363.49
Maximum	$3,705,377.24
Mean	$1,827,389.71
90% CI	± $7,893.08
Mode	$1,544,626.50
Median	$1,787,096.56
Std Dev	$479,820.62
Skewness	0.3790
Kurtosis	2.7933
Values	10000
Errors	0
Filtered	0
LSL	$2,081,135.5790
USL	$2,543,610.1520
Target	$2,312,372.8650
Cp	0.1606
Cpk	-0.1763
Sigma Level	0.2642

The *NPV Mean* is $1,827,389.71 with a *Standard Deviation* of $479,820.62, i.e., 26.257%. The Six Sigma target parameters are *TV* = $2,312,372.87; *LSL* = $2,081,135.58; and *USL* = $2,543,610.15. The Six Sigma process capability metrics are *Cp* = 0.1606; *Cpk* = -0.1763; and σ-*L* = 0.2642. There is a 5% probability that NPV will be below $1,106,000; a 90% probability that it will be in the range of $1,106,000 – $2,679,000; and a 5% probability that it will be above $2,679,000.

NPV Risk Attribution (DMAIC Analyse)

Sensitivity analysis provides for identifying and quantifying the main contributors to variability and risk. The regression coefficients graph (Figure 3) illustrates that if the top variable, the Use per Customer Year 1 (i.e., with a regression coefficient of 0.95), changes by one Standard Deviation, the NPV will change by 0.95 Standard Deviation. If the second top variable, Entrants Year 1 (i.e., with a regression coefficient of -0.46, which is negative), increases by one Standard Deviation, the NPV will decrease by 0.46 Standard Deviations. Other variables Entrants Year 2, etc. are less influential.

Figure 3. NPV regression coefficients

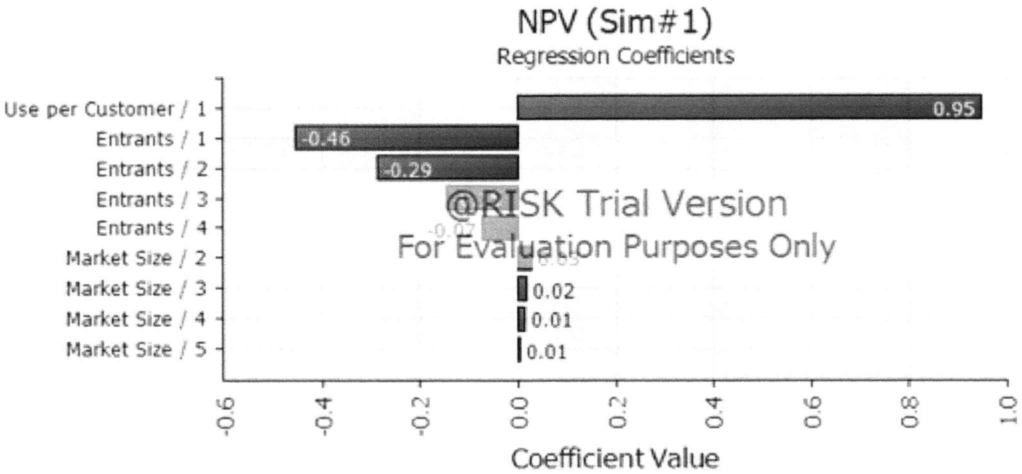

Simulation #2: Measuring Results (DMAIC Measure)

Simulation #2 is run and the results are presented below.

The Profits Vector results for five years are presented in Table 6.

Table 6. Profits vector results

Profits Vector for Five Years					
Year	**1**	**2**	**3**	**4**	**5**
Profits ($)	668,752.00	549,976.00	491,914.00	467,014.00	460,203.00

The Profits Vector results are graphically presented in Figure 4.

Figure 4. Summary trend of profits vector

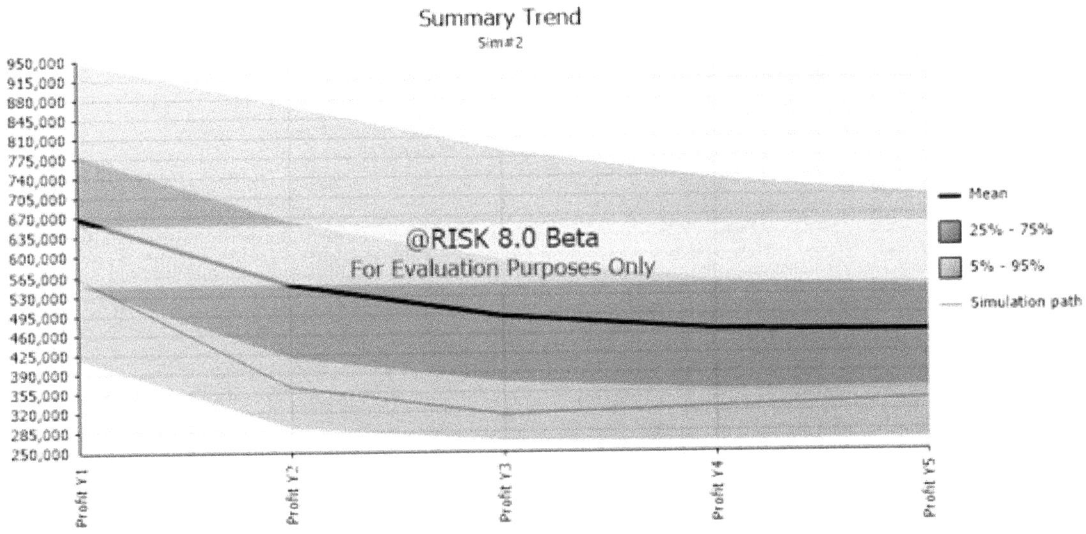

The results for the NPV Variables are shown in Table 7.

Table 7. NPV variables results

Net Present Value Variables	
Net Present Value ($)	**2,061,264.00**
NPV Value at Risk ($)	1,035,522.00

Simulation #2: Results Analysis, Evaluation, and Risk Attribution (DMAIC Analyse)

The results for NPV are presented below.

NPV Analysis and Evaluation

The NPV results are as follows (Figure 5). The *NPV Mean* is $2,062,723.18 with a *Standard Deviation* of $547,113.30, i.e., 26.524%. The Six Sigma target parameters are *TV* = $2,312,372.87; *LSL* = $2,081,135.58; and *USL* = $2,543,610.15. The Six Sigma process capability metrics are *Cp* = 0.1409; *Cpk* = -0.0112; and σ-*L* = 0.3332. There is a 5% probability that NPV will be below $1,241,000; a 90% probability that it will be in the range of $1,241,000 – $3,039,000; and a 5% probability that it will be above $3,039,000.

Figure 5. NPV distribution

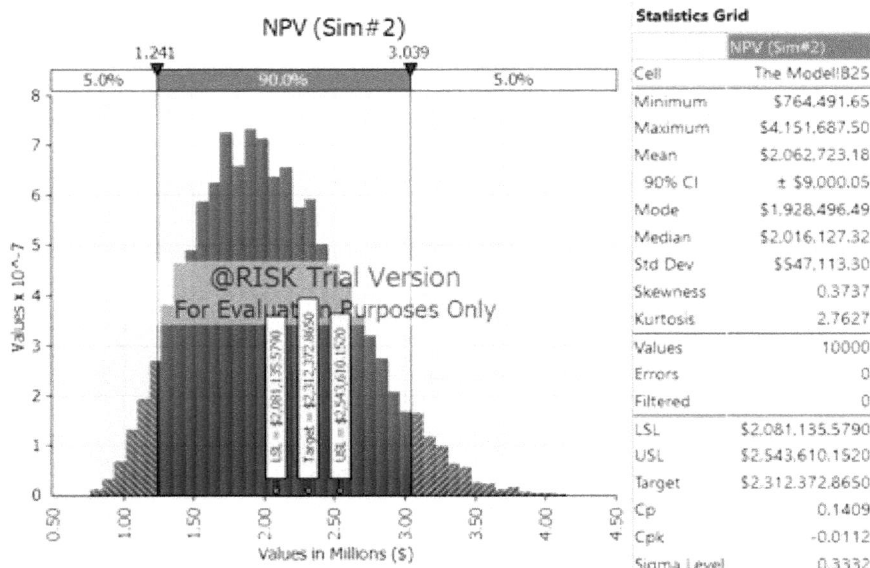

Statistics Grid

	NPV (Sim#2)
Cell	The Model!B25
Minimum	$764,491.65
Maximum	$4,151,687.50
Mean	$2,062,723.18
90% CI	± $9,000.05
Mode	$1,928,496.49
Median	$2,016,127.32
Std Dev	$547,113.30
Skewness	0.3737
Kurtosis	2.7627
Values	10000
Errors	0
Filtered	0
LSL	$2,081,135.5790
USL	$2,543,610.1520
Target	$2,312,372.8650
Cp	0.1409
Cpk	-0.0112
Sigma Level	0.3332

NPV Risk Attribution (DMAIC Analyse)

Sensitivity analysis provides for identifying and quantifying the main contributors to variability and risk. The regression coefficients graph (Figure 6) illustrates that if the top variable, the Use per Customer Year 1 (i.e., with a regression coefficient of 0.94), changes by one Standard Deviation, the NPV will change by 0.94 Standard Deviation. If the second top variable, Entrants Year 1 (i.e., with a regression coefficient of -0.49, which is negative), increases by one Standard Deviation, the NPV will decrease by 0.49 Standard Deviations. Other variables Entrants Year 2, etc. are less influential.

Figure 6. NPV regression coefficients

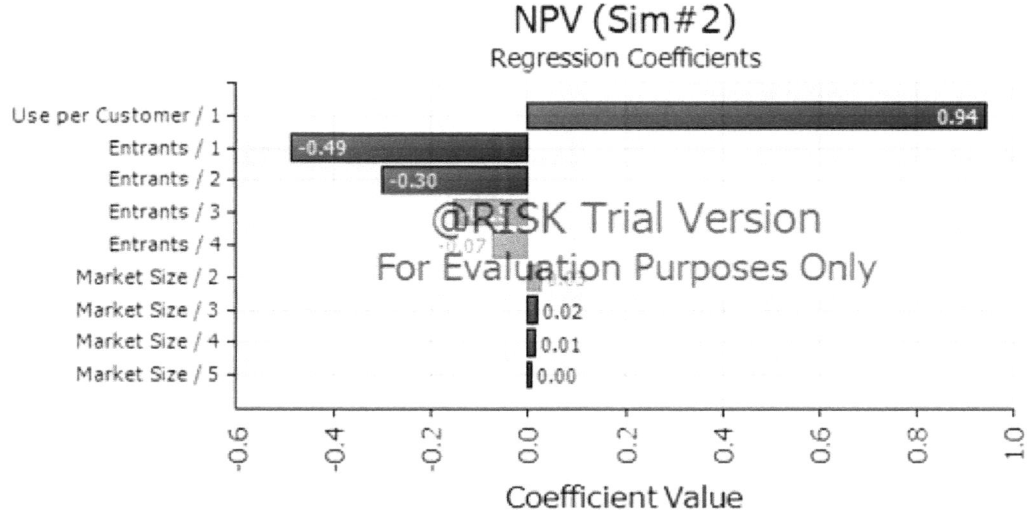

Simulation #3: Measuring Results (DMAIC Measure)

Simulation #3 is run and the results are presented below.

The Profits Vector results for five years are presented in Table 8.

Table 8. Profits vector results

Profits Vector for Five Years					
Year	**1**	**2**	**3**	**4**	**5**
Profits ($)	780,000.00	622,280.00	548,340.00	517,360.00	509,498.00

The Profits Vector results are graphically presented in Figure 7.

Figure 7. Summary trend of profits vector

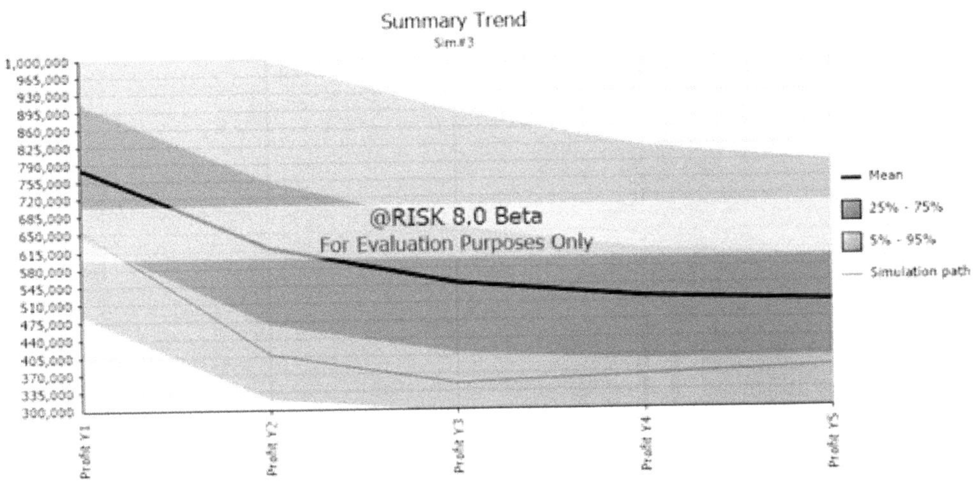

The results for NPV Variables are shown in Table 9.

Table 9. NPV variables results

Net Present Value Variables	
Net Present Value ($)	**2,305,069.00**
NPV Value at Risk ($)	1,143,160.00

Simulation #3: Results Analysis, Evaluation, and Risk Attribution (DMAIC Analyse)

The results for NPV are presented below.

NPV Analysis and Evaluation

The NPV results are as follows (Figure 6.8). The *NPV Mean* is \$2,306,755.51 with a *Standard Deviation* of \$620,344.36, i.e., 26.893%. The Six Sigma target parameters are TV = \$2,312,372.87; LSL = \$2,081,135.58; and USL = \$2,543,610.15. The Six Sigma process capability metrics are $Cp = 0.1243$; $Cpk = 0.1212$; and σ-$L = 0.3505$. There is a 5% probability that NPV will be below \$1,376,000; a 90% probability that it will be in the range of \$1,376,000 – \$3,414,000; and a 5% probability that it will be above \$3,414,000.

Figure 8. NPV distribution

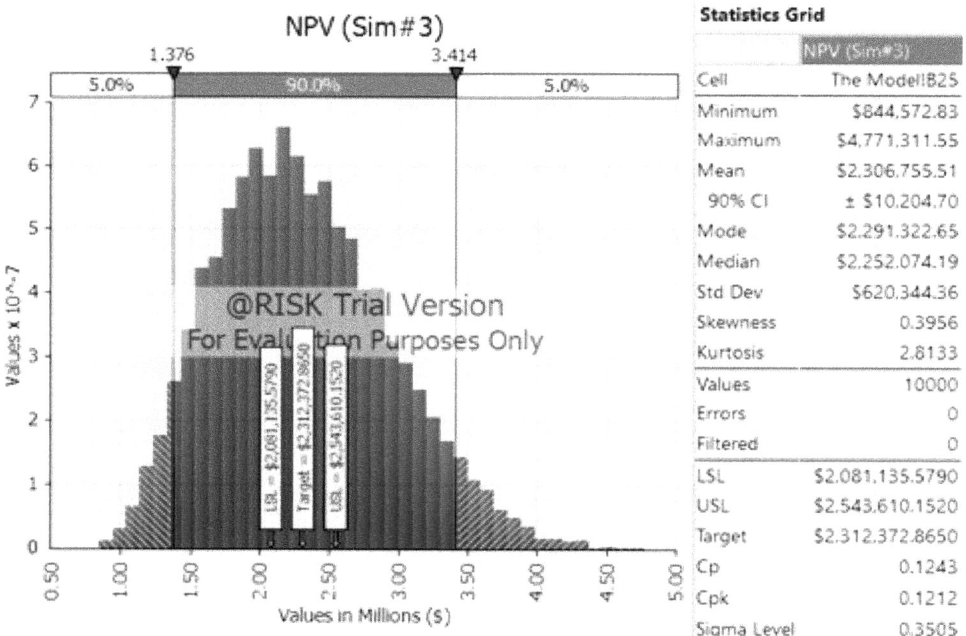

NPV Risk Attribution (DMAIC Analyse)

Sensitivity analysis provides for identifying and quantifying the main contributors to variability and risk. The regression coefficients graph (Figure 9) illustrates that if the top variable, the Use per Customer Year 1 (i.e., with a regression coefficient of 0.94), changes by one Standard Deviation, the NPV will change by 0.94 Standard Deviation. If the second top variable, Entrants Year 1 (i.e., with a regression coefficient of -0.52, which is negative), increases by one Standard Deviation, the NPV will decrease by 0.52 Standard Deviations. Other variables Entrants Year 2, etc. are less influential.

Figure 9. NPV regression coefficients

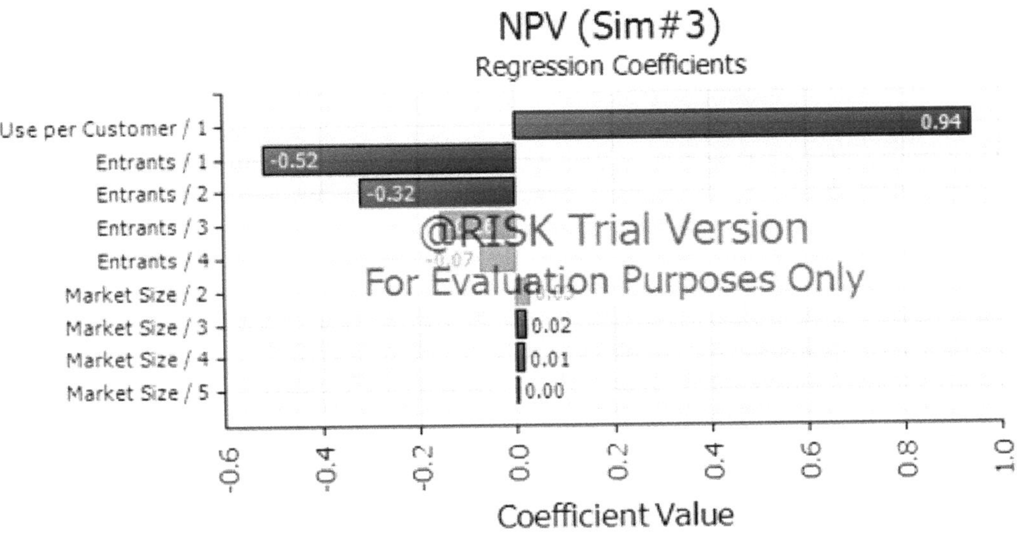

Simulation #4: Measuring Results (DMAIC Measure)

Simulation #4 is run and the results are presented below.

The Profits Vector results for five years are presented in Table 10.

Table 10. Profits vector results

Profits Vector for Five Years					
Year	**1**	**2**	**3**	**4**	**5**
Profits ($)	902,947.00	697,090.00	605,065.00	568,154.00	558,621.00

The Profits Vector results are graphically presented in Figure 10.

Figure 10. Summary trend of profits vector

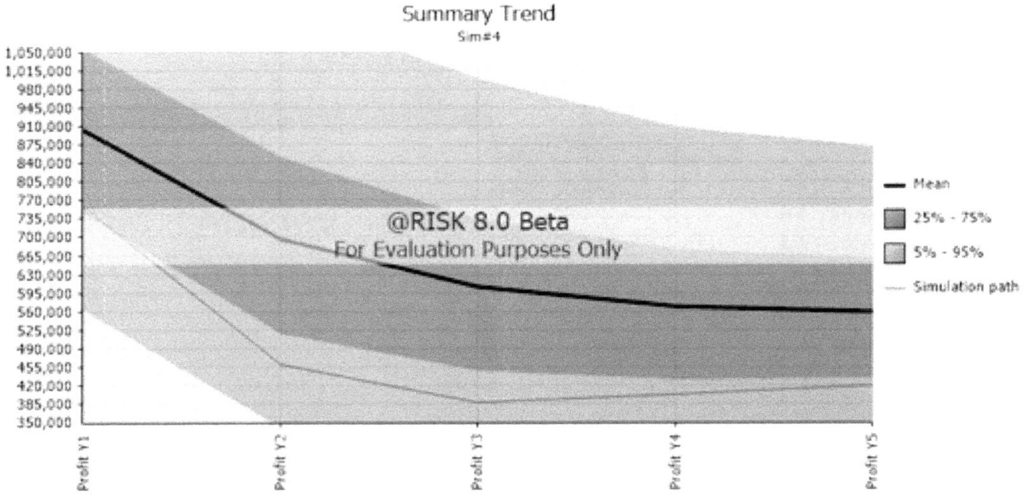

The results for NPV Variables are presented in Table 11.

Table 11. NPV variables results

Net Present Value Variables	
Net Present Value ($)	**2,556,668.00**
NPV Value at Risk ($)	1,250,663.00

Simulation #4: Results Analysis, Evaluation, and Risk Attribution (DMAIC Analyse)

The results for NPV are presented below.

NPV Analysis and Evaluation

NPV results are as follows (Figure 11). The *NPV Mean* is $2,557,379.90 with a *Standard Deviation* of $696,622.67, i.e., 27.240%. The Six Sigma target parameters are *TV* = $2,312,372.87; *LSL* = $2,081,135.58; and *USL* = $2,543,610.15. The Six Sigma process capability metrics are *Cp* = 0.1106; *Cpk* = -0.0066; and σ-*L* = 0.3259. There is a 5% probability that NPV will be below $1,513,000; a 90% probability that it will be in the range of $1,513,000 – $3,788,000; and a 5% probability that it will be above $3,788,000.

Figure 11. NPV distribution

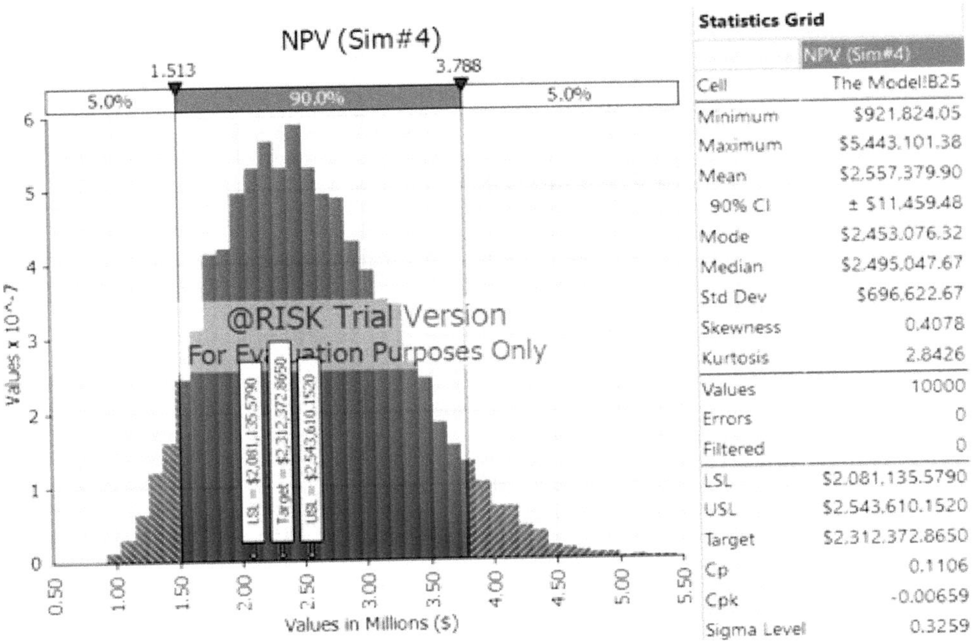
NPV (Sim#4)
1.513
3.788
5.0%
90.0%
5.0%
Values x 10^-7
Values in Millions ($)
@RISK Trial Version
For Evaluation Purposes Only
LSL = $2,081,135.5790
Target = $2,312,372.8650
USL = $2,543,610.1520
Statistics Grid
NPV (Sim#4)
Cell The Model!B25
Minimum $921,824.05
Maximum $5,443,101.38
Mean $2,557,379.90
90% CI ± $11,459.48
Mode $2,453,076.32
Median $2,495,047.67
Std Dev $696,622.67
Skewness 0.4078
Kurtosis 2.8426
Values 10000
Errors 0
Filtered 0
LSL $2,081,135.5790
USL $2,543,610.1520
Target $2,312,372.8650
Cp 0.1106
Cpk -0.00659
Sigma Level 0.3259

NPV Risk Attribution (DMAIC Analyse)

Sensitivity analysis provides for identifying and quantifying the main contributors to variability and risk. The regression coefficients graph (Figure 12) illustrates that if the top variable, the Use per Customer Year 1 (i.e., with a regression coefficient of 0.93), changes by one Standard Deviation, the NPV will change by 0.93 Standard Deviation. If the second top variable, Entrants Year 1 (i.e., with a regression coefficient of -0.55, which is negative), increases by one Standard Deviation, the NPV will decrease by 0.55 Standard Deviations. Other variables Entrants Year 2, etc. are less influential.

Figure 12. NPV regression coefficients

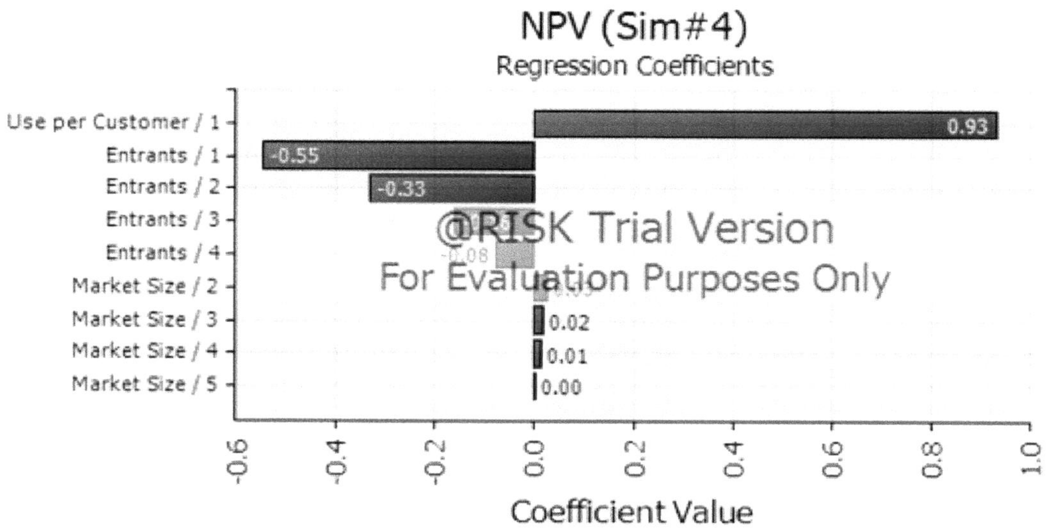

Simulation #5: Measuring Results (DMAIC Measure)

Simulation #5 is run and the results are presented below.

The Profits Vector results for five years are presented in Table 12.

Table 12. Profits vector results

Profits Vector for Five Years					
Year	**1**	**2**	**3**	**4**	**5**
Profits ($)	1.038180.00	773,353.00	661,163.00	617,423.00	606,933.00

The Profits Vector results are graphically presented in Figure 13.

Figure 13. Summary trend of profits vector

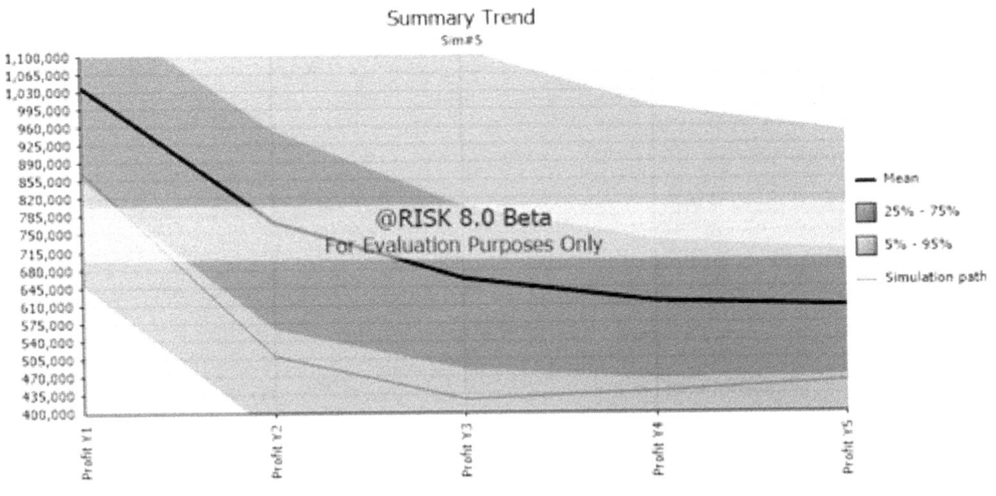

The results for NPV Variables are shown in Table 13.

Table 13. NPV variables results

Net Present Value Variables	
Net Present Value ($)	**2,813,305.00**
NPV Value at Risk ($)	1,356,787.00

Simulation #5: Results Analysis, Evaluation, and Risk Attribution (DMAIC Analyse)

The results for NPV are presented below.

NPV Analysis and Evaluation

NPV results are as follows (Figure 14). The *NPV Mean* is $2,813,519.52 with a *Standard Deviation* of $777,442.05, i.e., 27.632%. The Six Sigma target parameters are *TV* = $2,312,372.87; *LSL* = $2,081,135.58; and *USL* = $2,543,610.15. The Six Sigma process capability metrics are *Cp* = 0.0991; *Cpk* = -0.1157; and σ-*L* = 0.2767. There is a 5% probability that NPV will be below $1,650,000; a 90% probability that it will be in the range of $1,650,000 – $4,200,000; and a 5% probability that it will be above $4,200,000.

Figure 14. NPV distribution

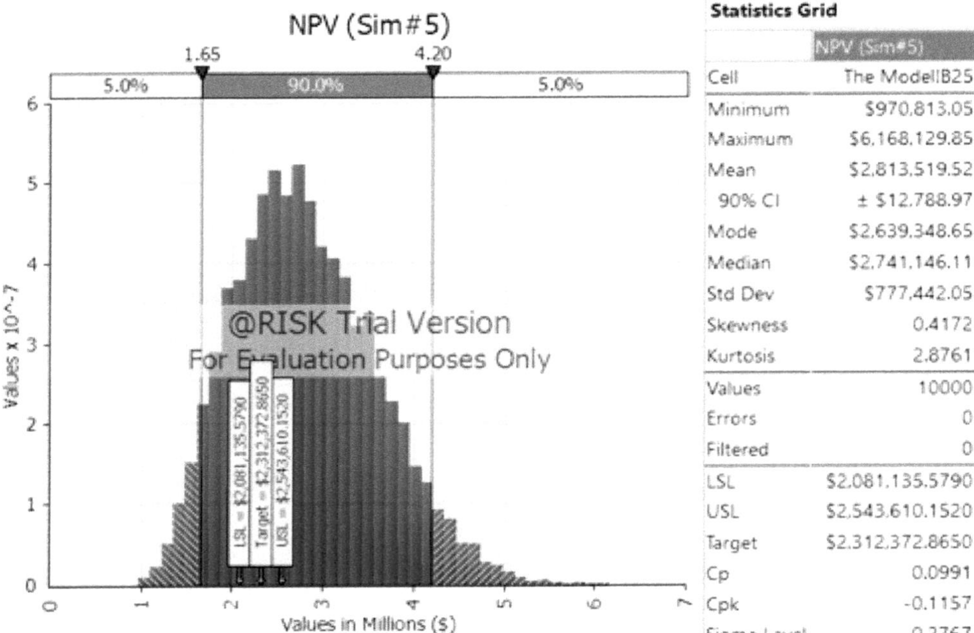

Statistics Grid	NPV (Sim#5)
Cell	The Model!B25
Minimum	$970,813.05
Maximum	$6,168,129.85
Mean	$2,813,519.52
90% CI	± $12,788.97
Mode	$2,639,348.65
Median	$2,741,146.11
Std Dev	$777,442.05
Skewness	0.4172
Kurtosis	2.8761
Values	10000
Errors	0
Filtered	0
LSL	$2,081,135.5790
USL	$2,543,610.1520
Target	$2,312,372.8650
Cp	0.0991
Cpk	-0.1157
Sigma Level	0.2767

Net Present Value (NPV) Risk Attribution (DMAIC Analyse)

Sensitivity analysis provides for identifying and quantifying the main contributors to variability and risk. The regression coefficients graph (Figure 15) illustrates that if the top variable, use per Customer Year 1 (i.e., with a regression coefficient of 0.93), changes by one Standard Deviation, the NPV will change by 0.93 Standard Deviation. If the second top variable, Entrants Year 1 (i.e., with a regression coefficient of -0.58, which is negative), increases by one Standard Deviation, the NPV will decrease by 0.58 Standard Deviations. Other variables Entrants Year 2, etc. are less influential.

Figure 15. NPV regression coefficients

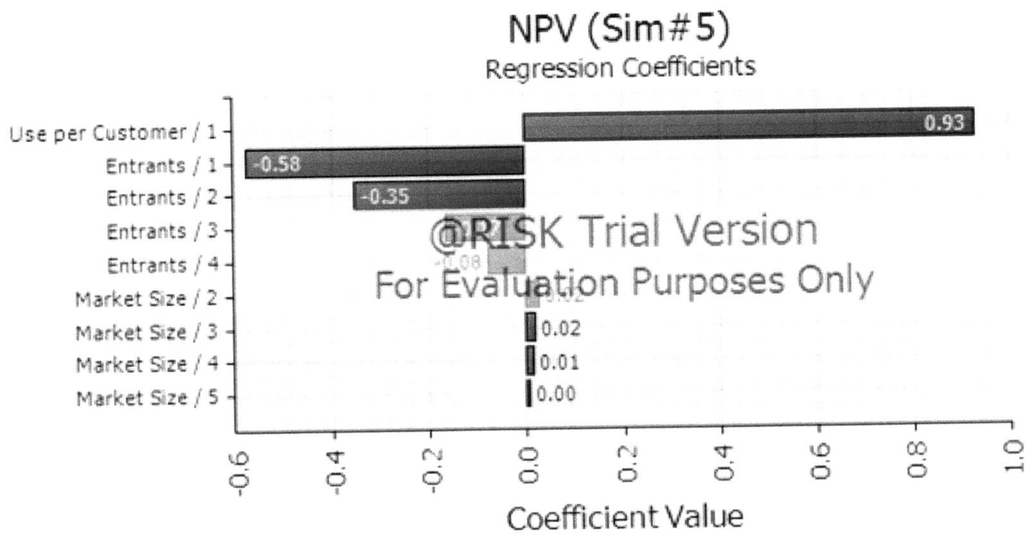

Comparison and Evaluation of Simulations Results (DMAIC Analyse)

The results of all the simulations are presented below for comparison.

The results of the Profits Vector are presented in Table 14.

Table 14. Profits vector results comparison

Profits Vector ($) for Five Years					
Year	**1**	**2**	**3**	**4**	**5**
Sim #1	568,620	480,855	436,330	416,655	411,611
Sim #2	668,752	549,976	491,914	467,014	460,203
Sim #3	780,000	622,280	548,340	517,360	509,498
Sim #4	902,947	697,090	605,065	568,154	558,621
Sim #5	1,038,180	773,353	661,163	617,423	606,933

The summary trend of Profit Vectors per simulation is presented in Figure 16. It is shown that the profit gradually increases from Sim #1 to Sim #5.

Figure 16. Summary trends of profit vectors per simulation

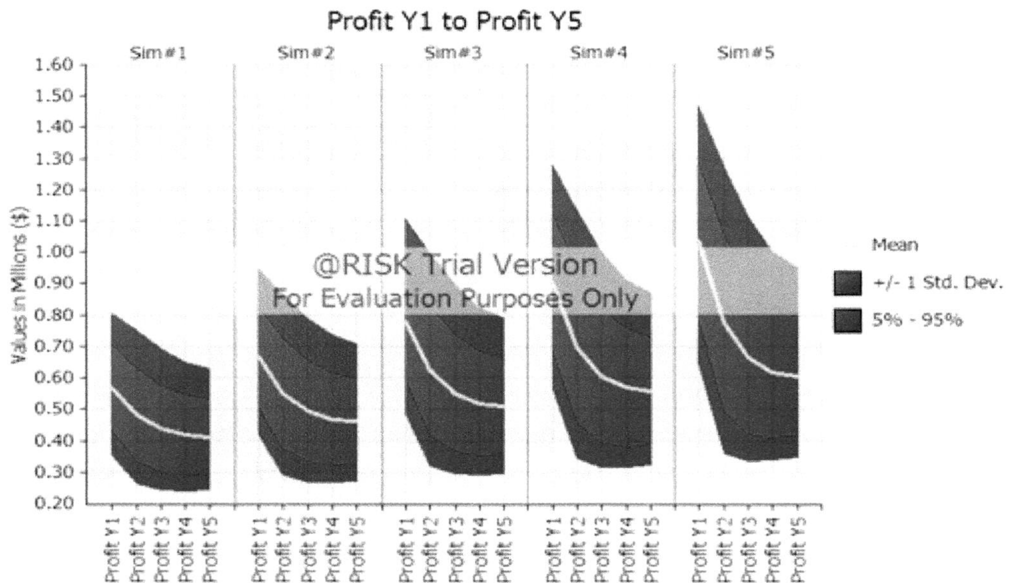

The trend of Profit Vectors per year is presented in Figure 17.

Figure 17. Trend of profit vectors per year

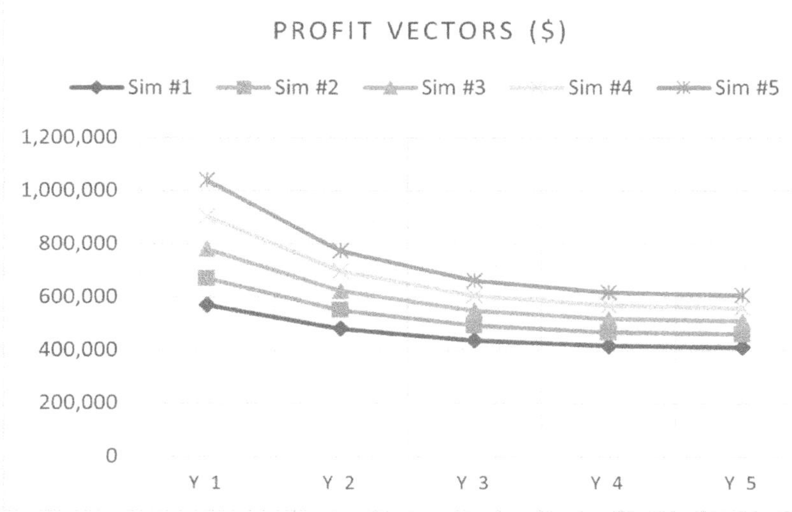

The results of the NPV Variables are shown in Table 15.

Table 15. NPV variables calculated values

Simulation No	Sim #1	Sim #2	Sim #3	Sim #4	Sim #5
Net Present Value ($)	1,826,007	2,061,264	2,305,069	2,556,668	2,813,305
NPV Value at Risk ($)	917,462	1,035,522	1,143,160	1,250,663	1,356,787

The trend of NPV Variables per simulation is presented in Figure 18. It is revealed that the NPV Variables gradually increase (in a linear approximation) from Sim #1 to Sim #5.

Figure 18. Trend of NPV variables per simulation

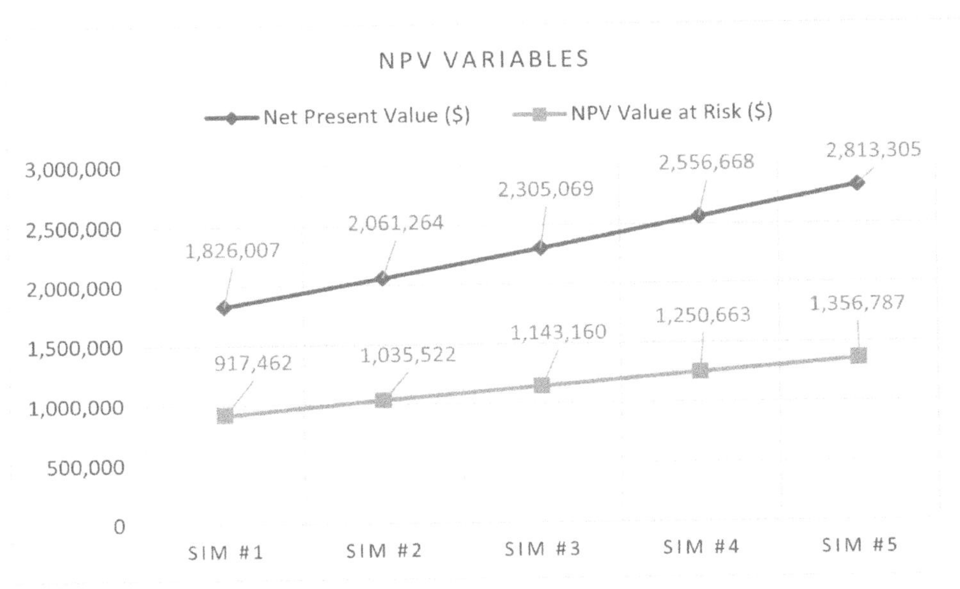

Conclusion (DMAIC Analyse)

The NPV Mean, Standard Deviation, and Six Sigma Level per simulation are presented in Table 16.

Table 16. NPV mean, standard deviation, and Six Sigma level

Simulation No	Sim #1	Sim #2	Sim #3	Sim #4	Sim #5
NPV Calculated ($)	1,826,007	2,061,264	2,305,069	2,556,668	2,813,305
NPV Mean ($)	1,827,390	2,062,735	2,306,756	2,557,380	2,813,520
Standard Deviation ($)	479,821	547,113	620,344	696,623	777,442
Standard Deviation (%)	26.257	26.524	26.983	27.240	27.632
Six Sigma Level	0.2642	0.3332	0.3505	0.3259	0.2767

Considering Standard Deviation, which is a major risk factor, the Sim #1 solution has the smallest risk of $479,821 (i.e., 26.257%), and the Sim #5 solution has the largest risk.

Considering the Six Sigma Level, which specifies the business's expected NPV, the Sim #3 solution has the best process capability of 0.3505 to achieve the anticipated NPV. Consequently, it seems that the Sim #3 solution is the most favoured for the business.

This analysis helps the company's management to decide whether to introduce the new product or not.

Verification of Results

The analysis presented in this chapter is comprehensive and delivers essential information to the business decision-makers. This acknowledges that the analysis is beneficial for business risk management, which is the ultimate goal. Therefore, the results of the method are satisfactorily verified.

CONCLUSION

This chapter presents an application of the DMAIC Stochastic Method to analyse the profitability of a new product. A company wants to launch a new product to the market. The profitability of the product is very uncertain when a company develops a new product. Thus, a comprehensive analysis is necessary to evaluate the profitability for five years. A stochastic model is used to provide for the analysis.

The model considers uncertain inputs such as the new product price, cost, as well as interest rate, probability of entry in the market, competition, market size, and share of the market. The simulation model evaluates the variables required for the marketing of the new product, for the five years. The variables include market size, product use per customer, competitors entering the market, market entrants, unit sales, revenues, costs, and profits. The simulation also calculates the NPV of profits over the five years and assesses the associated risks.

Five simulations are run with different values of the uncertain inputs to complete the analysis. The simulation results are evaluated, and sensitivity analysis is performed to identify and quantify the main contributors to variability and risk.

Considering Standard Deviation, which is a major risk factor, the Sim #1 solution has the smallest risk of $479,821 (i.e., 26.257%), and the Sim #5 solution has the largest risk. Also, considering the Six Sigma Level, which specifies the business's expected NPV, the Sim #3 solution has the best process capability of 0.3505 to achieve the anticipated NPV. Consequently, it seems that the Sim #3 solution is the most favoured for the business.

REFERENCES

Axson, D. J. A., & Rosander, K. (2014). *Measuring the True Profitability of Products, Services and Customers*. Accenture.

Cokins, G. (2017). *Strategic cost management for product.* Academic Press.

Daly, J. L. (2001). Pricing for Profitability: Activity-Based Pricing for Competitive Advantage. John Wiley & Sons.

Guide for Business Leaders. (2011). John Wiley & Sons.

Slywotzky, A. (2003). The Art of Profitability. Grand Central Publishing.

Chapter 7
Banks' Credit Losses Analysis

ABSTRACT

This chapter analyses the credit losses of 200 bank customers. The bank has classified the customers into eight credit rating categories, starting with 1 – Normal to 8 – Default, with associated default probabilities, which are empirically calculated as average values from historical data collected. Every customer begins a year in a certain credit rating category, with a certain amount of credit exposure at default. By the end of the year, each customer has either defaulted or not. In case of default, the percentage that can be recovered is uncertain. A stochastic model is applied to calculate the total loss amount from those customers and the percentage lost, which is the total loss percentage of the total amount of exposure at default. Also, it applies functions at several confidence levels to find the amounts of reserve required to be confident in covering the losses.

INTRODUCTION

This chapter demonstrates an analysis of credit risk for banks. A simulation model is designed to analyse the credit losses of 200 bank customers.

The model considers the Credit Loss Recovery Parameters, Credit Portfolio Profile, Customer Credit Losses, and simulation Outputs.

The Credit Loss Recovery Parameters are constants, that are empirical averages of historical data including Minimum, Most likely, and Maximum.

The Credit Portfolio Profile data includes Rating ID, Rating Category, Rating Default Probability, Customer Count, Customer Percentage of Total, Exposure at Default, and Exposure at Default Percentage of Total.

The Customer Credit Losses data comprises Customer ID, Customer Rating ID, Customer Rating Category, Customer Default Probability, Customer Exposure at Default, Customer Loss Recovery, Customer Default, and Customer Loss.

The simulation Outputs data are Total Loss, Total Loss Confidence Levels at 90%, 95% & 99%, and Percent Lost.

DOI: 10.4018/979-8-3693-3787-5.ch007

The simulation uses appropriate distributions with associated empirically estimated distribution parameters.

Literature

Some references for credit loss analysis in banking are provided below.

The chapter by Bubevski (2018) elaborates on Bank Credit Risk. The aim is to select the optimal loan portfolio that achieves the bank's investment objectives with an acceptable credit risk according to their predefined limits. Stochastic optimisation constructs an efficient frontier of optimal loan portfolios in banking with maximal profit and minimising loan losses, i.e., credit risk. Simulation stochastically calculates and measures mean gross profit, loan losses, variance, standard deviation, and the Sharpe ratio. The Six Sigma capability metrics determine if the loan portfolio complies with the bank's limits regarding the gross profit; loan losses, which quantify the credit risk; and Sharpe ratio, i.e., a risk-adjusted measure. Also, the bank regulation limits are applied based on the bank's capital to control the maximum loan amount per loan investment grade. The analysis allows for the selection of the best Efficient Frontier loan portfolio with the maximum Sharpe ratio. In their paper, Li & McMahan (2015) perform a case study on a community bank from the perspective of the structure of the terms of the bank's historical loan losses and the loan quality rating matrix used by the bank. The data source is from a small rural community bank located in the Midwestern state of the United States. The basic statistical analysis of the loan losses that is based on the bank's internal loan quality rating system is presented. Harris, Khan & Nissim (2018) reported that estimating the expected credit losses on banks' portfolios is difficult. The authors develop a method of the one-year-ahead expected rate of credit losses that combines various measures of credit risk disclosed by banks. The method uses cross-sectional analyses to obtain coefficients for estimating each period's measure of expected credit losses. The authors concluded that their approach is a better predictor of the provision for loan losses than analyst provision forecasts. Also, the method is useful for other credit risk metrics in predicting bank failure up to one year ahead.

The Basel Committee (1999) published a paper on the principles of credit risk management. This document was issued to encourage banking supervisors globally to promote sound practices for managing credit risk. Although the principles contained in this paper are most clearly applicable to the business of lending, they should be applied to all activities where credit risk is present. Chatterjee's (2015) handbook discusses a loan portfolio value model that is used by firms in their stress testing and is the basis of the Basel II risk weight formula. This book establishes that structural models are used to calculate the probability of default for a firm based on the value of its assets and liabilities. It discusses the reduced form models assuming an exogenous, random cause of default. For reduced form or default-intensity models, the book suggests that the fundamental modelling tool is a Poisson process. Finally, the book debates the counterparty credit risk in the over-the-counter derivatives market.

The article by Bhalla (2019) explains the basic concepts and methodologies of credit risk modelling and how it is important for financial institutions. In the credit risk world, statistics and machine learning play an important role in solving problems related to credit risk. Hence the roles of predictive modelers and data scientists have become so important. ECB (2007) summarises the findings of the bank task force. The objectives of the task force were threefold: i) to conduct a stock-taking exercise as regards current practices at the ECB; ii) to share views and know-how among participants; and iii) to develop or agree on a "best practice" for central banks on certain central bank-specific modelling aspects and parameter choices. Two common portfolios were analysed by several task force members with different systems and the simulation results were compared. It is organised as follows. The report starts with a discussion of the relevance of credit risk for central banks. It is followed by a short introduction to credit risk models, parameters, and systems. Next, it focuses on models used by members of the task force. Furthermore, it presents the results of the simulation exercise undertaken by the task force. Lastly, the lessons from these simulations as well as other conclusions are discussed.

The Problem Statement

The problem is to analyse the credit risk for a bank. Create a simulation model to analyse the credit losses of 200 bank customers. Use the given data of the bank customer classification for eight credit rating categories. The simulation model should calculate the Total Loss amount from those customers and the Percentage Lost, which is the Total Loss percentage of the Total Amount of Exposure at Default. Also, it should calculate the Total Loss confidence levels at 90%, 95% and 99%. Evaluate the simulation results considering the risk factors. Apply sensitivity analysis to identify and quantify the major contributors to variability and risk. Discuss the results for a conclusion.

The scenario presented in this chapter is hypothetical, using data published by Palisade® Corporation.

The data for the simulation model are presented below. The Credit Loss Recovery Parameters are the known Inputs (Table 1), which are empirical averages of history data including: i) PERT Minimum; ii) PERT Most likely; and iii) PERT Maximum.

Table 1. Known inputs

PERT Minimum	PERT Most Likely	PERT Maximum
0%	25%	90%

The Credit Portfolio Profile includes constant and calculated data presented in Table 2.

Table 2. Credit portfolio profile constant data

Rating ID	Rating Category	Default Probability
1	Normal	0.000087280
2	Special Mention 1	0.000119640
3	Special Mention 2	0.001842785
4	Subnormal 1	0.016429244
5	Subnormal 2	0.045791972
6	Doubtful 1	0.201255768
7	Doubtful 2	0.228174506
8	Default	0.717562189

The constant data is i) Rating ID Vector (*RatingIdV(i)*); ii) Rating Category Vector (*RatingCatgrV(i)*); and iii) Rating Default Probability Vector (*RatingDefltProbV(i)*). There are eight Rating Categories, so *i = 1, 2, …, 8.*

The calculated data is i) Customers Count Vector (*CustmrsCntV(i)*); ii) Customers Percentage of Total Vector (*Custmrs%OfTotlV(i)*); iii) Exposure at Default Vector (*Expsr@DefltV(i)*); and iv) Exposure at Default Percentage of Total Vector (*Expsr@Deflt%OfTotlV(i)*), where, *i = 1, 2, …, 9*, *i = 1, 2, …, 8* refers to the eight Rating IDs and *i = 9* refers to the Totals of these vectors.

The Customer Credit Losses also include constant and calculated data.

The constant data is i) Customer ID Vector (*CustmrIdV(i)*); ii) Customer Rating ID Vector (*CustmrRatingIdV(i)*); and iii) Customer Exposure at Default Vector (*CustmrExpsr@DefltV(i)*). There are 200 customers, so *i = 1, 2, …, 200* refers to the Customer ID.

The calculated data is i) Customer Loss Recovery Vector (*CustmrLossRcvrV(i)*); ii) Customer Loss Vector (*CustmLossV(i)*); and iii) Customer Default Vector (*CustmrDefltV(i)*). Where, *i = 1, 2, …, 200* refers to the Customer ID.

The Customer Credit Losses constant data is presented in Table 3. It is made up of the Customer ID and Customer Rating ID Vectors.

Table 3. Customer ID & customer rating ID data

Cust ID	Cust Rtng	Cust ID	Cust Rtng	Cust ID	Cust Rtng	Cust ID	Cust Rtng	Cust ID	Cust Rtng	Cust ID	Cust Rtng
1	1	35	1	69	1	103	1	137	1	171	1
2	1	36	4	70	1	104	1	138	1	172	1
3	1	37	1	71	1	105	1	139	1	173	1
4	1	38	1	72	1	106	1	140	7	174	5
5	2	39	1	73	1	107	1	141	6	175	6
6	1	40	3	74	1	108	1	142	1	176	7
7	1	41	1	75	3	109	1	143	1	177	1
8	1	42	1	76	1	110	1	144	5	178	2
9	1	43	1	77	2	111	1	145	2	179	1
10	1	44	1	78	1	112	1	146	1	180	4
11	1	45	1	79	1	113	1	147	1	181	4
12	1	46	1	80	1	114	1	148	1	182	2
13	3	47	3	81	1	115	2	149	6	183	1
14	1	48	1	82	3	116	1	150	1	184	2
15	1	49	1	83	1	117	1	151	2	185	1
16	1	50	1	84	1	118	3	152	4	186	1
17	1	51	1	85	1	119	1	153	1	187	1
18	1	52	1	86	1	120	1	154	3	188	1
19	1	53	1	87	1	121	1	155	1	189	1
20	1	54	1	88	1	122	1	156	1	190	1
21	5	55	1	89	1	123	1	157	1	191	1
22	1	56	1	90	3	124	1	158	1	192	1
23	2	57	1	91	1	125	1	159	3	193	2
24	1	58	1	92	5	126	1	160	6	194	2
25	1	59	1	93	1	127	1	161	1	195	1
26	1	60	2	94	1	128	1	162	1	196	1
27	1	61	1	95	1	129	1	163	2	197	2
28	1	62	1	96	2	130	1	164	7	198	1
29	1	63	1	97	1	131	1	165	1	199	1
30	1	64	1	98	3	132	1	166	5	200	1
31	1	65	1	99	1	133	1	167	5	-	-
32	1	66	3	100	1	134	7	168	4	-	-
33	1	67	1	101	5	135	1	169	2	-	-
34	1	68	1	102	2	136	4	170	1	-	-

The Customer Credit Losses data presented in Tables 4 & 5 includes Customer ID and Customer Exposure at Default (EAD) Vectors.

Table 4 shows the data for Customer IDs from 1 to 136.

Table 4. Customer ID & customer exposure at default data

Cust ID	Customer EAD	Cust ID	Customer EAD	Cust ID	Customer EAD	Cust ID	Customer EAD
1	$1,907,316	35	$4,153,072	69	$1,542,523	103	$2,336,059
2	$1,900,672	36	$1,705,383	70	$2,390,013	104	$8,078,044
3	$1,498,115	37	$4,168,234	71	$1,236,082	105	$2,773,255
4	$348,487	38	$9,582,638	72	$3,430,089	106	$3,734,150
5	$1,082,604	39	$3,227,850	73	$657,946	107	$5,389,994
6	$1,732,663	40	$386,158	74	$3,485,561	108	$5,512,769
7	$4,676,358	41	$522,297	75	$2,599,886	109	$617,093
8	$1,926,850	42	$718,133	76	$1,819,035	110	$1,477,668
9	$4,582,049	43	$3,641,618	77	$18,179,974	111	$3,245,435
10	$3,011,482	44	$3,109,875	78	$2,589,263	112	$2,148,669
11	$719,658	45	$3,681,002	79	$2,242,481	113	$1,940,406
12	$1,045,229	46	$2,033,390	80	$3,560,649	114	$2,626,689
13	$626,044	47	$4,224,292	81	$1,822,179	115	$24,613,893
14	$1,926,834	48	$2,419,418	82	$1,310,692	116	$1,114,534
15	$2,190,251	49	$426,862	83	$748,856	117	$975,279
16	$2,724,769	50	$2,373,815	84	$526,907	118	$462,238
17	$905,670	51	$296,331	85	$1,815,232	119	$4,804,542
18	$2,168,544	52	$1,767,779	86	$8,429,798	120	$1,799,467
19	$1,383,881	53	$3,975,848	87	$1,919,019	121	$1,772,445
20	$563,219	54	$8,715,195	88	$2,214,735	122	$1,200,876
21	$3,089,344	55	$3,419,843	89	$1,621,400	123	$596,070
22	$1,209,864	56	$2,405,363	90	$5,352,461	124	$2,582,727
23	$3,232,510	57	$1,311,542	91	$762,595	125	$3,642,593
24	$1,267,670	58	$4,119,503	92	$4,383,426	126	$203,247
25	$2,434,734	59	$1,125,038	93	$971,972	127	$1,964,762
26	$1,896,416	60	$1,537,006	94	$1,284,517	128	$1,230,809
27	$2,205,694	61	$1,558,348	95	$1,129,386	129	$786,471
28	$1,804,970	62	$870,329	96	$6,792,104	130	$846,194
29	$1,764,592	63	$998,228	97	$2,881,663	131	$9,877,466
30	$1,940,506	64	$1,471,620	98	$8,227,450	132	$1,239,928
31	$1,924,816	65	$2,644,260	99	$1,904,110	133	$2,784,600
32	$1,677,649	66	$3,586,146	100	$485,203	134	$2,162,897
33	$1,962,430	67	$1,485,642	101	$4,708,742	135	$2,527,095
34	$2,430,431	68	$2,430,907	102	$2,045,958	136	$1,010,332

Table 5 presents the data for Customer IDs from 137 to 200.

Table 5. Customer ID & customer exposure at default vectors

Cust ID	Customer EAD	Cust ID	Customer EAD	Cust ID	Customer EAD	Cust ID	Customer EAD
137	$2,325,338	153	$2,946,628	169	$3,461,743	185	$1,295,346
138	$516,274	154	$2,312,607	170	$2,051,671	186	$594,271
139	$1,463,269	155	$577,252	171	$5,017,704	187	$3,132,947
140	$1,989,852	156	$1,239,402	172	$1,975,281	188	$7,421
141	$2,471,392	157	$4,398,751	173	$1,861,112	189	$2,057,315
142	$5,135,704	158	$5,051,470	174	$1,761,533	190	$3,742,646
143	$1,465,070	159	$5,190,828	175	$5,530,005	191	$4,623,556
144	$3,994,537	160	$3,210,272	176	$2,686,551	192	$773,681
145	$1,113,796	161	$4,944,896	177	$2,597,334	193	$379,942
146	$83,341	162	$2,972,760	178	$2,180,719	194	$3,289,667
147	$3,572,135	163	$1,130,054	179	$4,981,629	195	$1,517,013
148	$1,466,798	164	$1,093,110	180	$1,686,287	196	$1,155,557
149	$9,295,514	165	$2,191,895	181	$2,446,077	197	$1,395,726
150	$1,239,590	166	$355,223	182	$1,851,117	198	$677,737
151	$5,572,586	167	$376,197	183	$1,308,131	199	$3,639,961
152	$2,105,923	168	$2,901,893	184	$1,756,666	200	$3,017,871

Calculations (DMAIC Define)

Microsoft™ Excel® and Palisade™ @RISK® formulae are used for the calculations presented in this section.

Credit Portfolio Profile Vector Calculations

The Credit Portfolio Profile Vectors to be calculated are i) Customers Count Vector (*CustmrsCntV(i)*); ii) Customers Percentage of Total Vector (*Custmrs%OfTotlV(i)*); iii) Exposure at Default Vector (*Expsr@DefltV(i)*); and iv) Exposure at Default Percentage of Total Vector (*Expsr@Deflt%OfTotlV(i)*), where $i = 1, 2, \ldots, 9$; $i = 1, 2, \ldots, 8$ refers to the eight Rating IDs and $i = 9$ refers to the Totals of these vectors. The calculations are given below.

Customers Count Vector:

CustmrsCntV(i)=COUNTIF(CustmrRatingIdV(1): CustmrRatingIdV(200), RatingIdV(i)) (1)

CustmrsCntV(9)=SUM(CustmrsCntV(1):CustmrsCntV(8)) (2)

where *CustmrRatingIdV(i)* is the Customer Rating ID Vector and *RatingIdV(i)* is the Rating ID Vector.

Customers Percentage of Total Vector:

Custmrs%OfTotlV(i)= CustmrsCntV(i)/CustmrsCntV(9) (3)

Custmrs%OfTotlV(9)=SUM(Custmrs%OfTotlV(1): Custmrs%OfTotlV(8)) (4) where *CustmrsCntV(i)* is the Customers Count Vector.

Exposure at Default Vector:

Expsr@DefltV(i)=SUMIF(CustmrRatingIdV(1):CustmrRatingIdV(200), RatingIdV(i), CustmrExpsr@DefltV(1):CustmrExpsr@DefltV(200)) (5)

Expsr@DefltV(9)=SUM(Expsr@DefltV(1):Expsr@DefltV(8)) (6)

where *CustmrRatingIdV(i)* is the Customer Rating ID Vector, *RatingIdV(i)* is the Rating ID Vector, and *CustmrExpsr@DefltV(i)* is the Customer Exposure at Default Vector.

Exposure at Default Percentage of Total Vector:

Expsr@Deflt%OfTotlV(i)= Expsr@DefltV(i)/Expsr@DefltV(9) (7)

Expsr@Deflt%OfTotlV(9)=SUM(Expsr@Deflt%OfTotlV(1): Expsr@Deflt%OfTotlV(8)) (8)

where *Expsr@DefltV(i)* is the Exposure at the Default Vector.

Customer Credit Losses Vectors Calculations

The Customer Credit Losses Vectors to calculate are i) Customer Loss Recovery Vector (*CustmrLossRcvrV(i)*); ii) Customer Default Vector (*CustmrDefltV(i)*); and iii) Customer Loss Vector (*CustmLossV(i)*). Where, *i = 1, 2, …, 200* refer to the Customer ID. The calculations are given below.

Customer Loss Recovery Vector:

CustmrLossRcvrV(i)=RiskPert(PertMinimum,PertMostLikely, PertMaximum) (9)

where *RiskPert* is the @RISK Distribution, *PertMinimum, PertMostLikely,* and *PertMaximum* are the associated parameters, which are the known Inputs given in Table 71.

Customer Default Vector:

CustmrDefltV(i)=RiskBernoulli(SUMIF(RatingIdV(1):RatingIdV(8), CustmrRatingIdV(i),RatingDefltProbV(1):RatingDefltProbV(8))) (10)

where *RiskBernoulli* is the @RISK Distribution, *RatingIdV(i)* is the Rating ID Vector, *CustmrRatingIdV* is the Customer Rating ID Vector and *RatingDefltProbV(i)* is the Rating Default Probability Vector.

Customer Loss Vector:

CustmLossV(i)= IF(CustmrDefltV(i)=0,0, CustmrExpsr@DefltV(i)* (1 - CustmrLossRcvrV(i))) (11)

where *CustmrDefltV(i)* is the Customer Default Vector, *CustmrExpsr@DefltV(i)* is the Customer Exposure at Default Vector and *CustmrLossRcvrV(i)* is the Customer Loss Recovery Vector.

Simulation Outputs Calculations

The simulation Outputs comprise i) Total Loss (*TotalLoss*); ii) Total Loss Confidence Level at 90% (*TotalLossConf@90%*); iii) Total Loss Confidence Level at 95% (*TotalLossConf@95%*); iv) Total Loss Confidence Level at 99% (*TotalLossConf@99%*); and v) Percent Lost (*PercentLost*). The calculations are given below.

Total Loss:

TotalLoss=RiskOutput("Total-Loss",, RiskSixSigma(4833664*0.5, 4833664*1.5,4833664,0,3))+ SUM(CustmLossV(1):CustmLossV(200)) (12)

where *RiskOutput* & *RiskSixSigma* are the @RISK functions and *CustmLossV(i)* is the Customer Loss Vector.

Total Loss Confidence Level at 90%:

TotalLossConf@90%= RiskPercentile(TotalLoss,90%) (13)

Total Loss Confidence Level at 95%:
TotalLossConf@95%= RiskPercentile(TotalLoss,95%) (14)
Total Loss Confidence Level at 99%:
TotalLossConf@99%= RiskPercentile(TotalLoss,99%) (15)
where *RiskPercentile* is the @RISK function.
Percent Lost:
PercentLost=RiskOutput("Percent-Lost",, RiskSixSigma(0.9152%*0.5,0.9152%*1.5,0.9152%,0,3))+ TotalLoss / Expsr@DefltV(9) (16)

where *RiskOutput* & *RiskSixSigma* are the @RISK functions and *Expsr@DefltV(9)* is the Total of Exposure at Default Vector.

Measure Total Loss and Percent Lost (DMAIC Measure)

The calculated simulation Outputs of Total Loss and Percent Lost are presented in Table 6 below.

Table 6. Total loss and percent lost results

Simulation Output	Value
Total Loss	$4,833,664.47
Total Loss Confidence Level at 90%	$10,258,442.42
Total Loss Confidence Level at 95%	$12,028,788.54
Total Loss Confidence Level at 99%	$15,173,954.52
Percent Lost	0.9152%

The Total Loss Confidence Levels are interpreted as follows.

1. Total Loss Confidence Level at 90%: there is a 90% probability that the Total Loss will be equal to, or below $10,258,442.42;
2. Total Loss Confidence Level at 95%: there is a 95% probability that the Total Loss will be equal to, or below $12,028,788.54;
3. Total Loss Confidence Level at 99%: there is a 99% probability that the Total Loss will be equal to, or below $15,173,954.52.

Total Loss and Percent Lost Evaluation, and Risk Attribution (DMAIC Analyse)

The simulation results are analysed below.

Total Loss Analysis, Evaluation, and Risk Attribution

Figure 1 displays the Total Loss distribution. The *Mean* is $4,838,180.53 and the *Standard Deviation* is $3,736,215.75, i.e., 77.224%. The Six Sigma target parameters are *TV* = $4,833,664; *LSL* = $2,416,832; and *USL* = $7,250,496. The Six Sigma process capability metrics are *Cp* = 0.2156; *Cpk* = 0.2152; and *σ-L* = 0.5836. There is a hypothetical 5% probability that the *Mean* will be below zero (i.e., negative); a 90% probability that it will be in the range of \$0.00 MM – \$12.03 MM; and a 5% probability that it will be above \$12.03 MM.

Figure 1. Total loss distribution

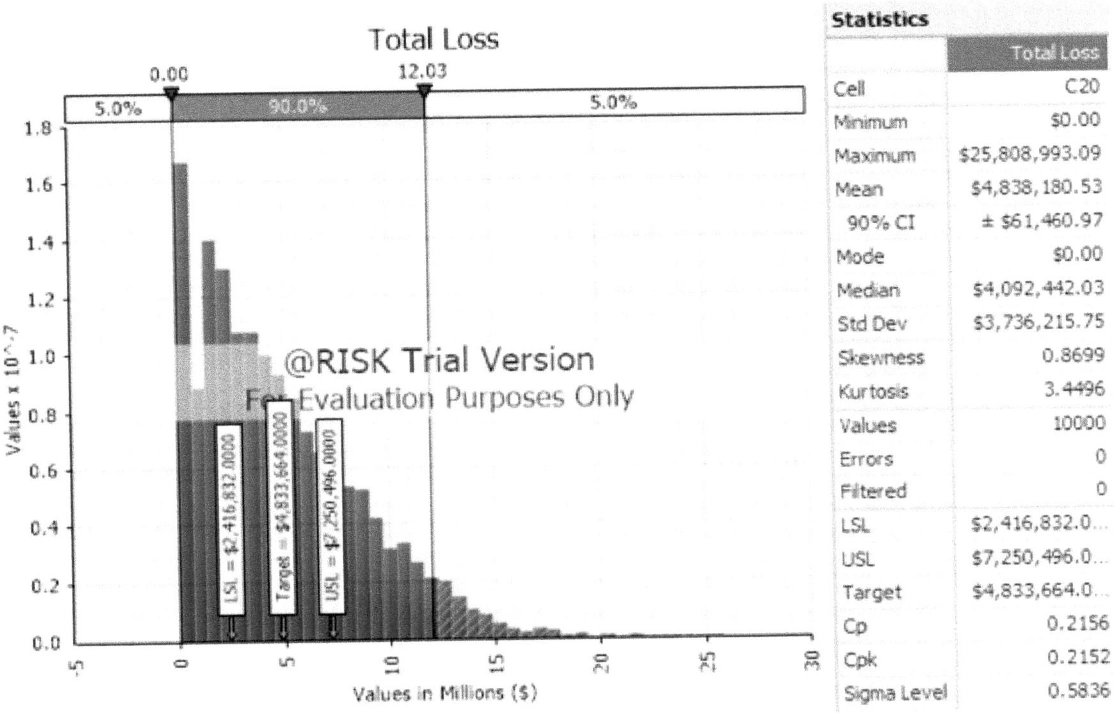
Total Loss
0.00
12.03
5.0%
90.0%
5.0%
@RISK Trial Version
For Evaluation Purposes Only
LSL = $2,416,832.0000
Target = $4,833,664.0000
USL = $7,250,496.0000
Values x 10^-7
Values in Millions ($)
Statistics
Total Loss
Cell C20
Minimum $0.00
Maximum $25,808,993.09
Mean $4,838,180.53
90% CI ± $61,460.97
Mode $0.00
Median $4,092,442.03
Std Dev $3,736,215.75
Skewness 0.8699
Kurtosis 3.4496
Values 10000
Errors 0
Filtered 0
LSL $2,416,832.0...
USL $7,250,496.0...
Target $4,833,664.0...
Cp 0.2156
Cpk 0.2152
Sigma Level 0.5836

Sensitivity analysis provides for identifying and quantifying the main contributors to variability and risk. The correlation coefficients graph (Figure 2) illustrates that if the top variable, Customer 149 Default (i.e., ID 149, with Rating Category of Doubtful 1 (H173)), increases by one unit, the Total Loss will change by 0.61 units, which is the most influential variable. The other variables are less influential as their correlation coefficients are in the range of 0.41 to 0.05 from top to bottom.

It should be noted that the customers with higher risk rating categories are more influential, which are the categories from Special Mention 2 to Doubtful 2 as shown in Figure 2.

Figure 2. Total loss correlation

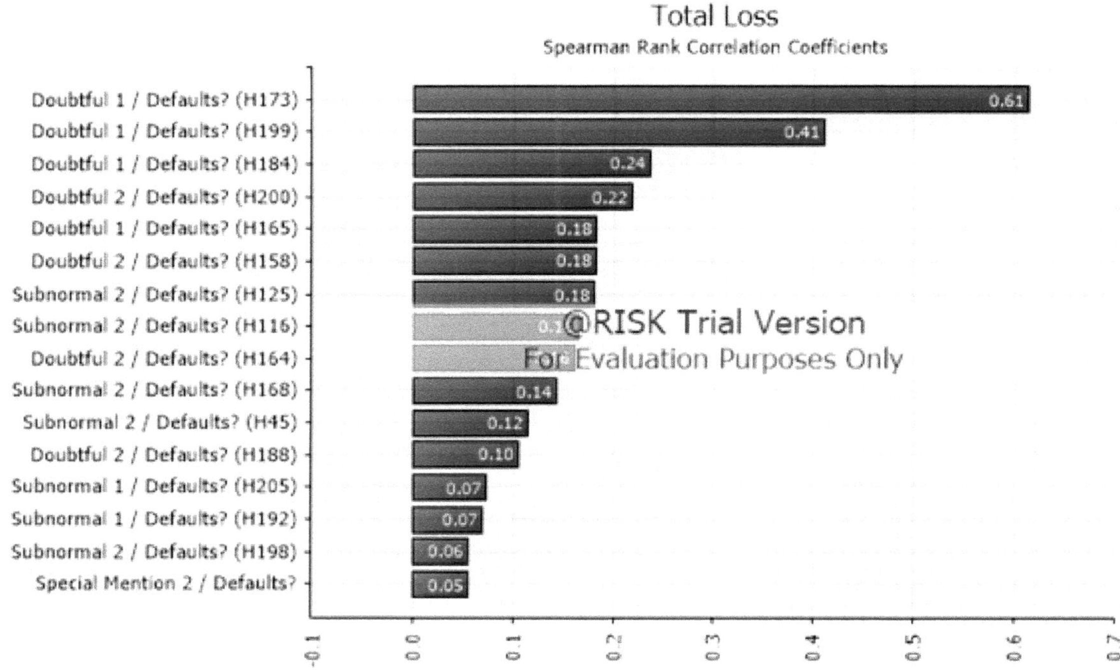

Percent Lost Analysis, Evaluation, and Risk Attribution

Figure 3 displays the Percent Lost distribution.

Figure 3. Percent lost distribution

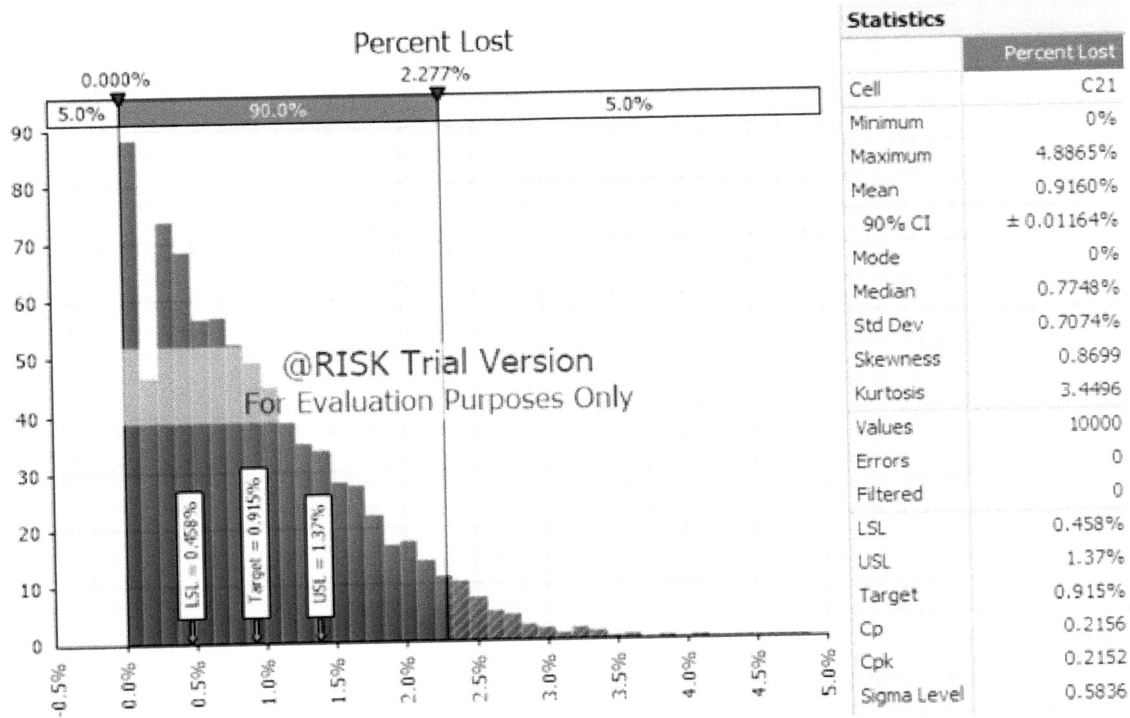

The *Mean* is 0.9160% and the *Standard Deviation* is 0.7074% (Figure 3), i.e., 77.227%. The Six Sigma target parameters are *TV* = 0.915%; *LSL* = 0.458%; and *USL* = 1.37%. The Six Sigma process capability metrics are *Cp* = 0.2156; *Cpk* = 0.2152; and *σ-L* = 0.5836. There is a hypothetical 5% probability that the *Mean* will be below zero percent (i.e., negative); a 90% probability that it will be in the range of 0.000% – 2.277%; and a 5% probability that it will be above 2.277%

Sensitivity analysis provides for identifying and quantifying the main contributors to variability and risk. The correlation coefficients graph shown in Figure 4 illustrates that if the top variable, Customer 149 Default (i.e., ID 149, with Rating Category of Doubtful 1 (H173)), increases by one unit, the Total Loss will change by 0.61 units, which is the most influential variable. The other variables are less influential as their correlation coefficients are in the range of 0.41 to 0.05 from top to bottom.

Figure 4. Percent lost correlation

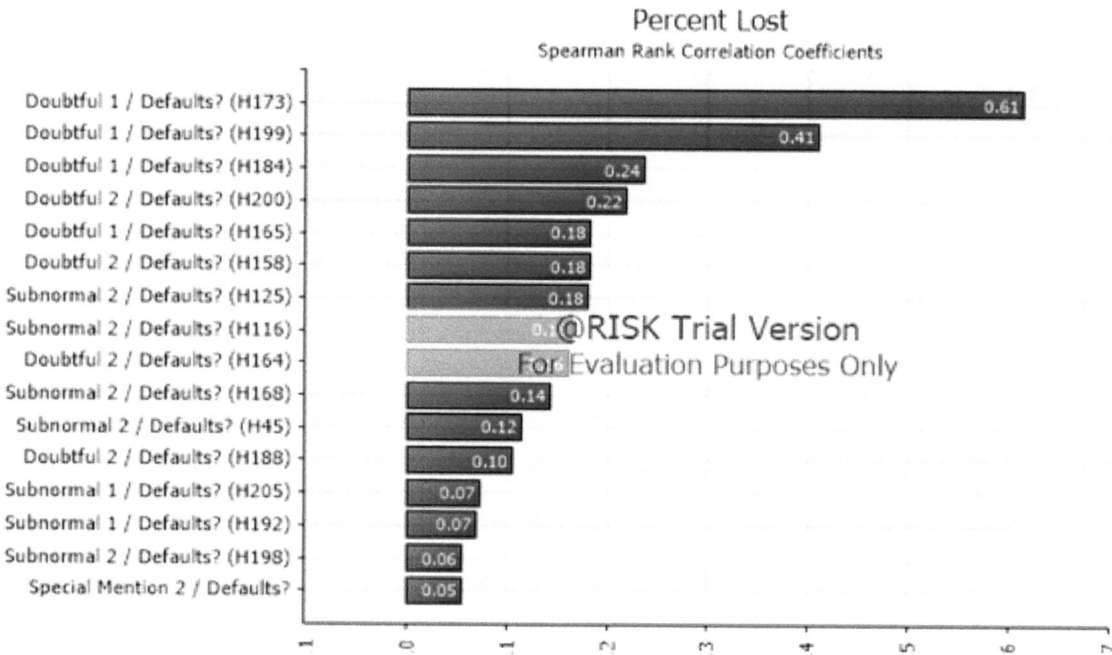

Once more, the customers with higher risk rating categories are more influential, which are the categories from Special Mention 2 to Doubtful 2 (Figure 4).

Verification of Results

Considering the results in Table 7.6 above, the conclusion is that the Total Loss Confidence Levels are satisfactorily good, which is important information for the banks' credit risk management. This recognises that the simulation analysis improves the banks' credit risk management process, which is the ultimate goal. Therefore, the results are satisfactorily verified.

CONCLUSION

This chapter applied a stochastic model to analyse credit risk in banking. A simulation model was designed to analyse the credit losses of 200 bank customers.

The model considered data such as Credit Loss Recovery Parameters, Credit Portfolio Profile, Customer Credit Losses, and Simulation Outputs.

The simulation model calculated Total Loss, Total Loss Confidence Levels at 90%, 95% & 99%, and Percent Lost. The simulation used appropriate distributions with associated empirically estimated distribution parameters. The simulation results were evaluated, including the associated risk factors. Sensitivity analysis was performed to identify and quantify the major contributors to variability and risk.

It was concluded that the Total Loss Confidence Levels were satisfactorily good, which is important information for the bank's credit risk management. This recognised that the simulation analysis improved the bank's credit risk management, which was the ultimate objective.

REFERENCES

Bhalla, D. (2019). *A complete guide to credit risk modelling*. ListenData.

Bubevski, V. (2018). Managing Credit Risk in Bank Loan Portfolio. In V. Bubevski (Ed.), *Six Sigma Improvements for Basel III and Solvency II in Financial Risk Management* (pp. 10–36). IGI Global.

Chatterjee, S. (2015). *Modelling credit risk*. Bank of England.

ECB. (2007). *The use of portfolio credit risk models in central banks. European Central Bank (ECB).*

Harris, T. S., Khan, U., & Nissim, D. (2018). The Expected Rate of Credit Losses on Banks' Loan Portfolios. *The Accounting Review*, *93*(5), 2018. doi:10.2308/accr-52012

Li, W., & McMahan, P. (2015, December). A case study on loan loss analysis of a community bank. *The Journal of Finance and Data Science*, *1*(1), 11–32. doi:10.1016/j.jfds.2015.07.001

The Basel Committee. (1999). *Principles for the Management of Credit Risk*. The Basel Committee.

Chapter 8
Discounted Cash Flow Projection

ABSTRACT

A risk analysis of a copper mining discounted cash flow projection is presented. Financial projection for 10 years is done to decide upon and undertake its initiative. The projection calculates the profit per year, total profit, and NPV. The inputs required include copper price per pound, mining cost per pound, pounds mined and sold, and investment cost, which impact the profit per year, total profit, and NPV. Historical data provide the inputs and to consider the risk involved, probability distributions with empirical parameters are applied, which are derived from the historical data. A simulation is run to calculate the profit for the 10 years, the total profit, and NPV. What-if and sensitivity analysis provided a comprehensive insight into the probability of the outputs and quantified the sensitivity of the outputs based on changes in the associated inputs. The risk analysis provided management with valuable information for decision-making.

INTRODUCTION

This chapter presents a Risk Analysis of a Discounted Cash Flow (DCF) projection in mining. A copper mine is making a financial projection for ten years to decide upon and undertake its initiative. The projection calculates the Profit per Year, Total Profit, and NPV. The stochastic analysis is performed for ten years.

To introduce the variability of the inputs, probability distributions with empirical parameters are applied, which are projections from historical data. The Discount Rate input is an average estimate from the historical data.

The financial variables required to derive DCF are calculated each year, i.e., from Year 2021 to Year 2030. The financial variables are Year, Copper Price per Pound, Mining Cost per Pound, Pounds Mined and Sold, Investment Cost, and Profit.

Finally, the outputs of the stochastic analysis are Total Profit and NPV. They are calculated from the Profit from all years.

DOI: 10.4018/979-8-3693-3787-5.ch008

A simulation model is designed and run to calculate the variables for the analysis. What-If and Sensitivity Analysis are applied, which provide a comprehensive view of the probability of the outputs and quantify the sensitivity of the outputs based on the variability of the associated inputs and financial variables.

This risk analysis is purposed to help management decide whether to invest in mining over the next ten years.

Literature

This chapter considers Cash Flow and NPV, some references for which are given below. Fight (2005) outlines the techniques required to undertake a detailed analysis of the cash flow dynamics of the business from both a historical and forward-looking perspective. The book presents i) the determination of appropriate cash flow figures from pro forma financial statements; ii) the interpretation of detailed cash flow forecasts and understanding of the difference between profit and cash flow; iii) the preservation and generation of cash in the short term; iv) evaluation of different methods of project evaluation; and v) recognition of the limitations of accounting information in valuing companies.

Tham & Velez-Pareja's (2001) book provides a comprehensive and practical, market-based framework for the valuation of finite cash flows derived from a set of integrated financial statements, namely, the income statement, balance sheet, and cash budget. Miller, Vandome & McBrewster (2011) in their book elaborate on NPV. Establishing that NPV is a central tool in discounted cash flow analysis, and is a standard method for using the time value of money to appraise long-term projects. This book describes the NPV usage for measuring the excess or shortfall of cash flows in present-value terms, in capital budgeting, economics, finance, and accounting. Sekhar's (2016) book covers capital budgeting methods, estimating project cash flows, and project analysis. It also illustrates the Payback period, Discounted Payback Period, Average Rate of Return, Net Present Value, Profitability Index, Internal Rate of Return, and Modified Internal Rate of Return. Sekhar (2018) in his book elaborates on the Capital Budgeting Decision Methods. This book demonstrates decision methods including the relevant concepts and theories. The book covers an introduction to Capital Budgeting, Capital Budgeting methods, and estimating project Cash Flows and elaborates on project analysis. The book considers the major aspects of Capital Budgeting including amongst others the NPV. Shapiro (2004) in his book on Capital Budgeting presents the theory and practice by providing numerous real-world examples of its applications. The book elaborates on the subject principles and techniques, estimating project cash flows, biases in cash flow estimates, foreign investment analysis, real options, and project analysis, risk and incorporating risk in capital budgeting analysis, estimating project cost, financing side effects, discount rates for foreign investments, corporate strategy, and capital budgeting decision. Peterson & Fabozzi (2002) in their book explore and illustrate all aspects of the capital budgeting decision process examining the critical issues and the limitations of capital budgeting techniques. The book presents an in-depth analysis of i) classifying capital budgeting proposals; ii) determining the relevant cash flows for capital budgeting proposals; iii) assessing the economic value of a capital budgeting proposal using different techniques; iv) incorporating risk into the capital budgeting decision; and v) evaluating whether to lease or borrow-to-buy.

The Problem Statement: Perform a Risk Analysis of a Discounted Cash Flow projection in mining. Perform stochastic analysis for ten years. Simulate the financial variables to calculate them each year for ten years, including Profit. Finally, calculate the outputs of Total Profit and NPV. Perform What-If and Sensitivity Analysis to provide a comprehensive view of the probability of the outputs and quantify the sensitivity of the outputs based on the variability of associated inputs and financial variables. The objective of this risk analysis is to help management decide whether to implement their mining project.

The scenario presented in this chapter is hypothetical, using data published by Palisade® Corporation.

Model Data Definition: The data for the simulation model are presented below including the financial variables and simulation outputs.

The financial variables are calculated each year, i.e., from Year 2021 to Year 2030. They are: i) Year Vector (*YearV(i)*); ii) Copper Price per Pound Vector (*CopperPricePoundV(i)*); iii) Mining Cost per Pound Vector (*MiningCostPoundV(i)*); iv) Pounds Mined & Sold Vector (*PoundsMinedSoldV(i)*); v) Investment Cost Vector (*InvestmentCostV(i)*); and xi) Profit Vector (*ProfitV(i)*); where *i = 2021, 2022, ..., 2030.*

The variables calculated by the Normal Distribution have the following empirically projected parameters of Mean (*Mu*) and Standard Deviation (*SD*). The Standard Deviation for all variables is 20%, i.e., 0.2, which will be specified in the formulae. The Mean (*Mu*) parameters are i) Copper Price per Pound Mean Vector, (*CPPMuV(i)*); ii) Mining Cost per Pound Mean Vector, (*MCPMuV(i)*); iii) Pounds Mined & Sold Mean Vector, (*PMSMuV(i)*); and iv) Investment Cost Mean Vector, (*ICMuV(i)*). The Normal Distribution parameters are given in Table 1.

Lastly, the outputs of the stochastic analysis are: i) Total Profit (*TotalProfit*); and Net Present Value (*NPV*). They are calculated from the Profit Vector (*ProfitV(i)*).

Table 1. Normal distribution parameters

Year	'21	'22	'23	'24	'25
CPPMuV	1.1	1.2	1.35	1.5	1.3
MCPMuV	0.55	0.55	0.55	0.65	0.65
PMSMuV	30000	50000	70000	90000	90000
ICMuV	100000	50000	0	0	0
Year	**'26**	**'27**	**'28**	**'29**	**'30**
CPPMuV	1.1	1.2	1.3	1.3	1.4
MCPMuV	0.65	0.65	0.65	0.65	0.65
PMSMuV	90000	90000	90000	40000	30000
ICMuV	0	0	0	0	0

Calculations

Microsoft™ Excel®, Palisade™ @RISK®, and TopRank® are used for the calculations presented in this section.

Financial Variables per Year Vectors

The financial variables are given in the Model Data Definition section above. The calculations are the following.

Year Vector:

YearV (i)= i (1)

Copper Price per Pound Vector:
CopperPricePoundV(i)=RiskNormal(CPPMuV(i),0.2) (2)
Mining Cost per Pound Vector:
MiningCostPoundV(i)= RiskNormal(MCPMuV(i),0.2) (3)
Pounds Mined & Sold Vector:
PoundsMinedSoldV(i)=RiskNormal(PMSMuV(i),0.2) (4)
Investment Cost Vector:
InvestmentCostV(i)= RiskNormal(ICMuV(i),0.2) (5)
where RiskNormal is the @RISK Normal Distribution with specified parameters for Mean (*Mu*) and Standard Deviation (*SD*) of 0.2.
Profit Vector:
ProfitV(i)=RiskOutput(Concatenate("Profit-Year",YearV(i)))+ (CopperPricePoundV(i)-MiningCostPoundV(i))* PoundsMinedSoldV(i)- InvestmentCostV(i) (6)

Total Profit and NPV Outputs

The outputs of the stochastic analysis are i) Total Profit (*TotalProfit*) and Net Present Value (*NPV*).
Total Profit:
TotalProfit =SUM(ProfitV(2021):ProfitV(2030))+ RiskOutput("TotalProfit ($M)",, RiskSixSigma(200883.2, 373068.8, 286976.0,1.5,3)) (7)
Net Present Value:
NPV=NPV(DiscountRate,SUM(ProfitV(2021):ProfitV(2030))+ RiskOutput("NPV ($M)",, RiskSixSigma(81311.4, 189726.6, 135519.0,1.5,3)) (8)
where *RiskSixSigma* is the @RISK function for Six Sigma Limit parameters.

Measuring the Simulation Results

The calculated Profit per Year results are presented in Table 2.

Table 2. Profit per year ($M)

Year	2021	2022	2023	2024	2025
Profit ($M)	($83,500)	($17,500)	$56,000	$76,500	$58,500
Year	**2026**	**2027**	**2028**	**2029**	**2030**
Profit ($M)	$40,500	$49,500	$58,500	$26,000	$22,500

The calculated Profit per Year graph is presented in Figure 1 with value labels given in dollars ($M). The calculated Profit per Year starts at -$83,500,000 in the Year 2021 and linearly increases to $56,000,000 in the Year 2023. It reaches a maximum of $76,500,000 in Year 2024, from where it linearly decreases to a local minimum of $40,500,000 in Year 2026. From Year 2026 it linearly grows to a local maximum of $58,500,000 in Year 2028. Subsequently, it exponentially reduces to $22,500,000 in Year 2030.

Figure 1. Calculated profit per year graph

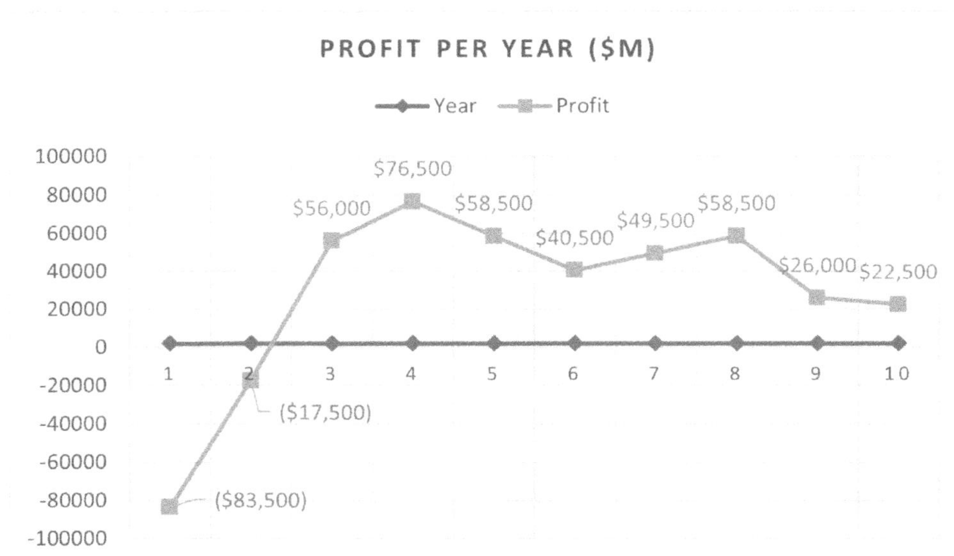

The Profit Per Year *Mean* is graphically presented in Figure 2.

Figure 2. Summary trend of profit per year mean

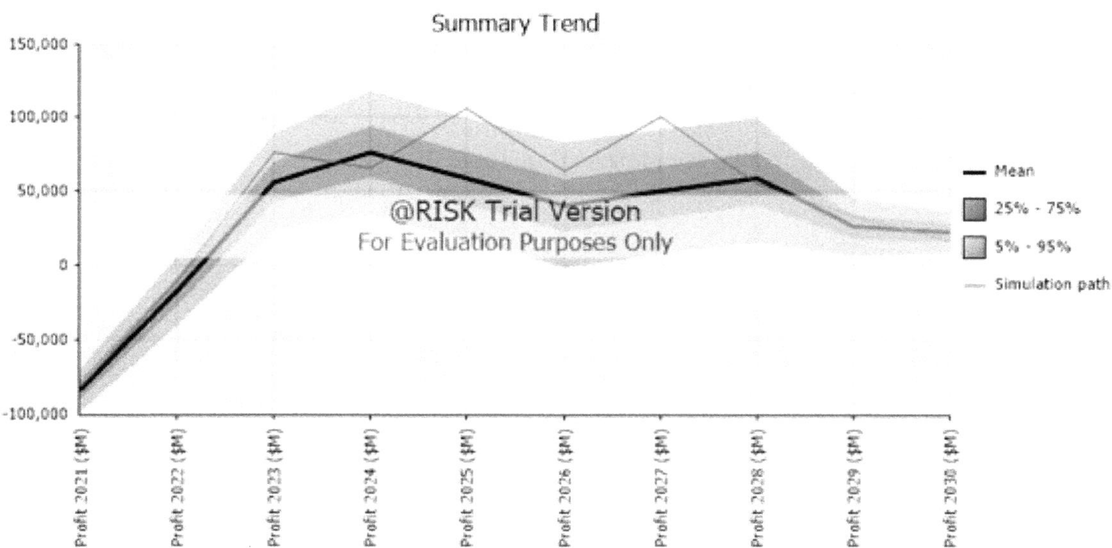

Note: The *Mean* results, which involve a *probability distribution* calculation, are equal to the calculated results, which also use the Normal Distribution to calculate the financial variables from which the Profit per Year is calculated (Ref. Formula (6))

Simulation Results Evaluation, Sensitivity, and What-If Analysis

The results are presented below.

Total Profit Evaluation, Sensitivity, and What-If Analysis

Evaluation

The Total Profit distribution is shown in Figure 3.

Figure 3. Total profit distribution

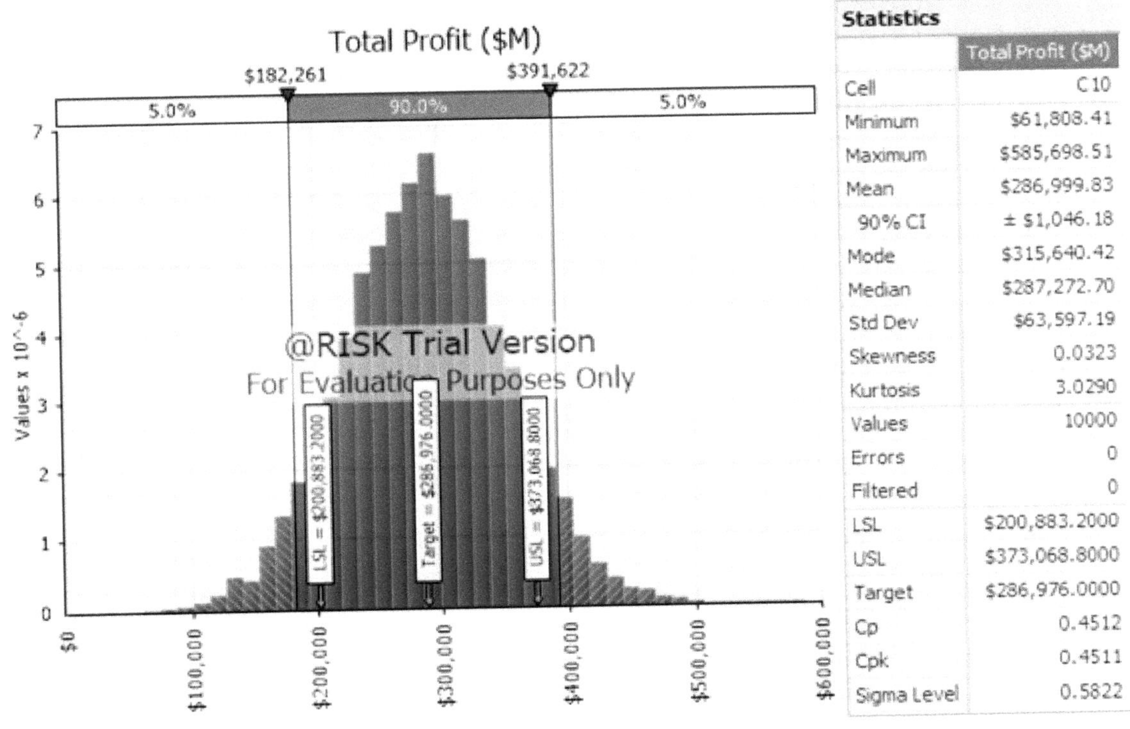

Statistics	Total Profit ($M)
Cell	C10
Minimum	$61,808.41
Maximum	$585,698.51
Mean	$286,999.83
90% CI	± $1,046.18
Mode	$315,640.42
Median	$287,272.70
Std Dev	$63,597.19
Skewness	0.0323
Kurtosis	3.0290
Values	10000
Errors	0
Filtered	0
LSL	$200,883.2000
USL	$373,068.8000
Target	$286,976.0000
Cp	0.4512
Cpk	0.4511
Sigma Level	0.5822

The Total Profit *Mean* (Figure 3) is $286,999,830 with a *Standard Deviation* of $63,597,190, i.e., 22.159%, which is a low risk. The Six Sigma target parameters are *TV* = $286,976,000; *LSL* = $200,883,200; and *USL* = $373,068,800. The Six Sigma process capability metrics are *Cp* = 0.4512; *Cpk* = 0.4511; and σ-*L* = 0.5822. There is a 5% probability that Total Profit will be below $182,261,000; a 90% probability that it will be in the range of $182,261,000 – $391,622,000; and a 5% probability that it will be above $391,622,000.

Sensitivity Analysis

Sensitivity analysis provides for identifying and quantifying the main contributors to variability and risk based on the probability distribution.

The Inputs Ranked by Effect on Output Mean are given in Figure 4.

Figure 4. Total profit inputs ranked by effect on output mean

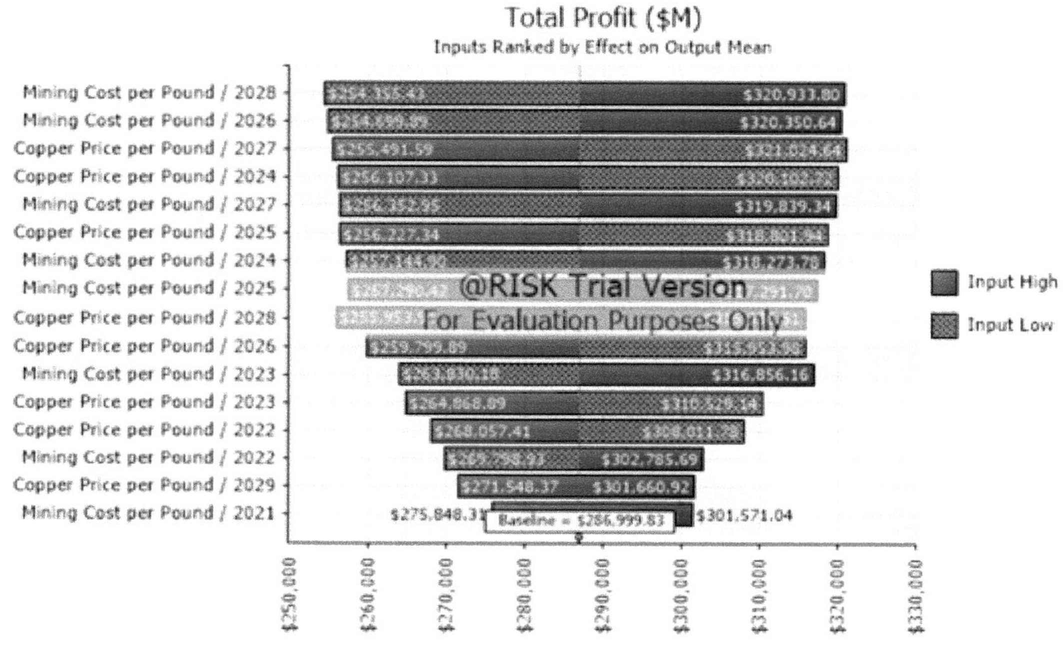

The graph illustrates that the effect of the top variable, Mining Cost per Pound Year 28, on the Total Profit is a change in the range of $254,355,430 to $320,933,800, which are respectively left and right from the Baseline of $286,999,800, which is marked on the graph. Other variables are less influential as their associated effects have smaller ranges.

The Regression Coefficients graph is shown in Figure 5.

Figure 5. Total profit regression coefficients

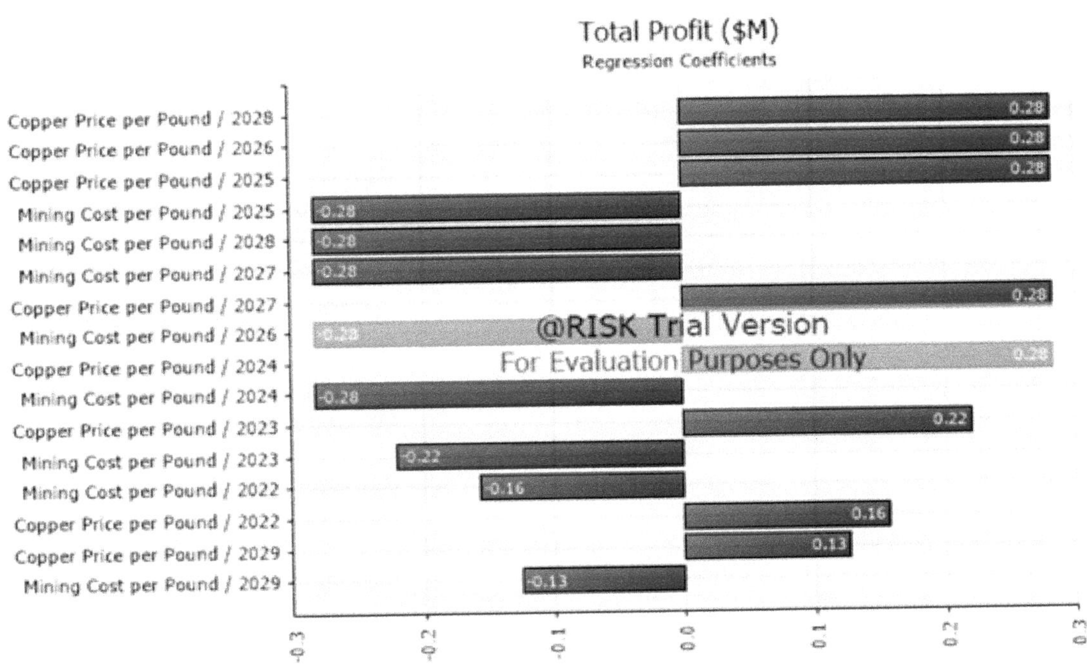

This graph illustrates that if the top five variables with equal positive coefficients of 0.28, from Copper Price per Pound Year 2028 to Copper Price per Pound Year 2024, increase by one Standard Deviation, the Total Profit will increase by 0.28 Standard Deviations. Also, if the top five variables with equal negative coefficients of -0.28, from Mining Cost per Pound Year 2025 to Mining Cost per Pound Year 2024, increase by one Standard Deviation, the Total Profit will decrease by 0.28 Standard Deviations. The other variables are less influential with regression coefficients in the range of 0.22 to -0.13 from top to bottom.

The Correlation Coefficients are presented in Figure 6.

Figure 6. Total profit correlation coefficients

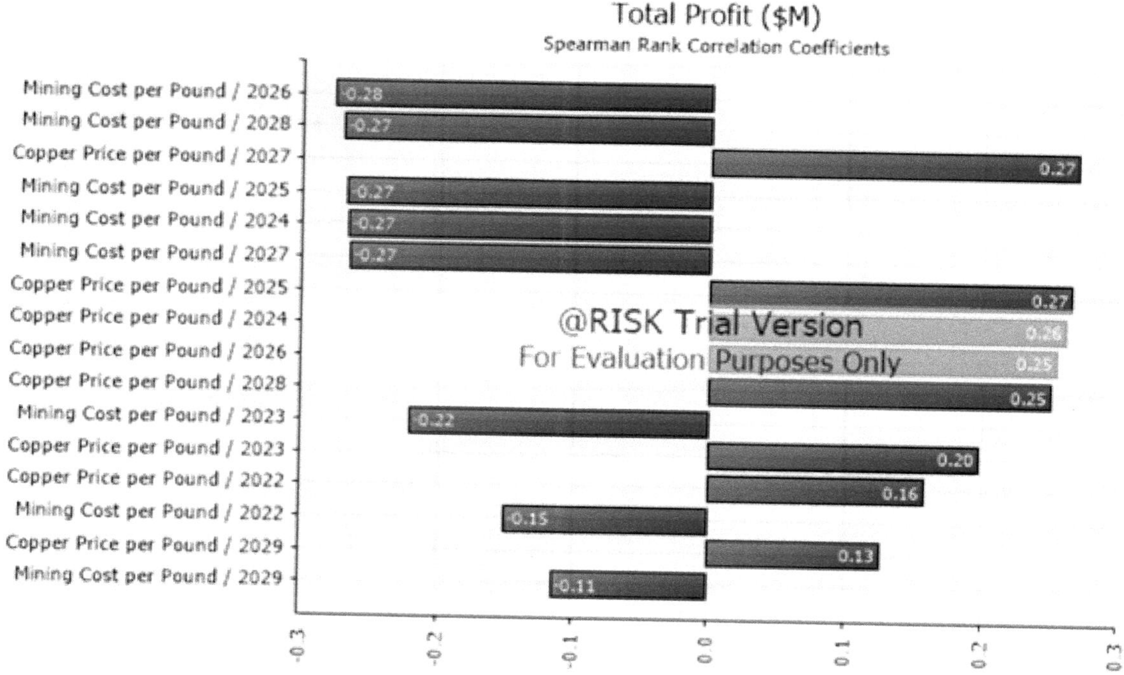

The graph shows that if the top variable, Mining Cost per Pound Year 2026, with a correlation coefficient of -0.28, increases by one unit, the Total Profit will decrease by 0.28 units. Other variables are less influential as their correlation coefficients are in the range of -0.27 to -0.11 from top to bottom.

The Contribution to Variance graph presented in Figure 7 illustrates that the top variable, Mining Cost per Pound Year 2026, has a contribution of 8.4% to the variance of Total Profit. Other variables are less influential as their contribution to variance is in the range of 8.2% to 1.6% from top to bottom.

Figure 7. Total profit contribution to variance

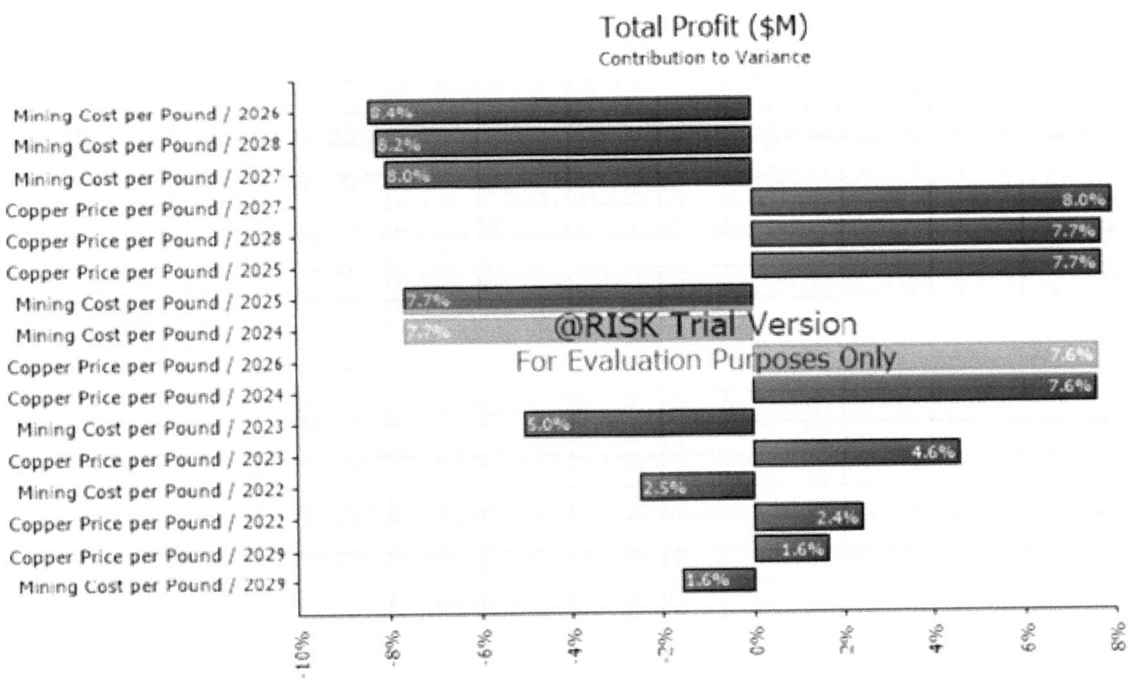

What-If Analysis

What-If analysis provides for ranking the inputs by variability of the output based on the simulation calculation. It also quantifies the minimum and maximum values and changes the percentage of the output for the associated minimum and maximum values of the input, as well as reporting the input base value.

The Total Profit tornado graph is given in Figure 8.

Figure 8. Total net profit tornado graph

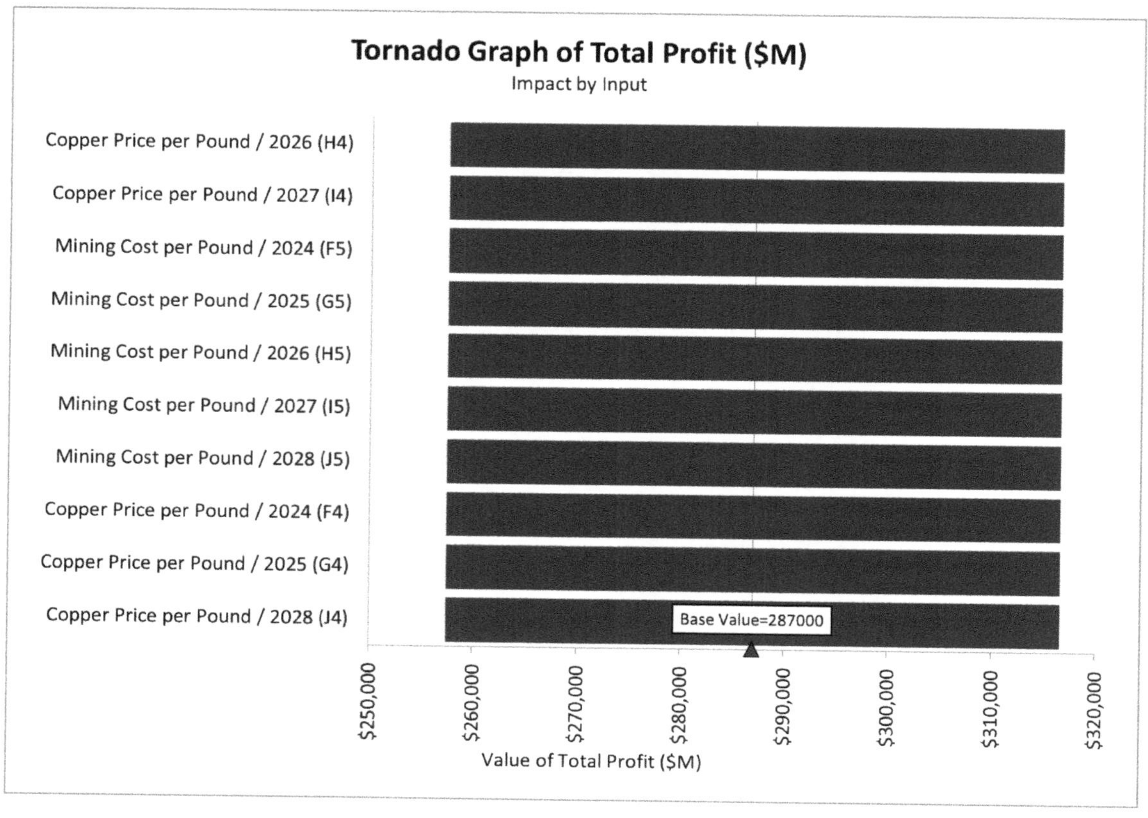

The graph shows the Total Profit values on the x-axis. It illustrates that the Total Profit Base Value is $287,000,000, which is marked on the graph and is calculated from the Profit Vector. The bars on the graph quantify the variability of the Total Profit based on every financial variable showing the Minimum and Maximum, which are respectively left and right from the Base value. The Total Net Profit Minimum and Maximum are respectively calculated from the financial variable Minimum and Maximum values.

Figure 8 also shows that the ten most influential financial variables are: Copper Price per Pound for Years 2026, 2027, 2024, 2025, and 2028; and Mining Cost per Pound for Years 2024, 2025, 2026, 2027, and 2028. It should be noted that all these ten variables specified in Point 1 and Point 2 have the same impact on Total Profit.

The What-If Analysis Summary for Total Profit is presented in Table 3.

Table 3. What-if analysis summary for total profit

What-If Analysis Summary for Output Total Profit ($M)								
Top 10 Inputs Ranked By Change in Actual Value								
		Minimum			Maximum			Input
		Output		Input	Output		Input	Base
Rank	**Input Name**	**Value**	**Change (%)**	**Value**	**Value**	**Change (%)**	**Value**	**Value**
1	Copper Price Pound Year 2026	$257,393	-10.32%	$0.77	$316,607	10.32%	$1.43	$1.10
2	Copper Price Pound Year 2027	$257,393	-10.32%	$0.87	$316,607	10.32%	$1.53	$1.20
3	Mining Cost Pound Year 2024	$257,393	-10.32%	$0.98	$316,607	10.32%	$0.32	$0.65
4	Mining Cost Pound Year 2025	$257,393	-10.32%	$0.98	$316,607	10.32%	$0.32	$0.65
5	Mining Cost Pound Year 2026	$257,393	-10.32%	$0.98	$316,607	10.32%	$0.32	$0.65
6	Mining Cost Pound Year 2027	$257,393	-10.32%	$0.98	$316,607	10.32%	$0.32	$0.65
7	Mining Cost Pound Year 2028	$257,393	-10.32%	$0.98	$316,607	10.32%	$0.32	$0.65
8	Copper Price Pound Year 2024	$257,393	-10.32%	$1.17	$316,607	10.32%	$1.83	$1.50
9	Copper Price Pound Year 2025	$257,393	-10.32%	$0.97	$316,607	10.32%	$1.63	$1.30
10	Copper Price Pound Year 2028	$257,393	-10.32%	$0.97	$316,607	10.32%	$1.63	$1.30

The Summary table quantifies the minimum and maximum values and change percentage of the output for the associated minimum and maximum values of the input, as well as the input base value. As stated above, all the ten variables specified in Column "Input Name" have the same impact on Total Profit.

For example, Copper Price Pound Year 2026: The input base value is $1.10. The input minimum value is $0.77, for which the Total Profit is $257,393,000, i.e., a change of -10.32% from the Total Profit Base Value of $287,000,000. The input maximum value is $1.43, for which the Total Profit is $316,607,000, i.e., a change of 10.32% from the Total Net Profit Base Value of $287,000,000. Again, it should be noted that all these ten variables specified in the Summary table have the same impact on Total Profit.

NPV Evaluation, Sensitivity, and What-If Analysis

Evaluation

The NPV distribution is shown in Figure 9.

Figure 9. NPV distribution

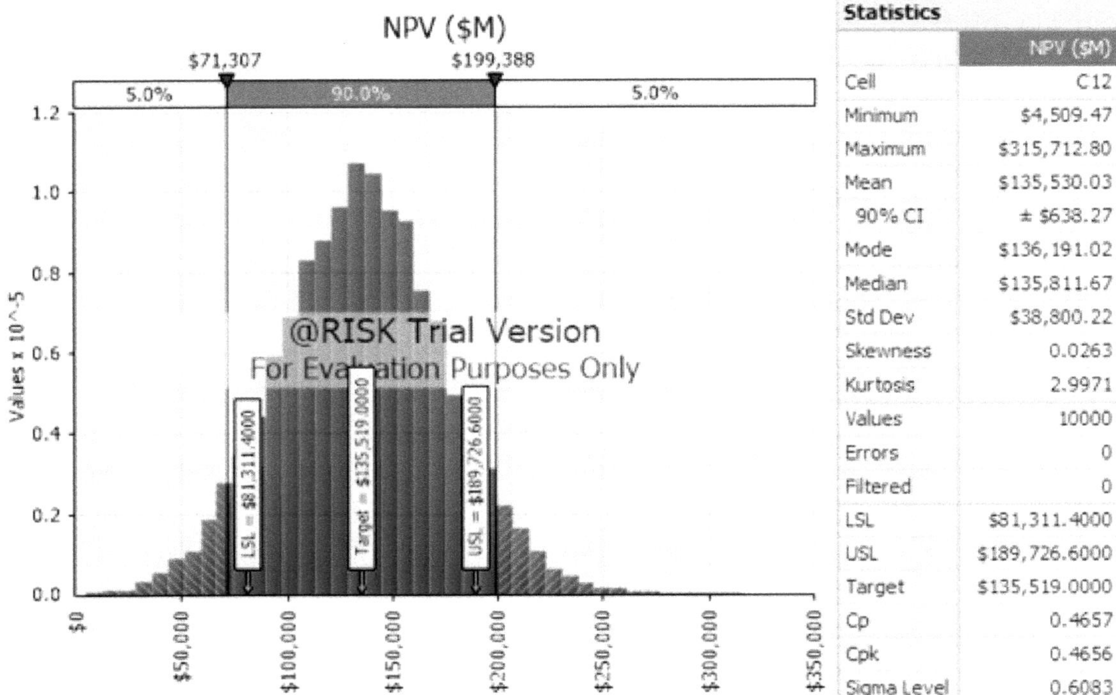

The NPV *Mean* is $135,530,030 with a *Standard Deviation* of $38,800,220, i.e., 28.629%, which is a small risk. The Six Sigma target parameters are *TV* = $135,519,000; *LSL* = $81,311,400; and *USL* = $189,725,600. The Six Sigma process capability metrics are *Cp* = 0.4657; *Cpk* = 0.4656; and σ-*L* = 0.6083. There is a 5% probability that NPV will be below $71,307,000; a 90% probability that it will be in the range of $71,307,000 – $199,388,000; and a 5% probability that it will be above $199,388,000.

Sensitivity Analysis

Sensitivity analysis provides for identifying and quantifying the main contributors to variability and risk based on the probability distribution.

The Inputs Ranked by Effect on Output Mean graph in Figure 10 illustrates that the effect of the top variable, Copper Price per Pound, on the NPV in dollar ($) terms is a change in the range of $114,382,150 to $158,083,880, which are respectively left and right from the Baseline of $135,530,030, which is marked on the graph. Other variables are less influential as their associated effects have smaller ranges.

Figure 10. NPV inputs ranked by effect on output mean

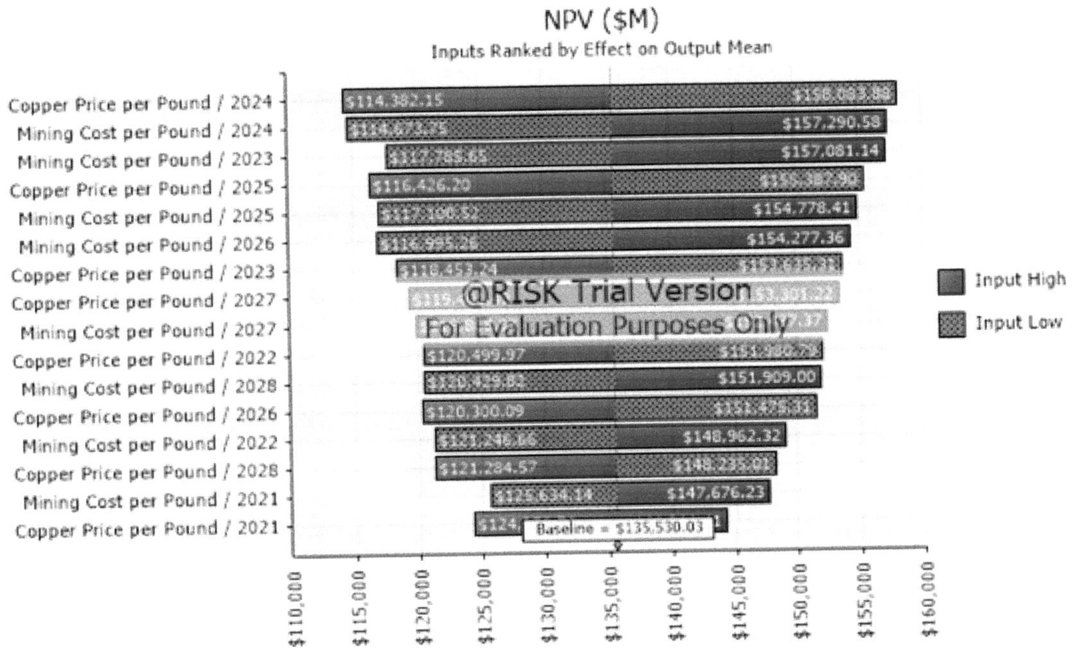

The <u>Regression Coefficients</u> graph is shown in Figure 11.

Figure 11. NPV regression coefficients

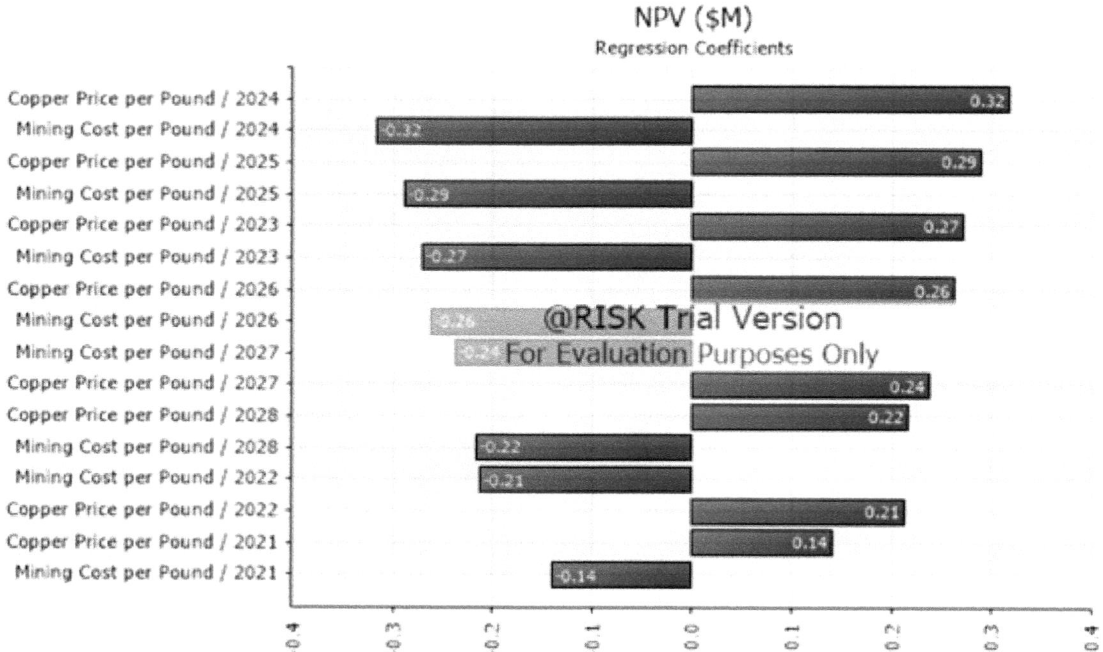

It illustrates (Figure 11) that if the top variable, Copper Price per Pound Year 2024 (with a regression coefficient of 0.32), increases by one Standard Deviation, the NPV will increase by 0.32 Standard Deviations. Also, if Mining Cost per Pound (with a regression coefficient of -0.32) increases by one Standard Deviation, the NPV will decrease by 0.32 Standard Deviations (i.e., because of the negative coefficient). Other variables are less influential as their regression coefficients are in the range from 0.29 to -0.14 from top to bottom.

The Correlation Coefficients are presented in Figure 12.

The graph shows that if the top variable, Mining Cost per Pound Year 2024 (i.e., with a correlation coefficient of -0.30), increases by one unit, the NPV will decrease by 0.30 units. Other variables are less influential as their correlation coefficients are in the range from 0.29 to 0.13 from top to bottom.

Figure 12. NPV correlation coefficients

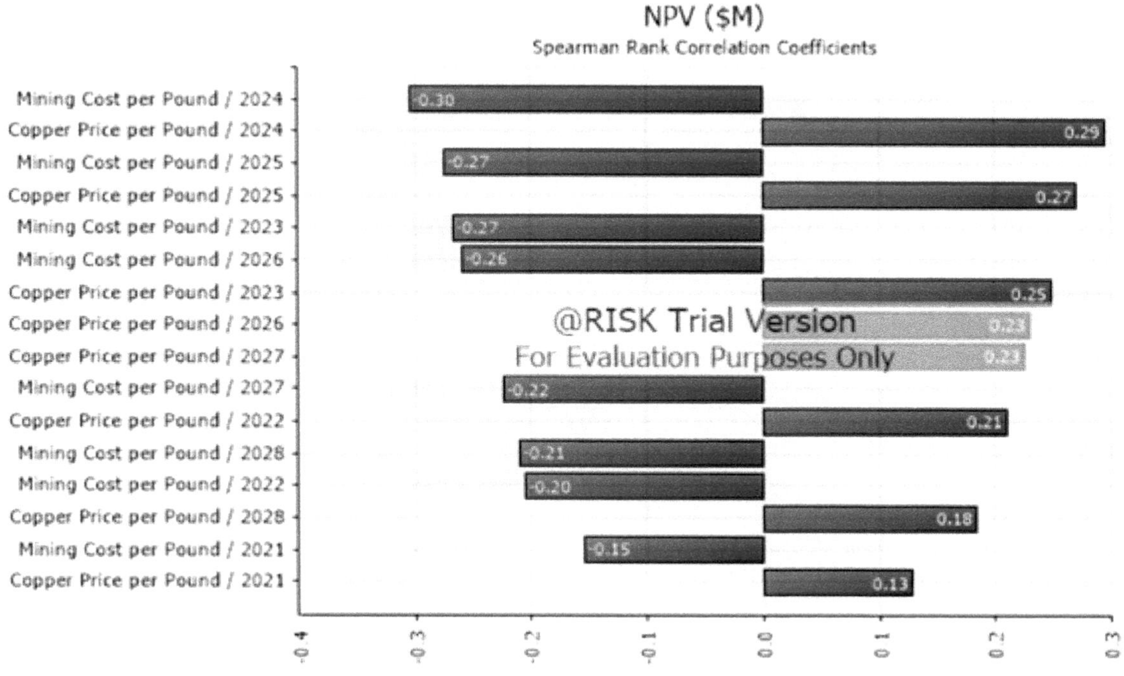

<u>Contribution to Variance</u> is presented in Figure 13.

This graph illustrates that the top variable, Mining Cost per Pound Year 2024, has a 9.8% contribution to the variance of NPV. Other variables are less influential as their contribution to variance is in the range of 9.5% – 2.0% from top to bottom.

Figure 13. NPV contribution to variance

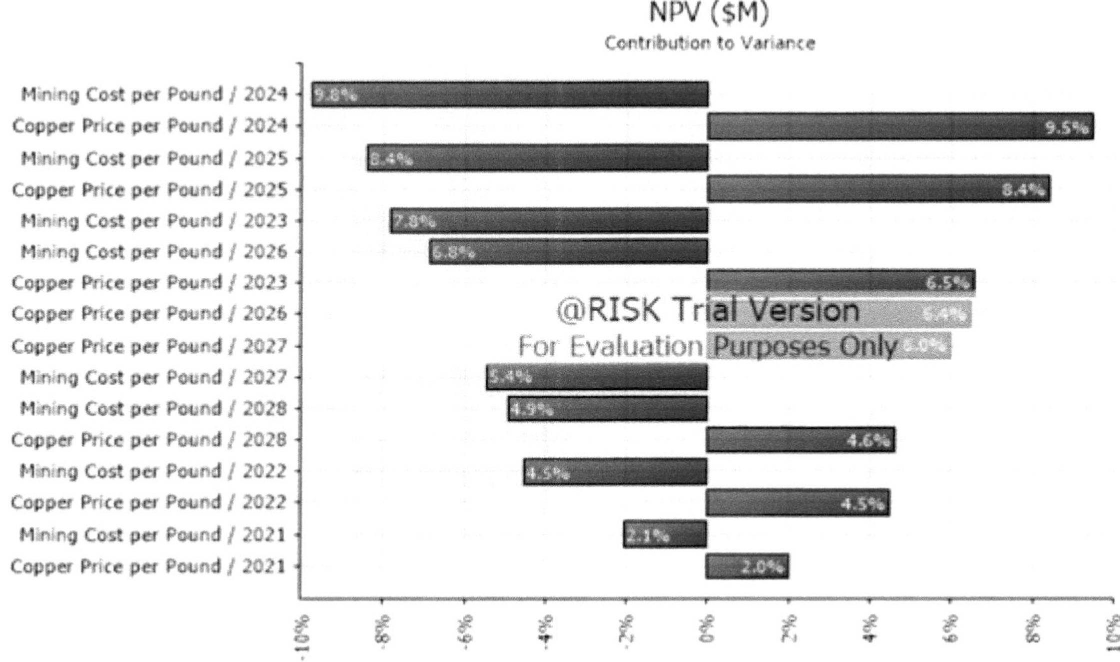

What-If Analysis

The NPV tornado graph is given in Figure 14.

The graph shows the NPV values on the x-axis. It illustrates that the NPV Base Value is $135,530,620, which is marked on the graph and is calculated from the Profit Vector. The bars on the graph quantify the variability of the NPV from every financial variable, showing the Minimum and Maximum, which are respectively left and right from the Base value. The NPV Minimum and Maximum are respectively calculated from the related Profit Vector Minimum and Maximum values.

Figure 14 also shows that the most influential variables are the five pairs of following financial variables, having the same impact per pair on NPV: 1) Copper Price and Mining Cost per Pound Year 2024; 2) Copper Price and Mining Cost per Pound Year 2025; 3) Copper Price & Mining Cost per Pound Year 2023; 4) Copper Price & Mining Cost per Pound Year 2026; and 5) Copper Price & Mining Cost per Pound Year 2027.

Figure 14. NPV tornado graph

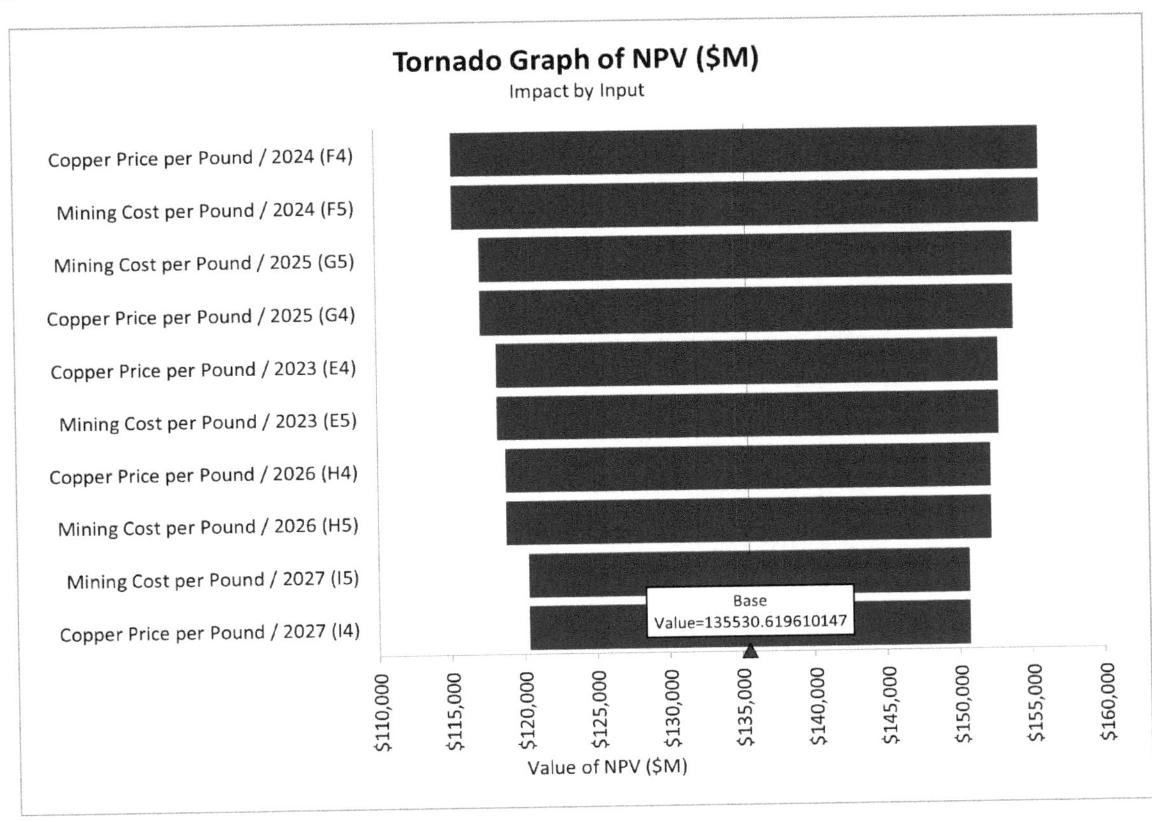

As in the Tornado graph in Figure 14 above, the NPV summary displays that the most influential are the five pairs of the following top-rank financial variables, having the same impact per pair on NPV: 1) Copper Price & Mining Cost per Pound Year 2024; 2) Copper Price & Mining Cost per Pound Year 2025; 3) Copper Price & Mining Cost per Pound Year 2023; 4) Copper Price & Mining Cost per Pound Year 2026; and 5) Copper Price & Mining Cost per Pound Year 2027. For example, Copper Price & Mining Cost per Pound Year 2024: The input base values, as well as the input minimum and maximum values are different as given in the table. However, the NPV minimum and maximum values and the related change (%) are the same for the pair, i.e., $115,308,000 & -14.92%, and $155,753,000 & 14.92% respectively. The same applies to all the other less influential pairs of financial variables.

The What-If Analysis Summary for NPV is presented in Table 4. The Summary table quantifies the minimum and maximum values and change percentage of the output for the associated minimum and maximum values of the input, as well as the input base value.

Table 4. What-if analysis summary for NPV

What-If Analysis Summary for Output NPV ($M)								
Top 10 Inputs Ranked By Change in Actual Value								
		Minimum			Maximum			Input
		Output		Input	Output		Input	Base
Rank	**Input Name**	**Value**	**Change (%)**	**Value**	**Value**	**Change (%)**	**Value**	**Value**
1	Copper Price Pound Year 2024	$115,308	-14.92%	$1.17	$155,753	14.92%	$1.83	$1.50
2	Mining Cost Pound Year 2024	$115,308	-14.92%	$0.98	$155,753	14.92%	$0.32	$0.65
3	Mining Cost Pound Year 2025	$117,147	-13.56%	$0.98	$153,914	13.56%	$0.32	$0.65
4	Copper Price Pound Year 2025	$117,147	-13.56%	$0.97	$153,914	13.56%	$1.63	$1.30
5	Copper Price Pound Year 2023	$118,229	-12.77%	$1.02	$152,832	12.77%	$1.68	$1.35
6	Mining Cost Pound 2023	$118,229	-12.77%	$0.88	$152,832	12.77%	$0.22	$0.55
7	Copper Price Pound Year 2026	$118,818	-12.33%	$0.77	$152,243	12.33%	$1.43	$1.10
8	Mining Cost Pound Year 2026	$118,818	-12.33%	$0.98	$152,243	12.33%	$0.32	$0.65
9	Mining Cost Pound Year 2027	$120,337	-11.21%	$0.98	$150,724	11.21%	$0.32	$0.65
10	Copper Price Pound Year 2027	$120,337	-11.21%	$0.87	$150,724	11.21%	$1.53	$1.20

CONCLUSION

This chapter presented a Risk Analysis of the DCF projection in mining. A copper mine was making a financial projection for ten years to decide upon and undertake their initiative for mining. The projection calculated the Profit per Year, Total Profit, and NPV. The stochastic analysis was performed for ten years starting with Year 2021 to Year 2030.

To introduce the variability of the inputs, probability distributions with empirical parameters were applied, which were projections from historical data. The Discount Rate input was an average estimate from the historical data. The financial variables required to derive DCF were calculated each year. The financial variables were Year, Copper Price per Pound, Mining Cost per Pound, Pounds Mined and Sold, Investment Cost, and Profit.

Finally, the outputs of the stochastic analysis were Total Profit and NPV. They were calculated from the Profit per Year.

A simulation model was designed and run to calculate the variables for the analysis. What-If and Sensitivity Analysis were applied, which provided a comprehensive view of the probability of the outputs and quantified the sensitivity of the outputs based on the variabilities of the associated inputs and financial variables. This risk analysis was purposed to help management decide whether to invest in mining for the next ten years.

To recap, the Total Profit *Mean* was $286,999,830 with a *Standard Deviation* of $63,597,190, i.e., 22.159%, which was a low risk. Also, the NPV *Mean* was $135,530,030 with a *Standard Deviation* of $38,800,220, i.e., 28.629%, also a small risk.

Standard Deviation is the major risk factor. Considering that the major risks for both Total Profit and NPV are low, the technical conclusion is that the company should invest in its mining project for the next ten years. However, the company's management needs to decide whether to invest in the project based on their risk appetite. This risk analysis will help management to decide whether to invest in the project.

REFERENCES

Fight, A. (2005). Cash Flow Forecasting. Butterworth-Heinemann – Elsevier.

Miller, F. P., Vandome, A. F., & McBrewster, J. (2011). Net Present Value. VDM Publishing.

Peterson, P. P., & Fabozzi, F. J. (2002). Capital Budgeting. Wiley.

Sekhar, C. (2016). Capital Budgeting Decisions: PBP, DPBP, ARR, NPV, PI, IRR & MIRR (Theory & interpretation Book 1). Academic Press.

Sekhar, C. (2018). *Capital Budgeting Decision Methods*. Independently Published.

Shapiro, A. C. (2004). Capital Budgeting and Investment Analysis. Pearson.

Tham, J., & Velez-Pareja, I. (2004). Principles of Cash Flow Valuation. Academic Press – Elsevier.

Chapter 9
Comprehensive Investment Risk Assessment

ABSTRACT

The Six Sigma DMAIC is applied to improve risk management in investment portfolios. The objective is to select the optimal portfolio achieving investment objectives with acceptable risk. Optimization constructs an efficient frontier of optimal portfolios with an expected return in a predefined range with a determined increment. Simulation stochastically calculates and measures expected return, variance, standard deviation, and the major risk factors. Six Sigma capability metrics of expected return, value at risk, sharpe ratio, and beta are calculated versus desired specified limits. The analysis allows for the selection of the best efficient frontier portfolio with a maximum Sharpe ratio. Simulation sensitivity analysis identifies the riskiest asset. Portfolio revision considers options to improve the portfolio and replaces the asset with an option to reduce risk. Portfolio execution implements the revised portfolio. Ongoing portfolio management evaluates portfolio performance regularly and, if required, revises the portfolio considering market changes and the investor position.

INTRODUCTION

Market risk is the risk of losses due to adverse market movements depressing the values of the positions held by market players. The market parameters fluctuating randomly are called "risk factors": they include all interest rates, equity indexes, or foreign exchange rates.

The market risk depends on the period required to sell the assets as the magnitude of market movements tends to be wider over longer periods. The liquidation period is lower for instruments easily traded in active markets, and longer for exotic instruments that are traded on a bilateral basis (over the counter). Market risk is price risk for traded instruments. Instruments that are not traded on organized markets are marked-to-market because their gains or losses are accounted for as variations of value whether or not materialized by a sale.

DOI: 10.4018/979-8-3693-3787-5.ch009

Literature

Bernstein and Damodaran (1998), in their book "Investment Management", presented and elaborated on the investment process. They emphasised the importance of the investment process; in particular that the process is generic regardless of what the investment philosophy is, which investment strategy is applied, or what assets are involved. Also, Maginn et al. (2007) presented and defined Portfolio Management as an ongoing process. According to Bernstein and Damodaran (1998), the investment process is multi-dimensional always considering that return on investment and associated risk are very closely coupled. Therefore, the investment process necessitates consideration of return on investment and associated risk measurement, evaluation, and attribution.

Utility functions are used to determine the value of the return on investment considering the investment horizon (Kritzman 1998). Also, taxes have a significant impact on returns (Jeffrey 1998a). The investment includes choices of investing in domestic versus foreign assets considering all the prohibitive and supporting factors (Brinson 1998). There are different aspects of asset allocation. For example, passive mix, where the investor's characteristics determine the right mix for the portfolio; or market timing, where depending on the market conditions the portfolio manager deviates from the passive mix to gain a better return (Arnott 1998a). Also, from an asset selection perspective, different strategies and valuation models are used considering the empirical evidence of the efficiency of each (Damodaran 1998b; Arnott 1998b).

Speed is another dimension of investment important to consider; for example, fast trade, i.e., short-term investment incurs much higher trading costs than long-term investment (Damodaran 1998c; Arnott 1998c). Also, derivatives are an important tool used for hedging the investment risk thus providing for greater returns over time (Clark 1998b).

The risk assessment requires defining the risk and understanding how to measure it. Different risk models are used for risk assessment, e.g., the Capital Asset Pricing Model (CAPM), Arbitrage Pricing Model (APM), and other multifactor risk models (Damodaran 1998a). Alternative measures of risk can also be used for risk assessment, e.g., Standard Deviation, Variance, Value at Risk (VAR), Conditional Value at Risk (CVAR), etc. (Clark 1998a).

The investment performance evaluation relies on absolute risk measures, e.g., Standard Deviation and Variance, and risk measures relative to a market index (i.e., a benchmark), for example, Beta. Also, risk-adjusted performance measures can be used such as the Sharpe Ratio and Treynor Ratio (Jacob 1998).

In his work, Plantinga (2007) discussed methodologies for measuring and evaluating performance to control the investment process. He elaborated methods for i) Measuring returns of investment portfolios; ii) Evaluating performance considering Sharpe Ratio, Jensen's Alpha, Treynor Ratio, and Information Ratio, as well as the downside risk measures, i.e., Sortino Ratio and Fouse Index; iii) Performance attribution considering portfolio composition and time series of returns; and iv) Liability driven performance attribution where the investment objectives are related to liabilities.

Lawton and Jankowski (2009) published a book, including a collection of works of some of today's most prominent industry professionals and academics focussing on investment performance evaluation.

Jacob (1998) presented an approach to evaluating the performance of portfolio managers considering i) Portfolio return; ii) The absolute risk measures Standard Deviation and Variance; iii) The risk measure relative to a market index Beta; & iv) Risk-adjusted performance measures such as Sharpe Ratio and Treynor Ratio.

Meier (2009) elaborated on how institutional investors evaluate portfolio managers. In addition to the return on investment, Standard Deviation and risk measures versus the market were utilised including Alpha, Beta Excess Return, Information Ratio, Sharpe Ratio, and Tracking Error.

Busse, Goyal, and Wahal (2010) used to aggregate and average estimates of alphas for performance measurement of institutional investment management considering the return on investment.

Bansal and Taneja (In Press) considered Standard Deviation, Sharpe Ratio, Bata, Alpha, R-Square, and Treynor Ratio in their comparative study of performance evaluation regarding the return on investment.

Advanced Financial Risk models involve stochastic optimisation of investment portfolios. The problem of asset allocation for portfolio optimisation was solved by Markowitz (1952; 1987) in the 1950s. Markowitz applied his Mean-Variance method to determine the minimum mean-variance portfolio that yields the expected return with minimal risk. Nowadays, stochastic optimisation is used to resolve the optimal portfolio. Stochastic optimisation models in Finance are elaborated in a book edited by Ziemba and Vickson (2006). Stochastic models necessarily use Monte Carlo Simulation. A comprehensive elaboration on general applications of Monte Carlo Simulation in Finance was published by Glasserman (2004).

Statement

As inspired by Bernstein, "We can approach the interaction between the portfolio and the markets, to frame strategies that will minimise risk and maximise the returns we expect. *But the risk will always be there, so we must explore many interesting tools that can help us to control risks we cannot avoid taking*" (Bernstein and Damodaran 1998), a practical Six Sigma approach to Investment Management is proposed. Six Sigma DMAIC is systematically used as a tactical framework to improve the investment process. In addition to conventional techniques, the new concept involves a) stochastic measurement of investment performance by using the Six Sigma process capability metrics considering Mean Return and associated risk factors; and b) continuous monitoring and control of investment performance on the market by iteratively and recursively applying the DMAIC framework. To simplistically demonstrate the method, only the Mean Return, Standard Deviation and Variance, VAR, Sharpe Ratio, and Beta are considered. If appropriate, the method can be easily extended to consider the other risk measures such as Alfa, R-Square, Treynor Ratio, etc., by applying the same techniques that are used for VAR, Sharp Ratio, and Beta.

The DMAIC stage is specified in the text topics for easy understanding.

THE METHOD: PORTFOLIO CONSTRUCTION

The following sections demonstrate step-by-step the investment portfolio construction part of the method.

The problem statement is as follows:

1. Find the Efficient Frontier of eight minimal mean-variance portfolios. The expected return is at least 8.8%, 9%…, 10%, and 10.2% respectively.
2. Stochastically measure and evaluate the portfolios' performance; determine the investment improvements and accordingly revise the eight initial portfolios based on the respective performance attribution. Thus, find the Efficient Frontier of associated revised portfolios.

3. Stochastically calculate the Variance, Standard Deviation, VAR, Sharpe Ratio, and Beta of all 16 portfolios.
4. Determine the best technical portfolio, based on the criteria of Maximum Sharpe Ratio for example.
5. Summarise and report the results of the analysis to the Financial Executives for decision support. The executive summary should include comprehensive tabular and graphical info for all the Efficient Frontier portfolios to allow them to select the portfolio to invest in.
6. Select and execute the desired portfolio on the market.

It is important to note that there are eight initial and eight revised Efficient Frontier portfolios. Because the applied methods are the same for all portfolios, only the initial and the revised portfolio with a return of 9.2% is shown in the Portfolio Construction experiments.

Hypothetical Scenario (DMAIC Define)

To facilitate the method's demonstration, a simplistic approach is taken by using a hypothetical scenario. The assets' returns however are actual financial market data. The assumptions are the following.

1. Understanding the Client stage of the investment process is completed;
2. The client is a conservative investor. They aim to invest in a portfolio less volatile than the market index (i.e., Portfolio's Beta is positive and less than one). Their liabilities are estimated at 5%. The expected return is in the range of 8.8%–10.2%, which is sufficient to cover the liabilities and gain a surplus;
3. The actual market data for the assets considered are available from January 2010 to April 2017 inclusive;
4. Only the data from January 2010 to October 2016 are used for Portfolio Construction;
5. The data from November 2016 to April 2017 are used for verification of the method's results;
6. The present date is 1 November 2016;
7. The objective is to construct and execute an optimal portfolio for a time horizon of one year;
8. Trading costs and trading speed, as well as options pricing and options premiums, are not considered for simplicity.

Determination of Initial Efficient Frontier Portfolios (DMAIC Define)

It is assumed that the Asset Allocation and Asset Selection of the Portfolio Construction process are completed and four specific assets are selected, i.e., Asset 1, Asset 2, Asset 3, and Asset 4.

Financial Market Data

At this stage, the market data for the selected assets are considered.

The Monthly Return (*MR*) of the four selected assets is available for the period from January 2010 to October 2016 (Ref. Appendix, Table 9.7). Considering these data, portfolio construction continues.

Calculating Compounded Monthly Return

The Compounded Monthly Return (*CMR*) is calculated for each month and each asset (i.e., *CMR1, CMR2, CMR3,* and *CMR4*) from the respective given asset's *MR* using the following formula:

$$CMR = \ln(1 + MR) \quad (1)$$

Fitting Distributions

For the Monte Carlo method, the distribution of the *CMR* for each asset is required. Thus, for each asset, the best-fit distribution is determined based on the Chi-Square measure. The standard "fit distribution to data" feature of Palisade™ @RISK® is used. For example, the best-fit distribution for the *CMR* of Asset 4 (i.e., *CMR4*) is the normal distribution, with a Mean Return of 0.6% and a Standard Deviation of 4.7%. Similarly, the best-fit distribution is determined for all selected assets for the portfolio.

Assets Correlation

The *MR* and *CMR* of the assets are correlated. This correlation needs to be determined to allow the Monte Carlo method to generate correlated random values for *CMR*. The assets correlation coefficients matrix is calculated from the assets available data (Ref. Appendix, Table 9.7) by using the standard data correlation feature of Microsoft™ Excel®, that is the Asset Correlation Matrix (*AssetCorrMat*).

Generating Compounded Monthly Return

The *CMR* is randomly generated for each asset from the best-fit distribution considering the correlations. The following distribution functions of Palisade™ @RISK® are used:

CMR1=RiskLogistic(0.0091429,0.044596, RiskCorrmat(AssetCorrMat)) (2)

CMR2=RiskLognorm(1.1261,0.077433,Shift(-1.1203), RiskCorrmat(AssetCorrMat)) (3)

CMR3=RiskWeibull(6.9531,0.46395,Shift(-0.42581), RiskCorrmat(AssetCorrMat)) (4)

CMR4= RiskNormal(0.0060531,0.047225, RiskCorrmat(AssetCorrMat)) (5)

Where "*RiskCorrmat*" is a Palisade™ @RISK® function to apply correlation.

Calculating Compounded Annual Return

The Compounded Annual Return (*CAR*) is calculated for each asset from the respective *CMR*, using the following formula:

CAR = 12*CMR (6)

Calculating Expected Annual Mean Return

The Expected Annual Return Mean (*EAR-Mean*) is calculated from the assets' Weights Vector (*Weights-V*) and the CAR Vector (*CAR-V*) by using the following Excel® formula:

EAR-Mean = SumProduct(Weights-V, CAR-V) (7)

Calculating Variance, Standard Deviation, and VAR

The Variance, Standard Deviation, and *VAR* (*VAR* is calculated with a Confidence Probability of 99.95%) of the portfolio are stochastically calculated from the distribution of the Expected Annual Return Mean (*EAR-Mean*) of the portfolio by using the following Palisade™ @RISK® functions:

Variance = RiskVariance(EAR-Mean) (8)

Standard-Deviation = RiskStdDev(EAR-Mean) (9)

VAR = RiskPercentile(EAR-Mean,0.005) (10)

Calculating Sharpe Ratio and Beta

The *Sharp Ratio* is a portfolio performance measure compared to the *Free Risk Rate* to the risk associated with it. A higher Sharp Ratio indicates a better portfolio performance in response to the risk involved. *Sharpe Ratio* is calculated by using the following formula.

Sharpe Ratio = $(\mu - r) / \sigma$ (11)

Where,
μ = Expected Annual Return Mean (*EAR-Mean*),
σ = Standard-Deviation,
r = *Risk-Free Rate*, which is estimated to be 5.35%.

Beta is a portfolio risk measure relative to the Market Index over a specific time horizon. Lower *Beta* indicates lower portfolio risk, which is suitable for conservative investors. Higher *Beta* relates to higher portfolio risk, which makes the portfolio more unpredictable (volatile) in nature. *Beta* is interpreted as the slope of the regression of the portfolio returns on those of the Market Index over the time horizon. *Beta* is calculated with the following formula.

$$\text{Beta} = \text{Correlation-PM}\ (\sigma\text{-P} / \sigma\text{-M}) \qquad (12)$$

Where,
Correlation-PM = Portfolio–Market Index Correlation Coefficient over the time horizon,
σ-*P* = Standard Deviation of Portfolio over the time horizon,
σ-*M* = Standard Deviation of the Market Index over the time horizon.

Process Performance Measurement and Metrics

To measure the investment process performance, the Six Sigma metrics are calculated from the simulation distribution. For this purpose, the following Six Sigma target parameters are specified for every measured attribute of the process: i) Lower Specified Limit (*LSL*); ii) Target Value (*TV*); and iii) Upper Specified Limit (*USL*).

The simulation model calculates the following Six Sigma process capability metrics: i) *Process Capability* (*Cp*); ii) *Probability of Non-Compliance* (P*NC*); and iii) *Sigma Level* (σ-*L*). Please for details refer to Introduction, Sec. The Six Sigma DMAIC Approach.

Resolution of Initial Efficient Frontier Portfolios

Stochastic optimisation is used to resolve the Efficient Frontier of minimal mean-variance portfolios, which yields sufficient return to cover the liabilities and gain a maximum surplus with minimal risk. Thus, the optimisation model minimises the mean-variance of the portfolios subject to the following specific constraints: i) The expected portfolio return is from 8.8% to 10.2% in 0.2% increments, i.e., eight Efficient Frontier portfolios; ii) All the money, i.e., 100% of the available funds, is invested; and iii) No short selling is allowed so all the fractions of the capital placed in each asset should be non-negative.

The simulation Model is used to predict the *Mean Return*, *Standard Deviation*, *Variance*, *VAR*, *Sharpe Ratio,* and *Beta* for all initial portfolios.

For example, the optimal portfolio which gains a 9.2% expected return has the following investment fractions: 32.42% in Asset 1; 0% in Asset 2; 30.89% in Asset 3; and 36.7% in Asset 4.

The probability distribution of this optimal portfolio is given in Figure 1.

Figure 1. Initial portfolio return distribution

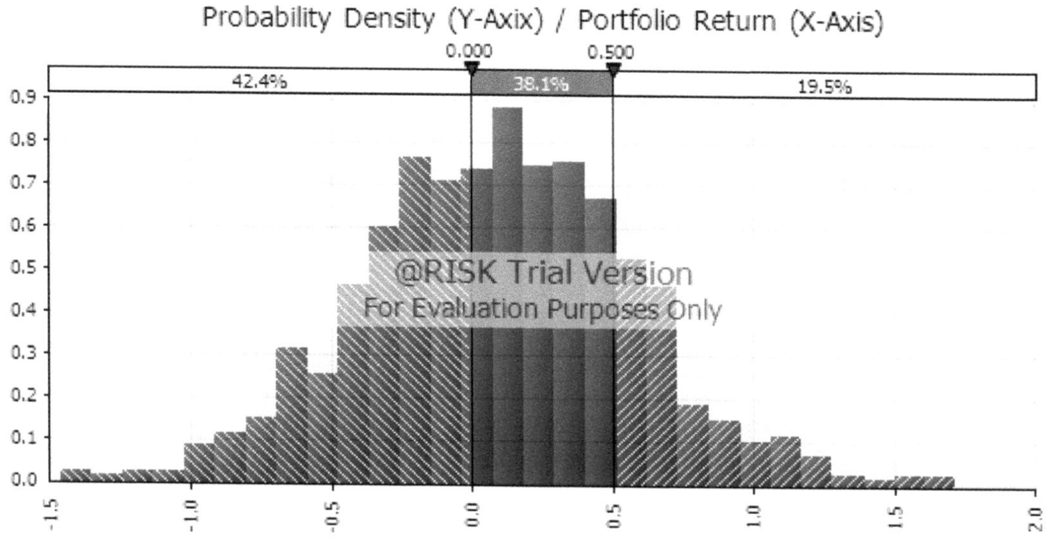

The *Mean Return* is 9.2% with *Variance* of 24.7%; *Standard Deviation*, 49.7%; *VAR*, -28.3%; *Sharpe Ratio*, 0.077; and *Beta*, 0.740. The probability that the portfolio return will be below zero (0%), i.e., negative, is 42.4%. There is a 38.1% probability that the return will be in the range of 0%–50% and a 19.5% probability that the return will be greater than 50%.

The complete results of the initial Efficient Frontier portfolios are as follows. Table 1 shows the *Mean Return* (μ) and the investment fractions of total funds invested in each asset.

Table 1. The initial efficient frontier portfolios' fractions

μ	Asset 1	Asset 2	Asset 3	Asset 4
0.088	0.25045	0.03481	0.26003	0.45470
0.090	0.28592	0.00699	0.28530	0.42179
0.092	0.32416	0	0.30889	0.36695
0.094	0.36329	0	0.33199	0.30472
0.096	0.40242	0	0.35509	0.24250
0.098	0.44155	0	0.37819	0.18027
0.100	0.48067	0	0.40129	0.11804
0.102	0.51980	0	0.42439	0.05581

Table 2 shows the *Mean Return* (μ), *Variance* (V), *Standard Deviation* (σ), *VAR*, *Sharpe Ratio* (*SR*), and *Beta* (β).

Table 2. The initial efficient frontier portfolios' details

μ	V	σ	VAR	SR	β
0.088	0.223	0.472	-0.204	0.073	0.723
0.090	0.232	0.482	-0.228	0.076	0.730
0.092	0.247	0.497	-0.283	0.077	0.740
0.094	0.266	0.515	-0.362	0.079	0.756
0.096	0.295	0.543	-0.454	0.078	0.777
0.098	0.332	0.576	-0.537	0.077	0.798
0.100	0.378	0.615	-0.625	0.076	0.820
0.102	0.429	0.655	-0.732	0.074	0.848

Performance Measurement of Initial Efficient Frontier Portfolios (DMAIC Measure)

The performance measurement of the initial optimal portfolio with a *Mean Return* of 9.2% is presented here as an example. The results of this measurement phase are discussed in more detail in the Performance Evaluation, i.e., the next stage.

Measuring Mean Return

The *Mean Return* of the portfolio is simulated to predict and measure the associated investment process considering the expected return of 9.2%. The predicted values are *Mean Return*, 9.2%; Return Maximum, 171.54%; Return Minimum, -146.95% theoretically; *Variance*, 24.7%; *Standard Deviation*, 49.7%; *VAR*, -28.31%; *Sharpe Ratio*, 0.077; and *Beta*, 0.740.

Figure 2. Portfolio return distribution vs. target range

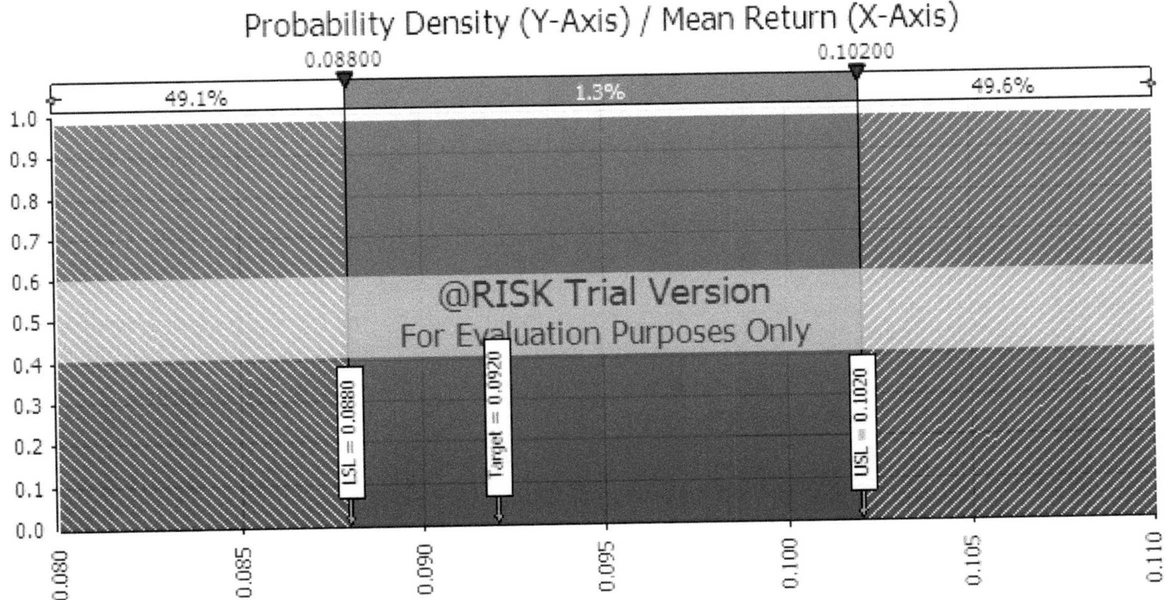

The simulation model also predicts the Six Sigma process capability metrics *Cp*, *PNC,* and *σ-L*. The Six Sigma target range parameters are *LSL*, 8.8%; *TV*, 9.2%; and *USL*, 10.2%. Figure 2 shows that the probability is 49.1% that the return will be less than 8.8%; 1.3%, within the target range of 8.8%–10.2%; and 49.6%, greater than 10.2%. The Six Sigma process capability metrics are *Cp*, 0.00473; *PNC*, 0.987; and *σ-L*, 0.02005.

Measuring VAR

The predicted *VAR* in the previous step is -28.3% with a confidence level of 99.95%. These two single figures are useful, but these figures are not sufficient for appropriate risk analysis particularly because the *Standard Deviation* is 49.7% (i.e., high). What is needed is the distribution of the *VAR*.

Therefore, the *VAR* is simulated using Normal Distribution with a Mean *VAR* of -28.31% and the same *Standard Deviation* as that for the *Main Return* simulation where the *VAR* is calculated (i.e., 49.7%). Normal Distribution is used for simplicity, but other distributions can be used if more appropriate.

Figure 3. VAR distribution

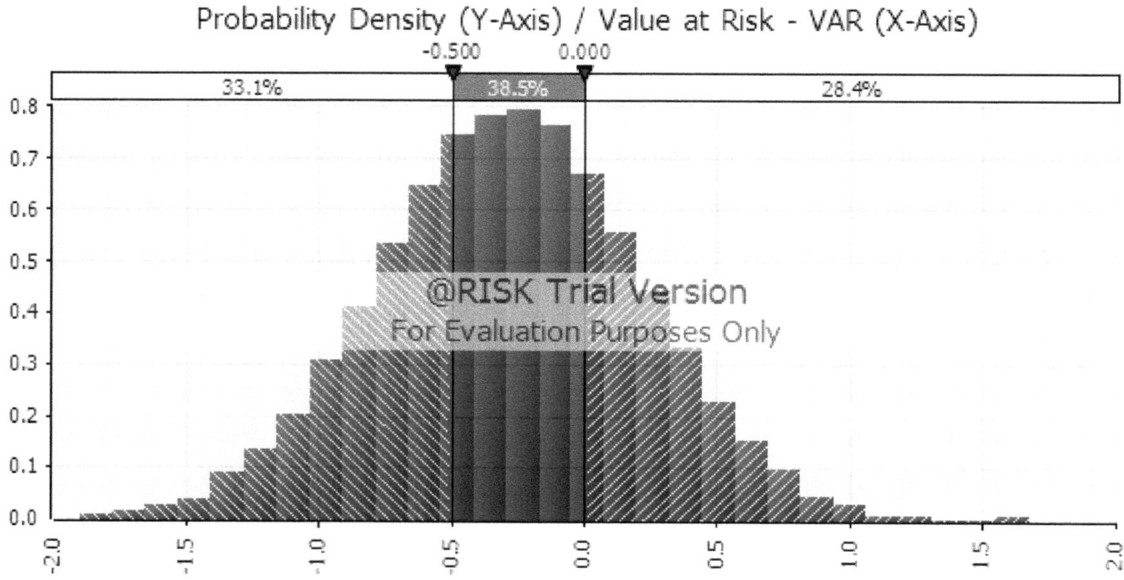

Figure 3 shows the *VAR* Distribution. The Mean *VAR* is -28.3%; the *VAR* Maximum is -155.62% theoretically (i.e., Maths Minimum); *VAR* Minimum, is 136.67% (i.e., Maths Maximum). This graph shows that the probability is 38.5% that VAR will be in the range -of 50.0%–0.0%. There is a 33.1% probability that the VAR will be losing more than -50.0%; and 28.4% that *VAR* is a positive number, i.e., the portfolio will gain a return.

The *VAR* distribution around the Sigma target range is shown in Figure 4. The target parameters are *LSL*, -40%; *TV*, -28.31%; and *USL*, 0.0%. The probability is 30.9% that *VAR* will be within the target range. The predicted process metrics are *Cp*, 0.1339; *PNC*, 0.691; and σ-*L*, 0.3975.

Figure 4. VAR distribution vs. target range

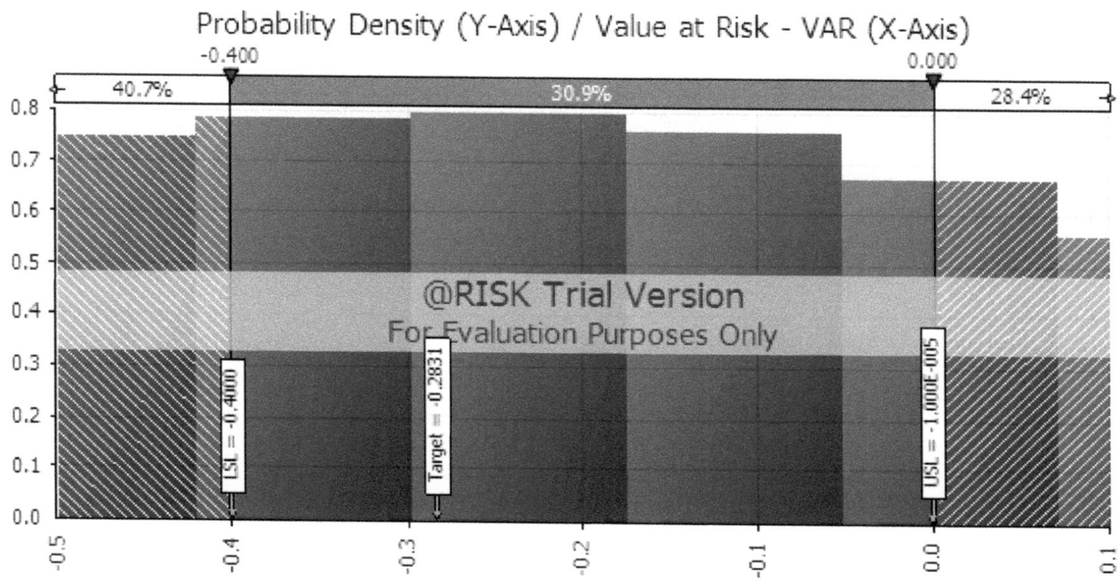

Measuring Sharpe Ratio

Figure 5 shows the *Sharpe Ratio* Distribution.

Figure 5. Sharpe ratio distribution

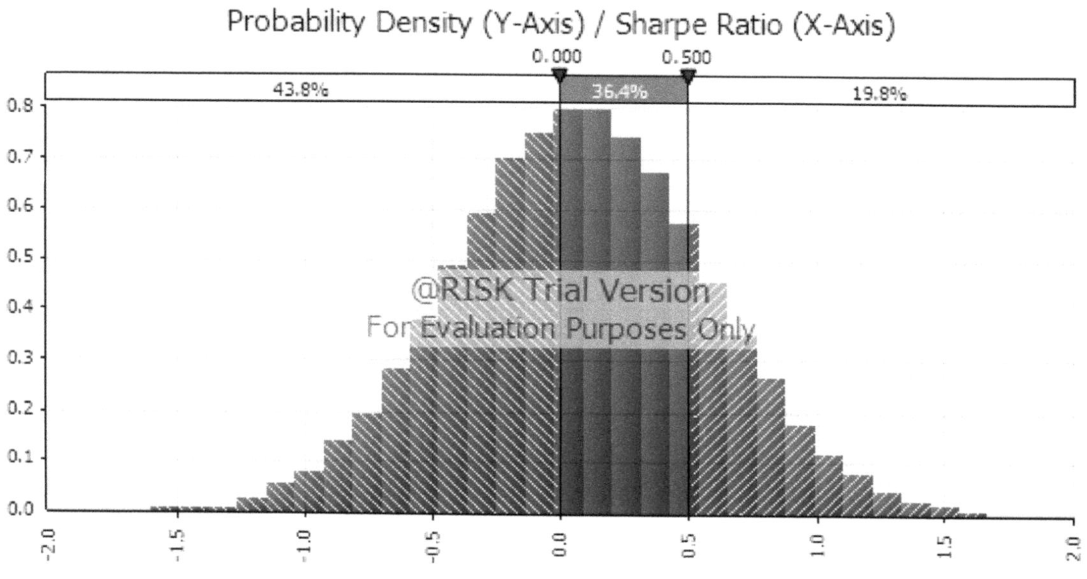

The predicted *Sharpe Ratio* is 0.077 (Figure 5). This again is a single figure, which is insufficient for analysis. So, the *Sharpe Ratio* is simulated using Normal Distribution (e.g., other distribution can be used if more appropriate) with a Mean of 0.077 and the same *Standard Deviation* with which the *Sharpe Ratio* is calculated (i.e., 49.7%). The *Sharpe Ratio* Distribution (Figure 5) shows that the probability of having a negative *Sharpe Ratio* is 43.8%; in the range of 0.0–0.5, 36.4%; and *Sharpe Ratio* greater than 0.5, 19.8%. *Sharpe Ratio* minimum and maximum values are -1.6 and 1.67 respectively.

The Six Sigma target parameters are *LSL*, zero; *TV*, 0.077; and *USL*, 0.3. The *Sharp Ratio* distribution around the target range is shown in Figure 6. The probability is 23.5% that the *Sharp Ratio* will be within the target range. The predicted process metrics are *Cp*, 0.1006; *PNC*, 0.765; and *σ-L*, 0.2989.

Figure 6. Sharp ratio distribution vs. target range

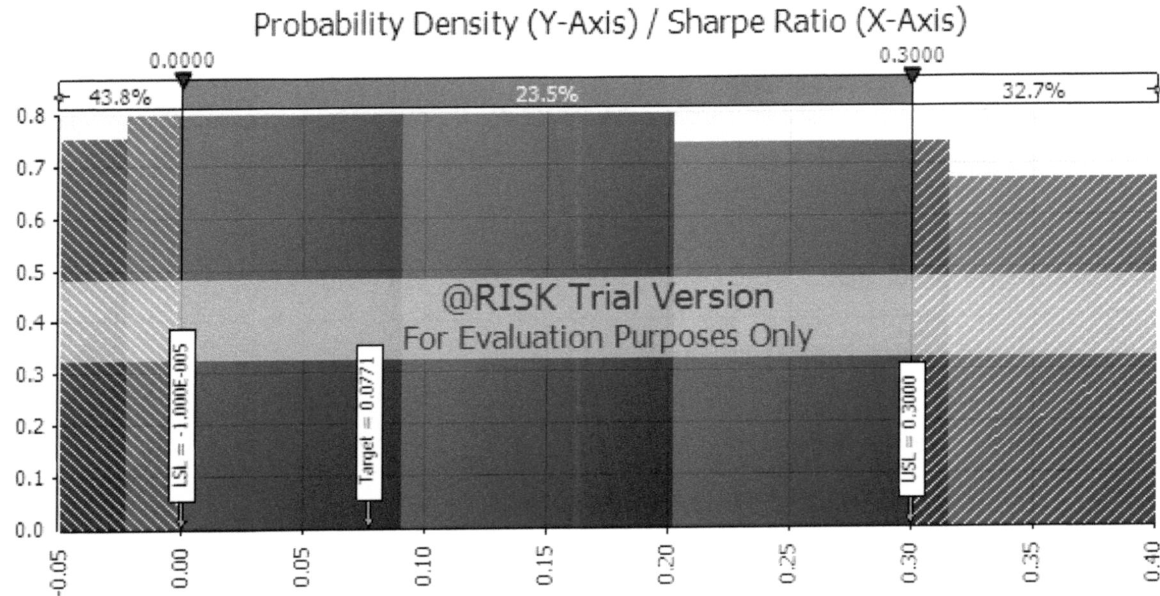

Measuring Beta

The predicted value of *Beta* is 0.74. This is inadequate for analysis. Thus, *Beta* is simulated using a Normal Distribution (Mean = 0.74, Standard Deviation = 49.7%); (e.g., again other distribution can be used if more appropriate).

Figure 7. Beta distribution

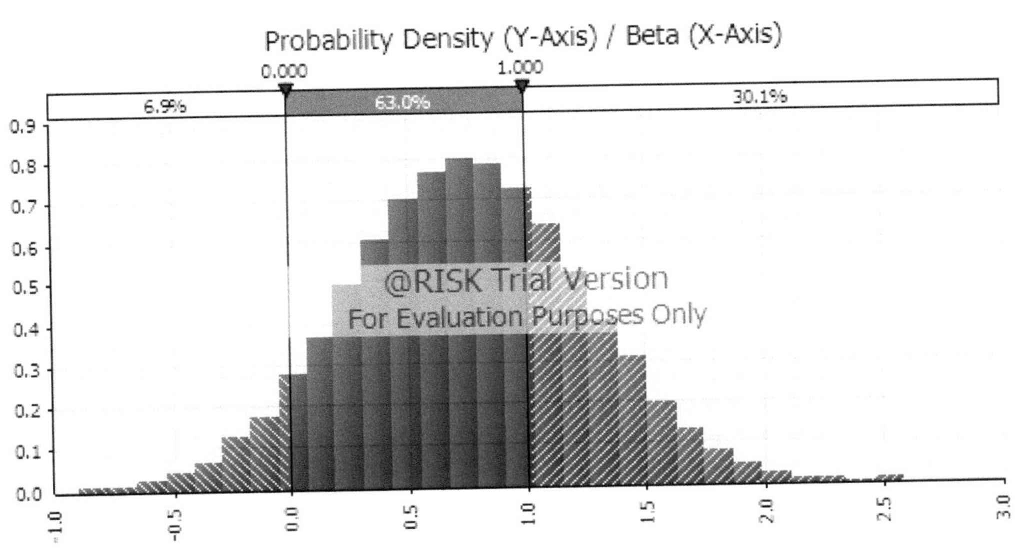

Beta's distribution (Figure 7) shows Mean *Beta*, 0.74; Maximum, 2.58; and Minimum, -0.895. The probability of having a negative *Beta* is 6.9%; *Beta* in the range of 0.0 – 1.0, 63.0%; and *Beta* being greater than 1.0, 30.1%.

Figure 8. Beta distribution vs. target range

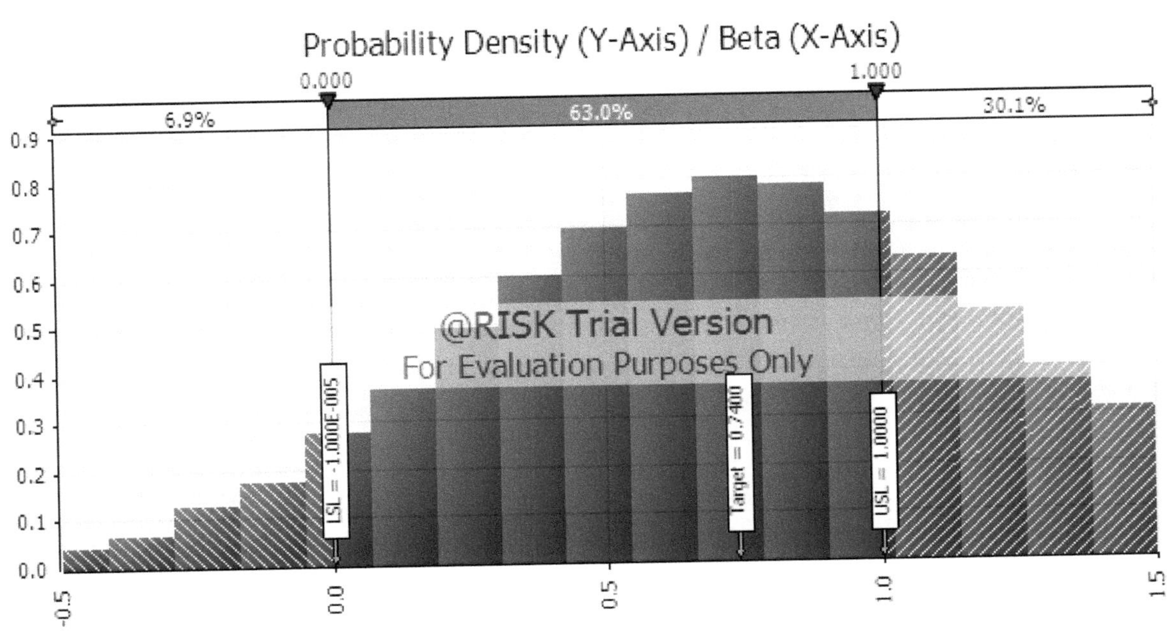

The *Beta*'s distribution versus the target parameters of *LSL*, zero; *TV*, 0.74; and *USL*, 1.0 is shown in Figure 8. The probability is 63.0% that *Beta* will be within the target range. The predicted process metrics are *Cp*, 0.335; *PNC*, 0.37; and σ-*L*, 0.896.

Performance Evaluation of Initial Efficient Frontier Portfolios (DMAIC Analyse)

For example, the performance evaluation of the portfolio which gains 9.2%, considering *Mean Return*, *VAR*, *Sharpe Ratio,* and *Beta* is as follows.

Evaluating Mean Return

The predicted *Mean Return* is 9.2%, with a *Variance*, of 24.7%; and a *Standard Deviation*, of 49.7%. The return maximum value is 171.54%; and the return minimum value is -146.95% theoretically; The Six Sigma investment process metrics are *Cp*, 0.00473; *PNC*, 0.987; and σ-*L*, 0.02005. These figures suggest that the financial risk for the portfolio is significant. For example, *Standard Deviation* and *PNC* are very high, i.e., 49.7% and 0.987 respectively. This indicates high risk and poor performance. Therefore, portfolio revision should be considered.

Evaluating VAR

The predicted Mean *VAR* is -28.3% with a *Standard Deviation* of 49.7%. The *VAR* maximum is -190.01% theoretically (i.e., Maths Minimum); and the minimum, is 171.54% (i.e., Maths Maximum). The Six Sigma investment process metrics are *Cp*, 0.1339; *PNC*, 0.691; and σ-*L*, 0.3975. The probability of losing more than 50% is 33.1%; and the 38.5% probability of losing up to 50%. There is a 28.4% chance that the portfolio will gain a return on investment. *Standard Deviation*, 49.7%; and *PNC*, 0.691; are quite high. Again, this shows the risk is high and the performance is poor. Once more, the portfolio amendment should be considered.

Evaluating Sharpe Ratio

The *Sharpe Ratio* predicted value is 0.077 with a Standard Deviation of 49.7%. The probability that the portfolio will underperform compared with the Free Risk Rate (i.e., *Sharpe Ratio* is negative) is 43.8%. The probability of gaining up to 50% more return than the *Free Risk Rate* is 36.4% and over 50% more return than the *Free Risk Rate* is 19.8%. The Six Sigma investment process metrics are *Cp*, 0.1006; *PNC*, 0.765; and σ-*L*, 0.2989. Considerably high *Standard Deviation* and *PNC* suggest poor performance and high risk. Consequently, portfolio improvement should be considered.

Evaluating Beta

The value predicted for *Beta* is 0.74 with a Standard Deviation of 49.7%. The probability that the portfolio will be less volatile than the Market Index (i.e., positive *Beta* less than one) is 63%. The probability that the portfolio will be more volatile than the Market Index (i.e., *Beta* greater than one) is 30.1%. The probability that *Beta* is negative, i.e., the portfolio will gain return when the index is going down, is 6.9%. The probability that the portfolio will move like the index is 93.1%. The Six Sigma investment process metrics are *Cp*, 0.335; *PNC*, 0.37; and *σ-L*, 0.896. Considerably high values for *Standard Deviation* and *PNC* suggest that the performance will be poor with a high risk. Therefore, consideration of the portfolio revision is needed.

Performance Attribution of Initial Efficient Frontier Portfolios (DMAIC Analyse)

The objective of this stage is to identify the major contributors to portfolios' risk by quantifying the impact of the change in return of every asset, to the portfolio *Mean Return*. Correlation coefficients and regression-mapped values quantitatively define these impacts. Thus, sensitivity analysis is used to stochastically calculate the correlation coefficients and regression-mapped values based on the statistics of the simulation distribution. For example, the sensitivity analysis for the portfolio which gains 9.2% follows.

The correlation sensitivity graph (Figure 9) shows that the portfolio return is most dependent on Asset 4 with a correlation coefficient of 0.67. Asset 1 and Asset 3 are less influential with correlation coefficients of 0.60 and 0.51 respectively.

Figure 9. Correlation sensitivity

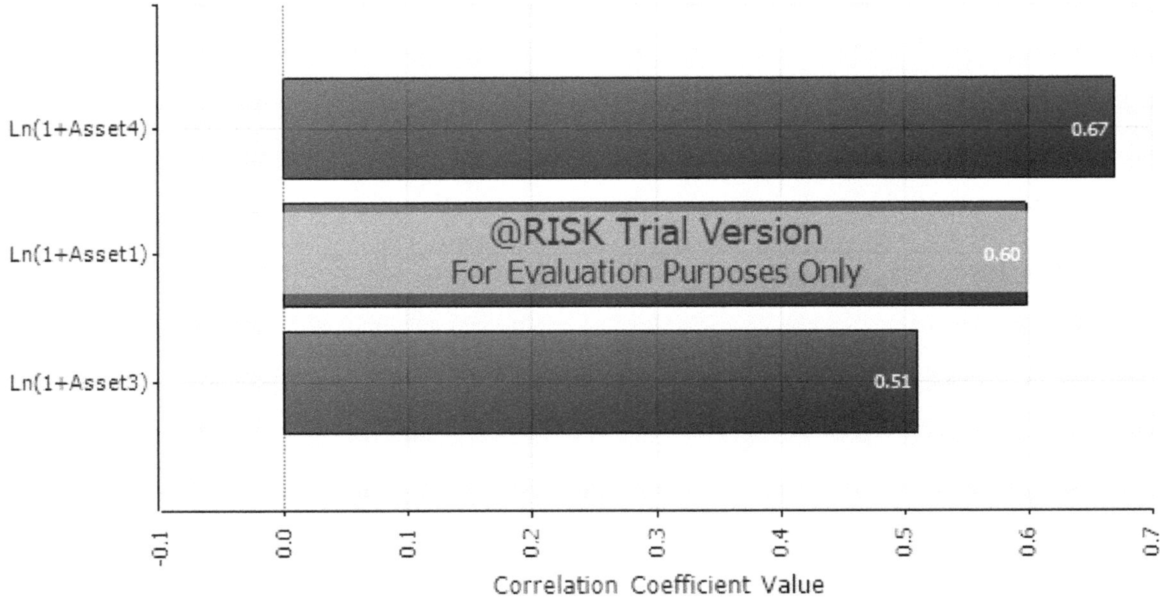

The regression sensitivity graph (Figure 10) illustrates that if Asset 4 return changes by one Standard Deviation, the portfolio return will change by 0.315 Standard Deviations. Again, Asset 1 and Asset 3 are less influential with regression-mapped values of 0.272 and 0.208 respectively.

This analysis suggests that this initial portfolio can be improved if the riskiest asset, Asset 4, is hedged with an option (i.e., Option 4) for example.

Figure 10. Regression mapped values sensitivity

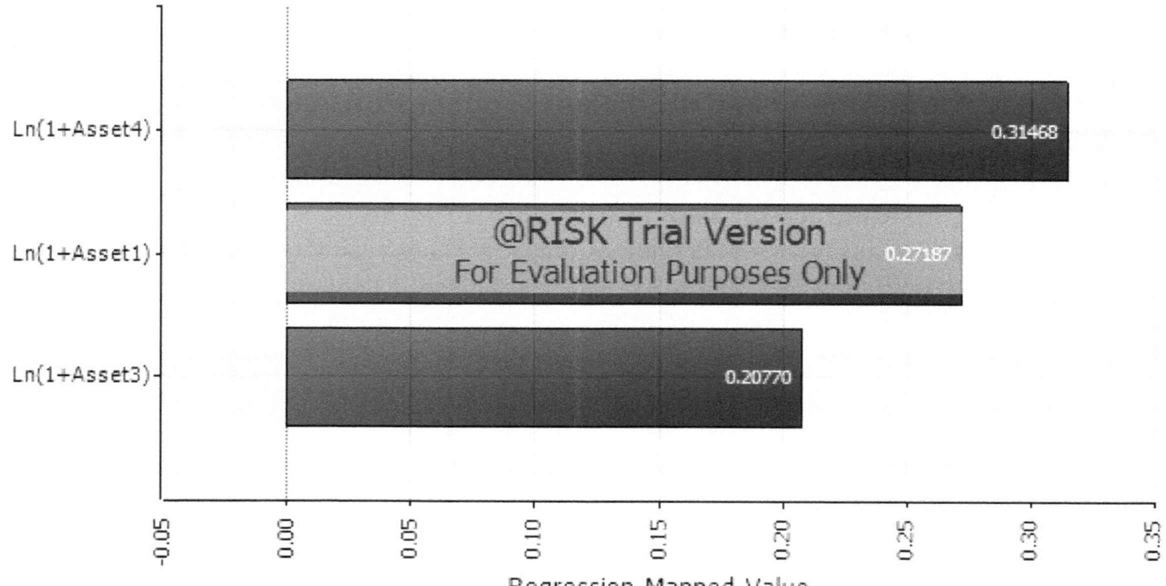

Revision of Initial Efficient Frontier Portfolios (DMAIC Improve)

Again, the method is demonstrated on one portfolio as an example because it is the same for all portfolios. It is assumed that Asset 4 is the riskiest asset for all initial portfolios. It is also assumed that Option 4 is purchased on 100% of Asset 4 for all revised portfolios.

Determination of Initial Efficient Frontier Portfolios' Improvements (DMAIC Define)

The sensitivity analysis in the previous phase identified that the initial portfolio with a return of 9.2% can be improved if Asset 4 is hedged with Option 4, which is an American Put option for example.

It should be noted that the market data for Option 4 are unavailable. Therefore, to simplify the elaboration of the method, the Option 4 data are hypothetically crafted by applying basic assumptions: i) Option pricing is not applied; ii) Option premium is ignored; iii) Option intrinsic value is only considered; iv) Option is purchased on 100% of the asset; v) *MR* of Option 4 (i.e., *MRO4*) is derived from the *MR* of Asset 4 (i.e., *MR4*); vi) The negative returns are truncated (i.e., *MRO4* is zero where *MR4* is negative); and vii) The positive returns are modified to ensure that the average return of Option 4 is equal to the average return of Asset 4; that is for *MR4* greater than zero, $MRO4 = MR4 * F$ where $F = AVERAGE(MR4) / AVERAGE(MR4 > 0)$.

The *CMR* of Option 4 – *CMRO4* is calculated by using Formula 1. The Average *CMRO4* is 0.61% and the yearly return is 7.28%. The best-fit distribution to *CMRO4* is an Exponential Distribution with the Mean slightly shifted to 0.0060635. In the simulation model, the *CMRO4* is generated by using the following Palisade™ @Risk® function.

CMRO4 = RiskExpon(0.0060635,Shift(-7.4e-005)) (13)

Determination of Revised Efficient Frontier Portfolios (DMAIC Define)

The stochastic optimisation model is used to resolve the Efficient Frontier of the revised portfolios. This model will hedge the riskiest asset for every portfolio as defined by the respective sensitivity analysis.

For example, the investment fractions of the revised portfolio with a 9.2% return are 32.42% in Asset 1; 0% in Asset 2; 30.89% in Asset 3; and 36.7% in Option 4. The *Mean Return* is 9.2% with *Variance*, 19.3%; *Standard Deviation*, 43.9%; *VAR*, -12.4%; *Sharpe Ratio*, 0.088; and *Beta*, 0.671.

The probability distribution (Figure 11) shows the probability is 40.5% that the portfolio return will be negative. There is a 43.5% probability that the return will be in the range of 0%–50% and a 16.0% probability that the return will be greater than 50%.

Figure 11. Revised portfolio return distribution

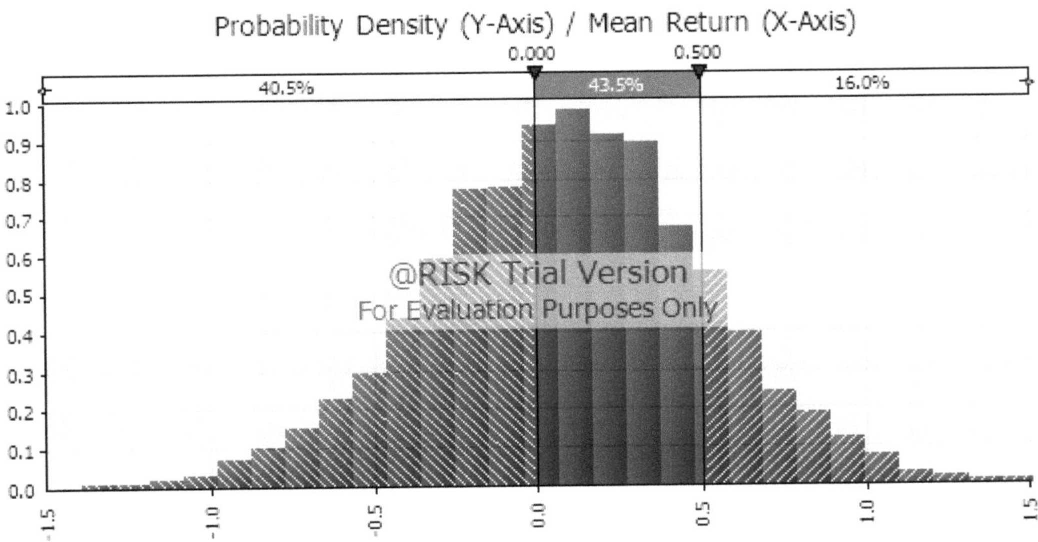

The results of Efficient Frontier's revised portfolios are presented here.

Table 3 shows the *Mean Return* (μ) and the investment fractions of total funds invested in each asset.

Table 3. The revised efficient frontier portfolios' fractions

μ	Asset 1	Asset 2	Asset 3	Option 4
0.088	0.25045	0.03481	0.26003	0.45470
0.090	0.28592	0.00699	0.28530	0.42179
0.092	0.32416	0	0.30889	0.36695
0.094	0.36329	0	0.33199	0.30472
0.096	0.40242	0	0.35509	0.24250
0.098	0.44155	0	0.37819	0.18027
0.100	0.48067	0	0.40129	0.11804
0.102	0.51980	0	0.42439	0.05581

Table 4 shows the *Mean Return* (μ), *Variance* (V), *Standard Deviation* (σ), *VAR*, *Sharpe Ratio* (*SR*), and *Beta* (β).

Table 4. The revised efficient frontier portfolios' details

μ	V	σ	VAR	SR	β
0.088	0.174	0.417	-0.036	0.083	0.655
0.090	0.181	0.425	-0.066	0.086	0.661
0.092	0.193	0.439	-0.124	0.088	0.671
0.094	0.217	0.466	-0.212	0.087	0.691
0.096	0.252	0.502	-0.326	0.085	0.724
0.098	0.298	0.546	-0.446	0.082	0.761
0.100	0.348	0.590	-0.565	0.079	0.799
0.102	0.410	0.640	-0.687	0.076	0.840

Performance Measurement of Revised Efficient Frontier Portfolios (DMAIC Measure)

Only the measurement of the revised portfolio with a return of 9.2% is presented here as an example.

Measuring Mean Return

The mean Return of the portfolio is simulated to measure the portfolio performance. The simulation model also calculates the Six Sigma process capability metrics *Cp*, *PNC,* and σ-*L* of the investment process. The investment fractions are: 32.41% in Asset 1; 31.89% in Asset 3; and 36.7% in Option 4.

The expected range of return is 8.8%–10.2% and the target is 9.2% (Figure 12).

The probability is 48.7% that the return will be less than 8.8%; 1.6%, within the target range of 8.8%–10.2%; and 49.7%, greater than 10.2%. The simulation results are *Mean Return*, 9.2%; Return Maximum, 171.38%; Return Minimum, -117.65% theoretically; *Variance*, 19.3%; *Standard Deviation*, 43.90%; *VAR*, -12.37%; *Sharpe Ratio*, 0.0876; and *Beta*, 0.6706. The Six Sigma investment process metrics are *Cp*, 0.00545; *PNC*, 0.984; and σ-*L*, 0.02382.

Figure 12. Portfolio return distribution vs. target

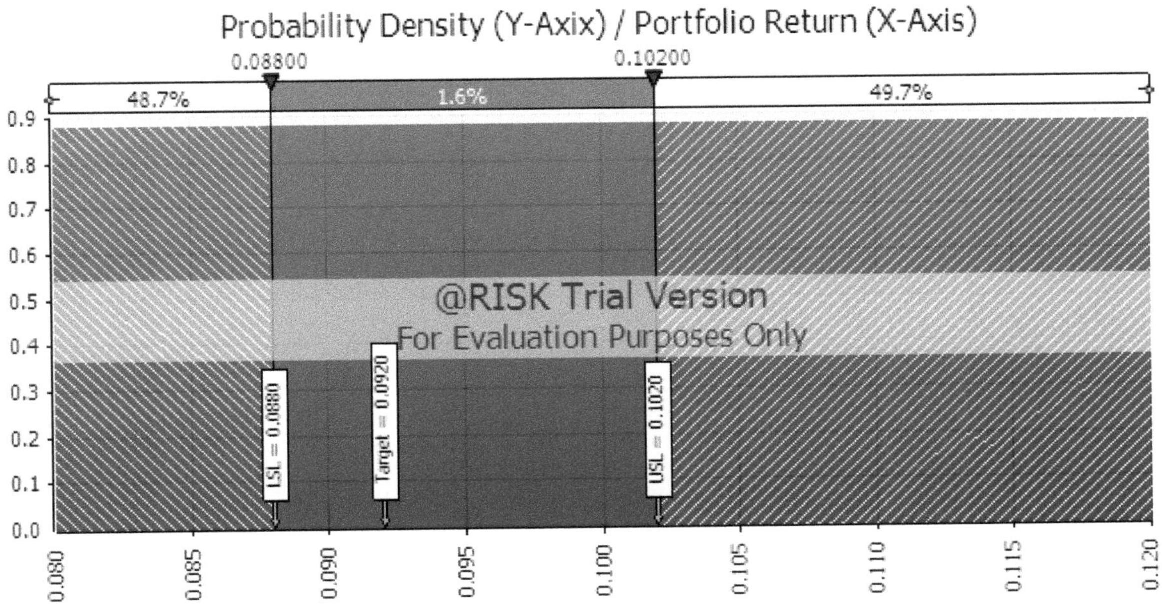

Probability Density (Y-Axix) / Portfolio Return (X-Axis)

0.08800 0.10200

48.7% 1.6% 49.7%

LSL = 0.0880 Target = 0.0920 USL = 0.1020

Measuring VAR

The predicted *VAR* in the previous step is -12.37% with a confidence level of 99.95%, but we need distribution for measurement.

To get the *VAR* distribution, *VAR* is simulated (Figure 13) using Standard Distribution with a Mean *VAR* of -12.37% and the same *Standard Deviation* as that for the *Main Return* simulation where the *VAR* is calculated (i.e., 43.90%).

Figure 13. VAR distribution

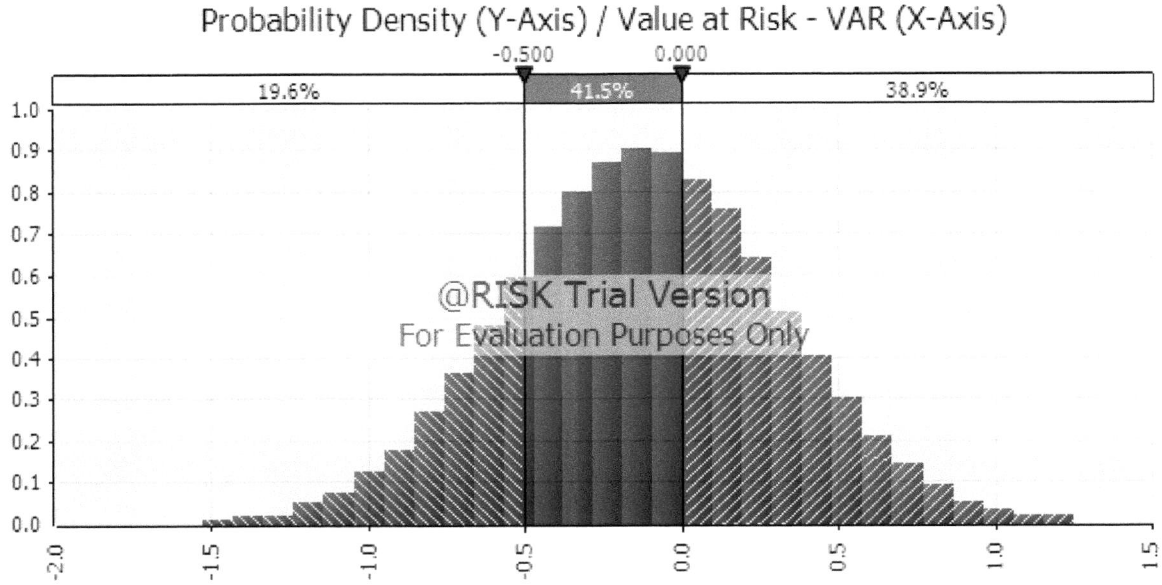

Figure 13 shows the *VAR* Distribution. The Mean *VAR* is -12.37%; the *VAR* Maximum is -153.29% theoretically (i.e., Maths Minimum); the *VAR* Minimum is 124.99% (i.e., Maths Maximum).

This graph shows that the probability of losing more than 50% is 19.6%; of losing 50%–0% is 41.5%, and of gaining (i.e., *VAR* greater than zero) is 38.9%.

Figure 14. VAR distribution vs. target range

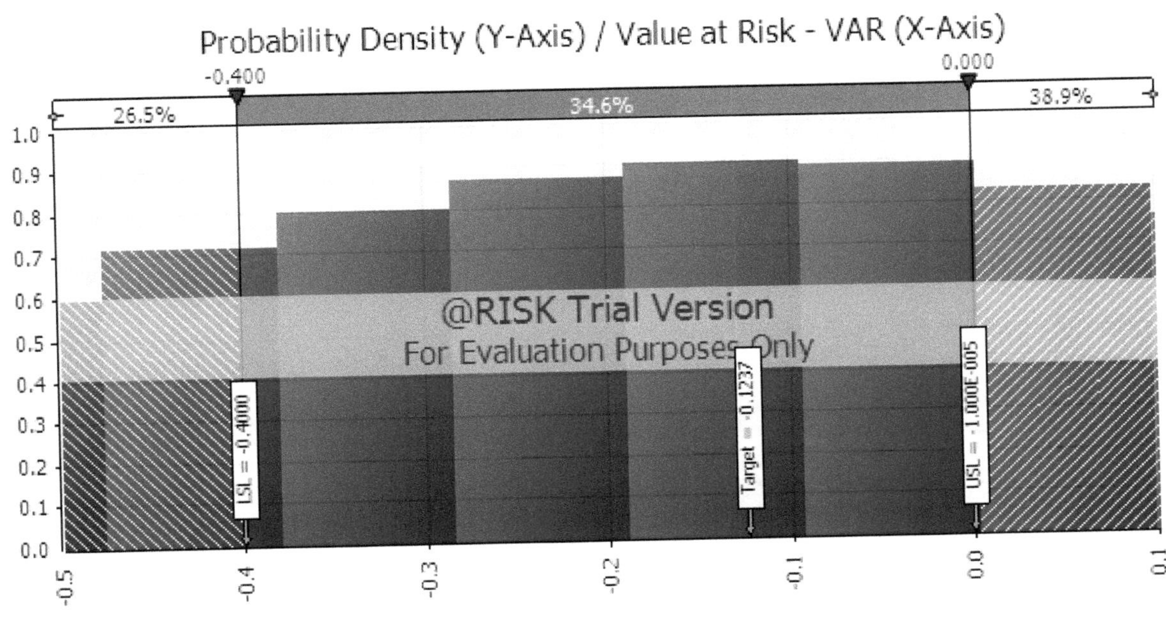

Let's have a closer look at the *VAR* Six Sigma target range (Figure 14). The Six Sigma target range is -40%–0% with a target value of -12.37%. The probability is 34.6% that *VAR* will be within the target range. The predicted process metrics are *Cp*, 0.15193; *PNC*, 0.654; and *σ-L*, 0.44821.

Measuring Sharpe Ratio

Figure 15 shows the *Sharpe Ratio* Distribution.

Figure 15. Sharpe ratio distribution

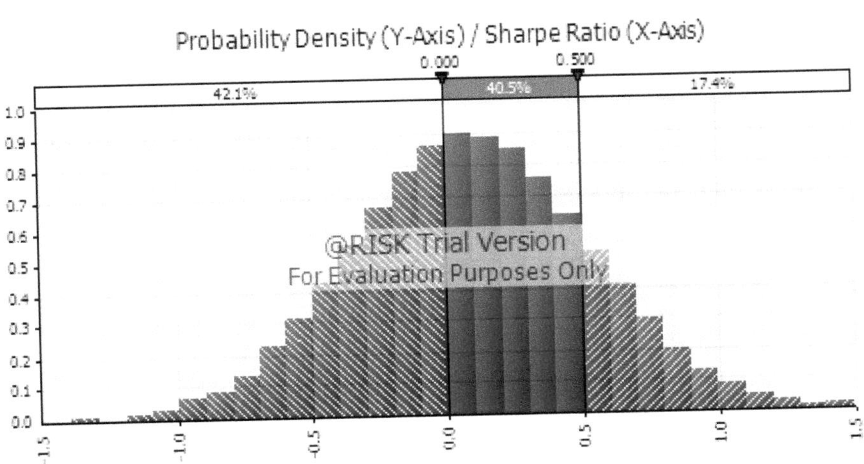

The predicted *Sharpe Ratio* is 0.0876 (Figure 15).

To get the distribution around the target range, the *Sharpe Ratio* is simulated using Normal Distribution (Mean, 0.0876 and *Standard Deviation,* 43.90%). The *Sharp Ratio* distribution versus the target is shown in Figure 16.

The Mean *Sharpe Ratio* is 0.0876; *SR* Maximum, 1.492; *SR* Minimum, -1.394. The probability of having a negative *Sharpe Ratio* is 42.1%; in the range of 0–0.5, 40.5%; and *Sharpe Ratio* greater than 0.5, 17.4%.

Figure 16. Sharp ratio distribution vs. target range

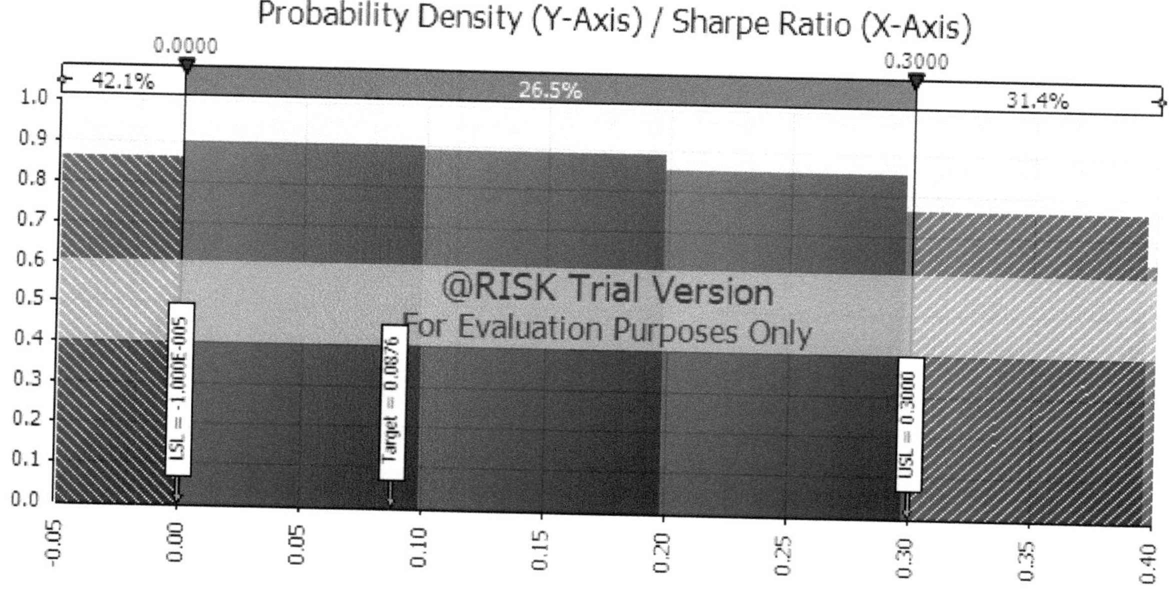

The Six Sigma target range is 0–0.3 with a target of 0.0876 (Figure 16). The probability is 20.5% that the *Sharp Ratio* will be in the target range. The calculated process metrics are *Cp*, 0.11386; *PNC*, 0.735; and *σ-L*, 0.3385.

Measuring Beta

The predicted value of *Beta* is 0.6706.

Beta is simulated using the Normal Distribution with Mean = 0.6706 and Standard Deviation = 43.90%. Figure 17 shows *Beta*'s Distribution. The Mean *Beta* is 0.6706; the Maximum is 2.11, and the Minimum is -0.7586. The probability is 90% of having *Beta* in the range -0.054–1.389; and 5% of *Beta* being less than -0.054, or greater than 1.389.

Figure 17. Beta distribution

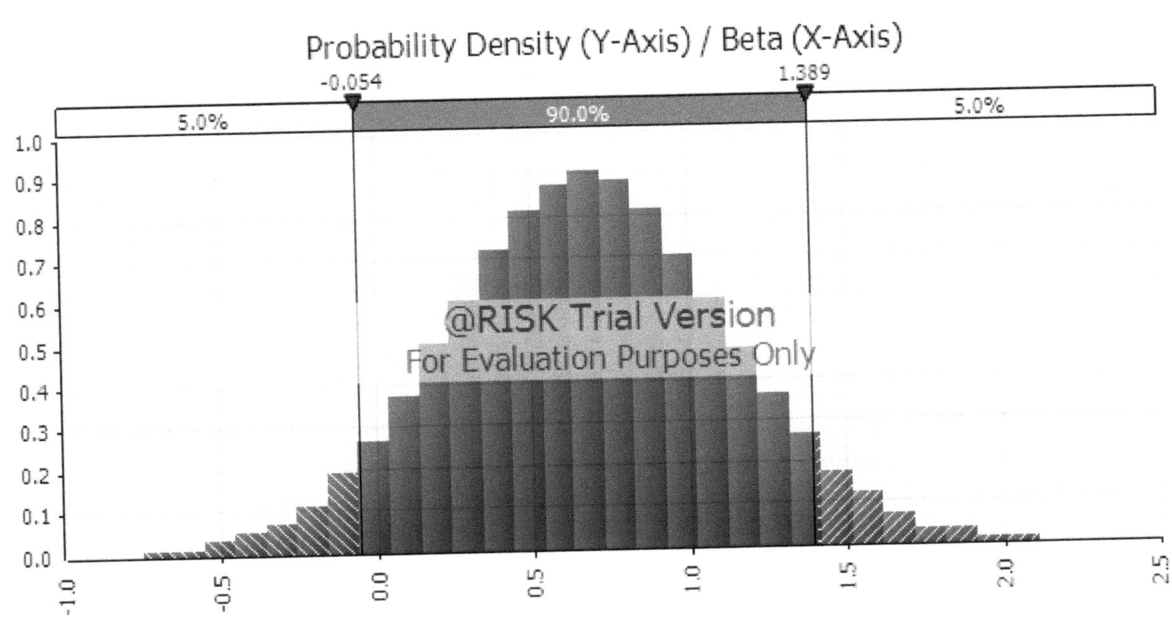

In Figure 18, the Six Sigma target range is 0.0–1.0 with a target of 0.6706. The *Beta* will be within the target range with a 71.1% probability. The predicted process metrics are *Cp*, 0.3798; *PNC*, 0.289; and σ-*L*, 1.0603.

Figure 18. Beta distribution vs. target range

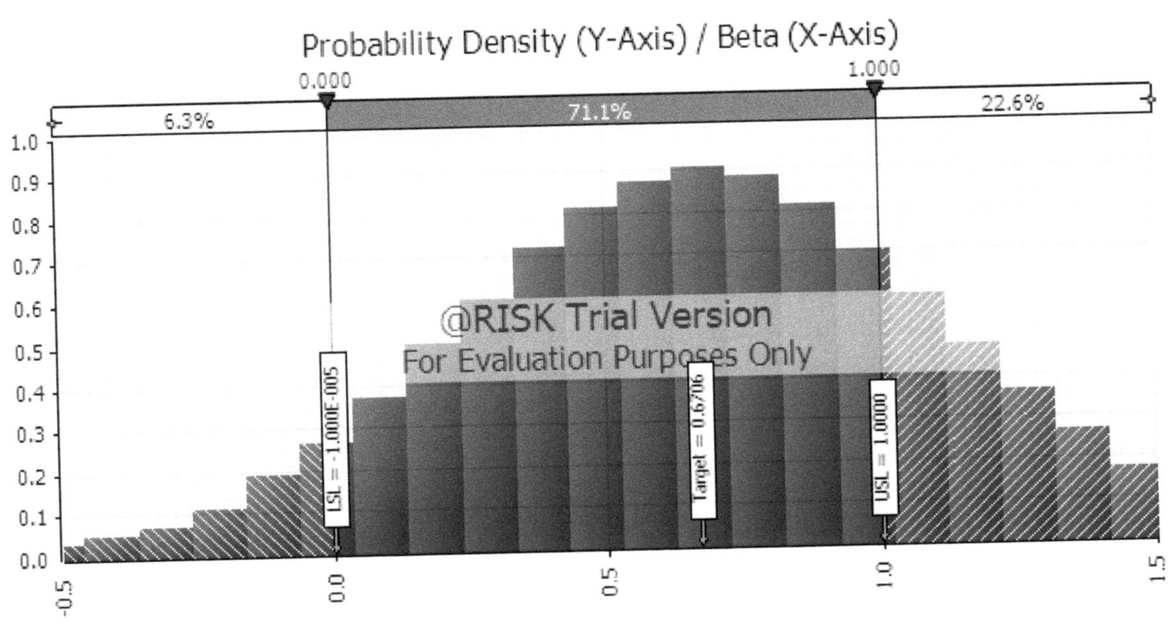

Performance Evaluation of Revised Efficient Frontier Portfolios (DMAIC Analyse)

The predicted future values of the portfolio's return and risks are: *Mean Return*, 9.2%; *Variance*, 19.3%; *Standard Deviation*, 43.90%; *VAR*, -12.37%; Sharpe Ratio, 0.0876; and *Beta*, 0.6706. The *Mean Return*, *VAR*, *Sharpe Ratio,* and *Beta* of the portfolio are discussed in the following sections.

Evaluating Mean Return

The predicted *Mean Return* is 9.2%, with a *Variance*, of 19.3%; and a *Standard Deviation*, of 43.90%. The return maximum value is 171.39%; and the return minimum value is -117.65% theoretically; The Six Sigma investment process metrics are *Cp*, 0.0361; *PNC*, 0.984; and σ-*L*, 0.1081.

Compared with the initial portfolio, the *Variance* is reduced from 24.7% to 5.4%; and the *Standard Deviation* is reduced from 49.7% to by5.8%; which is a noticeable reduction of risk. Consequently, the return maximum value (i.e., maximum gain) is reduced from 171.54% by 0.15%; and the return minimum value (i.e., maximum loss) is reduced by 29.3% from -146.95% theoretically.

Comparing the Six Sigma investment process metrics, *Cp* is increased by 7.63 times from 0.00473; *PNC* is 0. 984, i.e., reduced from 0.987, and σ-*L* is increased by 5.39 times from 0.02005; which is a significant investment process improvement.

Evaluating VAR

The predicted Mean *VAR* is -12.37% with a *Standard Deviation* of 43.90%. The *VAR* maximum is -153.29% theoretically (i.e., Maths Minimum); and the minimum, is 125% (i.e., Maths Maximum). The Six Sigma investment process metrics are *Cp*, 0.1519; *PNC*, 0.654; and σ-*L*, 0.4482.

Compared with the initial portfolio, *VAR* is reduced by 15.93% from -28.3%, which is a good risk reduction. Also, the *VAR* maximum is reduced by 36.71% from -190% theoretically (i.e., Maths Minimum); and the minimum is reduced by 43% from 168% (i.e., Maths Maximum).

The investment process is noticeably improved as well, i.e., *Cp* is increased by 13.44% from 0.1339; *PNC* is 0.654, i.e., reduced from 0.691; and σ-*L* is increased by 12.75% from 0.3975.

Evaluating Sharpe Ratio

The *Sharpe Ratio* predicted value is 0.0876 with a Standard Deviation of 43.90%. The probability that the portfolio will underperform compared with the Free Risk Rate (i.e., *Sharpe Ratio* is negative) is 42.1%. The probability of gaining up to 50% more return than the *Free Risk Rate* is 40.6% and over 50% more return than the *Free Risk Rate* is 17.3%. The Six Sigma investment process metrics are *Cp*, 0.0759; *PNC*, 0.735; and σ-*L*, 0.2275.

Compared with the initial portfolio, the *Sharpe Ratio* increased by 13.77% from 0.077. Thus, the revised portfolio will outperform the Free Risk Rate by 13.77% more than the initial portfolio.

The investment process metrics are also improved, i.e., *Cp* is increased by 13.19% from 0.1006; *PNC* is 0.735, i.e., reduced from 0.765; and σ-*L* is increased by 13.24% from 0.2989.

Evaluating Beta

The value predicted for Beta is 0.6706 with a Standard Deviation of 43.90%. The probability that the portfolio will be riskier (i.e., volatile) than the Market Index is 22.6%, and less risky than the Market

Index is 71.1%. The probability that Beta is negative, i.e., the portfolio will gain return when the index is going down, is 6.3%. The probability that the portfolio will move like the index is 93.7%. The Six Sigma investment process metrics are *Cp*, 0.3798; *PNC*, 0.289; and *σ-L*, 1.06.

Compared with the initial portfolio, *Beta* is reduced by 9.38% from 0.74. Thus, the revised portfolio will be less volatile than the Market Index by 9.38% compared with the initial portfolio. Therefore, the Market Index associated risk is reduced, which is an improvement. The investment process is improved too, i.e., *Cp* is increased by 13.38% from 0.335; *PNC* is reduced to 0.289 from 0.37, and *σ-L* is increased by 18.34% from 0.896.

Performance Attribution of Revised Efficient Frontier Portfolios (DMAIC Analyse)

Figure 19 shows the correlation sensitivity graph.

Figure 19. Correlation sensitivity

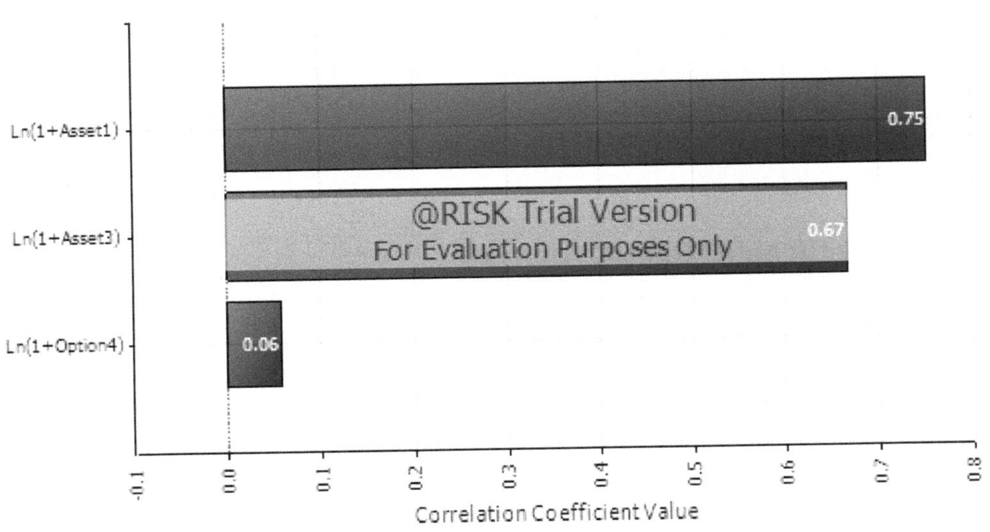

The correlation sensitivity graph (Figure 19) shows that the portfolio return is most dependent on Asset 1 with a correlation coefficient of 0.75. Asset 3 and Option 4 are less influential with correlation coefficients of 0.67 and 0.06 respectively.

The regression-mapped value graph (Figure 20) shows that the portfolio return is most dependent on Asset 1 with a regression coefficient of 0.31350. Asset 3 and Option 4 are less influential with regression coefficients of 0.27178 and 0.026851 respectively.

Figure 20. Regression mapped values sensitivity

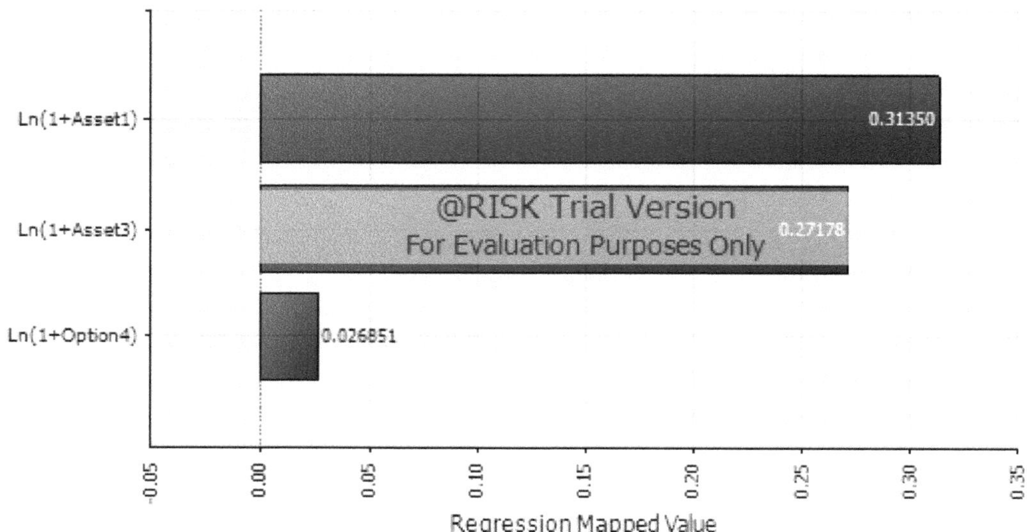

This analysis suggests that this portfolio could be further improved if Asset 1, is hedged with Option 1, but this is not considered here.

Results and Discussion (DMAIC Analyse)

Overall Results for Efficient Frontier Portfolios

The overall results of all the portfolios on the Efficient Frontier including the initial and the associated revised portfolios (shown in Blue) are presented in Table 5 showing the *Mean Return* (μ), *Variance* (V), *Standard Deviation* (σ), *VAR*, *Sharpe Ratio* (*SR*) and *Beta* (β) of the optimal portfolios.

Table 5. The overall results

μ	V	σ	VAR	SR	β
0.088	0.223	0.472	-0.204	0.073	0.723
0.088	0.174	0.417	-0.036	0.083	0.655
0.090	0.232	0.482	-0.228	0.076	0.730
0.090	0.181	0.425	-0.066	0.086	0.661
0.092	0.247	0.497	-0.283	0.077	0.740
0.092	0.193	0.439	-0.124	0.088	0.671
0.094	0.266	0.515	-0.362	0.079	0.756
0.094	0.217	0.466	-0.212	0.087	0.691
0.096	0.295	0.543	-0.454	0.078	0.777
0.096	0.252	0.502	-0.326	0.085	0.724
0.098	0.332	0.576	-0.537	0.077	0.798
0.098	0.298	0.546	-0.446	0.082	0.761
0.100	0.378	0.615	-0.625	0.076	0.820
0.100	0.348	0.590	-0.565	0.079	0.799
0.102	0.429	0.655	-0.732	0.074	0.848
0.102	0.410	0.640	-0.687	0.076	0.840

The Efficient Frontier of Portfolios

The Efficient Frontier of the optimal portfolios is presented in Figure 21. The Efficient Frontier curves show that an increase in the expected return of the portfolio causes an increase in the portfolio *Standard Deviation*. Also, the Efficient Frontiers get flatter as expected. This shows that each additional unit of *Standard Deviation* allowed, increases the portfolio *Mean Return* by less and less. To emphasise, the *Standard Deviation* (i.e., the risk) of revised portfolios for a given return is less than the risk of the original portfolios, thus the revised Efficient Frontier is shifted to the left. Also, the Efficient Frontier (i.e., the risk) of revised portfolios asymptotically converges to the Efficient Frontier of the original portfolios for higher returns.

Figure 21. Efficient frontier of optimal portfolios

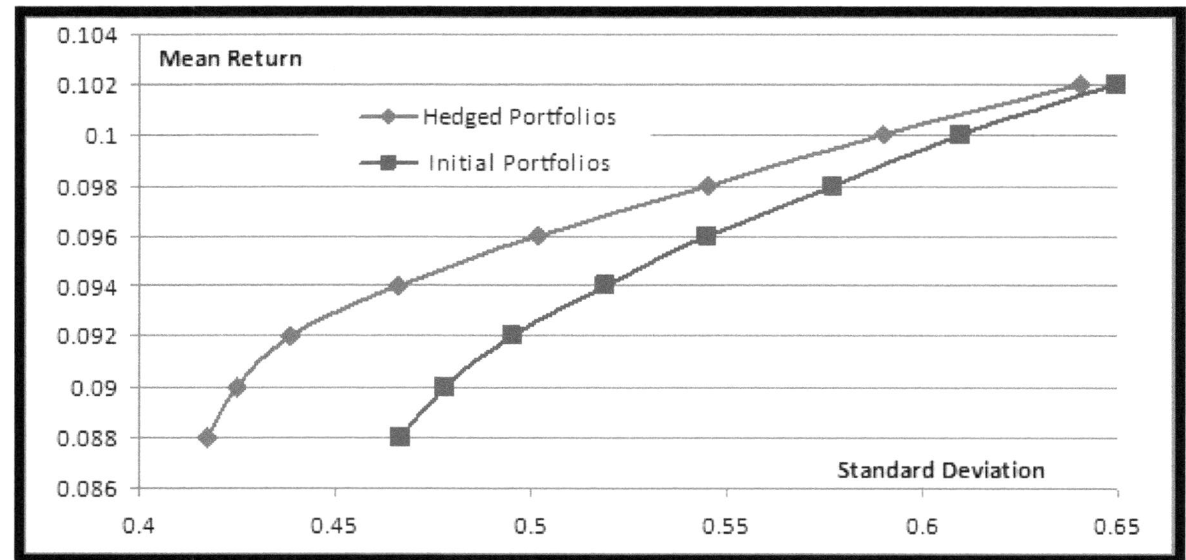

Portfolios Expected Mean Return vs. VAR

Figure 22 shows the dependency of the expected portfolio returns against *VAR*.

Figure 22. Portfolios return versus VAR

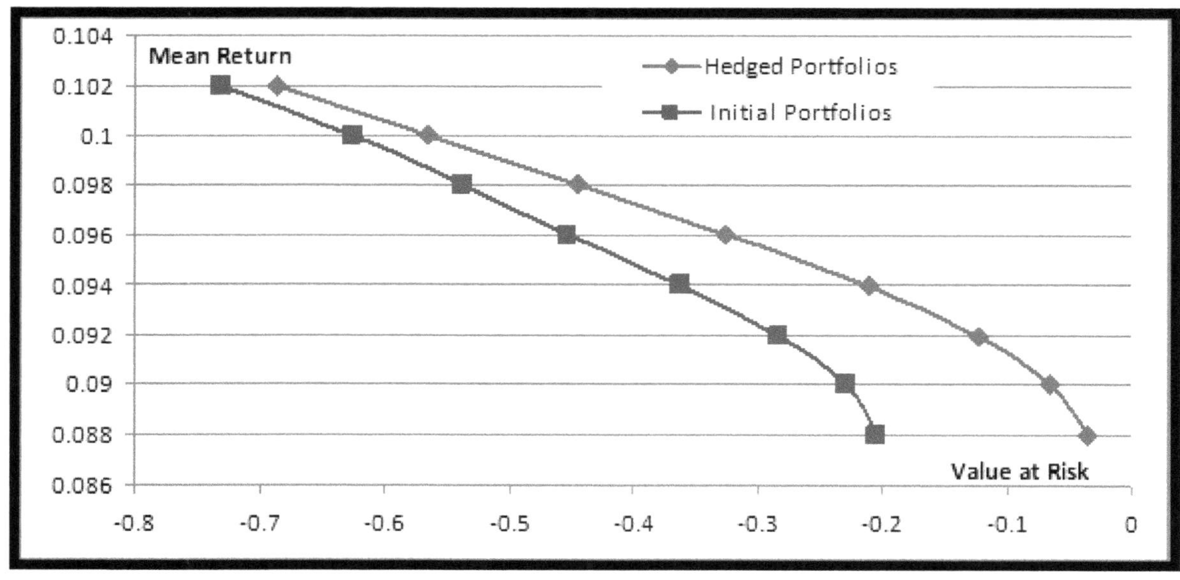

From the graph (Figure 22), it is possible to see that an increase in the expected return of the portfolio causes an increase in portfolio *VAR* in terms of money. (It should be noted that mathematically, VAR is a negative number, which decreases when the return increases.) Also, the curves on the graph get flatter, again as expected. This shows that each additional unit of *VAR* allowed increases the portfolio *Mean Return* by less and less.

Like the *Standard Deviation*, the *VAR* of revised portfolios for a given return is less than the *VAR* of the original portfolios, so the revised curve is shifted to the right. Also, the *VAR* of revised portfolios asymptotically converges to the VAR of the original portfolios for higher returns.

Portfolios Sharpe Ratio

Figure 23 shows that the *Sharpe Ratio* of the revised portfolios is greater than the ratio of the original portfolios, so the revised curve is shifted to the right.

Figure 23. Sharpe ratio of the efficient portfolios

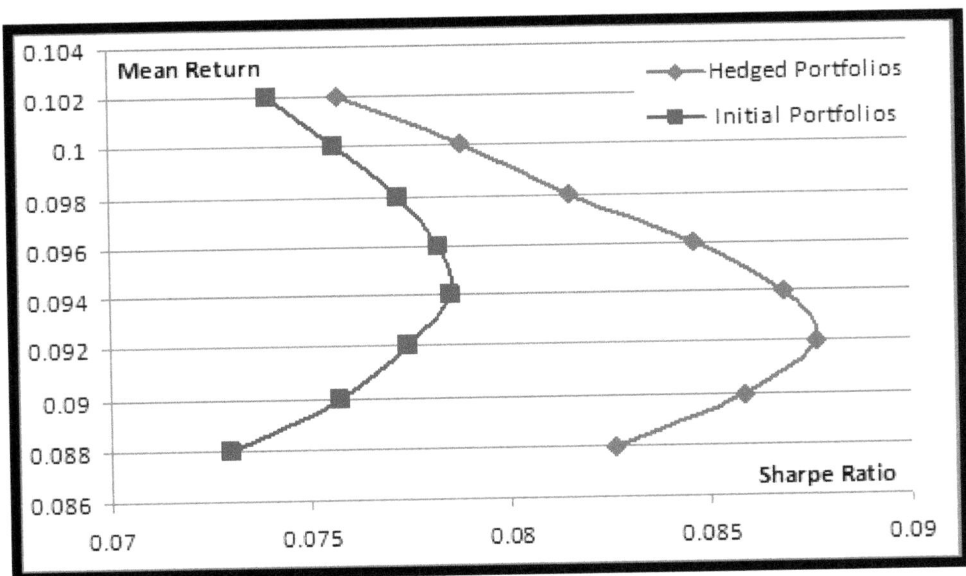

For example, a common goal in investments is to choose a portfolio that maximises the *Sharpe Ratio*. From the graph (Figure 23), it is possible to see that the revised portfolio with a *Mean Return* of 9.2% and a *Sharpe Ratio* of 0.088 (shown in Table 9.5 in Red) is technically the best investment portfolio considering the *Sharpe Ratio* criteria. Therefore, this portfolio should be recommended to Financial Executives.

Portfolios Beta

Figure 24 shows that regarding the *Mean Return*, *Beta* behaves like the *Standard Deviation* (i.e., Efficient Frontier), i.e., an increase in the expected return of the portfolio causes an increase in portfolio Beta.

Also, the Beta curve gets flatter as expected. This shows that each additional unit of risk (i.e., *Beta*), increases the portfolio *Mean Return* by less and less.

To emphasise, the *Beta* of revised portfolios for a given return is less than the *Beta* of the original portfolios (i.e., the revised curve is shifted to the left), which is expected. Also, the *Beta* curve of revised portfolios asymptotically converges to the *Beta* curve of the original portfolios for higher returns.

Figure 24. Beta of the efficient portfolios

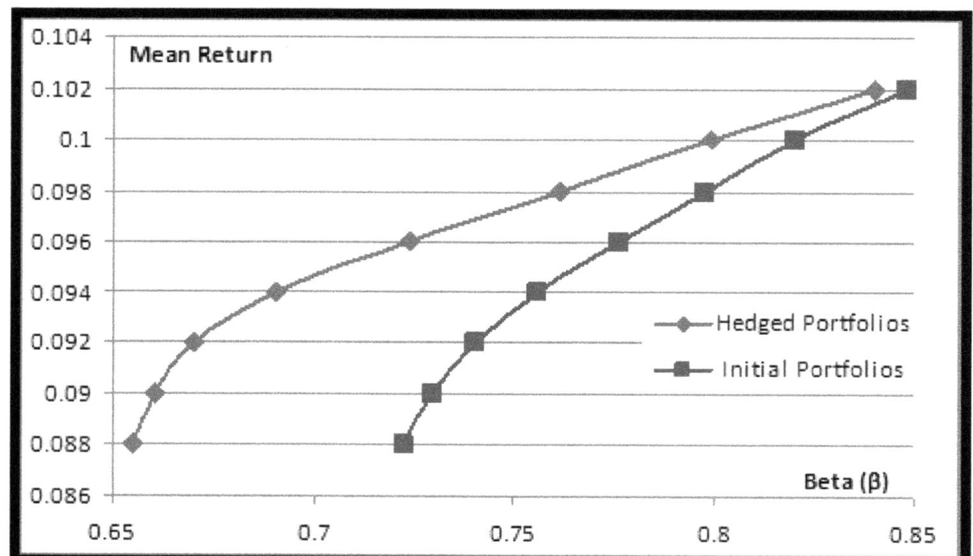

Decision Support

The results presented above provide for comprehensive and reliable decision support for the decision-makers, i.e., the financial risk executives of the financial institution. In particular, considering the Efficient Frontier of portfolios and the dependencies between portfolio expected *Mean Return*, *Standard Deviation*, *VAR*, *Sharpe Ratio,* and *Beta* (Figure 11–14), the decision-makers can decide in which portfolio to invest according to the expected return and risk appetite, considering *Standard Deviation*, *VAR*, *Sharpe Ratio* and *Beta*.

Portfolio Selection and Execution (DMAIC Improve)

It is assumed that the selected and executed portfolio on the market is the revised portfolio with investments of 32.41% in Asset 1; 31.89% in Asset 3; and 36.7% in Option 4; *Mean Return* 9.2%; and *Sharpe Ratio*, 0.088. This portfolio is recognised as technically the best portfolio based on the Maximal *Sharpe Ratio* criteria.

THE METHOD: ONGOING PORTFOLIO MANAGEMENT

Ongoing Portfolio Management applies the DMAIC Control stage to the executed portfolio regularly (i.e., half-yearly) to perform portfolio performance measurement, evaluation, and attribution. If deviations from the expected return and risk are found, corrective action should be undertaken such as the revision of the portfolio considering changes in the market and the position of the investor.

Hypothetical Scenario (DMAIC Define)

In this hypothetical scenario, it is assumed as follows: i) This stage is applied half-yearly; ii) The present date is 1 May 2014; iii) The market data are available for the last six months, i.e., from November 2013 to April 2014 inclusive; iv) Only these data (i.e., November/2013–April/2014 data) are used for portfolio performance measurement, evaluation, and attribution, and portfolio revision; and v) The investor's positions remained unchanged.

It should be noted that only *Mean Return* is considered for Ongoing Portfolio Management. *VAR*, *Sharpe Ratio,* and *Beta* are not presented because the respective techniques are the same as the ones elaborated in Portfolio Construction. This approach simplifies the article and avoids repetition.

However, to preserve the integrity of the method's presentation, the topics for *VAR*, *Sharpe Ratio,* and *Beta* are given but without any details; only references are provided to the sections where the respective technique is elaborated.

Performance Measurement of Executed Portfolio (DMAIC – Measure)

Measuring Mean Return

The *Mean Return* of the portfolio is simulated to measure the portfolio performance for the last six months and predict the annual return by using the data available from November 2013 to April 2014 inclusive. The simulation model also predicts the *Variance, Standard Deviation, VAR*, *Sharpe Ratio,* and *Beta* of the portfolio. In addition, Six Sigma process capability metrics *Cp*, *PNC,* and *σ-L* are predicted to measure the future performance of the investment process.

The executed portfolio has the following investment fractions: 32.41% in Asset 1; 31.89% in Asset 3; and 36.7% in Option 4. The expected range of return is 8.8%–10.2% and the target is 9.2%. The simulation results are as follows. Figure 25 shows the probability distribution for the portfolio return.

Figure 25. Portfolio return distribution

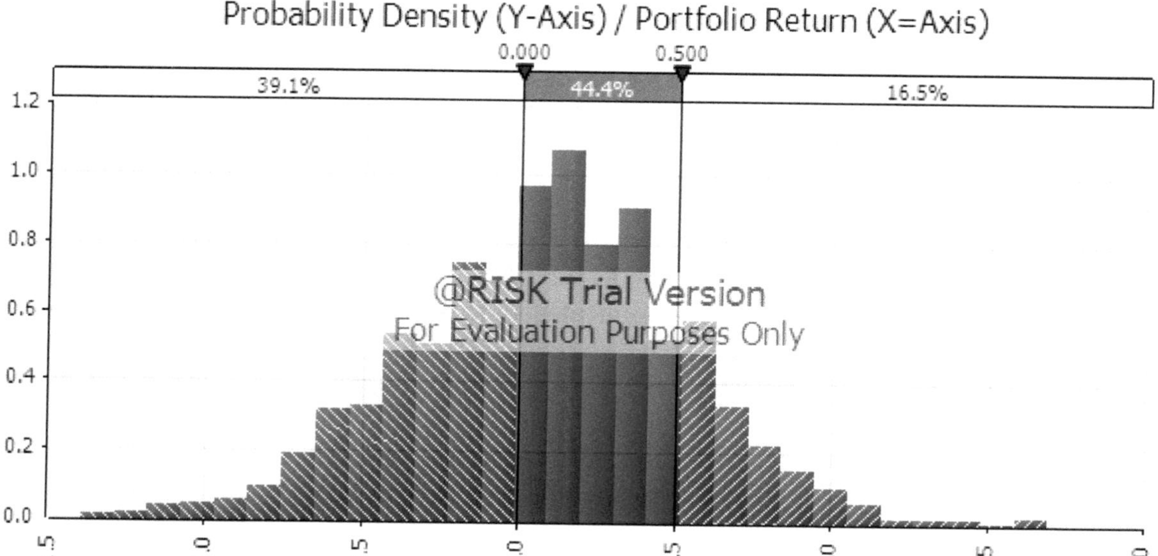

The predicted annual values (Figure 25) are *Mean Return*, 8.78%, which is missing the target range; Return Maximum, 169.58%; Return Minimum, -140.1% theoretically; *Variance*, 19.31%; *Standard Deviation*, 43.95%; *VAR*, -13.98%; *Sharpe Ratio*, 0.078; and *Beta*, 0.6771. The probability is 39.1% that the return will be negative (i.e., loss); 44.4%, within 0%–50%; and 16.5%, greater than 50%.

Let's have a closer look at the *Mean Return* Six Sigma target range (Figure 26). The probability is only 1.3% that the *Mean Return* will be within the target range. The predicted process metrics are *Cp*, 0.0053; *PNC*, 0.987; and *σ-L*, 0.0020.

Figure 26. Return distribution vs. target range

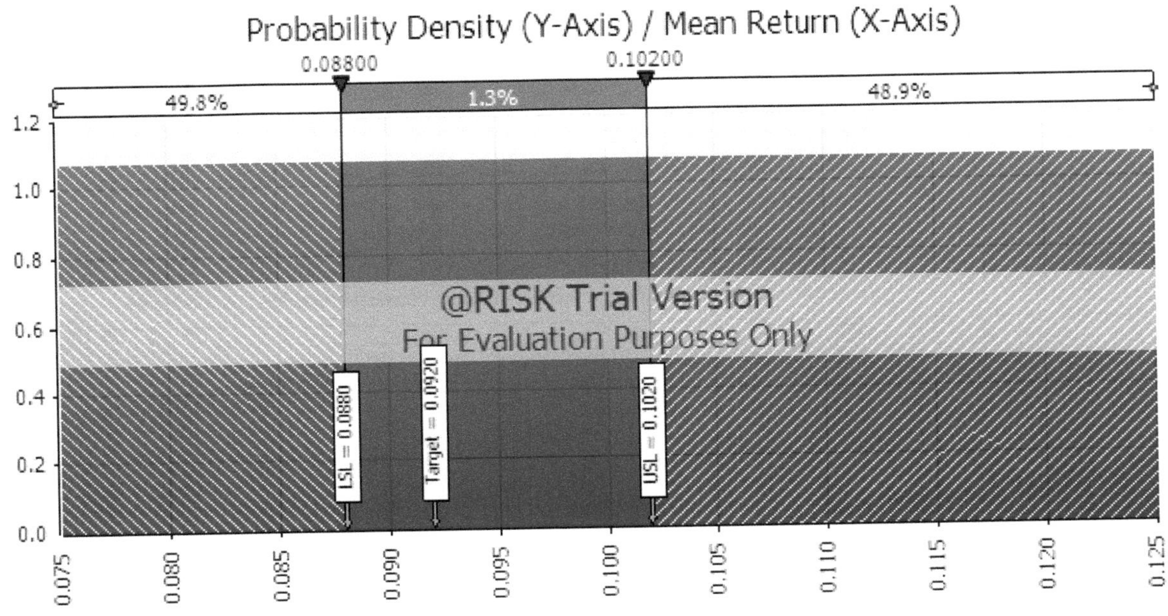

Performance Evaluation of Executed Portfolio (DMAIC – Analyse)

Evaluating Mean Return

The predicted annual *Mean Return* is 8.78%. Thus, the *Mean Return* of 8.78% does not meet the target of 9.2%. Moreover, it is out of the target range of 8.8%–10.2%, which is unacceptable.

The Six Sigma investment process metrics are *Cp*, 0.0053; *PNC*, 0.987; and *σ-L*, 0.0020. *PNC* is almost one (i.e., 98.7% deviation). The metrics confirm the poor capability of the investment process (i.e., not capable of gaining 9.2%). Therefore, the portfolio should be revised.

Performance Attribution of Executed Portfolio (DMAIC – Analyse)

The correlation sensitivity graph (Figure 27) shows that the portfolio return is most dependent on Asset 1 with a correlation coefficient of 0.72. Asset 3 and Option 4 are less influential with correlation coefficients of 0.69 and 0.04 respectively.

Figure 27. Correlation sensitivity

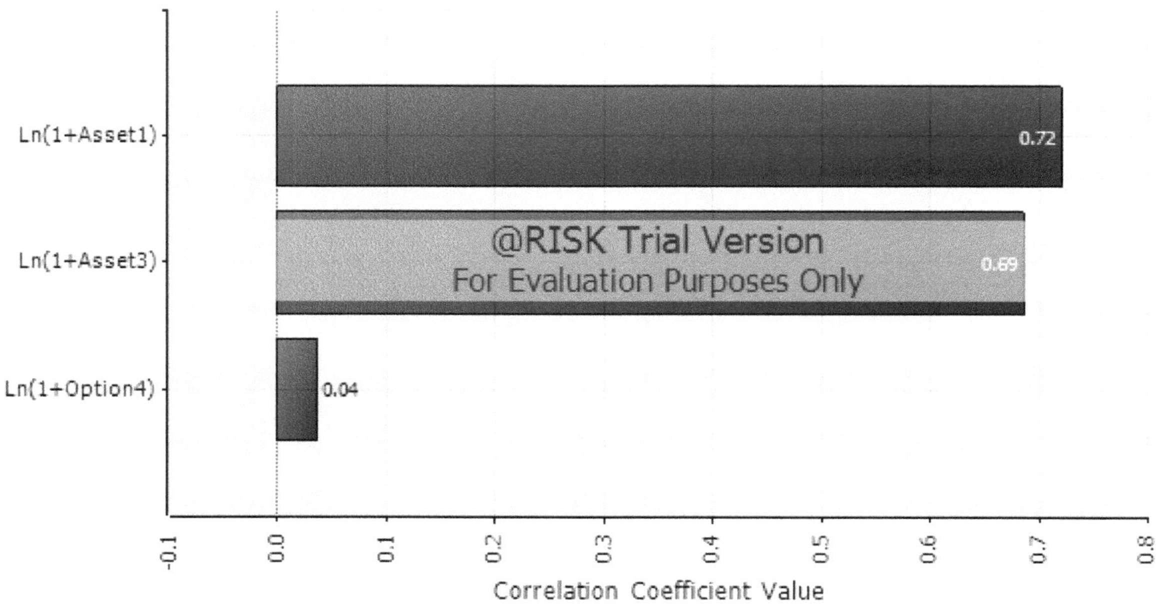

The regression sensitivity graph is presented in Figure 28.

Figure 28. Regression mapped values sensitivity

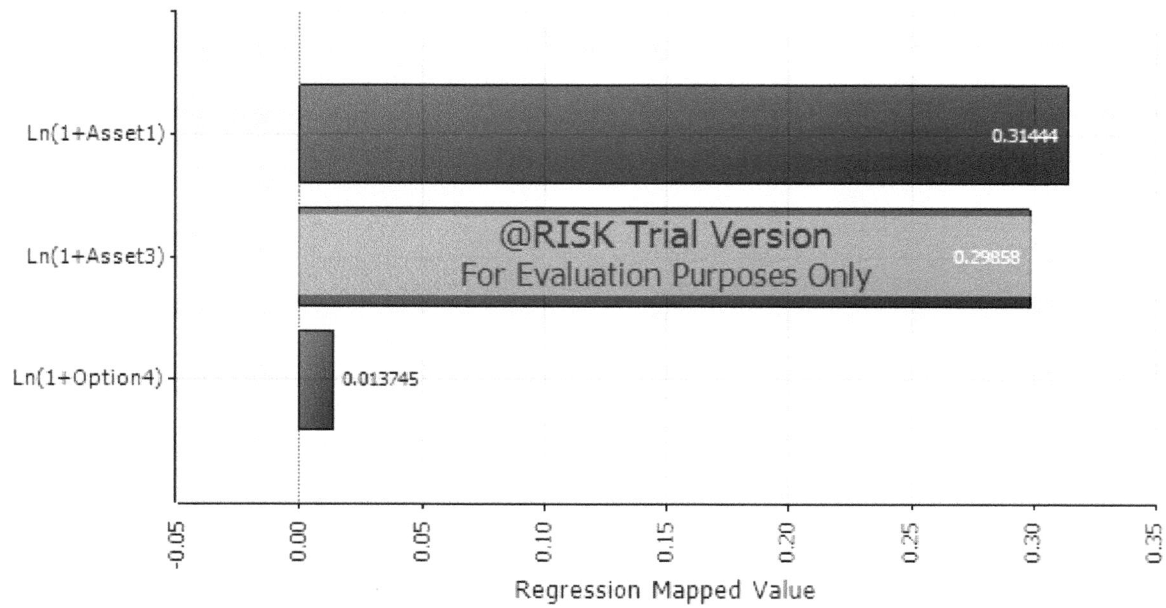

The regression sensitivity graph (Figure 28) illustrates that if Asset 1 return changes by one Standard Deviation, the portfolio return will change by 0.314 Standard Deviations. Again, Asset 1 and Option 4 are less influential with regression-mapped values of 0.299 and 0.0137 respectively.

Revision of Executed Portfolio (DMAIC Improve)

Determination of Portfolio Improvement (DMAIC Define)

The sensitivity analysis identified that the risk of the executed portfolio can be reduced if Asset 1 is hedged with Option 1, but this option is not considered because it is discussed in Sec. 3.6.1. The ultimate objective is to revise the portfolio to gain the expected annual return of 9.2%.

Determination of Revised Minimal Mean-Variance Portfolio (DMAIC Define)

A stochastic optimisation model resolves the minimal mean-variance portfolio which gains 9.2%. The investment fractions of the revised portfolio with a 9.2% return are 37.81% in Asset 1; 25.69% in Asset 3; and 36.5% in Option 4.

Performance Measurement of Revised Portfolio (DMAIC Measure)

Measuring Mean Return

Figure 29 presents the revised portfolio.

This revised portfolio is simulated to measure the performance (Figure 29). The predicted *Mean Return* is 9.2% with *Variance*, 20.21%; *Standard Deviation*, 44.96%; *VAR*, -15.33%; *Sharpe Ratio*, 0.0855; and *Beta*, 0.7426. Figure 29 shows the probability that the portfolio return will be negative (i.e., loss) is 41.2%; in the range of 0%–50%, 42.5%; and greater than 50%, 16.3%.

Figure 29. Revised portfolio return distribution

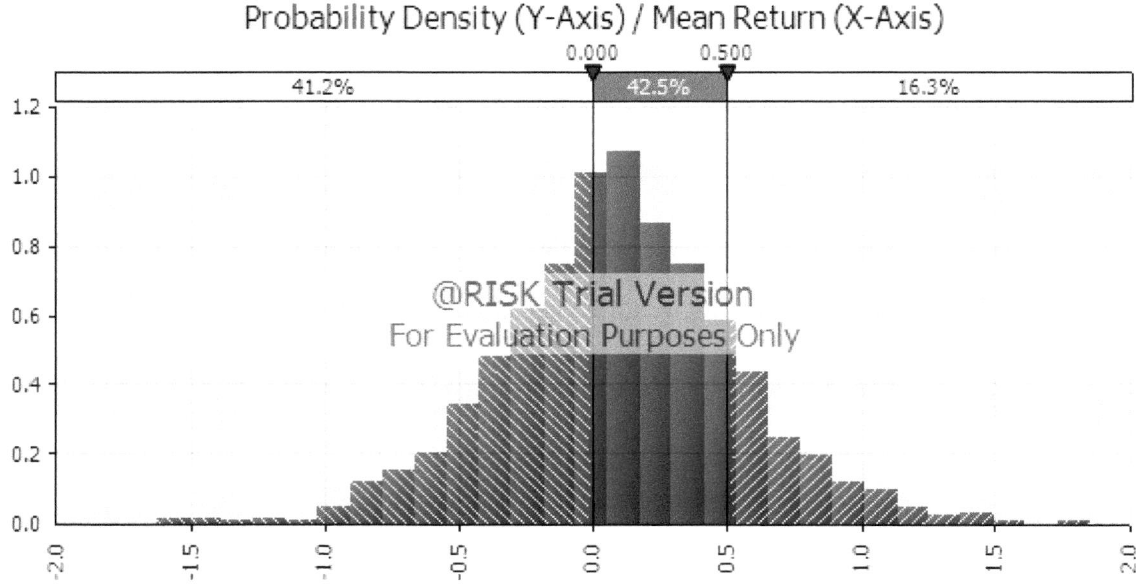

The expected return range is 8.8%–10.2% and the target is 9.2% (Figure 30). The predicted Six Sigma process capability metrics are: *Cp,* 0.0082; *PNC*, 0.984; and *σ-L*, 0.0163.

Figure 30. Mean return distribution vs. target range

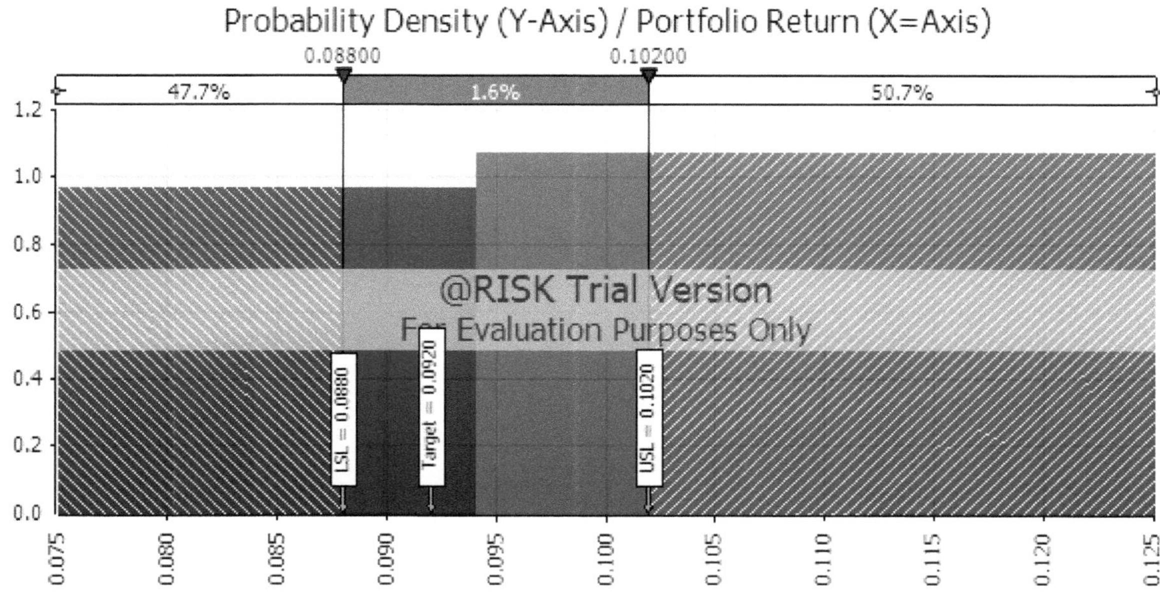

Performance Evaluation of Revised Portfolio (DMAIC Analyse)

Evaluating Mean Return of Revised Portfolio

The predicted *Mean Return* is 9.2% with *Variance*, 20.21%; *Standard Deviation*, 44.96%; *VAR*, -15.33%; *Sharpe Ratio*, 0.0855; and *Beta*, 0.7426. Therefore, the ultimate objective is achieved. The risk measures for the revised portfolio are slightly increased in comparison with the original portfolio's risk measures, which are: *Variance*, 19.31%; *Standard Deviation*, 43.95%; *VAR*, -13.98%; *Sharpe Ratio*, 0.078; and *Beta*, 0.6771. It is assumed that the risk measures are acceptable. The calculated process metrics for the revised portfolio are *Cp*, 0.0082; *PNC*, 0.984; and *σ-L*, 0.0163. The investment process capability is slightly improved compared with the original portfolio metrics, which are *Cp*, 0.0053; *PNC*, 0.987; and *σ-L*, 0.0020. It is assumed that the metrics are acceptable.

Performance Attribution of Revised Portfolio (DMAIC Analyse)

The correlation sensitivity graph (Figure 31) shows that the portfolio return is most dependent on Asset 1 with a correlation coefficient of 0.79. Asset 3 is less influential with correlation coefficients of 0.53. Option 4 has a very small negative correlation of -0.03.

Figure 31. Correlation sensitivity

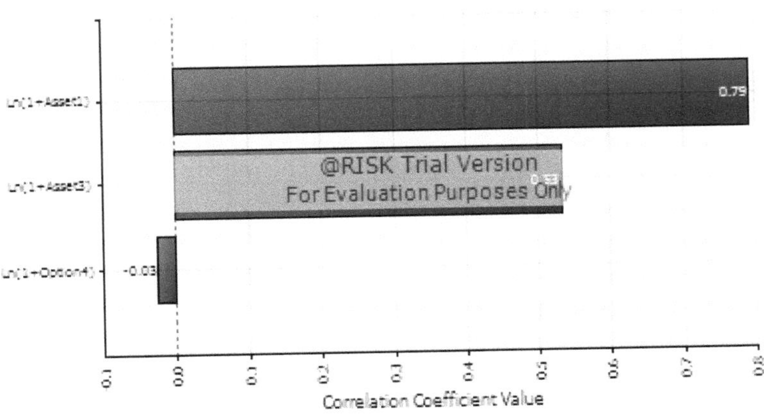

Figure 32 presents the regression sensitivity graph.

Figure 32. Regression mapped values sensitivity

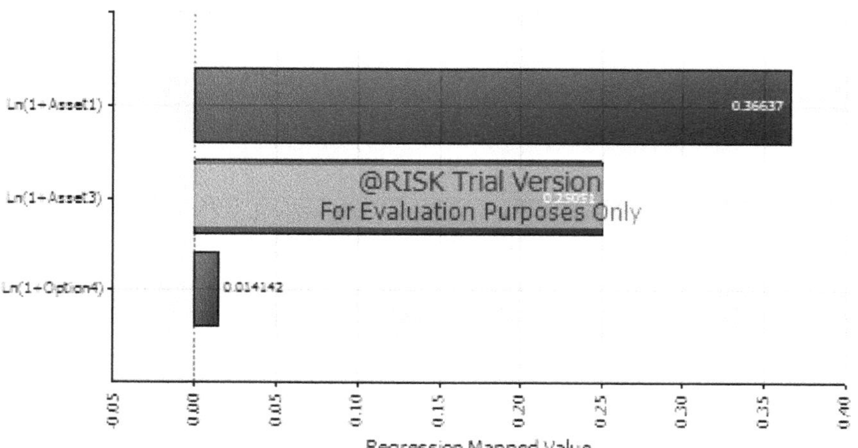

The regression sensitivity graph (Figure 32) illustrates that if Asset 1 return is changed by one Standard Deviation, the portfolio return will change by 0.366 Standard Deviations. Asset 3 and Option 4 are less influential with regression-mapped values of 0.251 and 0.014 respectively.

This analysis suggests that the revised portfolio could still be further improved if Asset 1 is hedged with Option 1, but this is not discussed here.

Revised Portfolio Execution (DMAIC Improve)

It is assumed that this revised portfolio was executed. This newly executed portfolio will be revised again after six months.

VERIFICATION OF THE METHOD'S RESULTS

A comparison of the method's predicted results based on the market history data versus the actual results based on the actual market data is done to verify the method's results.

In Portfolio Construction the method uses the market history data from January 2010 to October 2016 inclusive to construct and execute the optimal portfolio. The predicted results are the annual *Mean Return*, 9.02%; *VAR*, -12.4%; *Sharpe Ratio*, 0.088; and *Beta*, 0.671 (Ref. Sec. 3.6.2).

Subsequently, in Ongoing Portfolio Management, the method uses the actual market data from November 2016 to April 2017 inclusive to measure the performance of the portfolio for the last six months. The actual results of the measurement are the annual *Mean Return*, 8.78%; *VAR*, -13.98%; *Sharpe Ratio*, 0.078; and *Beta*, 0.677 (Ref. Sec. 4.2.1).

The comparisons of the predicted versus actual results are presented in Table 6 showing the *Mean Return* (μ), *VAR*, *Sharpe Ratio* (*SR*), and *Beta* (β), and the associated absolute and percentage (%) errors.

Table 6. The comparison of actual vs. predicted results

Result	Actual	Predicted	Error	Error %
μ	0.0878	0.0902	0.0273	2.73
VAR	-0.1398	-0.1240	-0.1130	-11.30
SR	0.0780	0.0880	0.1282	12.82
β	0.6770	0.6710	-0.0089	-0.89

For example, the *Mean Return* is overestimated by 2.73% which is a very good result. *VAR* is underestimated by 11.30% which is not a bad result at all. All in all, the results are reasonably good and acceptable. Therefore, the method results are successfully verified.

CONCLUSION

This chapter presents a Six Sigma practical approach to Market Risk management in an investment portfolio. In addition to the conventional methodologies, the method systematically applies Six Sigma DMAIC to define, measure, analyse, improve, and control the risk and performance of the investment portfolio selection processes. In synergy with conventional methodologies, this complementary method offers important enhancements to financial institutions.

The method conventionally uses stochastic optimisation to determine a minimal mean-variance portfolio according to the investor's objectives and constraints. It applies the Monte Carlo simulation model to stochastically calculate portfolio returns as well as to calculate the absolute, relative, and risk-adjusted performance measures. In addition, it utilises the DMAIC framework to systematically measure the performance of the portfolio to find deviations in expected return and accepted risks; and to apply corrective measures to improve the investment process if deviations are detected, thus accordingly revising the portfolio. Ultimately, the optimal portfolio is constructed and executed.

Also, the method establishes regular monitoring and corrective mechanisms to continuously control the portfolio performance on the market. It dynamically applies stochastic optimisation and Monte Carlo simulation in the DMAIC framework again to measure and evaluate the performance of the portfolio. If deviations from the investment objectives and constraints are found, the portfolio is revised to address the new market conditions as well as the changes in the investor's positions. The method systematically achieves the optimal portfolio, which is the crucial objective. This method is generally applicable to Investment Management and can be specifically applied to ALM. In particular, from Basel III and Solvency II perspectives, it proposes internal models' options to banks and (re)insurers, which can help them to reduce their capital requirements and VAR. The saved capital can be invested thus providing for higher business capabilities and increasing the competitive position, which is the ultimate objective.

REFERENCES

Brinson, G. P. (1998). Global Management and Asset Allocation. In P. L. Bernstein & A. Damodaran (Eds.), *Investment Management* (pp. 117–161). John Wiley & Sons.

Busse, J. A., Goyal, A., & Wahal, S. (2010). Performance and Persistence in Institutional Investment Management. *The Journal of Finance*.

Clark, R. G. (1998a). Alternative Measures of Risk. In P. L. Bernstein & A. Damodaran (Eds.), *Investment Management* (pp. 81–98). John Wiley & Sons.

Clark, R. G. (1998b). Managing Portfolio Risk. In P. L. Bernstein & A. Damodaran (Eds.), *Investment Management* (pp. 274–326). John Wiley & Sons.

Damodaran, A. (1998a). Models of Risk. In P. L. Bernstein & A. Damodaran (Eds.), *Investment Management* (pp. 58–80). John Wiley & Sons.

Damodaran, A. (1998b). Asset Selection: Strategies and Evidence. In P. L. Bernstein & A. Damodaran (Eds.), *Investment Management* (pp. 185–229). John Wiley & Sons.

Damodaran, A. (1998c). The Hidden Costs of Trading. In P. L. Bernstein & A. Damodaran (Eds.), *Investment Management* (pp. 259–273). John Wiley & Sons.

Glasserman, P. (2004). *Monte Carlo Methods in Financial Engineering*. Springer Science.

Jacob, N. L. (1998). Evaluating Investment Performance. In P. L. Bernstein & A. Damodaran (Eds.), *Investment Management* (pp. 329–371). John Wiley & Sons.

Jeffrey, R. H. (1998a). Tax Considerations in Investing. In P. L. Bernstein & A. Damodaran (Eds.), *Investment Management* (pp. 99–111). John Wiley & Sons.

Jeffrey, R. H. (1998b). Taxes and Performance Evaluation. In P. L. Bernstein & A. Damodaran (Eds.), *Investment Management* (pp. 372–386). John Wiley & Sons.

Kritzman, M. (1998). Risk and Utility Basics. In P. L. Bernstein & A. Damodaran (Eds.), *Investment Management* (pp. 27–57). John Wiley & Sons.

Lawton, P., & Jankowski, T. (2009). Investment Performance Measurement: Evaluating and Presenting Results. CFA Institute.

Maginn, J. P. (2007). Managing Investment Portfolios: A Dynamic Process (3rd ed.). John Wiley & Sons.

Markowitz, H. M. (1952). Portfolio Selection. *The Journal of Finance*, *7*, 77–91.

Markowitz, H. M. (1987). *Mean-Variance Analysis in Portfolio Choice and Capital Markets*. Basil Blackwell.

Meier, J. P. (2009). Investment Performance Appraisal. In Investment Performance Measurement: Evaluating and Presenting Results. CFA Institute.

Personal RePEc Archive (MPRA). (2007). MPRA Paper No 5048.

Plantinga, A. (2007). *Performance Measurement and Evaluation*.

Ziemba, W. T., & Vickson, S. W. (Eds.). (2006). Stochastic Optimization Models in Finance. World Scientific.

APPENDIX

Financial Market Data

The monthly return of the four selected assets for the period January 2010–April 2017 is given in Table 7 (Source: Legal & General Investment Management)

Table 7. Monthly return of selected assets

Date (mm/yy)	Asset 1	Asset 2	Asset 3	Asset 4
01/10	0.0468	-0.0097	-0.065	-0.0079
02/10	0.0646	0.0655	0.0383	0.0385
03/10	0.0209	0.0148	0.1244	0.0154
04/10	0.0262	-0.0231	-0.0188	-0.0358
05/10	0.113	0.0795	0.1278	0.0754
06/10	-0.0197	-0.0135	-0.0393	-0.0063
07/10	-0.0476	-0.0138	-0.0391	0.1011
08/10	-0.0696	-0.0831	-0.1904	0.0522
09/10	0.0431	-0.0565	-0.0729	-0.0037
10/10	-0.0089	0.0092	-0.0979	-0.0326
11/10	0.0896	0.009	0.1511	-0.001
12/10	-0.0052	-0.0377	0.0548	-0.0389
01/11	0.1234	0.0367	0.1495	-0.0344
02/11	0.0245	0.0688	0.0492	0.0984
03/11	-0.1046	-0.0288	0.0266	-0.027
04/11	-0.0873	-0.0344	0.0722	0.0317
05/11	0.0411	0.1545	0.0759	-0.0393
06/11	-0.0779	-0.0357	-0.1098	-0.0727
07/11	0.0414	-0.0161	-0.038	0.0664
08/11	-0.0294	-0.0222	0.1448	-0.0163
09/11	0.0689	-0.0108	-0.0678	-0.0252
10/11	-0.0484	-0.039	-0.1291	0.0313
11/11	-0.0432	-0.072	-0.0993	-0.1306
12/11	-0.0355	-0.0395	0.0813	0.0402
01/12	0.0108	0.0833	0.0544	-0.0152
02/12	-0.0201	0.1193	0.0538	-0.0059
03/12	-0.0365	-0.0153	-0.0891	-0.0436
04/12	0.0865	0.0919	-0.0166	0.1305
05/12	0.0128	-0.0255	0.1186	0.0381
06/12	0.0779	0.0778	-0.0133	-0.0579
07/12	-0.0301	-0.035	-0.0212	0.0499

Continued on following page

Table 7. Continued

Date (mm/yy)	Asset 1	Asset 2	Asset 3	Asset 4
08/12	-0.0674	-0.0994	0.0178	0.0343
09/12	-0.0628	-0.0466	0.0527	0.0486
10/12	-0.1515	-0.0279	0.1022	-0.0454
11/12	0.0376	0.0372	0.0339	-0.0432
12/12	-0.2215	0	-0.0394	0.0491
01/13	0.0216	0.1192	0.0273	0.0196
02/13	0.0654	-0.0052	-0.003	0.0299
03/13	-0.0597	0.0067	0.0722	-0.0252
04/13	-0.0414	0.0587	-0.1408	0.071
05/13	0.0961	-0.0088	0.024	0.0111
06/13	-0.0593	0.0747	-0.0855	-0.0653
07/13	-0.0901	0.0612	0.035	-0.0043
08/13	0.0327	-0.0192	-0.0278	0.0086
09/13	-0.0754	-0.0697	0.0389	-0.0087
10/13	0.0953	0.0974	0.0075	-0.0361
11/13	0.1839	0.0766	0.0339	-0.0465
12/13	0.0477	0.027	-0.0688	0.0145
01/14	0	0.0797	-0.0136	0.0499
02/14	-0.0555	-0.0297	0.0973	-0.0758
03/14	0.0321	-0.0484	0.0217	-0.0571
04/14	0.0516	0.0359	0.0852	0.0039
05/14	0.1003	-0.0321	0.0006	0.0721
06/14	-0.0625	-0.0421	0.0313	0.0136
07/14	0.0522	0.0149	0.0192	0.055
08/14	0.1121	-0.0118	0.0335	0.0058
09/14	0.0158	-0.0434	-0.1006	-0.0583
10/14	0.0692	-0.0987	0.0135	0.0743
11/14	-0.0439	-0.0195	0.0608	-0.0323
12/14	0.0379	0.0717	-0.1376	-0.0169
01/15	-0.0177	-0.0497	-0.0311	0.0467
02/15	0.0457	0.0694	0.0346	0.0423
03/15	0.0913	0.0215	0.0147	0.049
04/15	0.1566	0.017	-0.0633	-0.0043
05/15	-0.0138	0.0476	0.0647	0.0262
06/15	0.0313	-0.0154	0.0128	-0.0549
07/15	0.1368	0.0268	0.056	0.0501
08/15	-0.0451	-0.0178	-0.0282	-0.0403
09/15	-0.0788	-0.0035	0.0389	-0.016

Continued on following page

Table 7. Continued

Date (mm/yy)	Asset 1	Asset 2	Asset 3	Asset 4
10/15	0.0282	-0.0431	-0.097	-0.0058
11/15	-0.0037	0.0792	0.065	0.0281
12/15	-0.0506	0.0614	0.0339	0.0219
01/16	0.1962	-0.0031	-0.0103	0.026
02/16	0.135	-0.0122	0.0079	-0.0242
03/16	-0.0849	0.0261	0.1465	0.0868
04/16	-0.0296	0.0125	0.1298	-0.0105
05/16	-0.0058	0.0156	0.0753	0.0276
06/16	-0.067	-0.0324	0.0114	-0.0115
07/16	0.0855	-0.0447	-0.1239	-0.019
08/16	0.0664	0.0174	0.1513	0.0183
09/16	0.0883	-0.0214	-0.045	0.0921
10/16	0.0352	0.0805	0.051	0.0392
11/16	-0.0024	0.0064	0.0303	0.0113
12/16	-0.0282	-0.0135	0.0047	-0.0047
01/17	0.0344	-0.0186	-0.053	-0.0079
02/17	0.0268	0.0071	0.0597	0.0075
03/17	0.0354	-0.0089	-0.0188	0.0369
04/17	0.0143	0.0324	0.0207	0.016

Chapter 10
Risk Assessment in Investment Portfolio

ABSTRACT

A practical risk analysis in investment management for portfolio selection is presented. The purpose is to achieve investment objectives by controlling risk. Stochastic optimization and simulation are used to perform the risk analysis. Optimization is applied to resolve the efficient frontier of optimal portfolios with an expected return in a predefined range with a determined increment. The simulation calculates and measures the portfolio return, standard deviation, value at risk (VAR), Sharpe ratio, and beta of efficient frontier portfolios. The simulation sensitivity analysis identifies the riskiest asset. The what-if analysis ranks the inputs by the variability of the output based on the calculation and quantifies the minimum and maximum values, and the change percentages of the output for the associated minimum and maximum values of the input, reporting the input base value. This analysis provides for the selection of technically the best efficient frontier portfolio with maximum Sharpe ratio.

INTRODUCTION

This chapter presents a practical approach to Risk Analysis of Investment Management. The presented model is generic, considering the major financial aspects of Investment Management.

According to Bernstein and Damodaran (1998), the investment process comprises the following sub-processes: Understanding the Investor/Client (not presented); Portfolio Construction involving Asset Allocation, Asset Selection, Portfolio Optimisation, and Portfolio Selection (presented); Portfolio Execution (not presented); Ongoing Portfolio Management including Performance Evaluation, Financial Risk Portfolio and Portfolio Revision (not presented).

Portfolio Construction is as follows:

a) Determine the Efficient Frontier of minimal mean-variance portfolios;
b) Calculate/measure expected return and associated risk factors;
c) Select the portfolio with the maximal Sharpe Ratio as an optimal portfolio;

DOI: 10.4018/979-8-3693-3787-5.ch010

d) Apply Sensitivity analysis for risk attribution of the optimal portfolio.

The optimisation model should construct the Efficient Frontier of minimal mean-variance portfolios with an expected return in the range of 9.1%, 9.2%…, and 9.5% (i.e., with an increment of 0.1%).

The simulation model should calculate and measure the expected return, Variance, Standard Deviation, VAR, Sharpe Ratio, and Beta. Select the optimal portfolio from the Efficient Frontier based on the criteria of maximum Sharpe Ratio. Apply Sensitivity analysis for risk attribution of the optimal portfolio.

It should be noted that there are five Efficient Frontier portfolios, for which the Portfolio Return Mean is presented. Because the applied methods are the same for all portfolios, only the optimal portfolio with a return of 9.3% is fully demonstrated.

To facilitate the approach's demonstration, a simplistic approach is taken by using a hypothetical scenario. The assets' returns however are actual financial market data. The assumptions are the following.

a) The client is a conservative investor. They aim to invest in a portfolio less volatile than the market index (i.e., Portfolio's Beta is positive and less than one). Their liabilities are estimated at 5%.
b) The expected return is in the range of 9.1%–9.5%, which is sufficient to cover the liabilities and gain a surplus;
c) The actual market data for the assets considered are available from January 2009 to April 2016 inclusive; Only the data from January 2009 to October 2015 are used for Portfolio Construction; The data from November 2015 to April 2016 are used for verification of the approach's results; The present date is 1 November 2015; The objective is to construct and select an optimal portfolio for a time horizon of one year;

A simulation model is designed and run to calculate the variables for the risk analysis. What-if and Sensitivity Analysis are applied, which provide a comprehensive view of the probability of the outputs and quantify the sensitivity of the outputs based on the variability of the associated inputs and financial variables.

This risk analysis helps management to decide whether to execute the optimal portfolio.

Literature

Some references for Risk Analysis and Investment Management are given below. Bernstein and Damodaran (1998) elaborated on the investment process emphasizing the importance of the process; in particular, the process is generic regardless of what the investment philosophy is or which investment strategy is applied, or what assets are involved. Also, Maginn et al. (2007) presented and defined Investment Management as an ongoing process. Asset and Liability Management (ALM) originated from the duration analysis a long while ago (Macaulay 1938, Redington 1952). Subsequently, ALM has evolved into a powerful and integrated tool for analysis of assets and liabilities to value not only the interest rate risk but the liquidity risk, solvency risk, firm strategies, and asset allocation as well (Bloomsbury 2012). The frontier of ALM is based on stochastic optimisation and Monte Carlo Simulation (Bourdeau 2009). Mitra & Schwaiger (2011) published ALM quantitative decision models. Also, Adam (2007) presented advanced ALM stochastic models.

The problem of asset allocation for portfolio optimisation was solved by Markowitz (1952; 1987) in the 1950s. Markowitz applied his award-winning Mean Variance method. Nowadays, stochastic optimisation is used to resolve the optimal portfolio. Stochastic optimisation models in Finance are elaborated in a book edited by Ziemba & Vickson (2006). Also, advanced Financial Risk models are stochastic and use Monte Carlo Simulation. A comprehensive elaboration on general applications of Monte Carlo Simulation in Finance was published by Glasserman (2004). Performance Evaluation and Risk Attribution are important aspects to emphasize. Plantinga (2007) discussed methodologies for measuring and evaluating the investment process performance considering Sharpe Ratio, Jensen's Alpha, Treynor Ratio, Information Ratio, and downside risk measures. Lawton & Jankowski (2009) edited a collection of today's most prominent industry professionals and academic works focusing on investment performance evaluation. Busse, Goyal & Wahal (2010) used to aggregate and average estimates of alphas for performance measurement of institutional investment management. Jorion (2011), in his book on financial risk management, presented the utilisation of the Monte Carlo Simulation for options' valuation and Value at Risk (VAR) calculation. He also generally elaborated on Optimal Hedging, applying the Optimal Hedge Ratio, i.e., the minimal variance hedge ratio. In addition, he specifically described the application of Optimal Hedging in two important cases: Duration Hedging and Beta Hedging.

The Problem Statement: Perform an Investment Management Risk Analysis. Create The optimisation model should construct the Efficient Frontier of minimal mean-variance portfolios with an expected return in the range of 9.1%, 9.2%..., and 9.5% (i.e., with an increment of 0.1%). The simulation model should calculate and measure the expected return, Variance, Standard Deviation, VAR, Sharpe Ratio, and Beta. Select the optimal portfolio from the Efficient Frontier based on the criteria of maximum Sharpe Ratio. Apply Sensitivity analysis for risk attribution of the optimal portfolio.

The Compounded Monthly Return (CMR) is calculated for each month and each asset (i.e., CMR1, CMR2, CMR3, and CMR4) from the respective given asset's Monthly Return (MR) using the following formula: *CMR = ln (1 + MR) (1)*

Fitting Distributions

For the Monte Carlo method, the distribution of the CMR for each asset is required. Thus, for each asset, the best-fit distribution is determined based on the Chi-Square measure. The standard "fit distribution to data" feature of Palisade™ @RISK® is used. For example, the best-fit distribution for the CMR of Fund 2 (i.e., *CMR2*) is the normal distribution, with a Mean Return of 0.6% and a Standard Deviation of 4.7%. Similarly, the best-fit distribution is determined for all selected assets for the portfolio.

Asset Correlation

The MR and CMR of the assets are correlated. This correlation needs to be determined to allow the Monte Carlo method to generate correlated random values for CMR. The correlation coefficients matrix is calculated by using the standard data correlation feature of Microsoft™ Excel®.

Generating Compounded Monthly Return

The CMR is randomly generated for each asset from the best-fit distribution considering the correlations. The correlation is applied by using the *"RiskCorrmat"* function of the Palisade™ *@RISK®*. The following distribution functions of the Palisade™ @RISK® are used: *CMR1= RiskWeibull(6.9531,0.46395, Shift(-0.42581)) (2)*

CMR2= RiskNormal(0.0060531,0.047225) (3)

CMR3= RiskLogistic(0.0091429,0.044596)) (4)

CMR4= RiskLognorm(1.1261,0.077433, Shift(-1.1203)) (5)

Calculating Compounded Annual Return

The Compounded Annual Return (*CAR*) is calculated for each asset from the respective *CMR*, using the following formula:

CAR = 12*CMR (6)

Calculating Expected Annual Return – Mean

The Expected Annual Return – Mean (*EARMean*) is calculated from the assets' Weights Vector (*WeightsV*) and the CAR Vector (*CARV*) by using the following Excel® formula:

EARMean = SumProduct(WeightsV, CARV) (7)

Calculating Variance, Standard Deviation, and Value at Risk

The Variance, Standard Deviation, and VAR of the portfolio are stochastically calculated from the distribution of the Expected Annual Return Mean (EAR- Mean) of the portfolio. So, the following Palisade™ @RISK® functions are used:

Variance = RiskVariance(EARMean) (8)

StandardDeviation = RiskStdDev(EARMean) (9)

VAR = RiskPercentile(EARMean,0.005) (10)

Note: VAR is calculated with a Confidence Probability of 99.95%.

Calculating Sharpe Ratio and Beta

Sharpe Ratio is a portfolio performance measure compared to the Free Risk Rate concerning the risk associated with it. A higher Sharpe Ratio indicates a better portfolio performance in response to the risk involved. Sharpe Ratio is calculated by using the following formula:

$$\text{SharpeRatio} = (\mu - r) / \sigma \quad (11)$$

where, μ = *EARMean* (i.e., Expected Annual Return Mean), σ = *StandardDeviation*, r = *RiskFreeRate*, which is estimated to be 5.35%.

Beta is a portfolio risk measure relative to the Market Index over a specific time horizon. Lower Beta indicates lower portfolio risk, which is suitable for conservative investors. Higher Beta relates to higher portfolio risk, which makes the portfolio more unpredictable (volatile) in nature. Beta is interpreted as the slope of the regression of the portfolio returns on those of the Market Index over the time horizon. Beta is calculated with the following formula:

$$\text{Beta} = \text{CorrelationPM} (\sigma P / \sigma M) \quad (12)$$

where, *CorrelationPM* is the Portfolio–Market Index Correlation Coefficient over the time horizon, σP is the Standard Deviation of the Portfolio over the time horizon, and σM is the Standard Deviation of the Market Index over the time horizon.

Measuring Efficient Frontier Portfolios

The simulation is run and the results are presented below. It is assumed that Asset Allocation and Selection are completed and Fund 1, Fund 2, Fund 3, and Fund 4 are selected. The Monthly Return (MR) of the four selected assets is available for the period from January 2009 to October 2015 (Ref. Appendix). Stochastic optimisation is used to resolve the Efficient Frontier of minimal mean-variance portfolios, which yields sufficient return to cover the liabilities and gain a maximum surplus with minimal risk.

The stochastic optimisation model minimising the mean-variance of the portfolios subject to the following specific constraints: a) the expected portfolio return is from 9.1% to 9.5% in 0.1% increments, i.e., five Efficient Frontier portfolios; b) All the money, i.e., 100% of the available funds, are invested; and c) No short selling is allowed so all the fractions of the capital placed in each asset should be non-negative.

Table 1 shows the Mean Return (μ) and the investment fractions.

Table 1. The efficient frontier portfolios' investment fractions

µ	Fund 1	Fund 2	Fund 3	Fund 4
0.091	0.29440	0.40323	0.30237	0
0.092	0.30565	0.37249	0.32186	0
0.093	0.31689	0.34175	0.34136	0
0.094	0.32814	0.31101	0.36085	0
0.095	0.33938	0.28027	0.38035	0

Table 2 shows the Mean Return (μ), Variance (V), Standard Deviation (σ), *VAR*, Sharpe Ratio (*SR*), and Beta (β).

Table 2. The efficient frontier portfolios' details

µ	V	ó	VAR	SR	â
0.091	0.233	0.473	-0.188	0.0776	0.723
0.092	0.242	0.491	-0.225	0.0784	0.730
0.093	0.252	0.502	-0.291	0.0787	0.740
0.094	0.267	0.517	-0.375	0.0784	0.756
0.095	0.293	0.541	-0.491	0.0767	0.777

Efficient Frontier Optimal Portfolios

The Efficient Frontier of the optimal portfolios is presented in Figure 1. The Efficient Frontier curve shows that an increase in the expected return of the portfolio causes an increase in the portfolio Standard Deviation. To emphasise, the Efficient Frontier gets flattered as expected. This shows that each additional unit of Standard Deviation (i.e., risk) allowed, increases the portfolio Mean Return by less and less.

Figure 1. Efficient frontier of optimal portfolios

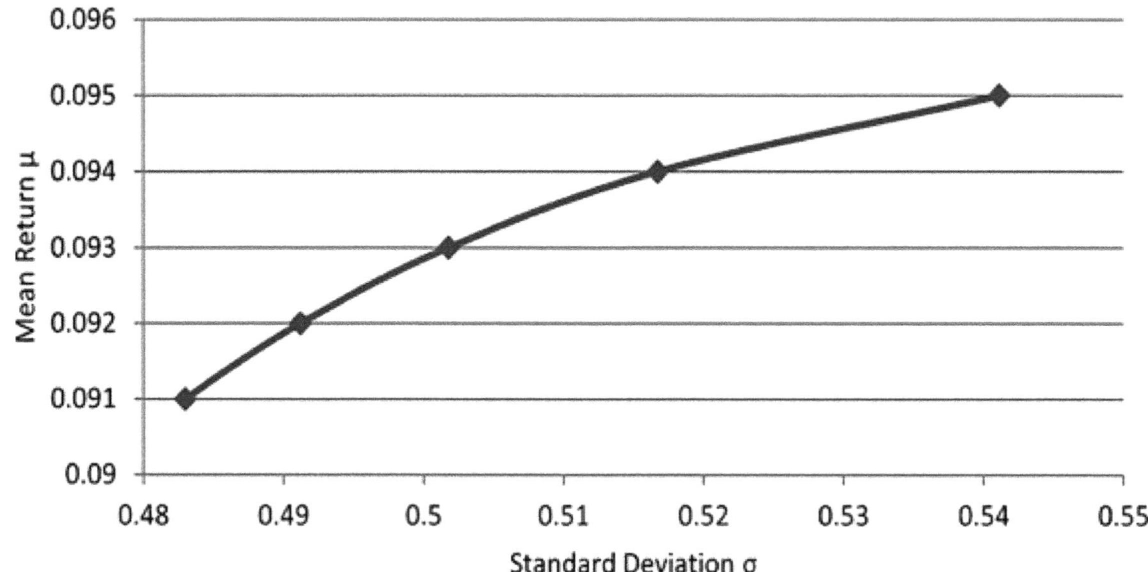

Expected Mean Return vs. VAR

Expected Mean Return vs. VAR is presented in Figure 2.

Figure 2. Expected mean return vs. VAR

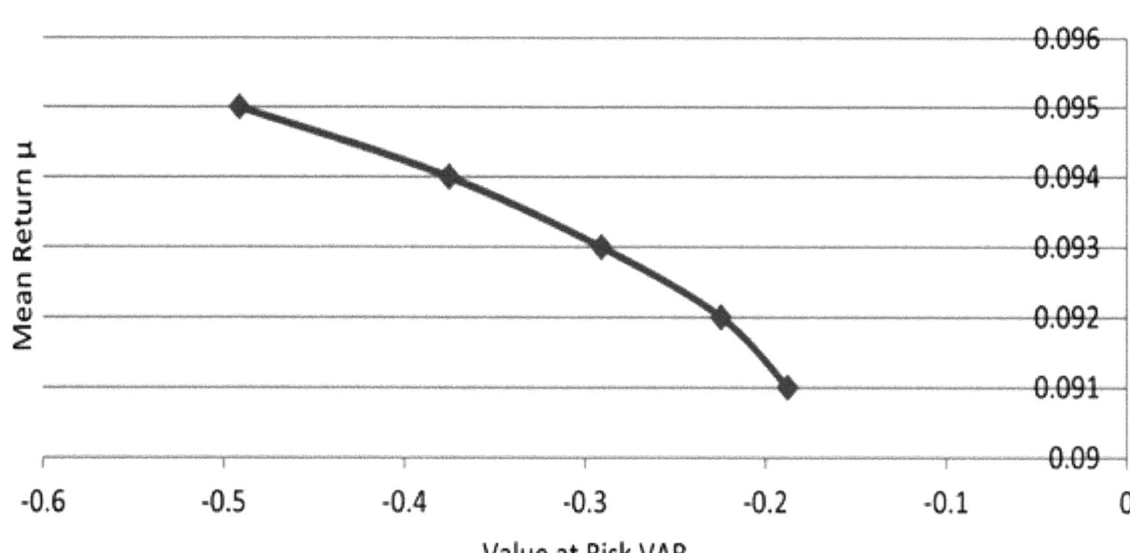

This graph shows that an increase in the expected return of the portfolio causes an increase in the portfolio VAR (Note: VAR is mathematically a negative number). As the return increases, the curve gets flattered as expected showing that each additional unit of VAR, increases the portfolio Mean Return by less and less.

Sharpe Ratio

Figure 3 shows the Sharpe Ratio of the frontier portfolios. Usually, a common goal in investments is to choose a portfolio that maximises the Sharpe Ratio. From the graph, it is possible to see that this is the portfolio with a Mean Return of 9.3% and the Sharpe Ratio of 0.07872 is technically the best investment portfolio considering the Sharpe Ratio criteria. Therefore, this portfolio should be selected for execution in the market.

Figure 3. Sharpe ratio of the efficient portfolios

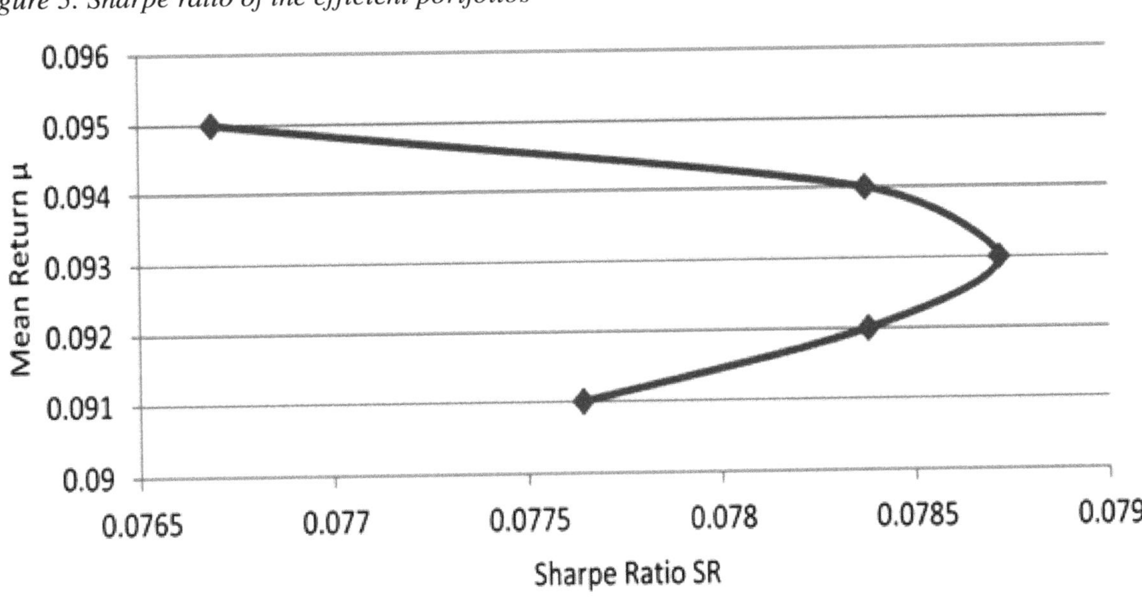

Evaluation of Optimal Portfolio with Mean Return of 0.091

The distribution of the Optimal Portfolio with a *Mean* Return of 0.091 is shown in Figure 4.

Figure 4. Portfolio mean return 0.091 distribution

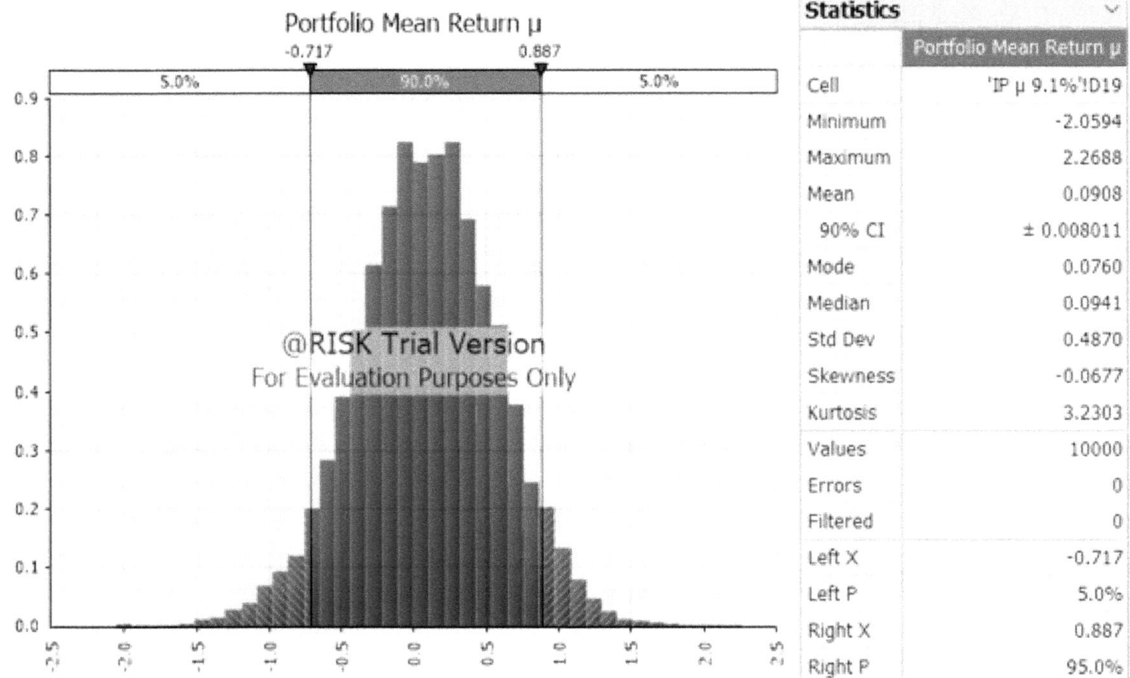

Statistics	Portfolio Mean Return μ
Cell	'IP μ 9.1%'!D19
Minimum	-2.0594
Maximum	2.2688
Mean	0.0908
90% CI	± 0.008011
Mode	0.0760
Median	0.0941
Std Dev	0.4870
Skewness	-0.0677
Kurtosis	3.2303
Values	10000
Errors	0
Filtered	0
Left X	-0.717
Left P	5.0%
Right X	0.887
Right P	95.0%

Figure 4 shows that the *Mean* is 0.0908 with a *Standard Deviation* of 0.4870, i.e., 536.344%, which is a very high risk. There is a 5.0% probability that the *Mean* will be below -0.717; a 90.0% probability that it will be in the range -0.717 – 0.887; and a 5.0% probability that it will be above 0.887.

Evaluation of Optimal Portfolio with Mean of 0.092

The distribution of the Optimal Portfolio with a *Mean* Return of 0.092 is shown in Figure 5. The *Mean* is 0.0918 with a *Standard Deviation* of 0.4953, i.e., 539.542%, which is a very high risk. There is a 5.0% probability that the *Mean* will be below -0.729; a 90.0% probability that it will be in the range -0.729 – 0.892; and a 5.0% probability that it will be above 0.892.

Figure 5. Portfolio mean return 0.092 distribution

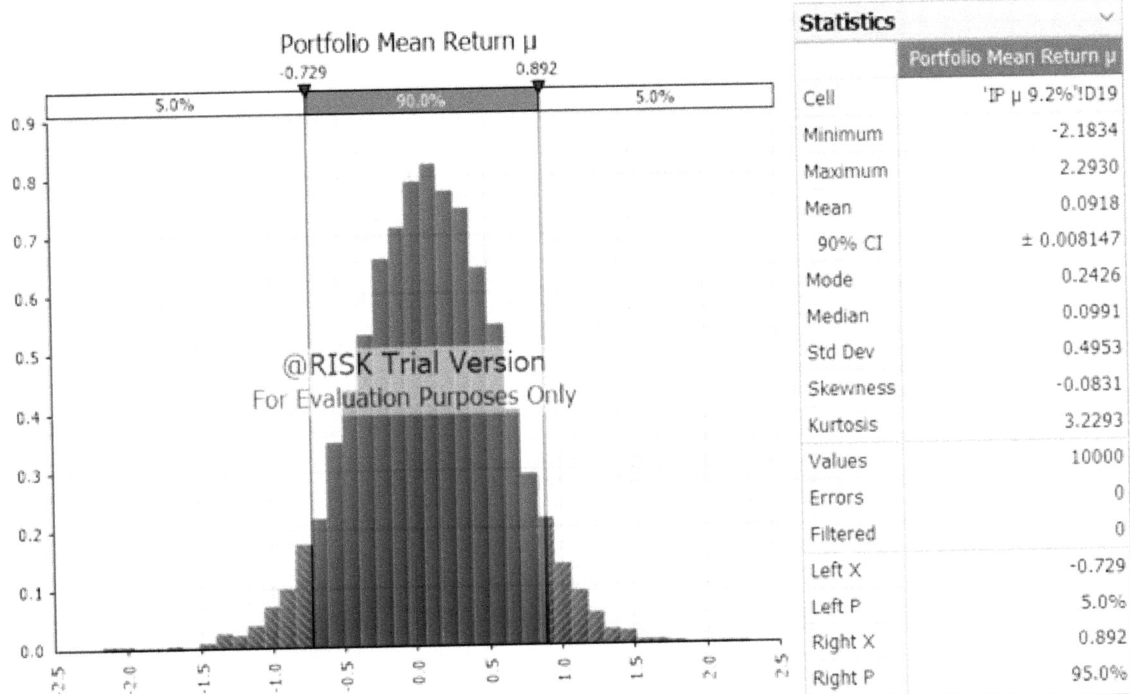

Evaluation of Optimal Portfolio with Mean of 0.093

The distribution of the Optimal Portfolio with a *Mean* Return of 0.093 is shown in Figure 6. The *Mean* is 0.0929 with a *Standard Deviation* of 0.5067, i.e., 545.425%, which is a very high risk. There is a 5.0% probability that the *Mean* will be below -0.754; a 90.0% probability that it will be in the range -0.754 – 0.910; and a 5.0% probability that it will be above 0.910.

Figure 6. Portfolio mean return 0.093 distribution

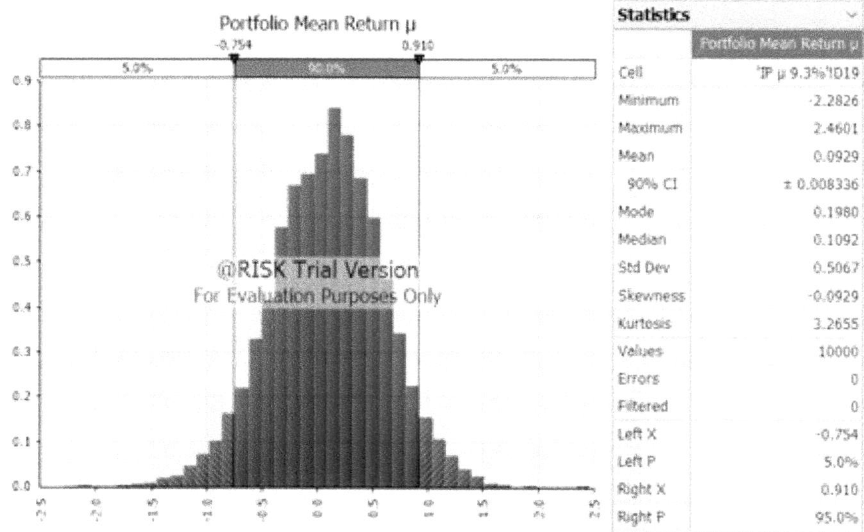

Evaluation of Optimal Portfolio with Mean of 0.094

The distribution of the Optimal Portfolio with a *Mean* Return of 0.094 is shown in Figure 7.

Figure 7. Portfolio mean return 0.094 distribution

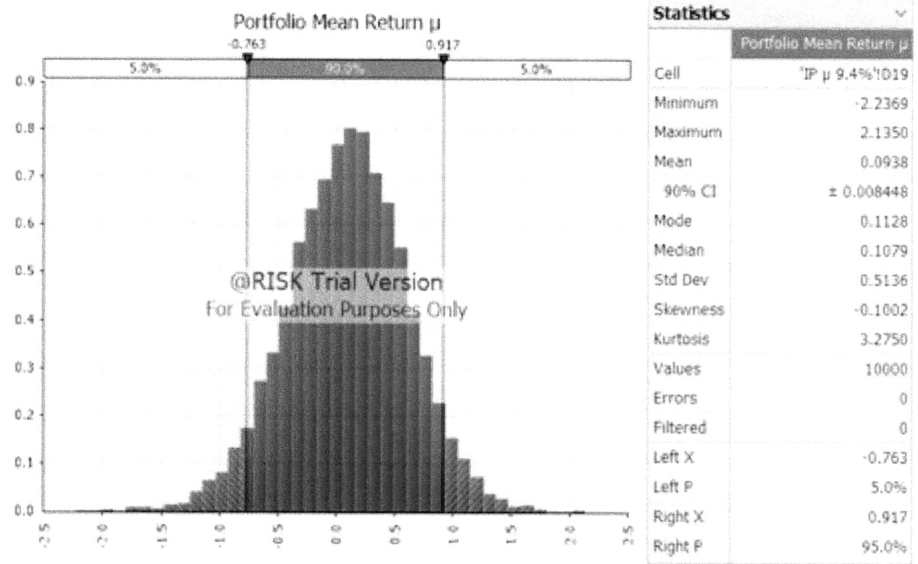

The *Mean* is 0.0938 with a *Standard Deviation* of 0.5136, i.e., 547.548%, which is a very high risk (Figure 7). There is a 5.0% probability that the *Mean* will be below -0.763; a 90.0% probability that it will be in the range -0.763 – 0.917; and a 5.0% probability that it will be above 0.917.

Evaluation of Optimal Portfolio with Mean of 0.095

The distribution of the Optimal Portfolio with a *Mean* Return of 0.095 is shown in Figure 8.

Figure 8. Portfolio mean return 0.095 distribution

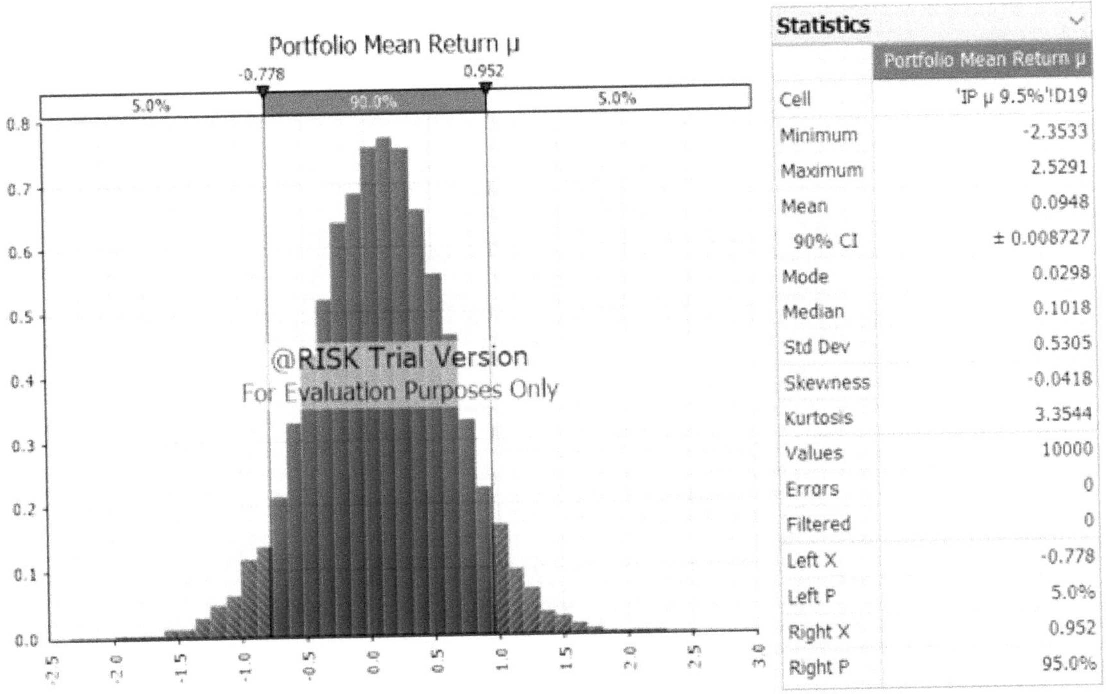
Portfolio Mean Return μ
-0.778
0.952
5.0%
90.0%
5.0%
@RISK Trial Version
For Evaluation Purposes Only
Statistics
Portfolio Mean Return μ
Cell 'IP μ 9.5%'!D19
Minimum -2.3533
Maximum 2.5291
Mean 0.0948
90% CI ± 0.008727
Mode 0.0298
Median 0.1018
Std Dev 0.5305
Skewness -0.0418
Kurtosis 3.3544
Values 10000
Errors 0
Filtered 0
Left X -0.778
Left P 5.0%
Right X 0.952
Right P 95.0%

Figure 8 shows the *Mean* is 0.0948 with a *Standard Deviation* of 0.5305, i.e., 559.599%, which is a very high risk. There is a 5.0% probability that the *Mean* will be below -0.778; a 90.0% probability that it will be in the range -0.778 – 0.952; and a 5.0% probability that it will be above 0.952.

The Best Portfolio Evaluation, Sensitivity, and What-If Analysis

It was established that the portfolio with a Mean Return of 9.3% and a Sharpe Ratio of 0.07872 is technically the best investment portfolio considering the Sharpe Ratio criteria, which is selected for execution in the market. Therefore, this portfolio is considered below.

Portfolio Mean Return 9.3% Evaluation, Sensitivity, and What-If Analysis

Evaluation

The Portfolio Mean Return of 9.3% evaluation is considered above (Figure 6). A closer look at the Mean Return 9.3% distribution is shown in Figure 9.

Figure 9. Portfolio mean return 9.3% distribution vs. target limits

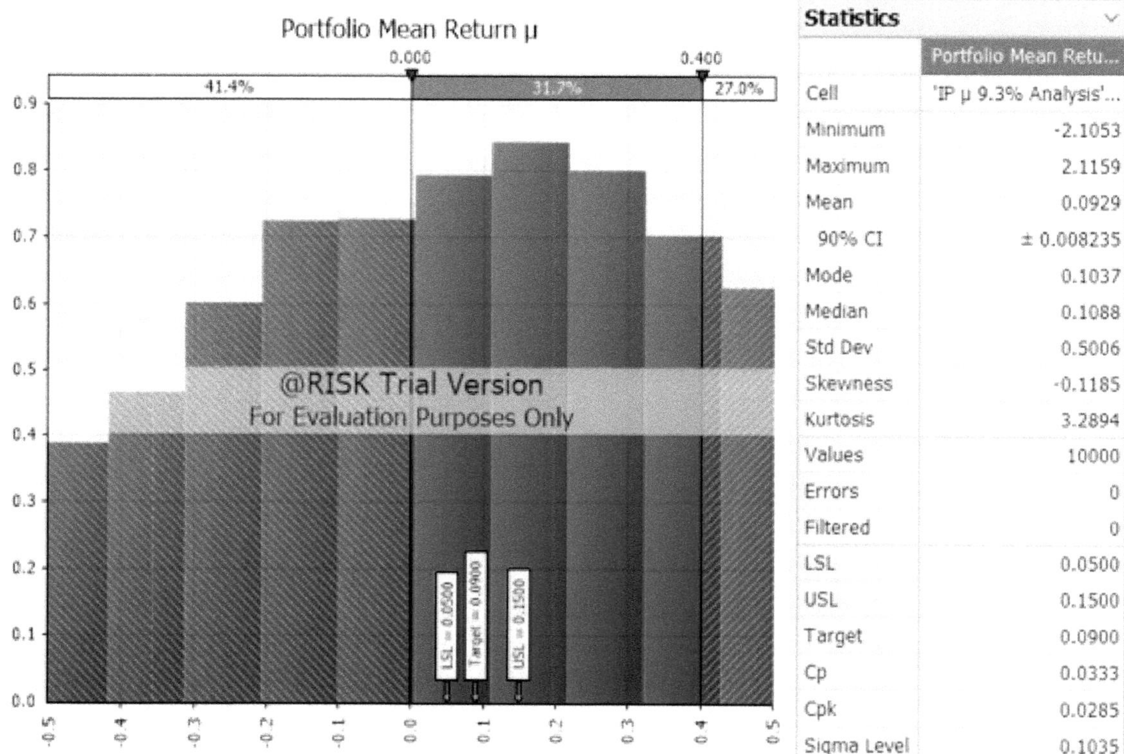

In Figure 9, the *Mean* is 0.0929 (i.e., 9.29%) with a *Standard Deviation* of 0.5006, i.e., 538.859%, which is a very high risk. The Six Sigma target parameters are $TV = 0.0900$; $LSL = 0.0500$; and $USL = 0.1500$. The Six Sigma process capability metrics are $Cp = 0.0333$; $Cpk = 0.0285$; and $\sigma\text{-}L = 0.1035$. There is a 41.4% probability that the *Mean* will be negative, i.e., below zero; 31.7% probability that it will be in the range \$0.00 – 0.400; and 27.0% probability that it will be above 0.400.

Sensitivity Analysis

Sensitivity analysis provides for identifying and quantifying the main contributors to variability and risk based on probability distribution.

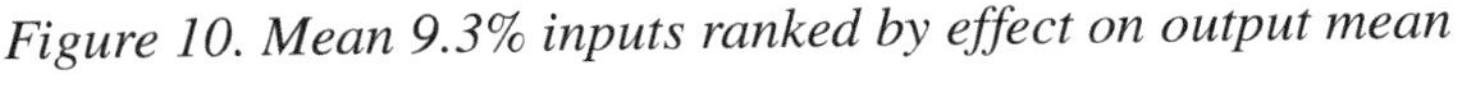

Figure 10. Mean 9.3% inputs ranked by effect on output mean

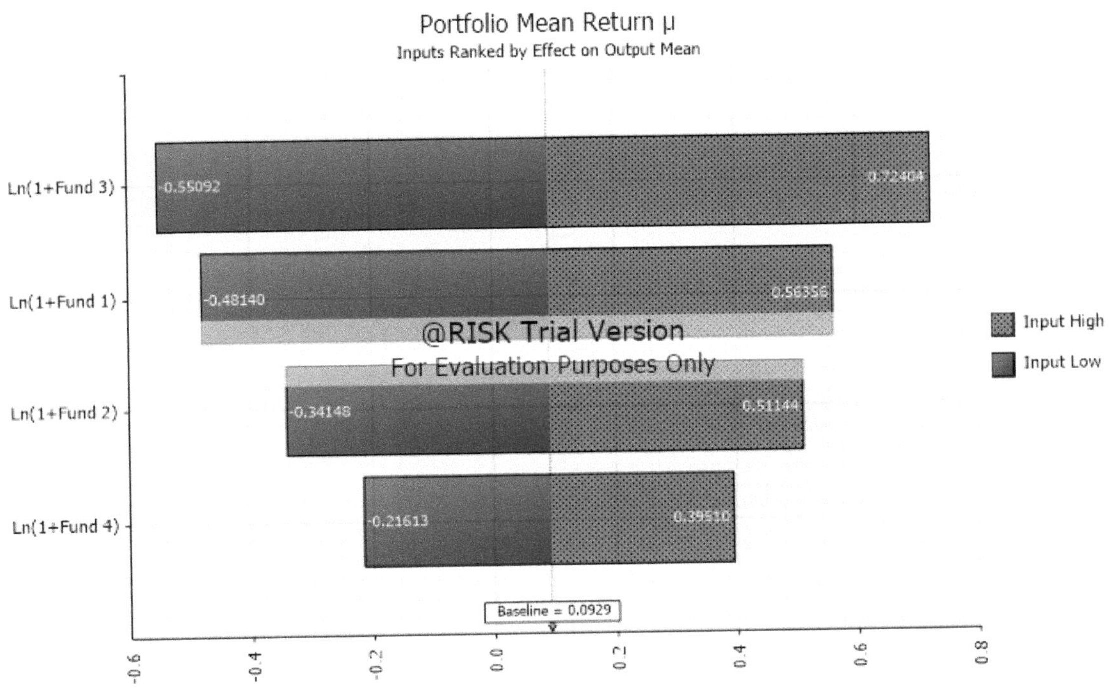

The Inputs Ranked by Effect on Output Mean graph in Figure 10.10 illustrates that the effect of the top variable, Fund 3 (i.e., the formula: Ln (1+Fund 3)), on the Portfolio Mean Return, is a change in the range of -0.55092 to 0.72404, which are respectively left and right from the Baseline of 0.0929, which is marked on the graph. Other variables are less influential as their associated effects have smaller ranges.

The Regression Coefficients graph (Figure 11) illustrates that if the top variable, Fund 3, with a regression coefficient of 0.66, changes by one Standard Deviation, the *Mean* will change by 0.66 Standard Deviations. The other two variables are less influential as their regression coefficients are 0.56 and 0.39.

Figure 11. Mean 9.3% regression coefficients

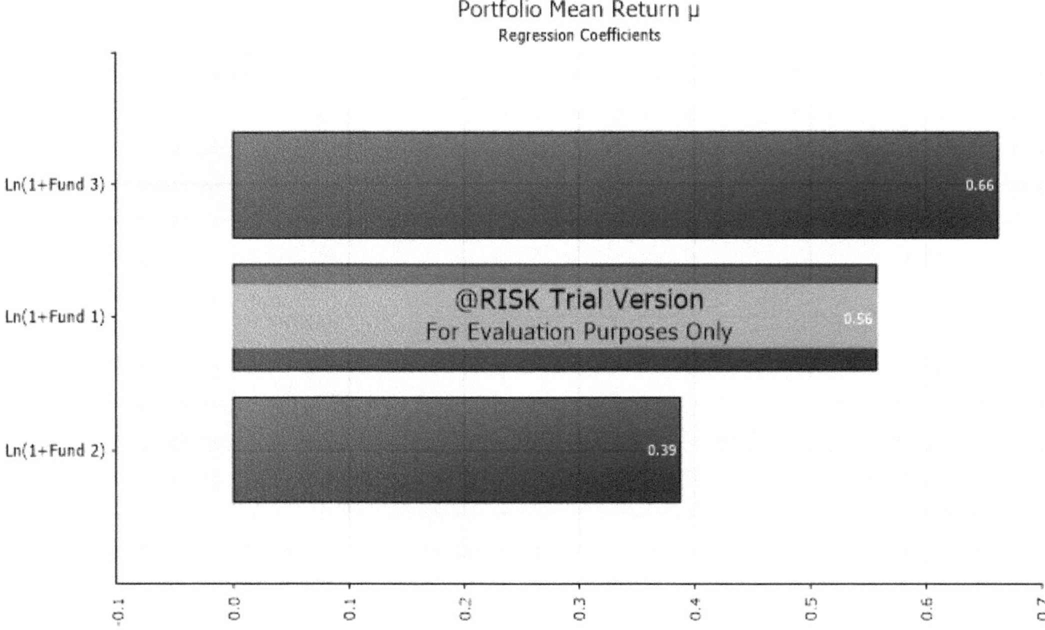

The Correlation Coefficients are presented in Figure 12.

Figure 12 shows that if the top variable, Fund 3, with a correlation coefficient of 0.68, changes by one unit, the *Mean* will change by 0.68 units. The other variables are less influential as their correlation coefficients are in the range of 0.60 to 0.33 from top to bottom.

Figure 12. Mean 9.3% correlation coefficients

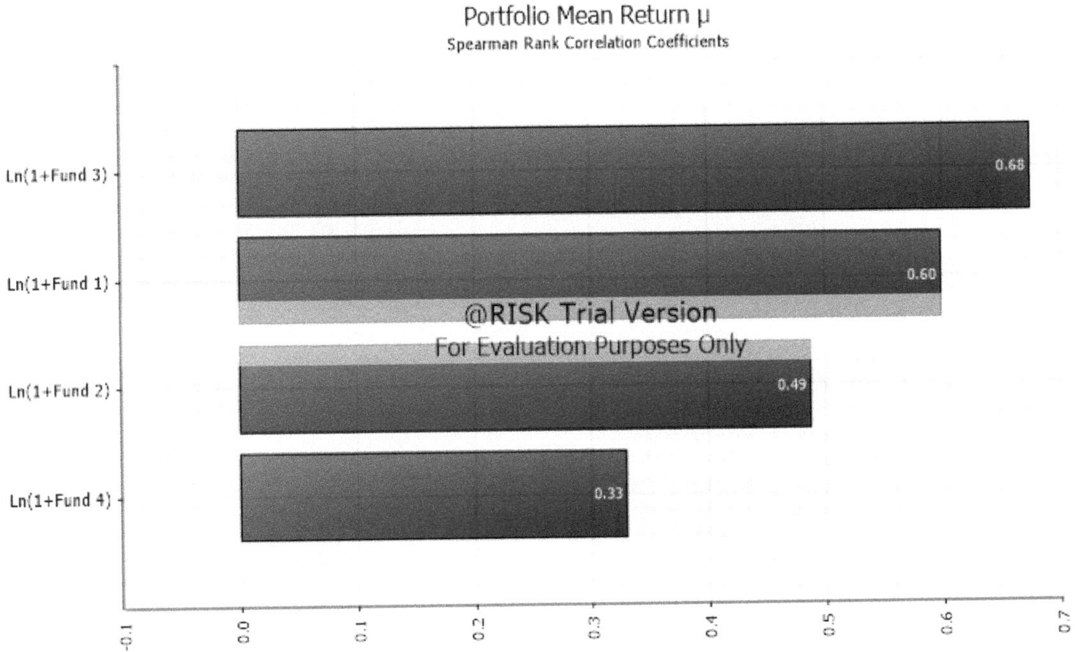

The Contribution to Variance is presented in Figure 13.

Figure 13. Mean 9.3% contribution to variance

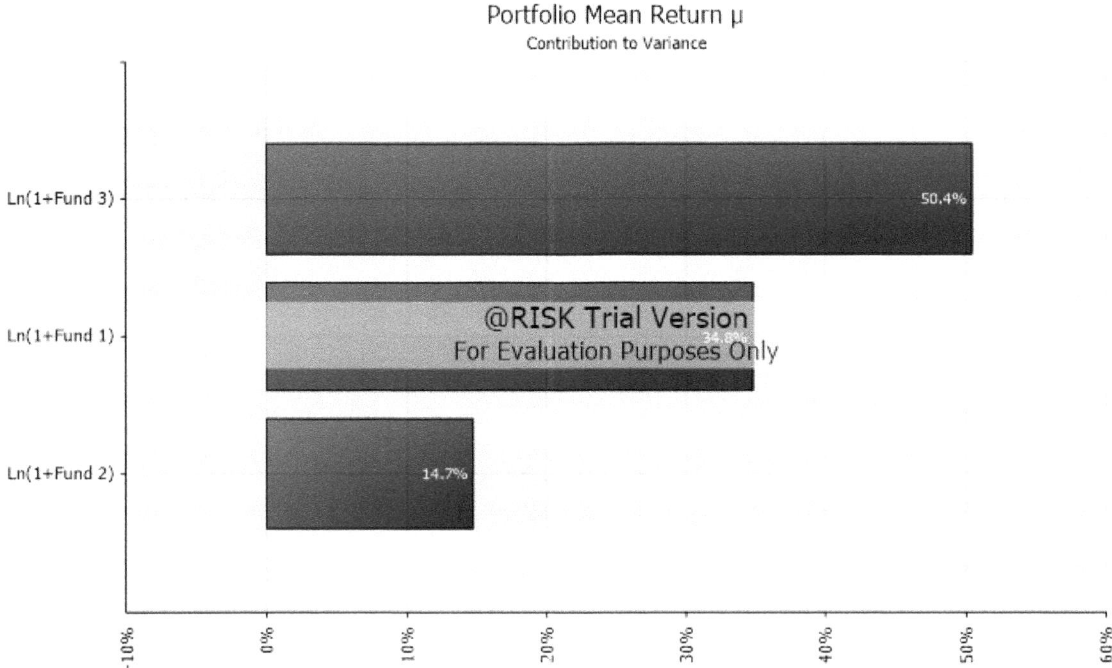

The graph illustrates that the top variable (Figure 13), Fund 3, has a contribution of 50.4% to the variance of the *Mean*. The other two variables are less influential as their contributions are 34.8% and 14.7%.

What-If Analysis

The What-If analysis provides for ranking the inputs by the variability of the output based on the calculation without a probability distribution. It also quantifies the minimum and maximum values and the percentage changes of the output for the associated minimum and maximum values of the input, reporting the input base value.

The Portfolio Return 9.3% tornado graph is given in Figure 14.

Figure 14. Portfolio return 9.3% tornado graph

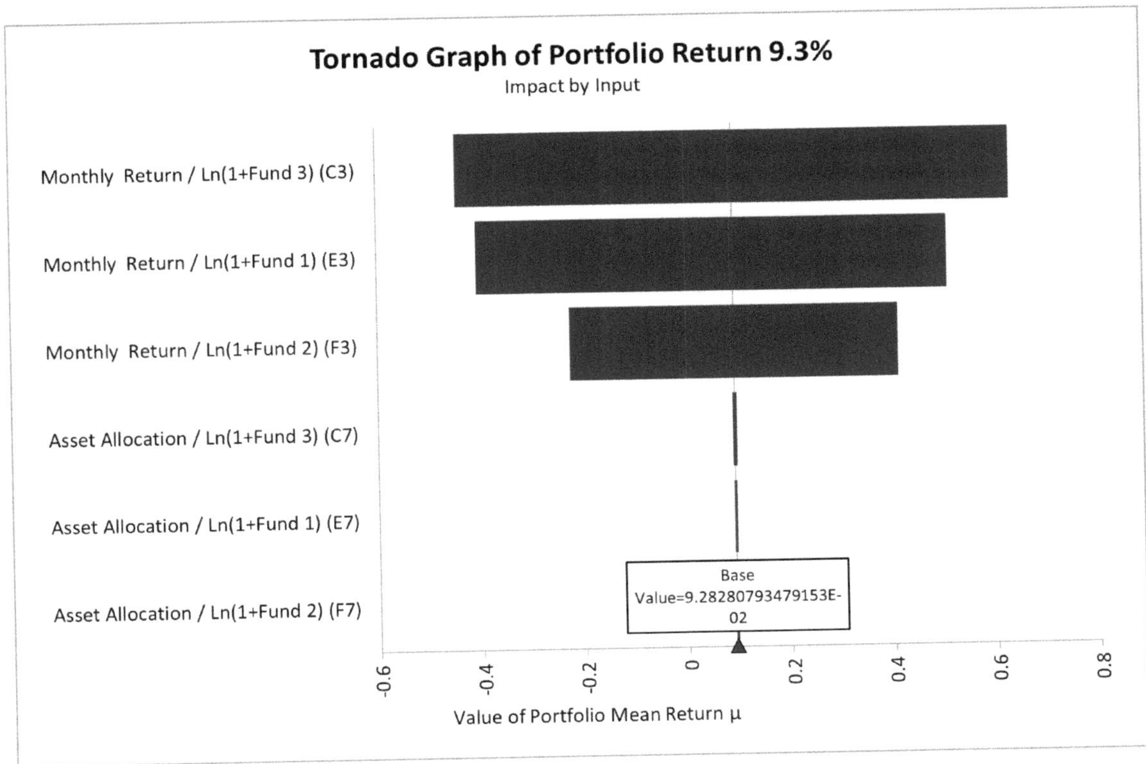

The graph shows the return values on the x-axis. It illustrates that the return Base Value is 9.2828%, which is marked on the graph and is calculated from the independent variable Base values given in Table 3. The bars on the graph quantify the variability of the return from every independent variable showing the Minimum and Maximum, which are respectively left and right from the Base value. The return Minimum and Maximum are respectively calculated from the independent variable Minimum and Maximum values are given in Table 3.

Figure 14 also shows that the three most influential input variables are: 1) Fund 3 Monthly Return; 2) Fund 1 Monthly Return; and 3) Fund 2 Monthly Return. The other input variables are insignificantly influential.

The What-If Analysis Summary for Portfolio Return 9.3% is presented in Table 3. The Summary table quantifies the minimum and maximum values and changes the percentage of the output for the associated minimum and maximum values of the input, as well as the input base value.

Table 3. What-if analysis summary for portfolio return 9.3%

What-If Analysis Summary for Output Portfolio Return 9.3%								
Top 3 Inputs Ranked by Change in Actual Value								
		Minimum			Maximum			
		Output		Input	Output		Input	Input
Rank	**Input Name**	**Value**	**Change (%)**	**Value**	**Value**	**Change (%)**	**Value**	**Base Value**
1	Month. Return Fund 3	-0.4451	-579.44%	-0.1222	0.6307	579.44%	0.1405	0.0091
2	Month. Return Fund 1	-0.4060	-537.41%	-0.1232	0.5089	448.19%	0.1174	0.0080
3	Month. Return Fund 2	-0.2257	-343.17%	-0.0716	0.4114	343.17%	0.0837	0.0061

1) Monthly Return Fund 3: The input base value is 0.91% (i.e., 0.0091). The input minimum value is -12.22%, for which the return has a minimum of -44.51%, i.e., a change of -579.44% from the Return Base Value of 9.2828%. The input maximum value is 14.05%, for which the Return has a maximum of 63.07%, i.e., a change of 479.44% from the return Base Value.
2) Monthly Return Fund 1: The input base value is 0.80% (i.e., 0.0080). The input minimum value is -12.32%, for which the return has a minimum of -40.60%, i.e., a change of -537.41% from the return Base Value of 9.2828%. The input maximum value is 11.74%, for which the return has a maximum of 50.89%, i.e., a change of 448.19% from the return Base Value.
3) Monthly Return Fund 2: The input base value is 0.61% (i.e., 0.0061). The input minimum value is -7.16%, for which the return has a minimum of -22.57%, i.e., a change of -343.17% from the return Base Value of 9.2828%. The input maximum value is 8.37%, for which the return has a maximum of 41.14%, i.e., a change of 343.17% from the return Base Value.

The other input variables are insignificantly influential, so they are not considered here.

Mean Return 9.3% VAR Evaluation, Sensitivity & What-If Analysis

Evaluation

The Mean Return of 9.3% VAR distribution is shown in Figure 15.

Figure 15. Portfolio mean return 9.3% VAR distribution vs. target limits

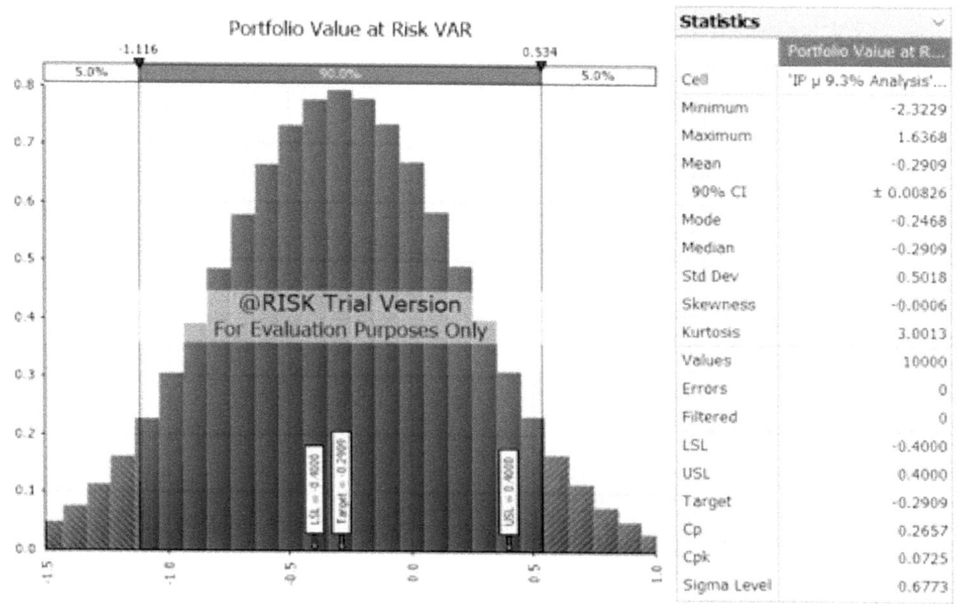

The *VAR Mean* (Figure 15) is -0.2909 (i.e., 9.29%) with a *Standard Deviation* of 0.5018, i.e., 172.499%, which is a very high risk. The Six Sigma target parameters are *TV* = -0.2909; *LSL* = -0.4000; and *USL* = 0.4000. The Six Sigma process capability metrics are *Cp* = 0.2657; *Cpk* = 0.0725; and σ-*L* = 0.6773. There is a 5.0% probability that the *VAR Mean* will be below -1.116; a 90% probability that it will be in the range -1.116 – 0.534; and a 5.0% probability that it will be above 0.534.

VAR Sensitivity and What-If Analysis

The VAR calculation has no independent input variables. Therefore, Sensitivity and What-If Analysis of VAR are not applicable.

CONCLUSION

This chapter presented a comprehensive Investment Management Risk Analysis. It was applied in Finance to manage the market risk of an investment portfolio, which is a part of Portfolio Management.

The market data were considered and calculations for the optimisation and simulation models were defined. Also, stochastic optimisation constructed the Efficient Frontier of five minimal mean-variance portfolios with an expected return in the range of 9.1%–9.5% with an increment of 0.1%. Monte Carlo simulation stochastically calculated and measured the expected mean return, Variance, Standard Deviation, VAR, Sharpe Ratio, and Beta of the Efficient Frontier portfolios.

The analysis of the simulation results determined technically the best optimal portfolio from the Efficient Frontier based on the criteria of maximum Sharpe Ratio. This optimal portfolio had a mean

Return, of 9.3%; Standard Deviation, of 50.06%; VAR, -of 29.09%; Sharpe Ratio, of 0.0787, and Beta, of 0.74. The major risk factor, Standard Deviation, indicated that the risk is high.

Sensitivity and What-If Analysis were applied, which provided a comprehensive view of the probability of the outputs, and quantified the sensitivity of the outputs based on the variability of the associated inputs and financial variables. The sensitivity analysis of the optimal portfolio identified that the riskiest asset was Fund 3.

The technically best optimal portfolio was recommended to the management to execute the portfolio on the market. It should be noted that Standard Deviation is a major risk factor. The Standard Deviation for Mean Return is 50.06%, and for VAR is 50.18%, which is high. The conclusion is that the management (i.e., decision-makers) needs to decide whether to execute the technically best optimal portfolio based on their risk appetite.

REFERENCES

Adam, A. (2007). *Handbook of Asset and Liability Management: From Models to Optimal Return Strategies*. John Wiley & Sons.

Bernstein, P. L., & Damodaran, A. (1998). *Investment Management*. John Wiley & Sons.

Bloomsbury. (2012). *Asset Liability Management for Financial Institutions: Balancing Financial Stability with Strategic Objectives*. Bloomsbury Information Ltd.

Bourdeau, M. (2009). Market Risk Measurement Under Solvency II. In M. Cruz (Ed.), *The Solvency II Handbook* (pp. 193–226). Risk Books–Incisive Media.

Bubevski, V. (2012). *A New Practical Approach to Asset Liability Management for Basel III and Solvency II*. European Modelling & Simulation.

Bubevski, V. (2016). *A Novel Approach to Investment Portfolio*. Academic Press.

Bubevski, V. (2016a). Solvency II Internal Models – An Alternative. Frontier in Finance. doi:10.14355/ff.2016.02.001

Busse, J. A., Goyal, A., & Wahal, S. (2010). Performance and Persistence in Institutional Investment Management. *The Journal of Finance*, *65*(2), 765–790. doi:10.1111/j.1540-6261.2009.01550.x

Fabozzi, F. J. (1998). *Bank Loans: Secondary Market and Portfolio Management, –(CFA Institute investment series)*. John Wiley & Sons.

Glasserman, P. (2004). *Monte Carlo Methods in Financial Engineering*. Springer Science.

Hayler, R., & Nichols, M. D. (2006). *Six Sigma for Financial Services: How Leading Companies Are Driving Results Using Lean, Six Sigma, and Process Management*. McGraw-Hill.

Jorion, P. (2011). *Financial Risk Manager Handbook*. John Wiley & Sons.

Lawton, P., & Jankowski, T. (2009). *Investment Performance Measurement: Evaluating and Presenting Results*. CFA Institute.

Markowitz, H. M. (1952). Portfolio Selection. *The Journal of Finance*, *7*, 77–91.

Markowitz, H. M. (1987). *Mean-Variance Analysis in Portfolio Choice and Capital Markets*. Basil Blackwell.

Mitra, G., & Schwaiger, K. (2011). *Asset and Liability Management Handbook*. Palgrave Macmillan. doi:10.1057/9780230307230

Plantinga, A. (2007). *Performance Measurement and Evaluation*. Munich Personal RePEc Archive (MPRA), MPRA Paper No 5048.

Redington, F. M. (1952). *Review of the Principles of Life Office Valuations*. Academic Press.

Stamatis, D. H. (2003). *Six Sigma for Financial Professionals*. Wiley.

Ziemba, W. T., & Vickson, S. W. (Eds.). (2006). *Stochastic Optimization Models in Finance*. World Scientific. doi:10.1142/6101

APPENDIX

The monthly return of the four selected funds for the period January 2009–April 2016 is given in Table 4 (Source: Legal & General Investment Management). The data from January 2009–October 2015 are used for the method demonstration presented, and the data from November 2009–April 2016 (In Blue) are used for verification of the method's results.

Table 4. Monthly return of selected funds

Date	Fund 1	Fund 2	Fund 3	Fund 4
31/01/2009	0.0273	0.0196	0.0216	0.1192
28/02/2009	-0.003	0.0299	0.0654	-0.0052
30/03/2009	0.0722	-0.0252	-0.0597	0.0067
30/04/2009	-0.1408	0.071	-0.0414	0.0587
31/05/2009	0.024	0.0111	0.0961	-0.0088
29/06/2009	-0.0855	-0.0653	-0.0593	0.0747
31/07/2009	0.035	-0.0043	-0.0901	0.0612
31/08/2009	-0.0278	0.0086	0.0327	-0.0192
28/09/2009	0.0389	-0.0087	-0.0754	-0.0697
31/10/2009	0.0075	-0.0361	0.0953	0.0974
30/11/2009	0.0339	-0.0465	0.1839	0.0766
31/12/2009	-0.0688	0.0145	0.0477	0.027
31/01/2010	0.1495	-0.0344	0.1234	0.0367
28/02/2010	0.0492	0.0984	0.0245	0.0688
28/03/2010	0.0266	-0.027	-0.1046	-0.0288
30/04/2010	0.0722	0.0317	-0.0873	-0.0344
31/05/2010	0.0759	-0.0393	0.0411	0.1545
28/06/2010	-0.1098	-0.0727	-0.0779	-0.0357
31/07/2010	-0.038	0.0664	0.0414	-0.0161
30/08/2010	0.1448	-0.0163	-0.0294	-0.0222
30/09/2010	-0.0678	-0.0252	0.0689	-0.0108
31/10/2010	-0.1291	0.0313	-0.0484	-0.039
29/11/2010	-0.0993	-0.1306	-0.0432	-0.072
31/12/2010	0.0813	0.0402	-0.0355	-0.0395
31/01/2011	0.0544	-0.0152	0.0108	0.0833
28/02/2011	0.0538	-0.0059	-0.0201	0.1193
31/03/2011	-0.0891	-0.0436	-0.0365	-0.0153
30/04/2011	-0.0166	0.1305	0.0865	0.0919
29/05/2011	0.1186	0.0381	0.0128	-0.0255
30/06/2011	-0.0133	-0.0579	0.0779	0.0778

Continued on following page

Table 4. Continued

Date	Fund 1	Fund 2	Fund 3	Fund 4
31/07/2011	-0.0212	0.0499	-0.0301	-0.035
31/08/2011	0.0178	0.0343	-0.0674	-0.0994
30/09/2011	0.0527	0.0486	-0.0628	-0.0466
30/10/2011	0.1022	-0.0454	-0.1515	-0.0279
30/11/2011	0.0339	-0.0432	0.0376	0.0372
31/12/2011	-0.0394	0.0491	-0.2215	0
29/01/2012	-0.065	-0.0079	0.0468	-0.0097
26/02/2012	0.0383	0.0385	0.0646	0.0655
31/03/2012	0.1244	0.0154	0.0209	0.0148
30/04/2012	-0.0188	-0.0358	0.0262	-0.0231
28/05/2012	0.1278	0.0754	0.113	0.0795
30/06/2012	-0.0393	-0.0063	-0.0197	-0.0135
30/07/2012	-0.0391	0.1011	-0.0476	-0.0138
31/08/2012	-0.1904	0.0522	-0.0696	-0.0831
30/09/2012	-0.0729	-0.0037	0.0431	-0.0565
29/10/2012	-0.0979	-0.0326	-0.0089	0.0092
30/11/2012	0.1511	-0.001	0.0896	0.009
31/12/2012	0.0548	-0.0389	-0.0052	-0.0377
31/01/2013	-0.0136	0.0499	0	0.0797
28/02/2013	0.0973	-0.0758	-0.0555	-0.0297
31/03/2013	0.0217	-0.0571	0.0321	-0.0484
29/04/2013	0.0852	0.0039	0.0516	0.0359
31/05/2013	0.0006	0.0721	0.1003	-0.0321
30/06/2013	0.0313	0.0136	-0.0625	-0.0421
29/07/2013	0.0192	0.055	0.0522	0.0149
31/08/2013	0.0335	0.0058	0.1121	-0.0118
30/09/2013	-0.1006	-0.0583	0.0158	-0.0434
31/10/2013	0.0135	0.0743	0.0692	-0.0987
30/11/2013	0.0608	-0.0323	-0.0439	-0.0195
30/12/2013	-0.1376	-0.0169	0.0379	0.0717
31/01/2014	-0.0311	0.0467	-0.0177	-0.0497
28/02/2014	0.0346	0.0423	0.0457	0.0694
31/03/2014	0.0147	0.049	0.0913	0.0215
28/04/2014	-0.0633	-0.0043	0.1566	0.017
31/05/2014	0.0647	0.0262	-0.0138	0.0476
30/06/2014	0.0128	-0.0549	0.0313	-0.0154
31/07/2014	0.056	0.0501	0.1368	0.0268
31/08/2014	-0.0282	-0.0403	-0.0451	-0.0178

Continued on following page

Table 4. Continued

Date	Fund 1	Fund 2	Fund 3	Fund 4
29/09/2014	0.0389	-0.016	-0.0788	-0.0035
31/10/2014	-0.097	-0.0058	0.0282	-0.0431
30/11/2014	0.065	0.0281	-0.0037	0.0792
29/12/2014	0.0339	0.0219	-0.0506	0.0614
31/01/2015	-0.0103	0.026	0.1962	-0.0031
28/02/2015	0.0079	-0.0242	0.135	-0.0122
29/03/2015	0.1465	0.0868	-0.0849	0.0261
30/04/2015	0.1298	-0.0105	-0.0296	0.0125
31/05/2015	0.0753	0.0276	-0.0058	0.0156
28/06/2015	0.0114	-0.0115	-0.067	-0.0324
31/07/2015	-0.1239	-0.019	0.0855	-0.0447
30/08/2015	0.1513	0.0183	0.0664	0.0174
30/09/2015	-0.045	0.0921	0.0883	-0.0214
31/10/2015	0.051	0.0392	0.0352	0.0805
30/11/2015	0.031	0.0115	-0.0024	0.0065
29/12/2015	0.0048	-0.0048	-0.0287	-0.0137
31/01/2016	-0.0541	-0.008	0.0351	-0.019
28/02/2016	0.061	0.0077	0.0274	0.0073
29/03/2016	-0.0191	0.0377	0.0362	-0.0090
30/04/2016	0.0211	0.0163	0.0146	0.033

Chapter 11
Estimating Loan Interest Rates and Payments

ABSTRACT

This chapter illustrates two models for estimating variable interest rates and loan payment schedules for 21 years. In the independent rates model, the yearly interest rates are generated independently of one another. The rates are normally distributed with a given mean and standard deviation. In the random walk model, only the first interest rate is normally distributed with a given mean and standard deviation, but each succeeding interest rate is normally distributed with a mean equal to the actual previous rate and the given standard deviation. The method by which the interest rates are generated makes a substantial difference in the distribution of the total payment. Interest rates can vary much more in the random walk model, which causes a larger variation in the total payment. Compared to loan payment schedules where all payments are equal, the schedules illustrated here pay a constant principal each year but have different yearly payments.

INTRODUCTION

This chapter presents two simulation models for projecting the variable interest rates and loan payment schedules for 21 years.

The Independent Rates Model (IRM) calculates the yearly interest rates independently of one another by applying a Log-normal distribution with a given Mean and Standard Deviation. In contrast, the Random Walk Model (RWM) calculates only the Year 1 Interest Rate by applying a log-normal distribution with a given mean and standard deviation, but each succeeding Year Interest Rate is calculated by a log-normal distribution with a Mean equal to the Previous Year's calculated Interest Rate and the given standard deviation. To provide extensive analysis, five simulations are run, each with a different Mean and Standard Deviation.

The model utilises the following given data: Loan Amount, Mean Interest Rate, and Standard Deviation Interest Rate. All the given values are empirical averages of the associated historical data.

DOI: 10.4018/979-8-3693-3787-5.ch011

The simulated data are Year, IRM Interest Rate, IRM Remaining Principal, IRM Principal Payment, IRM Interest Payment, IRM Net Payment, RWM Interest Rate, RWM Remaining Principal, RWM Principal Payment, RWM Interest Payment, and RWM Net Payment. All this data is annual for 21 years.

The simulation output data comprises the Total IRM Net Payment and Total RWM Net Payment.

The method by which the interest rates are generated makes a substantial difference in the distribution of the total payment. Specifically, interest rates can vary much more in the Random Walk model, which causes a larger variation in the total payment. Compared to most typical loan payment schedules where all payments are equal, the schedules illustrated in this chapter pay a constant principal each year but have varying yearly payments.

Literature

Some references for the subjects in this chapter are given here. A history of interest rates is published by Homer & Sylla (2011). Coyle's (2004) book presents topics such as interest-rate risk exposures, fixed or floating-rate interest, term of funding and the yield curve, forward rates and the yield curve and basis risk, gap exposure, and risk price. Anderson (2020) published a financial beginners' guide on managing personal credit, debt, and savings. The U.S. Congress Committee on Government Operations (1982) published specific guidelines for small businesses on the variable interest rate. Britten-Jones (1998) in his book considers interest rates and the analytical techniques of debt valuation. The book shows that the fundamentals of fixed income and interest rate analysis can be easily understood when seen as a small number of simple economic concepts.

Wahidudin (2011) in his book considers the interest rate in the subject such as single principal sum, multiple streams of cash flows, the rates of return, security valuation, cost of capital, and capital budgeting. Zagst (2013) in his book focuses on the interest rate within subjects such as mathematical finance background, modelling and pricing, and measuring and managing interest rate risk. Cornyn (1997) publishes a practical guide for interest rate risk modelling including models such as cash flows, net investment income versus net portfolio value, projections of interest rates, and volatility. Carmona & Tehranchi (2007) published a book that studies the mathematical issues that arise in modelling the interest rate term structure. These issues are approached by casting the interest rate models as stochastic evolution equations in infinite-dimensional function spaces.

The Problem Statement

The problem is to create and run two simulation models for projecting the variable interest rates and loan payment schedules for 21 years. The Independent Rates Model (IRM) should calculate the yearly interest rates independently of one another by applying a log-normal distribution with a given Mean and Standard Deviation. In contrast, the Random Walk Model (RWM) should compute only the Year 1 Interest Rate by applying a log-normal distribution with a given mean and standard deviation, but each succeeding Year Interest Rate should be calculated by a log-normal distribution with a Mean equal to the previous year calculated Interest Rate and the given standard deviation. To provide for a wide analysis, five simulations are run, each with a different Mean and Standard Deviation. The simulation results should be evaluated, including the sensitivity analysis, to determine the major risk factors. The results should be discussed and commented on for a conclusion.

ELABORATION

The scenario presented in this chapter is hypothetical, using data published by Palisade™ Corporation.

Loan Interest Rate and Payment Schedule Data (DMAIC Define)

The data for the simulation models are presented below. The known input data is presented in Table 1:

Table 1. Known input data

Data	Value
Loan Amount	$500,000
Mean Interest Rate	=RiskSimtable({0.08,0.09,0.1,0.11,0.12})
Standard Deviation Interest Rate	=RiskSimtable({0.008,0.009,0.01,0.011,0.012})

It should be noted that the Mean Interest Rate and Standard Deviation Interest Rate are specified with the SimTable @RISK function with five values each, which will be applied by the five simulations sequentially as defined by the RiskSimtable function.

The models use the log-normal distribution applying the given Mean and Standard Deviation with associated empirically estimated parameters.

Calculations (DMAIC Define)

Microsoft™ Excel® and Palisade™ @RISK® formulae are used for the calculations presented in this section.

Independent Rates Model Calculations

The simulated data is: i) Year Vector (*YearV(i)*); ii) IRM Interest Rate Vector (*IRMIntRateV(i)*); iii) IRM Remaining Principal Vector (*IRMRemPrincV(i)*); iv) IRM Principal Payment Vector (*IRMPrincPayV(i)*); v) IRM Interest Payment Vector (*IRMIntPayV(i)*); vi) IRM Net Payment Vector (*IRMNetPayV(i)*); vii) RWM Interest Rate Vector (*RWMIntRateV(i)*); viii) RWM Remaining Principal Vector (*RWMRemPrincV(i)*); ix) RWM Principal Payment Vector (*RWMPrincPayV(i)*); x) RWM Interest Payment Vector (*RWMIntPayV(i)*); and xi) RWM Net Payment Vector (*RWMNetPayV(i)*); where $i = 1, 2, \ldots, 21$ to cover the 21 years. Note: $i = 1, 2, \ldots, 21$ unless otherwise specified in the calculations below.

The calculations are given below.

Year Vector:

$$\text{YearV(i)} = \text{i} \tag{1}$$

IRM Interest Rate Vector:

IRMIntRateV(i) = RiskLognorm(MeanIR, StdDevIR) (2)

Where *RiskLognorm* is the log-normal @RISK distribution with the given parameters *MeanIR* & *StdDevIR*.

IRM Remaining Principal Vector:

IRMRemPrincV(1) = LoanAmount (3)

IRMRemPrincV(i) = IRMRemPrincV(i-1)- IRMPrincPayV(i-1) (4)

Where *IRMPrincPayV(i)* is the IRM Principal Payment Vector and *i = 2, 3, …, 21.*

IRM Principal Payment Vector:

IRMPrincPayV(i) = LoanAmount/20 (5)

IRM Interest Payment Vector:

IRMIntPayV(i) = IRMRemPrincV(i)* IRMIntRateV(i) (6)

IRM Net Payment Vector:

IRMNetPayV(i) = IRMIntPayV(i)+ IRMPrincPayV(i) (7)

Random Walk Model Calculations

RWM Interest Rate Vector:

RWMIntRateV(1) = RiskLognorm(MeanIR, StdDevIR) (8)

RWMIntRateV(i) = RiskLognorm(RWMIntRateV(i-1), StdDevIR) (9)

Where *RiskLognorm* is the log-normal @RISK distribution with the parameters *RWMIntRateV(i-1)* & *StdDevIR* and *i = 2, 3, …, 21.* Note: *RWMIntRateV(i-1)* is the previous Year's Interest Rate, which is different from the Independent Rates Model.

RWM Remaining Principal Vector:

RWMRemPrincV(1) = LoanAmount (10)

RWMRemPrincV(i) = RWMRemPrincV(i-1)- RWMPrincPayV(i-1) (11)

Where *RWMPrincPayV(i)* is the RWM Principal Payment Vector and $i = 2, 3, \ldots, 21$.
RWM Principal Payment Vector:

$$\text{RWMPrincPayV(i)} = \text{LoanAmount}/20 \tag{12}$$

RWM Interest Payment Vector:

$$\text{RWMIntPayV(i)} = \text{RWMRemPrincV(i)}^{*}\ \text{RWMIntRateV(i)} \tag{13}$$

RWM Net Payment Vector:

$$\text{RWMNetPayV(i)} = \text{RWMIntPayV(i)} + \text{RWMPrincPayV(i)} \tag{14}$$

Simulation Output Calculations

The simulation output data comprises i) Total IRM Net Payment (*TotalIRMNetPay*), and ii) Total RWM Net Payment (*TotalRWMNetPay*).

The calculations are given below.

Total IRM Net Payment:

TotalIRMNetPay=RiskOutput("Total-IRM", , RiskSixSigma(920000,1130000,1025000,1.5,3)) + SUM(IRMNetPayV(1): IRMNetPayV(21)) (15)

Where *RiskOutput* & *RiskSixSigma* are @RISK functions, and *IRMNetPayV(i)* is the IRM Net Payment Vector.

Total RWM Net Payment:

TotalRWMNetPay=RiskOutput("Total-RWM", , RiskSixSigma(920000,1130000,1025000,1.5,3)) + SUM(RWMNetPayV(1): RWMNetPayV(21)) (16)

Where *RiskOutput* & *RiskSixSigma* are @RISK functions, and *RWMNetPayV(i)* is the RWM Net Payment Vector.

Measuring Simulation Results (DMAIC Measure)

The five Total Net Payment simulation results of the two models, IRM and RWM, are presented below. The attained values for Total IRM Net Payment, Total IRM Net Payment Standard Deviation, Total RWM Net Payment, and Total RWM Net Payment Standard Deviation are given in Table 2.

Table 2. Five simulations of IRM and RWM results

Data	Sim #1	Sim #2	Sim #3	Sim #4	Sim #1
Total IRM Net Payment	$919,998	$972,498	$1,024,998	$1,077,497	$1,129,997
Total IRM Net Pay. SD	$11,122	$12,512	$13,903	$15,293	$16,683
Total RWM Net Payment	$919,998	$972,498	$1,024,998	$1,077,497	$1,129,997
Total RWM Net Pay. SD	$101,699	$107,503	$113,306	$119,109	$124,913

Figure 1 graphically presents the five Total Net Payment simulation results of the two models.

Figure 1. Total IRM and RWM net payment results

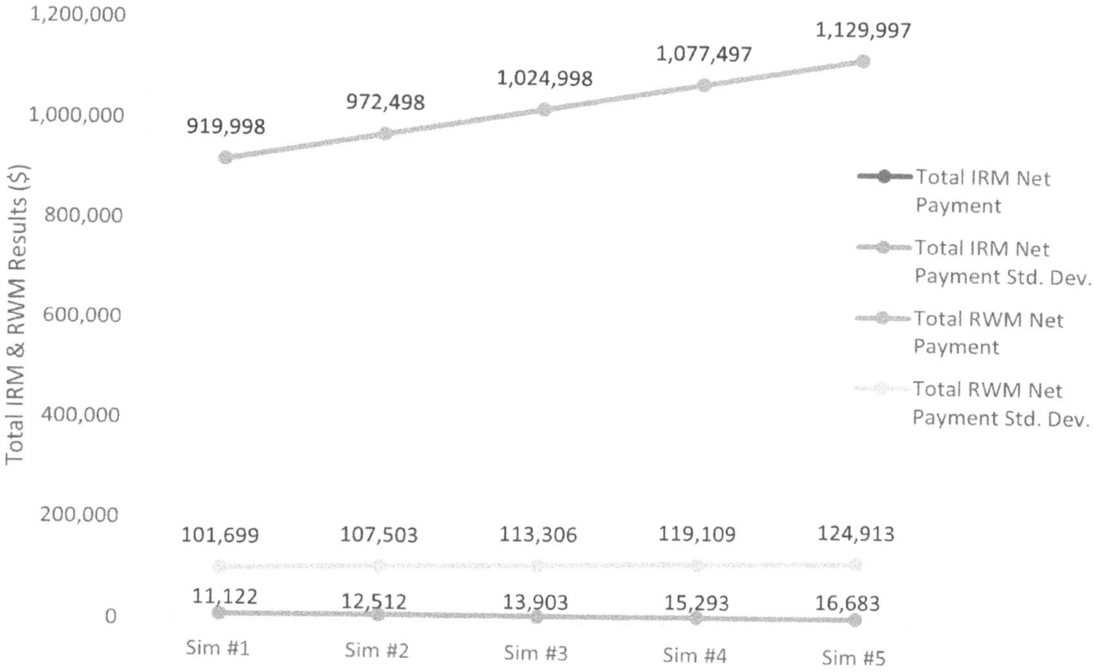

Total Net Payments (Figure 1) of IRM and RWM are the same (i.e., they overlap in the graph). Total Net Payment starts at $919,998 in Sim #1 and then increases to $1,129,997 in Sim #5 with linear approximation.

However, the Total Net Payment Standard Deviations of the IRM and RWM models are quite different. The RWM Standard Deviation is 9.144 times greater than the IRM Standard Deviation in Sim # 1, 8.592 times greater in Sim #2, 8.150 times greater in Sim #3, 7.788 times greater in Sim #4, and 7.487 times greater in Sim #5. Total Net Payment Standard Deviations start at $11,122 for IRM and $101,699 for RWM in Sim #1 and then increase to $16,683 and $124,913 respectively in Sim #5 with a linear approximation.

Figure 2 graphically presents the IRM Net Payment per Year in Sim #1. IRM Net Payment per Year starts at $65,000 in Year 1 and then decreases to $25,000 in Year 21 with a linear approximation.

Figure 2. IRM net payment per year in Sim #1

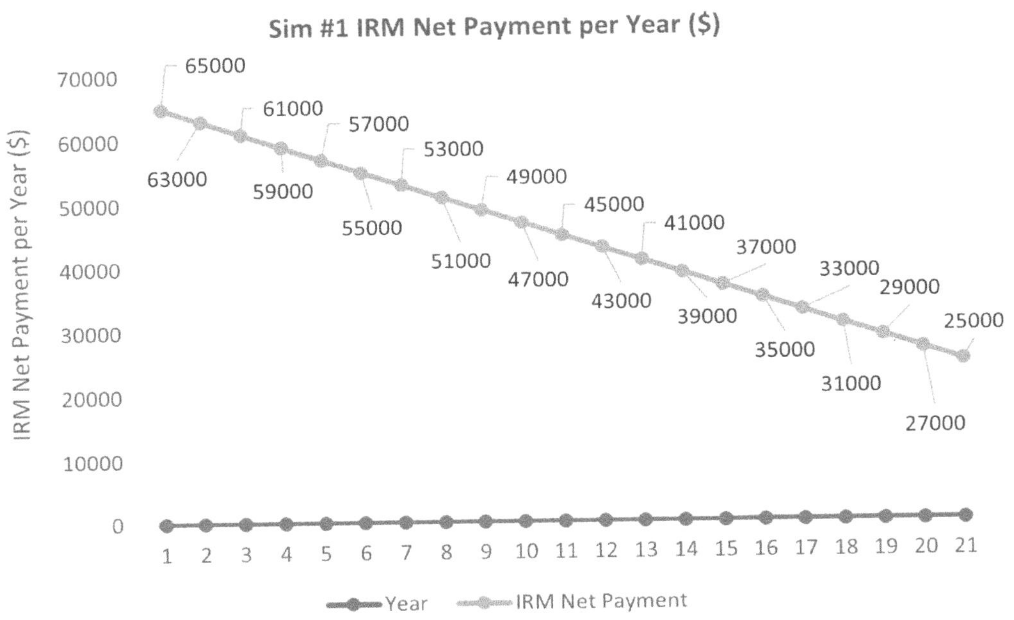

Figure 3 graphically presents the RWM Net Payment per Year in Sim #1. The RWM Net Payment per Year starts at $65,000 in Year 1 and then decreases to $25,000 in Year 21 with a linear approximation, which is the same as IRM for all years.

Figure 3. RWM net payment per year in Sim #1

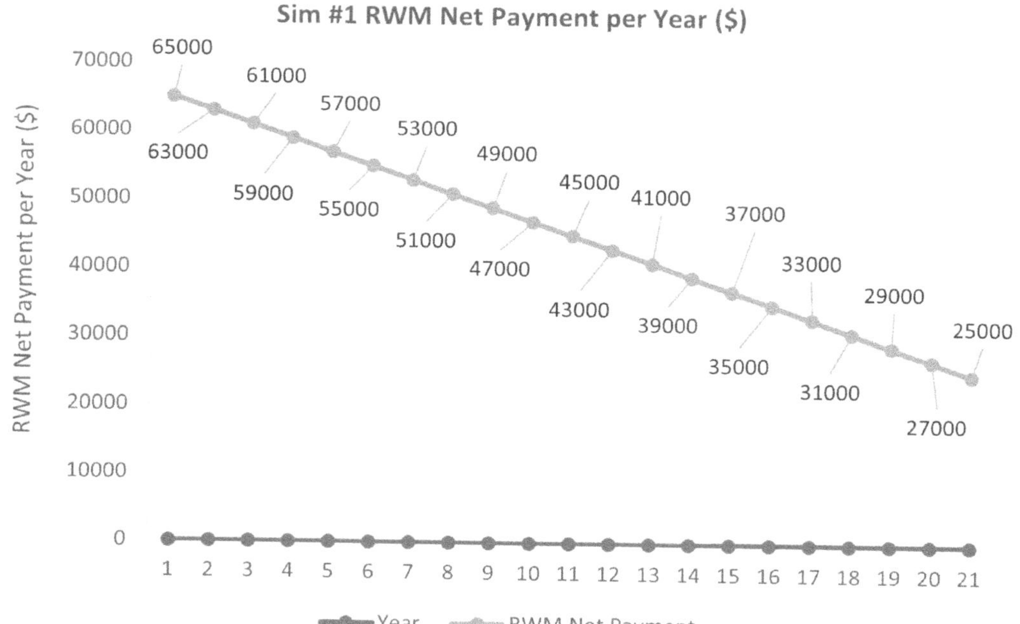

Results Analysis, Evaluation, and Risk Attribution (DMAIC Analyse)

The Simulation #3 results are analysed below. Simulation #3 is selected for demonstration purposes because it has a medium Mean Interest Rate and Standard Deviation Interest Rate, which means medium volatility.

Total IRM Net Payment Analysis, Evaluation, and Risk Attribution

Figure 4 displays the Total IRM Net Payment distribution. The *Mean* is $1,024,997.58 and the *Standard Deviation* is $13,902.77, i.e., 1.356%. The Six Sigma target parameters are *TV* = $1,025,000; *LSL* = $920,000; and *USL* = $1,130,000. The Six Sigma process capability metrics are *Cp* = 2.5175; *Cpk* = 2.5174; and σ-*L* = 6.1633. There is a 5% probability that the *Mean* will be below $1.0031 MM; a 90% probability that it will be in the range of $1.0031 MM – $1.0486 MM; and a 5% probability that it will be above $1.0486 MM.

Figure 4. Total IRM net payment distribution

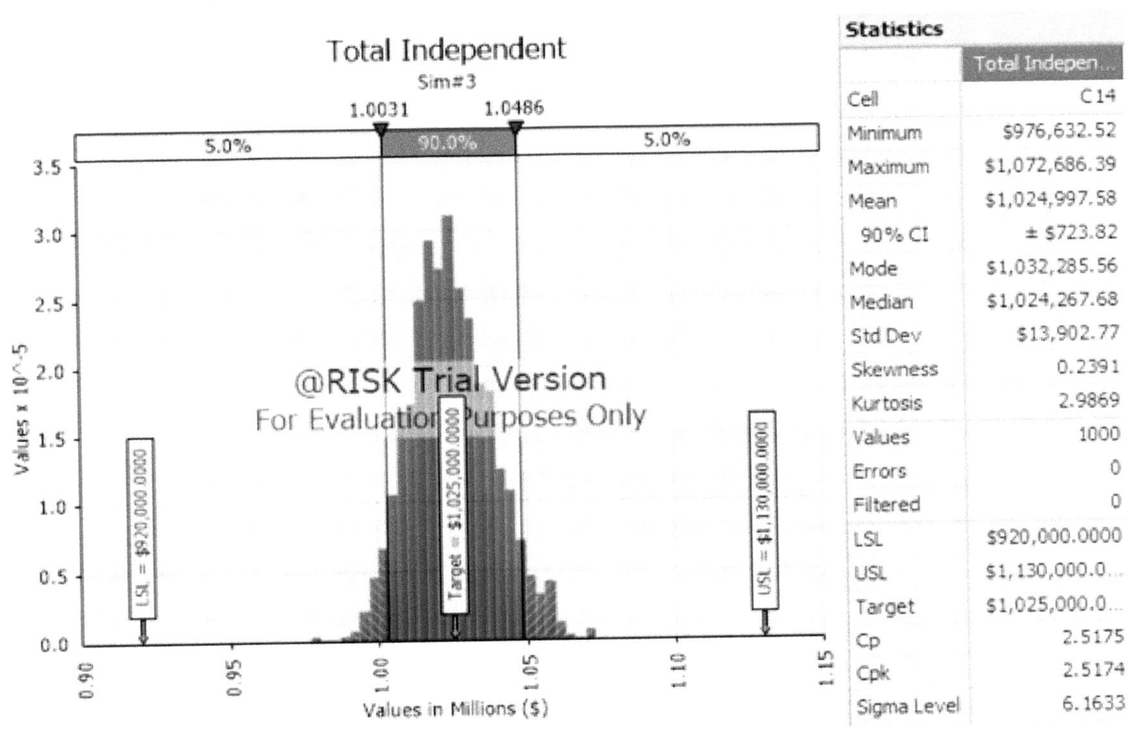

Sensitivity analysis provides for identifying and quantifying the main contributors to variability and risk, which is shown in Figure 5.

Figure 5. Total IRM net payment correlation

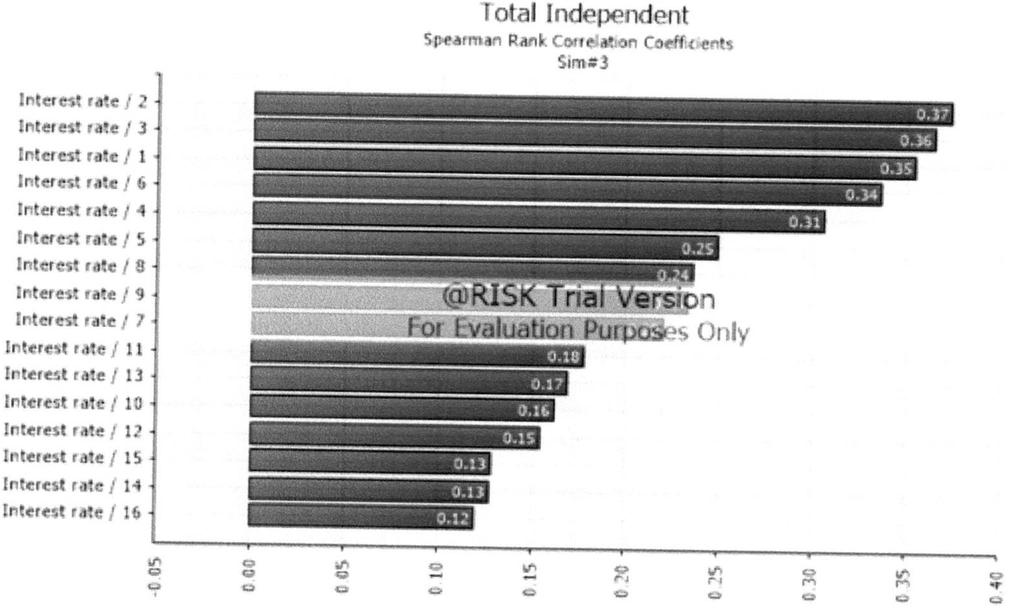

The correlation coefficients graph (Figure 5) illustrates that if the top variable, Interest Rate for Year 2, increases by one unit, the Total IRM Net Payment will increase by 0.37 units, so it is the most influential variable. The other variables are less influential as their correlation coefficients are in the range of 0.36 to 0.12 from top to bottom.

Total RWM Net Payment Analysis, Evaluation, and Risk Attribution

Figure 6 displays the Total RWM Net Payment distribution.

Figure 6. Total RWM net payment distribution

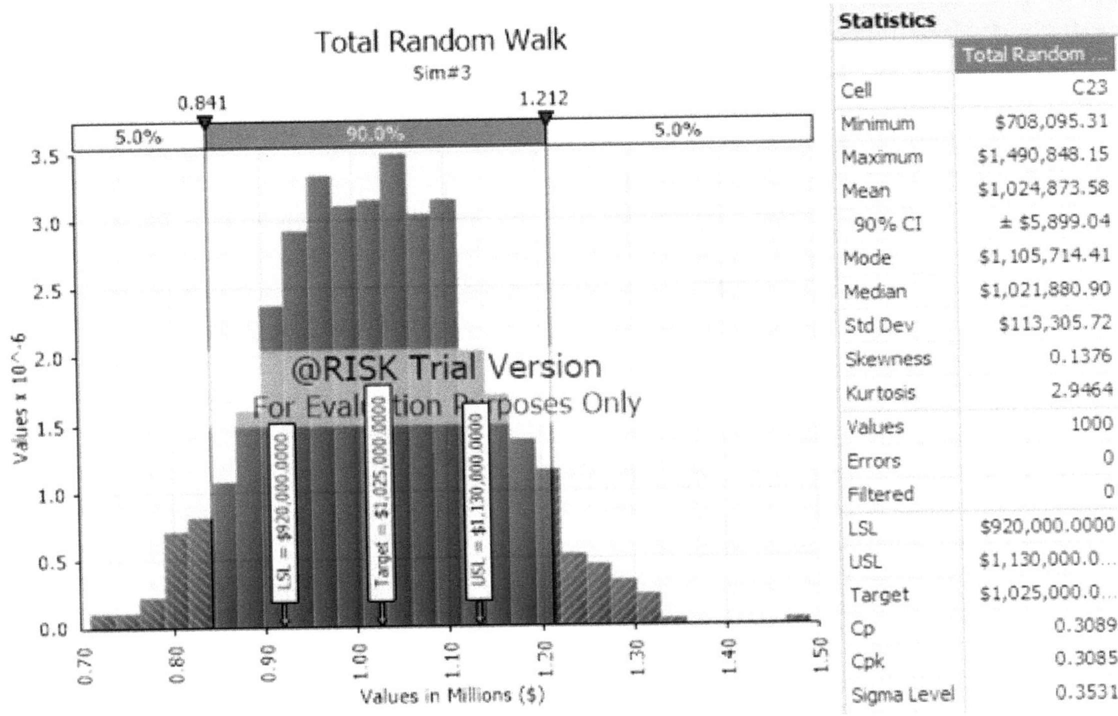

In Figure 6 the *Mean* is \$1,024,873.58 and the *Standard Deviation* is \$113,305.72, i.e., 11.056%. The Six Sigma target parameters are TV = \$1,025,000; LSL = \$920,000; and USL = \$1,130,000. The Six Sigma process capability metrics are $Cp = 0.3089$; $Cpk = 0.3085$; and $\sigma\text{-}L = 0.3531$. There is a 5% probability that the *Mean* will be below \$0.841 MM; a 90% probability that it will be in the range of \$0.841 MM – \$1.212 MM; and a 5% probability that it will be above \$1.212 MM.

Sensitivity analysis provides for identifying and quantifying the main contributors to variability and risk, which is shown in Figure 7.

Figure 7. Total RWM net payment correlation

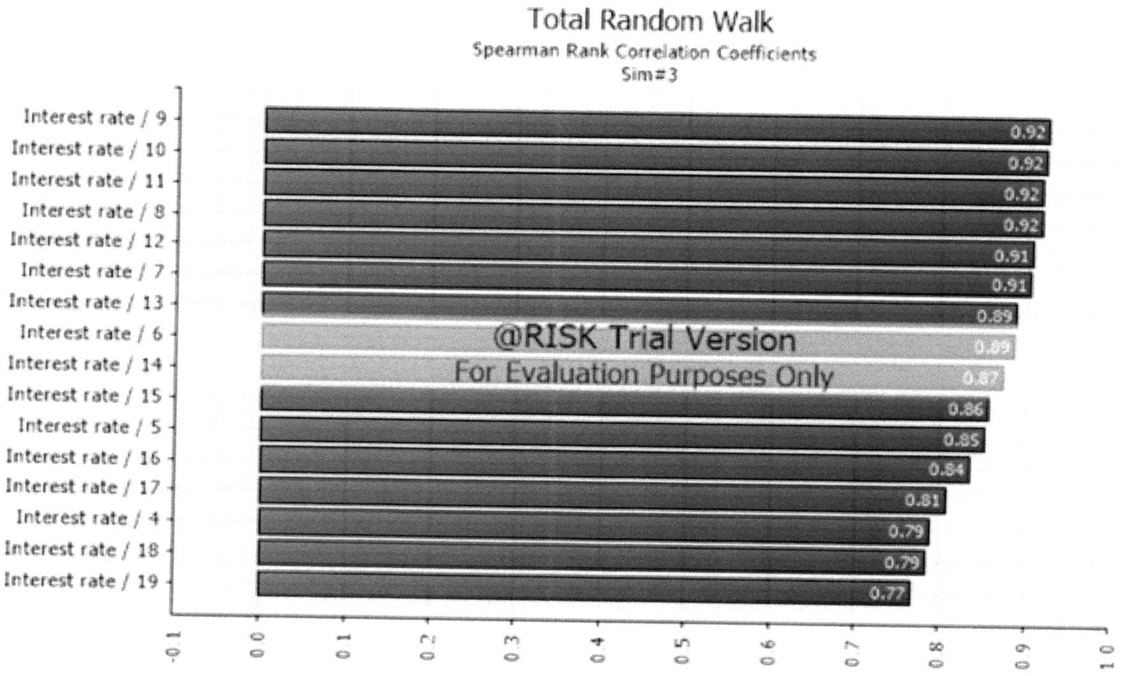

Total Random Walk
Spearman Rank Correlation Coefficients
Sim#3

Interest rate / 9 — 0.92
Interest rate / 10 — 0.92
Interest rate / 11 — 0.92
Interest rate / 8 — 0.92
Interest rate / 12 — 0.91
Interest rate / 7 — 0.91
Interest rate / 13 — 0.89
Interest rate / 6 — 0.89
Interest rate / 14 — 0.87
Interest rate / 15 — 0.86
Interest rate / 5 — 0.85
Interest rate / 16 — 0.84
Interest rate / 17 — 0.81
Interest rate / 4 — 0.79
Interest rate / 18 — 0.79
Interest rate / 19 — 0.77

-0.1 0.0 0.1 0.2 0.3 0.4 0.5 0.6 0.7 0.8 0.9 1.0

The correlation coefficients graph (Figure 7) illustrates that if the top variable, Interest Rate for Year 9, increases by one unit, the Total RWM Net Payment will increase by 0.92 units, so it is the most influential variable. The next three variables are less influential (despite having the same coefficient of 0.92, as this is an effect of rounding). The other variables are less influential as their correlation coefficients are in the range of 0.91 to 0.77 from top to bottom.

Comparison of Results

Table 3 shows Simulation #3 IRM and RWM Results for comparison. The Mean Total Net Payments are almost equal, i.e., \$1,024,998 for IRM and \$1,024,874 for RWM, but the Standard Deviations are very different, i.e., the Standard Deviation of RWM is 8.150 times greater than the Standard Deviation of IRM. Standard Deviation is a major risk factor, so RWM is much more volatile than IRM. This is also confirmed with the Six Sigma process metrics of Sigma Level (σ-L), which is 6.1633 for IRM and 0.3531 for RWM, i.e., the IRM Sigma Level is 17.455 times greater than the RWM Sigma Level.

Table 3. Simulation #3 IRM and RWM results comparison

Data	Mean	Standard Deviation	Standard Dev. %	Six Sigma σ-L
Total IRM Net Payment	\$1,024,998	\$13,903	1.356%	6.1633
Total RWM Net Payment	\$1,024,874	\$113,306	11.056%	0.3531

This is caused by the different methods that the interest rates are generated in the models, which makes a substantial difference in the distribution of the total payment. Interest rates can vary much more in the Random Walk Model, which causes a larger variation in the total payment.

CONCLUSION

This chapter presented two simulation models for projecting the variable interest rates and loan payment schedules for 21 years.

The Independent Rates Model (IRM) calculated the yearly interest rates independently of one another. In contrast, the Random Walk Model (RWM) calculated only the Year 1 Interest Rate independently. Each succeeding Year's Interest Rate was calculated based on the previous Year's calculated Interest Rate.

To provide for an extensive analysis, five simulations were run, each with a different Mean and Standard Deviation. The model used the known input data, the values of which are empirical averages of the associated historical data. The simulations calculated all the variables required for projecting the variable interest rates and loan payment schedules for 21 years.

The simulation results were evaluated and sensitivity analysis was performed. The Total IRM Net Payment and Total RWM Net Payment were compared and discussed.

It was concluded that interest rates vary much more in the Random Walk Model, which caused the larger variation in the total payment. This was a consequence of the different methods that the interest rates were generated in the models, which made a substantial difference in the distribution of the total payment.

Management needed to consider that RWM was much more volatile than IRM. Thus, the decision on which model to implement in practice depended on the risk tolerance of the decision-makers.

REFERENCES

Anderson, R. (2020). *Money Management & Financial Budgeting*. Academic Press.

Britten-Jones, M. (1998). *Fixed Income and Interest Rate Derivative*. Academic Press.

Carmona, R., & Tehranchi, M. R. (2007). *Interest Rate Models: An Infinite Dimensional Stochastic Analysis Perspective*. Springer.

Cornyn, A. G. (1997). *Interest Rate Risk Models: Theory and Practice*. Global Professional Publishing.

Homer, S., & Sylla, R. (2011). A History of Interest Rates. John Wiley & Sons.

U.S. Congress Committee on Government Operations, 1982. Small Business Administration's variable interest rate. (1982). U.S. Government Printing Office.

Wahidudin, A. N. (2011). *Interest Rates in Financial Analysis and Valuation*. Bookboon.

Zagst, R. (2013). *Interest-Rate Management*. Springer.

Chapter 12
Bank Loan Portfolio Credit Risk Analysis

ABSTRACT

This chapter illustrates an analysis of banking loan portfolio credit risk. The objective is to select the optimal loan portfolio that achieves the bank's investment objectives with an acceptable credit risk according to their predefined limits. Stochastic optimization constructs an efficient frontier of optimal loan portfolios in banking with maximal profit and minimizing loan losses (i.e., the credit risk). Simulation stochastically calculates and measures the gross profit and the objective profit. Also, the bank regulation limits are applied based on the bank's capital to control the maximum loan amount per loan investment grade. This analysis allows for the selection of the best efficient frontier loan portfolio which gains the maximum profit.

INTRODUCTION

This chapter presents an analysis of a loan portfolio credit risk by using optimisation and simulation. The optimisation model should calculate the Efficient Frontier of minimal mean-variance loan portfolios with maximal profit. The simulation model should calculate the Gross Profit, Objective Profit, and Loan Losses for all Efficient Frontier portfolios. The purpose is to select the portfolio which gains maximal profit. The selected portfolio should be measured and evaluated considering the Gross Profit and Objective Profit. Also, the bank regulation should be applied considering the limits based on the bank's capital to control the maximum loan amount per loan investment grade.

What-If analysis should be applied for risk attribution of the optimal portfolio. What-If Analysis provides a comprehensive view of the probability of the outputs and quantifies the sensitivity of the outputs based on the variability of the associated inputs and financial variables. Report the analysis results to the bank executives for decision support. This risk analysis helps bank executives to decide whether to execute the optimal loan portfolio.

This chapter specifically focuses on the credit risk associated with the loan portfolio of a bank. Credit risk is the risk of losses due to borrowers' default or deterioration of credit standing. Default is the event

DOI: 10.4018/979-8-3693-3787-5.ch012

that borrowers fail to comply with their debt obligations. The default triggers a total or partial loss of the amount lent to the counterparty.

Literature

Some references for a bank's loan portfolio are given below.

Wilson (1998) discussed how financial institutions are increasingly measuring and managing the risk from credit exposures at the portfolio level, in addition to the transaction level. This change in perspective has occurred for many reasons. First is the recognition that the traditional binary classification of credits into "good" credits and "bad" credits is not sufficient--a precondition for managing credit risk at the portfolio level is the recognition that all credits can potentially become "bad" over time given a particular economic scenario. The second reason is the declining profitability of traditional credit products, implying little room for error in terms of the selection and pricing of individual transactions, or portfolio decisions, where diversification and timing effects increasingly mean the difference between profit and loss. Finally, management has more opportunities to manage exposure proactively after it has originated, with the increased liquidity in the secondary loan market, the increased importance of syndicated lending, the availability of credit derivatives and third-party guarantees, and so on. Lending is the principal business activity for most commercial banks. The loan portfolio is typically the largest asset and the predominant source of revenue. As such, it is one of the greets sources of risk to banks' safety and soundness. Whether due to lax credit standards, poor portfolio risk management, or weakness in the economy, loan portfolio problems have historically been the major cause of bank losses and failures (Comptroller of the Currency Administrato, 2015). Credit Portfolio Management (Hünseler 2013) is a topical text on approaches to the active management of credit risks. The book is a valuable, up-to-date guide for portfolio management practitioners. Its content comprises three main parts: The framework for managing credit risks, Active Credit Portfolio Management in practice, and Hedging techniques and toolkits. A paper by Crouhya, Galaib & Marka (2000) reviewed the proposed industry-sponsored Credit Value-at-Risk methodologies. The credit migration approach, as proposed by JP Morgan with CreditMetrics, is based on the probability of moving from one credit quality to another, including default, within a given time horizon.

The approach proposed by Credit Suisse Financial Products (CSFP) with CreditRisk+ only focuses on default. The default for individual loans is assumed to follow an exogenous Poisson process. Also, McKinsey Research proposes Credit-Portfolio-View which is a discrete-time multi-period model where default probabilities are conditional on the macro- variables like unemployment, the level of interest rates, and the growth rate in the economy, which to a large extent drive the credit cycle in the economy. Modelling and management of credit risk are discussed by Lütkebohmert (2009) as the main topics within banks and other lending institutions. Historical experience shows that, in particular, the concentration of risk in credit portfolios has been one of the major causes of bank distress. Therefore, concentration risk is highly relevant to anyone who wants to go beyond the very basic portfolio credit risk models.

The bank loan market has increased dramatically in recent years and is now viewed by some as a distinct asset class (Fabozzi 1998). The author edited this comprehensive book, which covers the structure of the market, the secondary market in trading practices, and how to manage a bank loan portfolio.

The Problem Statement An analysis of a loan portfolio credit risk should be performed by using optimisation and simulation. The optimisation model, including simulation, should calculate the Efficient Frontier of minimal mean-variance loan portfolios with maximal profit considering Gross Profit and Objective Profit. The purpose is to select the portfolio which gains maximal profit. ELABORATION

The Model Definition A bank borrows money from its depositors and other sources at an average rate of 4.5%, which defines the Cost of Funds (*COF*).

The bank has seven investment grades for loans, i.e., A, B+, B, B-, C+, C, and C-, which defines the Investment Grade Vector (*IGV*).

The interest rates rise reflecting the underlying risk: A, 4.5%; B+, 5.0%; B, 6.0%; B-, 8.0%; C+, 10.0%; C, 11.0%; and C-, 12.0%, which defines the Interest Rate per Grade Vector (*IRpGV*). As loan creditworthiness declines, the Expected Loss Probability rises along with the Degree of Loss.

The model defines six vectors to specify the empirically estimated loss per loan grade from the bank's history data:

1. Minimum Expected Loss Probability per Grade Vector (*MinELPpGV*): A, 0.0%; B+, 0.0%; B, 0.0%; B-, 0.0%; C+, 0.0%; C, 0.0%; and C-, 0.0%.
2. Most Likely Expected Loss Probability per Grade Vector (*MLELPpGV*): A, 0.0%; B+, 0.25%; B, 0.50%; B-, 0.75%; C+, 1.00%; C, 1.50%; and C-, 2.00%.
3. Maximum Expected Loss Probability per Grade Vector (*MaxELPpGV*): A, 0.0%; B+, 0.50%; B, 1.00%; B-, 1.25%; C+, 1.50%; C, 2.50%; and C-, 3.00%.
4. Minimum Degree of Loss per Grade Vector (*MinDoLpGV*): A, 0.0%; B+, 0.0%; B, 5.0%; B-, 10.0%; C+, 15.0%; C, 20.0%; and C-, 40.0%.
5. Most Likely Degree of Loss per Grade Vector (*MLDoLpGV*): A, 0.0%; B+, 10.0%; B, 15.0%; B-, 20.0%; C+, 30.0%; C, 40.0%; and C-, 60.0%.
6. Maximum Expected Degreeof Lossper Grade Vector (*MaxDoLpGV*): A, 0.0%; B+, 20.0%; B, 25.0%; B-, 30.0%; C+, 40.0%; C, 50.0%; and C-, 80.0%.

Calculations

A specific loan reserve ratio is defined for each grade of loan. The required loan reserve ratio increases in concert with the level of risk: A, 15.0%; B+, 17.5%; B, 20.0%; B-, 22.5%; C+, 25.0%; C, 27.5%; and C-, 30.0%, which defines the Loan Reserve Ratio per Grade Vector (*LRRpGV*).

Also, the bank has $100 million in capital, which defines the Bank Capital. For example, if the bank holds only A loans, the maximum portfolio would be $667 million (i.e., the bank capital divided by loan reserve ratio). A loan portfolio made up of only C- loans cannot exceed $333 million. Therefore, it is not possible to fund as many risky loans as creditworthy loans.

Table 1 shows the available data for the bank's loan portfolio

Table 1. The available data for the bank's loan portfolio

Cost of Funds (COF)	**4.5%**						
Investment Grade Vector (IGV)	**A**	**B+**	**B**	**B-**	**C+**	**C**	**C-**
Interest Rate per Grade Vector (*IRpGV*)	4.5%	5.0%	6.0%	8.0%	10.0%	11.0%	12.0%
Minimum Expected Loss Probability per Grade Vector (*MinELPpGV*)	0.00%	0.00%	0.00%	0.00%	0.00%	0.00%	0.00%
Most Likely Expected Loss Probability per Grade Vector (*MLELPpGV*)	0.00%	0.25%	0.50%	0.75%	1.00%	1.50%	2.00%
Maximum Expected Loss Probability per Grade Vector (*MaxELPpGV*)	0.00%	0.50%	1.00%	1.50%	2.00%	3.00%	4.00%
Minimum Degree of Loss per Grade Vector (*MinDoLpGV*)	0%	0%	5%	10%	15%	20%	40%
Most Likely Degree of Loss per Grade Vector (*MLDoLpGV*)	0%	10%	15%	0%	30%	40%	60%
Maximum Expected Degree of Loss per Grade Vector (*MaxDoLpGV*)	0%	20%	25%	30%	40%	0%	80%
Loan Reserve Ratio per Grade Vector (*LRRpGV*)	15.0%	17.5%	0.0%	22.5%	25.0%	27.5%	30.0%
Bank Capital (*BankCap*)	$100						

Maximum Portfolio Size per Grade Vector

The Maximum Portfolio Size per Grade Vector (*MaxPSpGV*) is calculated by dividing Bank Capital (*BankCap*) by the Loan Reserve Ratio per Grade Vector (*LRRpGV*) given in Table 1, with the following formula:

$$MaxPSpGV(i) = BankCap / LRRpGV(i) \qquad (1)$$

Single Loan Amount per Grade Vector

The model provides for setting the bank regulation limits based on the bank's capital to control the maximum loan amount per loan investment grade. For this purpose, the Single Loan Amount per Grade Vector (*SLApGV*) is used. The Single Loan Amount per Grade Vector (*SLApGV*) is calculated as follows:

SLApGV(1) = 10 ($MM) (2)

The Single Loan Amount for Grade A is $10 MM as the maximum loan allowed by Bank Regulations for $100 (MM) Bank Capital. The Single Loan Amount for Grade C- is an adjustable variable, which is initially set to $10 MM, i.e., the maximum allowed amount.

SLApGV(7) = 10($MM) (3)

This variable is iteratively recalculated by the Stochastic Optimisation model until the optimal solution is reached, i.e., the Maximal Gross Profit of the portfolio.

It should be noted that the Punitive Charge associated with loan losses over a specific amount (e.g., $2 MM) is not considered in the model for simplicity. So, considered is Gross Profit instead of Net Profit, which is Gross Profit minus Punitive Charge.

The Single Loan Amount for Grades B+ to C is calculated by the following formula:

SLApGV(i) = SLApGV(i-1) – (SLApGV(1) - SLApGV(7)) / 6 (4)

where i is an integer value from 2 to 6.

Capital per Loan Grade Vector

The Capital per Loan Grade Vector (*CpLGV*) is an adjustable variable vector, which is initially set with values of minimum zero to maximum 50. This variable vector is iteratively recalculated by the Stochastic Optimisation model until the Maximal Gross Profit is reached.

0 <= CpLGV(i) <= 50, I = 1, 2, …, 7 (5)

Value of Portfolio Segment per Grade Vector

The Value of Portfolio Segment per Grade Vector (VoPSpGV) is calculated by the following formula:

VoPSpGV(i) = CpLGV(i) / LRRpGV(i) (6)

where Capital per Loan Grade Vector (*CpLGV*) is calculated by (5); and Loan Reserve Ratio per Grade Vector (*LRRpGV*) is given in Table 1.

Number of Loans per Grade Vector

The Number of Loans per Grade Vector (*NoLpGV*) is calculated by the following formula:

NoLpGV(i) = INT(VoPSpGV(i) / SLApGV(i) + 0.5) (7)

where Value of Portfolio Segment per Grade Vector (*VoPSpGV*) is calculated by (6); and Single Loan Amount per Grade Vector (*SLApGV*) is calculated by (2, 3, 4).

Interest Earnings per Loan Grade Vector

The Interest Earnings per Loan Grade Vector (*IEpLGV*) is calculated by the following formula:

IEpLGV(i) = VoPSpGV(i) / IRpGV (i) (8)

where the Value of Portfolio Segment per Grade Vector (VoPSpGV) is calculated by (6); and Interest Rate per Grade Vector (IRpGV) is given in Table 1.

Total Costs of Funds

The Total Costs of Funds (*TCoF*) are calculated by the following formula:

TCoF = (VoPSpGV(i) – BankCap) * COF (9)

where Value of Portfolio Segment per Grade Vector (*VoPSpGV*) is calculated by (6); and Cost of Funds (*COF*) and Bank Capital (*BankCap*) are given in Table 12.1.

Number of Defaulted Loans per Grade Vector

The Number of Defaulted Loans per Grade Vector (*NoDLpGV*) is calculated by the following formula:

NoDLpGV(i) = INT(NoLpGV(i) * RiskTriang(MinELPpGV(i), MLELPpGV(i), MaxELPpGV (i))+0.99) (10)

where Number of Loans per Grade Vector (*NoLpGV*) is calculated by (7); RiskTriang is the distribution function of Palisade™ @RISK®; and Minimum Expected Loss Probability per Grade Vector (*MinELPpGV*), Most Likely Expected Loss Probability per Grade Vector (*MLELPpGV*) and Maximum Expected Loss Probability per Grade Vector (*MaxELPpGV*) are given in Table 1.

Individual Loan Loss per Grade Vector

The Individual Loan Loss per Grade Vector (*ILLpGV*) is calculated by the following formula:

ILLpGV (i) = RiskTriang(MinDoLpGV(i), MLDoLpGV(i), MaxDoLpGV(i))* SLApGV(i) (11) where Single Loan Amount per Grade Vector (*SLApGV*) is calculated by (2, 3, 4); RiskTriang is the distribution function of Palisade™ @RISK®; and Minimum Degree of Loss per Grade Vector (*MinDoLpGV*), Most Likely Degree of Loss per Grade Vector (*MLDoLpGV*) and Maximum Degree of Loss per Grade Vector (*MaxDoLpGV*) are given in Table 1.

Total Loan Losses

The Total Loan Losses (*TLL*) are calculated by the following formula:

TLL = SUM(ILLpGV (i)) (12)

where Individual Loan Loss per Grade Vector (*ILLpGV*) is calculated by (11).

Total Interest Earnings

The Total Interest Earnings (*TIE*) are calculated by the following formula:

TIE = SUM(IEpLGV (i)) (13)

where Interest Earnings per Loan Grade Vector (*IEpLGV*) is calculated by (8).

Loan Portfolio Gross Profit

The Loan Portfolio Gross Profit (*LPGP*) is calculated by the following formula:

LPGP = TIE - TLL - TCoF (14)

where Total Interest Earnings (*TIE*) are calculated by (13); Total Loan Losses (*TLL*) are calculated by (12); and Total Costs of Funds (*TCoF*) are calculated by (9).

Loan Portfolio Objective Profit

The Loan Portfolio Objective Profit (*LPOP*) is calculated by the following formula:

LPOP = LPGP - IF(TLL >2, TLL -2,0) (15)

where Loan Portfolio Gross Profit (*LPGP*) is calculated by (14); and Total Loan Losses (TLL) is calculated by (12).

Measuring Loan Efficient Frontier Portfolios

The optimisation, including simulation, is run and the results are presented below.

Efficient Frontier Optimal Portfolios

Efficient Frontier Portfolios are presented in Table 2 and Figure 1.

Table 2. Efficient frontier portfolios' results

Portfolio	*Gross Profit Mean*	*Gross Profit Standard Deviation*	*Objective Profit Mean*	*Objective Profit Standard Deviation*
1	$22.891 MM	$0.8227 MM	$20.527 MM	$1.6450 MM
2	$23.291 MM	$0.5028 MM	$21.263 MM	$1.0056 MM
3	$24.419 MM	$0.7316 MM	$23.557 MM	$1.4224 MM
4	$24.727 MM	$0.5572 MM	$24.101 MM	$1.0600 MM

The results presented above show that the best Efficient Frontier portfolio is Portfolio No. 4 with a Gross Profit Mean of $24.727 MM. The Objective Profit Mean is $24.101 MM. The best Portfolio No. 4 will be discussed in detail in the following section. The Efficient Frontier Portfolios No 1, 2, and 3 are presented below.

Evaluation of Efficient Frontier Portfolio No. 1

The distributions of Optimal Portfolio No. 1 are shown in Figure 1 and Figure 2.

Figure 1. Portfolio 1 gross profit mean distribution

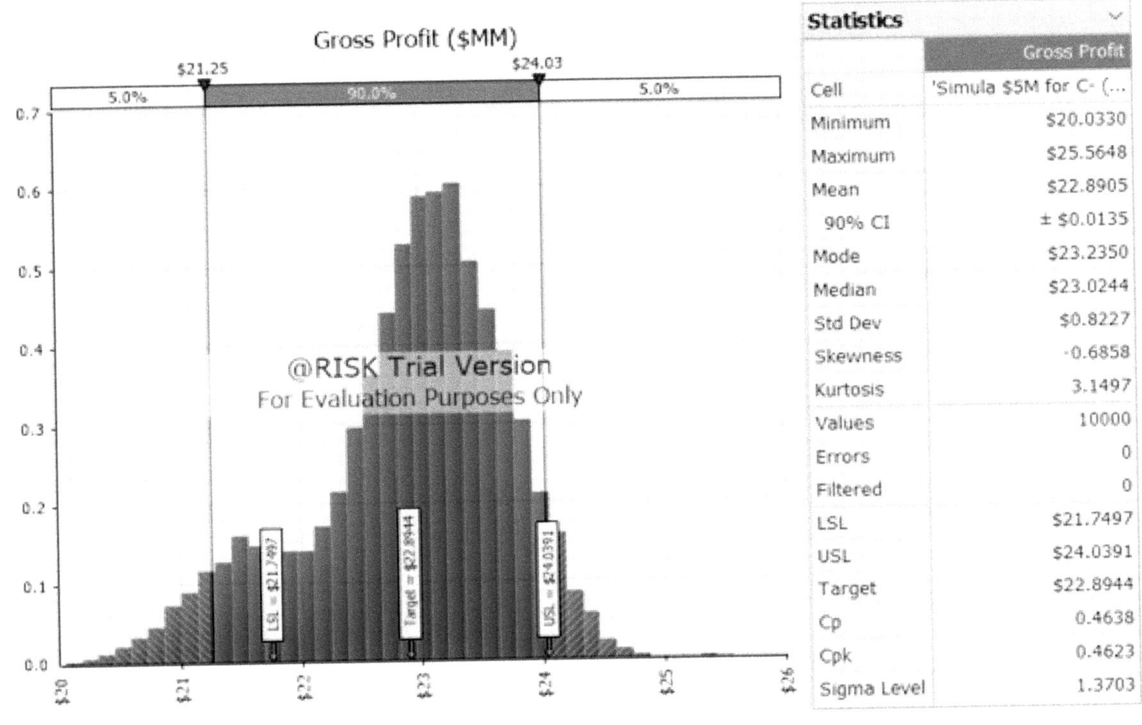

The Gross Profit *Mean* (Figure 1) is \$22.8905 MM with a *Standard Deviation* of \$0.8227 MM, i.e., 3.594%, which is a very low risk. The Six Sigma target parameters are TV = \$22.8944 MM; LSL = \$21.7497 MM; and USL = \$24.0391 MM. The Six Sigma process capability metrics are $Cp = 0.4638$; $Cpk = 0.4623$; and $\sigma\text{-}L = 0.13702$. There is a 5.0% probability that the *Mean* will be below \$21.25 MM; a 90.0% probability that it will be in the range of \$21.25 MM – \$24.03 MM; and a 5.0% probability that it will be above \$24.03 MM.

The Objective Profit *Mean* (Figure 2) is \$20.527 MM with a *Standard Deviation* of \$1.645 MM, i.e., 8.014%, which is a low risk. There is a 5.0% probability that the *Mean* will be below \$17.25 MM; a 90.0% probability that it will be in the range of \$17.25 MM – \$22.80 MM; and a 5.0% probability that it will be above \$22.80 MM.

Figure 2. Portfolio 1 objective profit mean distribution

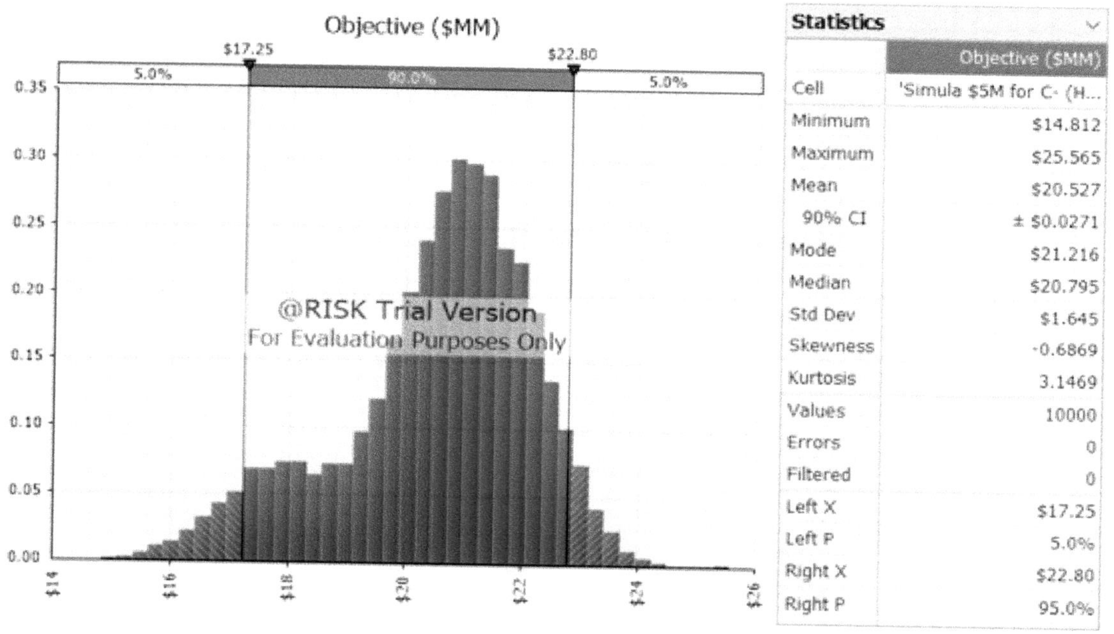
Objective ($MM)
$17.25
$22.80
5.0%
90.0%
5.0%
0.35
0.30
0.25
0.20
0.15
0.10
0.05
0.00
$14
$16
$18
$20
$22
$24
$26
@RISK Trial Version
For Evaluation Purposes Only
Statistics
Objective ($MM)
Cell 'Simula $5M for C- (H...
Minimum $14.812
Maximum $25.565
Mean $20.527
90% CI ± $0.0271
Mode $21.216
Median $20.795
Std Dev $1.645
Skewness -0.6869
Kurtosis 3.1469
Values 10000
Errors 0
Filtered 0
Left X $17.25
Left P 5.0%
Right X $22.80
Right P 95.0%

Evaluation of Efficient Frontier Portfolio No. 2

The distributions of Optimal Portfolio No. 2 are shown in Figure 3 and Figure 4.

Figure 3. Portfolio 2 gross profit mean distribution

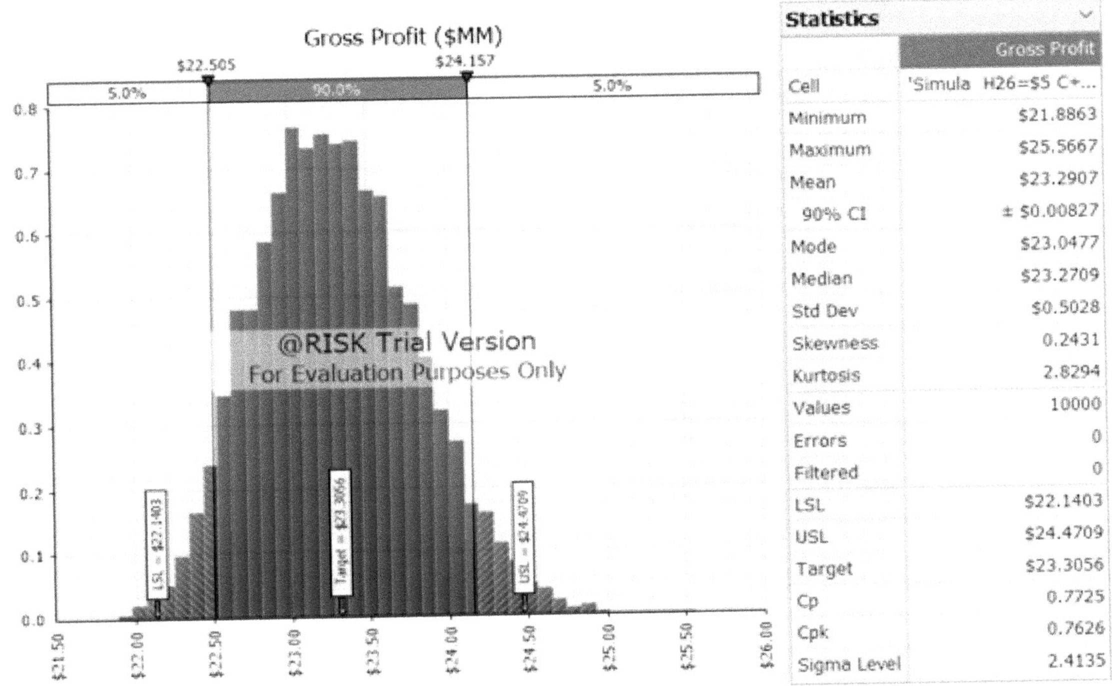

The Gross Profit *Mean* (Figure 3) is $23.2907 MM with a *Standard Deviation* of $0.5028 MM, i.e., 2.159%, which is a very low risk. The Six Sigma target parameters are *TV* = $23.3056 MM; *LSL* = $22.1403 MM; and *USL* = $24.4709 MM. The Six Sigma process capability metrics are *Cp* = 0.7725; *Cpk* = 0.7626; and *σ-L* = 2.4135. There is a 5.0% probability that the *Mean* will be below $22.505 MM; a 90.0% probability that it will be in the range of $22.505 MM – $24.157 MM; and a 5.0% probability that it will be above $24. 157 MM.

The Objective Profit *Mean* (Figure.4) is $21.2633 MM with a *Standard Deviation* of $1.0056 MM, i.e., 4.729%, which is a low risk. There is a 5.0% probability that the *Mean* will be below $19.69 MM; a 90.0% probability that it will be in the range of $19.69 MM – $23.00 MM; and a 5.0% probability that it will be above $23.00 MM.

Figure 4. Portfolio 1 objective profit mean distribution

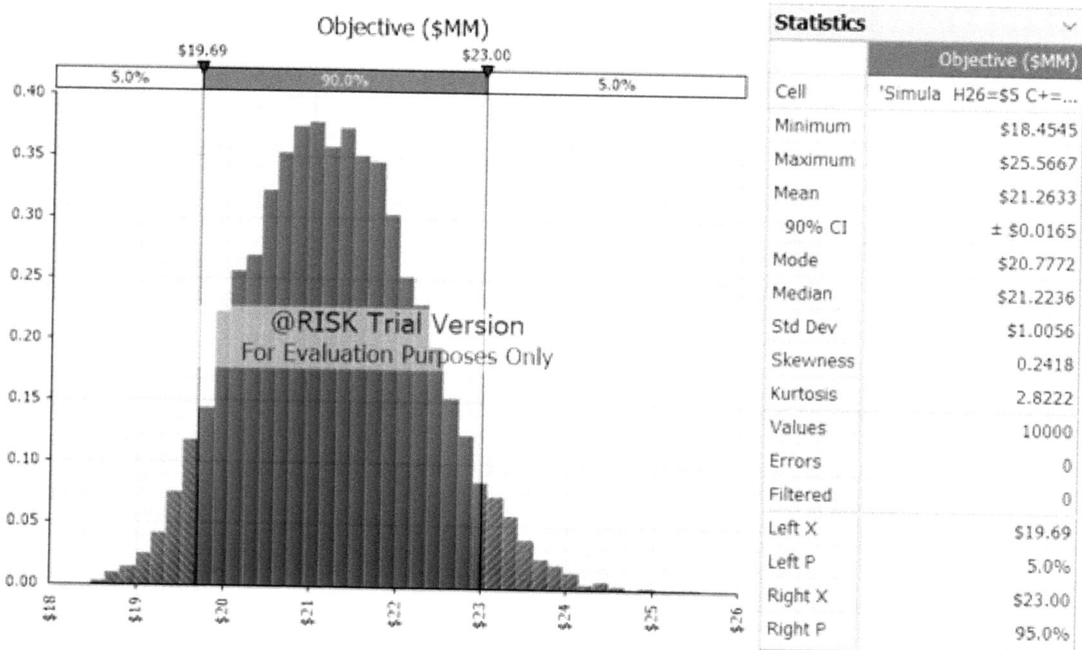

Evaluation of Efficient Frontier Portfolio No. 3

Figure 5. Portfolio 3 gross profit mean distribution

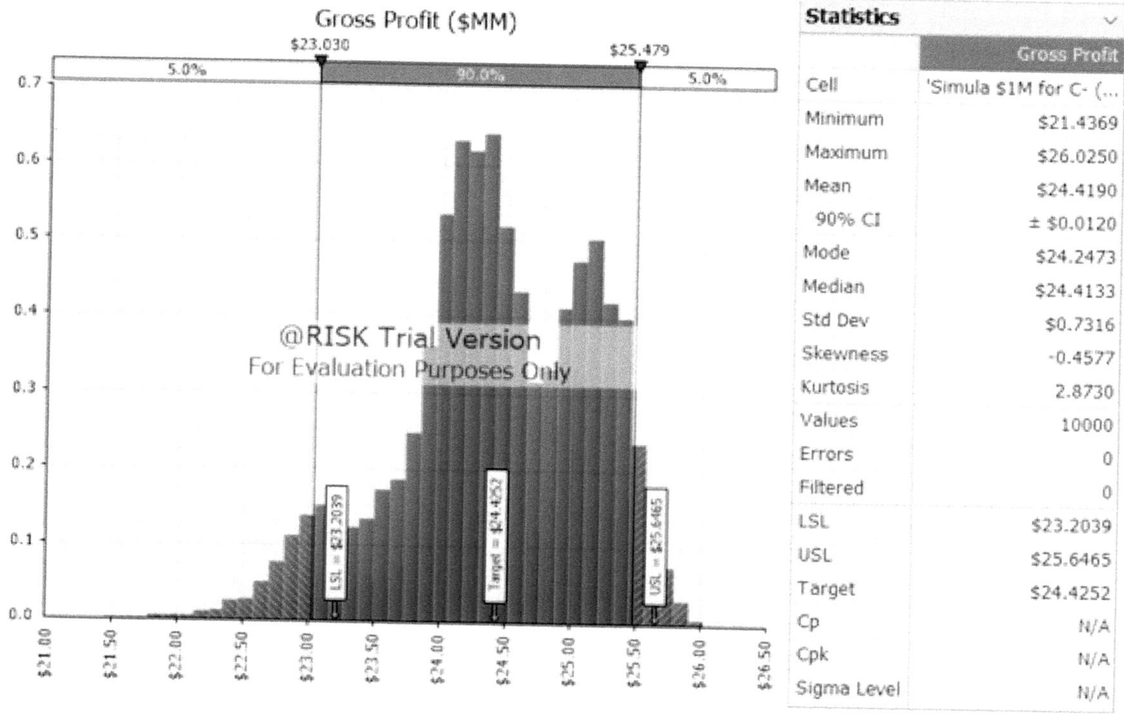

The distributions of the Optimal Portfolio No. 3 are shown in Figures 5 & 6.

The Gross Profit *Mean* (Figure 5) is \$24.4190 MM with a *Standard Deviation* of \$0.7316 MM, i.e., 2.996%, which is a very low risk. The Six Sigma target parameters are *TV* = \$24.4252 MM; *LSL* = \$23.2039 MM; and *USL* = \$25.6465 MM. The Six Sigma process capability metrics *Cp, Cpk*, and σ-*L* are not applicable. There is a 5.0% probability that the *Mean* will be below \$23.030 MM; a 90.0% probability that it will be in the range of \$23.030 MM – \$25.479 MM; and a 5.0% probability that it will be above \$25.479 MM.

Figure 6. Portfolio 3 objective profit mean distribution

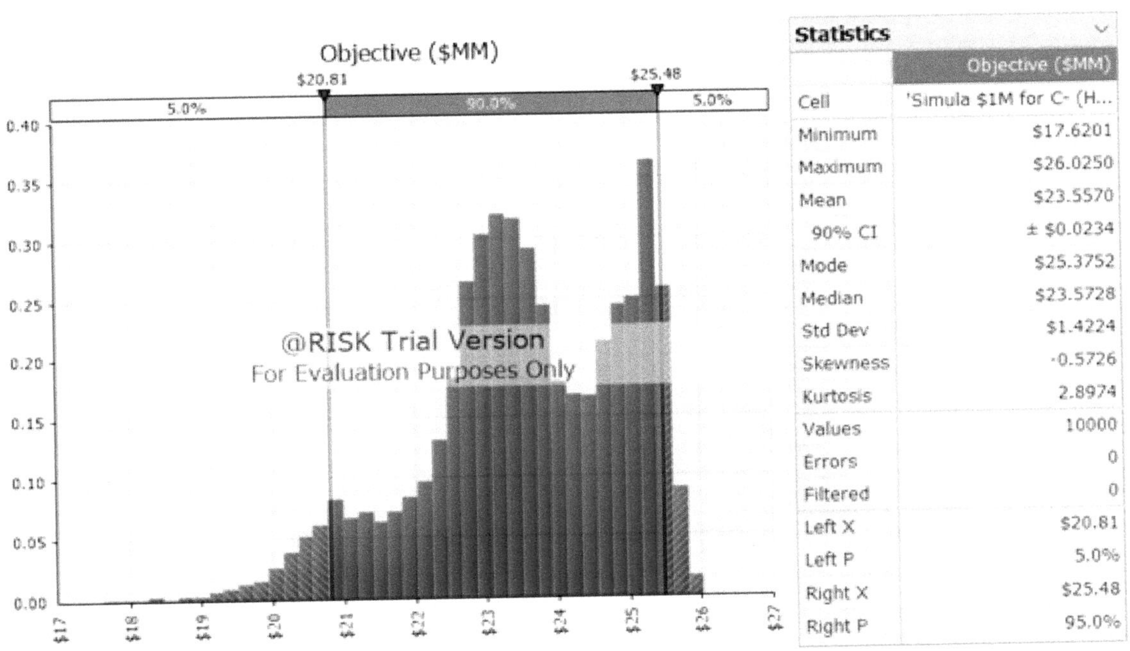

	Objective ($MM)
Cell	'Simula $1M for C- (H...
Minimum	$17.6201
Maximum	$26.0250
Mean	$23.5570
90% CI	± $0.0234
Mode	$25.3752
Median	$23.5728
Std Dev	$1.4224
Skewness	-0.5726
Kurtosis	2.8974
Values	10000
Errors	0
Filtered	0
Left X	$20.81
Left P	5.0%
Right X	$25.48
Right P	95.0%

The Objective Profit *Mean* (Figure 6) is \$23.5570 MM with a *Standard Deviation* of \$1.4224 MM, i.e., 6.038%, which is a low risk. There is a 5.0% probability that the *Mean* will be below \$20.81 MM; a 90.0% probability that it will be in the range of \$20.81 MM – \$25.48 MM; and a 5.0% probability that it will be above \$25.48 MM.

The Best Portfolio Evaluation and What-If Analysis

It was established that Efficient Frontier Portfolio No. 4 is technically the best. Therefore, this portfolio is considered below.

Efficient Frontier Portfolio No 4 Evaluation and What-If Analysis

Evaluation

The distributions of the Optimal Portfolio No 4 are shown in Figure 7 and Figure 8.

Figure 7. Portfolio 4 gross profit mean distribution

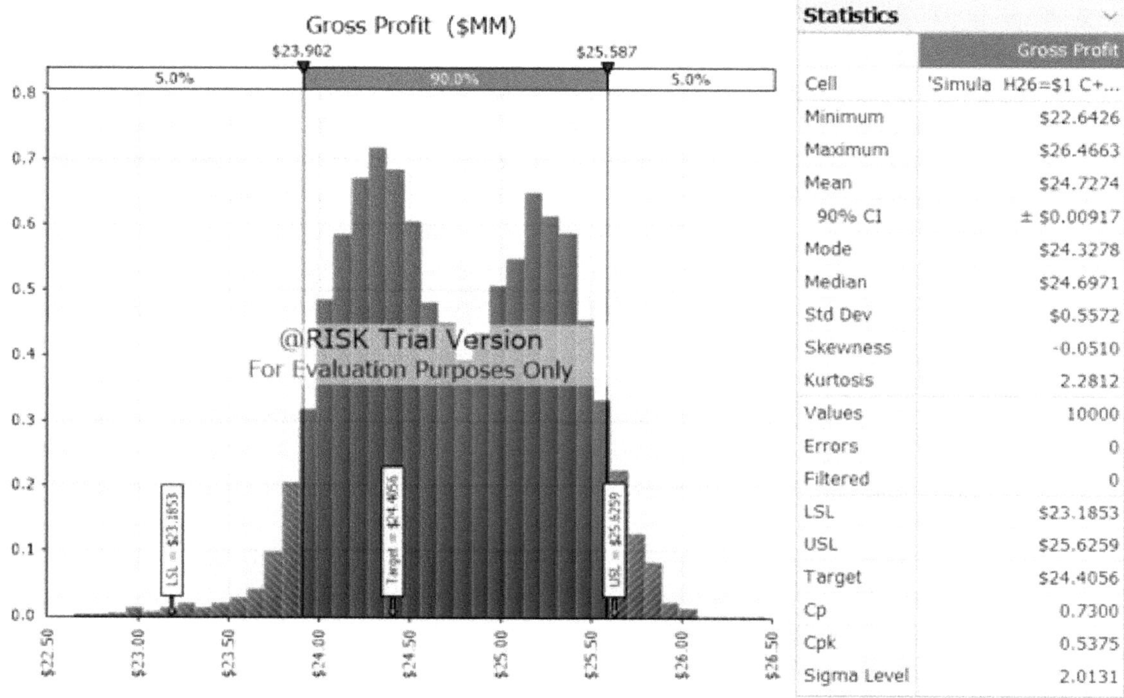

The Gross Profit *Mean* (Figure 7) is $24.7274 MM with a *Standard Deviation* of $0.5572 MM, i.e., 2.253%, which is a very low risk. The Six Sigma target parameters are *TV* = $24.4056 MM; *LSL* = $23.1853 MM; and *USL* = $25.6259 MM. The Six Sigma process capability metrics are *Cp* = 0.7300; *Cpk* = 0.5375; and σ-*L* = 2.0131. There is a 5.0% probability that the *Mean* will be below $23.902 MM; a 90.0% probability that it will be in the range of $23.902 MM – $25.587 MM; and a 5.0% probability that it will be above $25.587 MM.

Figure 8. Portfolio 4 objective profit mean distribution

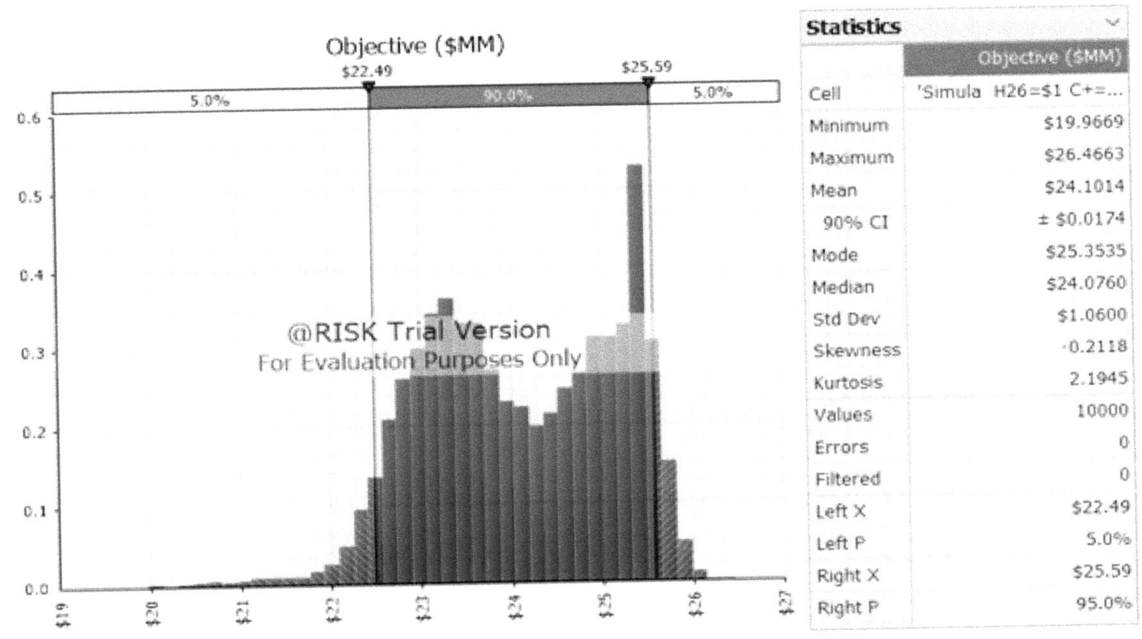

The Objective Profit *Mean* (Figure 8) is $24.1014 MM with a *Standard Deviation* of $1.0600 MM, i.e., 4.938%, which is a low risk. There is a 5.0% probability that the *Mean* will be below $22.49 MM; a 90.0% probability that it will be in the range of $22.49 MM – $25.59 MM; and a 5.0% probability that it will be above $25.59 MM.

What-If Analysis of Gross Profit

What-If Analysis provides for ranking the inputs by the variability of the output based on the calculation without a probability distribution. It also quantifies the minimum and maximum values and changes the percentage of the output for the associated minimum and maximum values of the input, reporting the input base value.

The Gross Profit tornado graph is given in Figure 9.

Figure 9. Gross profit tornado graph

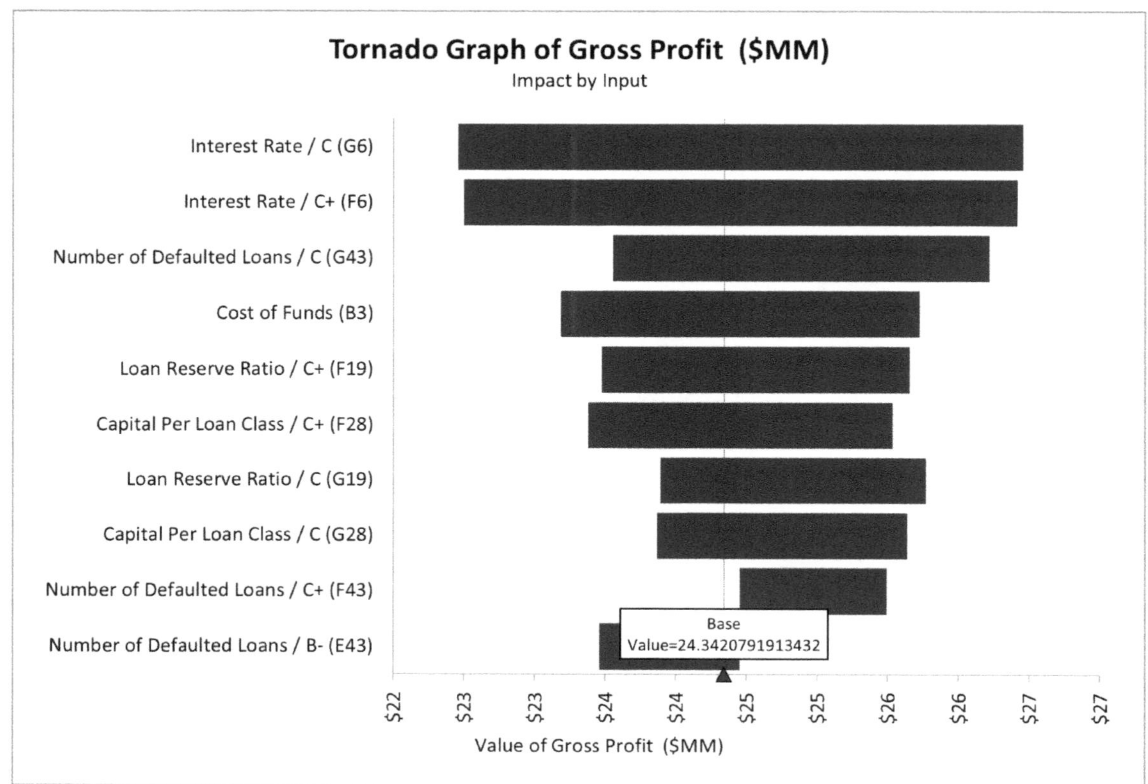

The graph shows the Gross Profit values on the x-axis. It illustrates that the Gross Profit Base Value is $24.342 MM, which is marked on the graph and is calculated from the independent variable Base values given in Table 3.

The bars on the graph quantify the variability of the profit from every independent variable showing the Minimum and Maximum, which are respectively left and right from the Base value. The profit Minimum and Maximum are respectively calculated from the independent variable Minimum and Maximum values given in Table 3.

Figure 9 also shows that the three most influential input variables are: 1) Interest Rate / Grade C; 2) Interest Rate / Grade C+; 3) Number of Defaulted Loans / Grade C. The other input variables are less influential.

The What-If Analysis Summary for Gross Profit is presented in Table 3. The Summary table quantifies the minimum and maximum values and changes the percentage of the output for the associated minimum and maximum values of the input, as well as the input base value.

Table 3. What-if analysis summary for gross profit

What-If Analysis Summary for Output Gross Profit ($MM)								
Top 3 Inputs Ranked by Change in Actual Value								
		Minimum			Maximum			
		Output		Input	Output		Input	Input
Rank	Input Name	Value	Change (%)	Value	Value	Change (%)	Value	Base Value
1	Interest Rate / C	$22	-7.75%	9.9%	$26	8.68%	12.1%	11.0%
2	Interest Rate / C+	$22	-7.58%	9.0%	$26	8.52%	11.0%	10.0%
3	Number of Defaulted Loans / C	$24	-3.24%	0.03	$26	7.70%	0	0.015

1) Interest Rate / Grade C: The input base value is 11.0% (i.e., 0.11). The input minimum value is 9.9%, for which the profit has a minimum of $22 MM, i.e., a change of -7.75% from the profit Base Value of $24.342 MM. The input maximum value is 12.1%, for which the profit has a maximum of $26 MM, i.e., a change of 8.68% from the profit Base Value.
2) Interest Rate / Grade C+: The input base value is 10.0%. The input minimum value is 9.0%, for which the profit has a minimum of $22 MM, i.e., a change of -7.58% from the profit Base Value of $24.342 MM. The input maximum value is 11.0%, for which the profit has a maximum of $26 MM, i.e., a change of 8.52% from the profit Base Value.
3) Number of Defaulted Loans / Grade C: The input base value is 0.015. The input minimum value is 0.03, for which the profit has a minimum of $24 MM, i.e., a change of -3.24% from the profit Base Value of $24.342 MM. The input maximum value is zero, for which the profit has a maximum of $26 MM, i.e., a change of 7.7% from the profit Base Value.

The other input variables are less influential, so they are not considered here.

What-If Analysis of Objective Profit

The Objective Profit tornado graph is given in Figure 10.

The graph shows the Objective Profit values on the x-axis. It illustrates that the Objective Profit Base Value is $23.430 MM, which is marked on the graph and is calculated from the independent variable Base values given in Table 4. The bars on the graph quantify the variability of the profit from every independent variable showing the Minimum and Maximum, which are respectively left and right from the Base value. The profit Minimum and Maximum are respectively calculated from the independent variable Minimum and Maximum values given in Table 12.4.

Figure 10 also shows that the three most influential input variables are: 1) Number of Defaulted Loans / Grade C; 2) Interest Rate / Grade C; 3). Interest Rate / Grade C+. The other input variables are less influential.

Figure 10. Objective profit tornado graph

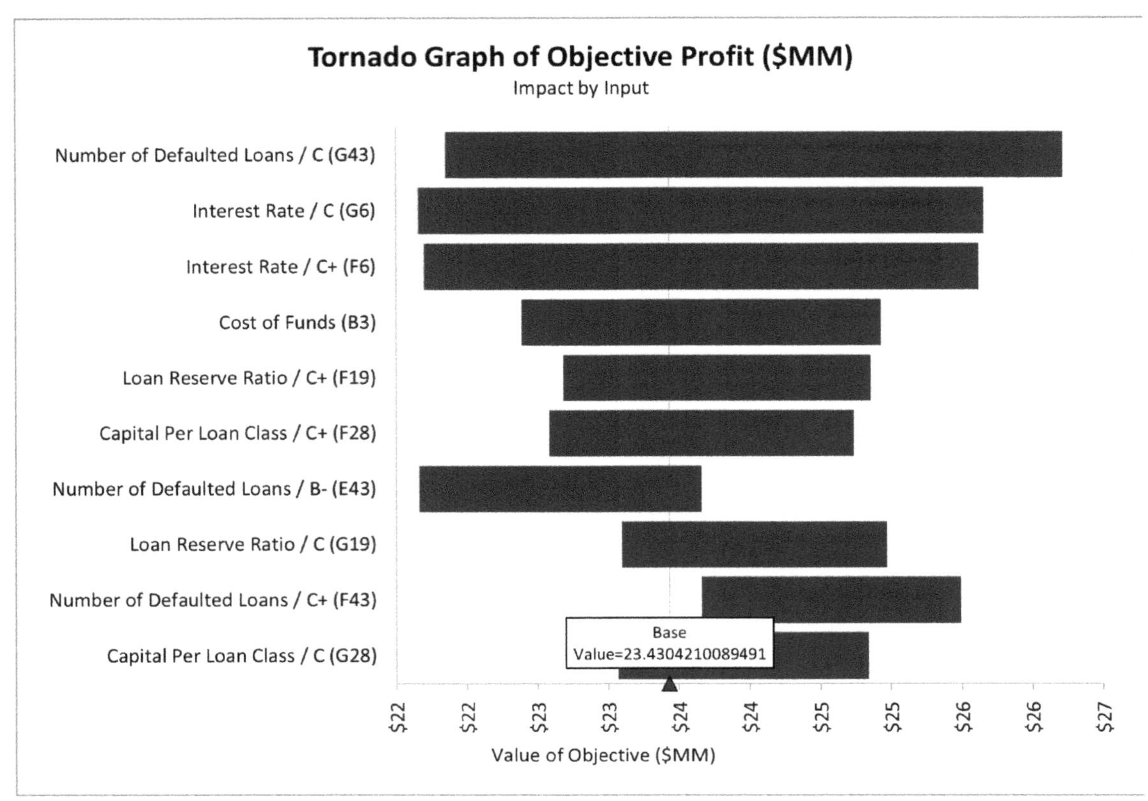

The What-If Analysis Summary for Objective Profit is presented in Table 4.

Table 4. What-if analysis summary for objective profit

What-If Analysis Summary for Output Objective Profit ($MM)								
Top 3 Inputs Ranked by Change in Actual Value								
		Minimum			Maximum			
		Output		Input	Output		Input	Input
Rank	**Input Name**	**Value**	**Change (%)**	**Value**	**Value**	**Change (%)**	**Value**	**Base Value**
1	Number of Defaulted Loans / C	$22	-6.74%	0.03	$26	11.89%	0	0.015
2	Interest Rate / C	$22	-7.56%	9.9%	$26	9.51%	12.1%	11.0%
3	Interest Rate / C+	$22	-7.39%	9.0%	$26	9.34%	11.0%	10.0%

The Summary table (Table 12.4) quantifies the minimum and maximum values and changes the percentage of the output for the associated minimum and maximum values of the input, as well as the input base value.

1) Number of Defaulted Loans / Grade C: The input base value is 0.015. The input minimum value is 0.03, for which the profit has a minimum of $22 MM, i.e., a change of -6.74% from the profit Base Value of $23.430 MM. The input maximum value is zero, for which the profit has a maximum of $26 MM, i.e., a change of 11.89% from the profit Base Value.
2) Interest Rate / Grade C: The input base value is 11.0%. The input minimum value is 9.9%, for which the profit has a minimum of $22 MM, i.e., a change of -7.56% from the profit Base Value of $23.430 MM. The input maximum value is 12.1%, for which the profit has a maximum of $26 MM, i.e., a change of 9.51% from the profit Base Value.
3) Interest Rate / Grade C+: The input base value is 10.0%. The input minimum value is 9.0%, for which the profit has a minimum of $22 MM, i.e., a change of -7.39% from the profit Base Value of $23.430 MM. The input maximum value is 11.0%, for which the profit has a maximum of $26 MM, i.e., a change of 9.34% from the profit Base Value.

The other input variables are less influential, so they are not considered here.

CONCLUSION

This chapter presented a credit risk analysis of a banking loan portfolio.

Firstly, the Efficient Frontier of four minimal mean-variance loan portfolios with maximal profit was determined. The Gross Profit, Objective Profit, and Loan Losses for Efficient Frontier portfolios were stochastically calculated.

The loan portfolios' performance was measured and evaluated considering Gross Profit and Objective. Bank regulation limits were applied, based on the bank's capital, to control the maximum loan amount per loan investment grade.

The best technical loan portfolio was determined based on the criterion of maximal profit.

The method conventionally used stochastic optimisation to determine the Efficient Frontier of minimal mean-variance loan portfolios. It applied Monte Carlo simulation to stochastically calculate and measure the loan portfolio attributes such as gross and objective profit, and loan losses, to quantify the credit risk.

The analysis of the simulation results determined technically the best optimal portfolio from the Efficient Frontier based on the criterion of maximum profit. This best portfolio had a Gross Profit *Mean* of $24.7274 MM with a *Standard Deviation* of $0.5572 MM, i.e., 2.253%, which is a very low risk. The Objective Profit *Mean* was $24.1014 MM with a *Standard Deviation* of $1.0600 MM, i.e., 4.938%, which is also a low risk.

What-if analysis was applied, which provided a comprehensive view of the probability of the outputs and quantified the sensitivity of the outputs based on the variability of the associated inputs. The analysis of the best optimal portfolio identified that the riskiest inputs were Interest Rate / Grade C, Interest Rate / Grade C+, and Number of Defaulted Loans / Grade C. The other input variables were less influential.

Standard Deviation is a major risk factor. The Standard Deviation for both, the Gross Profit of 2.253%, and the Objective Profit of 4.938% were very low. Consequently, the technical conclusion is that management should execute this loan portfolio. This risk analysis helped management to make an informed decision.

REFERENCES

Berger, A. N., & DeYoung, R. (1997). Problem loans and cost efficiency in commercial banks. *Journal of Banking & Finance*, *21*(6), 849–870. doi:10.1016/S0378-4266(97)00003-4

Bernstein, P. L., & Damodaran, A. (1998). *Investment Management*. John Wiley & Sons.

Bubevski, V. (2017). *Novel Six Sigma Approaches to Risk Assessment and Management*. IGI Global.

Comptroller of the Currency Administration. (2015). *Loan Portfolio Management: Comptroller's Handbook*. CreateSpace.

Crouhya, M., Galaib, D., & Marka, R. (2000). A comparative analysis of current credit risk models. *Journal of Banking & Finance*, *24*(1-2), 59–117. doi:10.1016/S0378-4266(99)00053-9

Fabozzi, F. J. (Ed.). (1998). *Bank Loans: Secondary Market and Portfolio Management*. John Wiley & Sons.

Glasserman, P. (2004). *Monte Carlo Methods in Financial Engineering*. Springer Science.

Gordy, M. B. (2003). A risk-factor model foundation for ratings-based bank capital rules. *Journal of Financial Intermediation*, *12*(3), 199–232. doi:10.1016/S1042-9573(03)00040-8

Hünseler, M. (2013). *Credit Portfolio Management: A Practitioner's Guide to the Active Management of Credit Risks*. Springer. doi:10.1057/9780230391505

Lütkebohmert, E. (2009). *Concentration Risk in Credit Portfolios*. Springer.

Markowitz, H. M. (1952). Portfolio Selection. *The Journal of Finance*, *7*, 77–91.

Markowitz, H. M. (1987). *Mean-Variance Analysis in Portfolio Choice and Capital Markets*. Basil Blackwell.

Merton, R. C. (1974). On the Pricing of Corporate Debt: The Risk Structure of Interest Rates. *The Journal of Finance*, *29*(2), 449–470.

Nersesian, R. L. (2011). *RISK Bank Credit and Financial Analysis* (2nd ed.). Palisade Corporation.

Rossia, S. P. S., Schwaigerc, M. S., & Winklerd, G. (2009). How loan portfolio diversification affects risk, efficiency and capitalization: A managerial behaviour model for Austrian banks. *Journal of Banking & Finance*, *33*(12), 2218–2226. doi:10.1016/j.jbankfin.2009.05.022

Seal, K. (2016). *Market Risk, International Monetary Fund*. In 2016 Seminar for Senior Bank Supervisors, Washington, DC. Retrieved from http://pubdocs. worldbank.org/en/253431477065134529/4-Minimum-Capital-Requirements- for-Market-Risk.pdf

Wilson, T. C. (1998). Portfolio Credit Risk. *Economic Policy Review*, *4*(3).

Ziemba, W. T., & Vickson, S. W. (Eds.). (2006). *Stochastic Optimization Models in Finance*. World Scientific. doi:10.1142/6101

Chapter 13
Price Evolution With Markov Chain Monte Carlo

ABSTRACT

This chapter presents a generic model for price evolution with the Markov Chain Monte Carlo (MCMC) method. MCMC is a stochastic simulation process observed through a time where the probability distribution of the next stage of the process, given the current state, is independent of the past states. MCMC simulation model is governed by the initial state at time zero and a one-step transition probability matrix. Each row of this matrix shows the probability distribution of the next state, given the current state for that row. An additional model illustrates the evolution of prices over time. It assumes that there is an underlying process, such as the state of the economy, that follows an MCMC with three states. Then for any given state, the price change is simulated with a probability distribution with parameters that depend on the state. The presented model is generic and applicable to all prices.

INTRODUCTION

This chapter presents a Price Evolution with the Markov Chain Monte Carlo method.

Here are some of Wikipedia's explanations relating to Markov Chains. A Markov Chain is a stochastic model describing a sequence of possible events in which the probability of each event depends only on the state attained in the previous event. A countably infinite sequence, in which the chain moves state at discrete time steps, gives a Discrete-Time Markov chain (DTMC). A continuous-time process is called a Continuous-Time Markov chain (CTMC). It is named after the Russian mathematician Andrey Markov.

Markov Chain Monte Carlo (MCMC) methods comprise a class of algorithms for sampling from a probability distribution. By constructing a Markov Chain that has the desired distribution as its equilibrium distribution, one can obtain a sample of the desired distribution by recording states from the chain. The more steps are included, the more closely the distribution of the sample matches the actual desired distribution.

DOI: 10.4018/979-8-3693-3787-5.ch013

Markov Chains have many applications as statistical models of real-world processes, such as studying cruise control systems in motor vehicles, queues or lines of customers arriving at an airport, currency exchange rates, animal population dynamics, etc.

Markov processes are the basis for general stochastic simulation methods known as Markov chain Monte Carlo, which are used for simulating sampling from complex probability distributions and have found application in Bayesian statistics, thermodynamics, statistical mechanics, physics, chemistry, economics, finance, signal processing, information theory, and artificial intelligence. The adjective "Markovian" is used to describe something related to a Markov process.

The presented Markov Chain Monte Carlo simulation model, for the prediction of the Price Evolution, is governed by the initial state at time zero and a one-step transition probability matrix. Each row of this matrix shows the probability distribution of the next state, given the current state for that row.

An additional model illustrates the evolution of prices through time. It assumes that there is an underlying process, such as the state of the economy, that follows a Markov Chain with three states. Then for any given state, the price change is simulated with a probability distribution with parameters that depend on the state.

Three simulations are applied to generate states and prices through time, starting with a given price, i.e., one simulation for any of the three possible starting states. The presented model is generic and applicable to all sorts of prices, including stock market prices, prices of goods in marketing, etc.

The initial state at time zero given inputs is i) State, which could be one (1), two (2), or three (3); ii) Initial Price, which is $1,000.00; iii) One-Step Transition Probability Matrix shown in Table 13.1; iv) Parameters of Price Changes in States incl. Mean and Standard Deviation (SD) are given in Table 2.

Table 1 shows the One-Step Transition Probability Matrix.

Table 1. One-step transition probability matrix

State	1	2	3
1	0.5	0.4	0.1
2	0.3	0.6	0.1
3	0.5	0.3	0.2

Table 2 shows the Parameters of Price Changes in States, i.e., Mean and Standard Deviation (SD).

Table 2. Parameters of price changes in states

State	1	2	3
Mean	0%	5%	-10%
Standard Deviation (SD)	5%	8%	15%

The simulation variables are vectors of 45 values: i) Time Vector; ii) Simulate State Vector; iii) Price Vector.

The simulation output vectors of three values, i.e., one for each state, are: i) State Vector; ii) First Visit Vector; iii) Average 1st Visit Start 1 Vector; iv) Average 1st Visit Start 2 Vector; v) Average 1st Visit Start 3 Vector; vi) Fraction Vector; vii) Average Fraction Start 1 Vector; viii) Average Fraction Start 2 Vector; ix) Average Fraction Start 3 Vector.

The simulation output variables are: i) Average Price; ii) Price @ Time 1; iii) Price @ Time 45.

A simulation model is designed and run to predict the Price Evolution with Markov Chain Monte Carlo. What-if and Sensitivity Analysis are applied, which provide a comprehensive view of the probability of the outputs and quantify the sensitivity of the outputs based on the variability of the associated inputs and financial variables.

This risk analysis helps management to decide on the prices of their business.

Literature

Some references for Markov Chains are given below. Behrends' (2000) book presents the mathematical concepts of Markov Chains. Besides the investigation of general chains, the book contains chapters that are concerned with eigenvalue techniques, conductance, stopping times, the strong Markov property, couplings, strong uniform times, Markov chains on arbitrary finite groups (including a crash course in harmonic analysis), random generation and counting, Markov random fields, Gibbs fields, the Metropolis sampler, and simulated annealing. Revuz (1984) published a classic book that is an introduction to sub-Markovian kernels on general measurable spaces and their associated homogeneous Markov chains. The first part, an expository text on the foundations of the subject, is intended for post-graduate students. A study of potential theory, the basic classification of chains according to their asymptotic behaviour, and the celebrated Chacon-Ornstein theorem are examined in detail. The second part of the book is at a more advanced level and includes a treatment of random walks on general locally compact abelian groups. Further chapters develop renewal theory, an introduction to Martin's boundary, and the study of chains recurrent in the Harris sense. Finally, the last chapter deals with the construction of chains starting from a kernel satisfying some kind of maximum principle.

The paper by Bhusal (2018) applied a Markov chain model to forecast the behaviour of the Nepal Stock Exchange (NEPSE) index. The application of the Markov chain model for forecasting future states is based on the strong feature of the randomness of the NEPSE index. This study explores the long-run behaviour of the NEPSE index, the expected number of visits to a particular state, and determines the expected first return time of various states. The NEPSE index showed three different states: Up (U), remains Same (S), and Down (D). The initial state vector and transition probability matrix, which were used to predict the behaviour of the index has been obtained from the close inspection of the number of transitions from one state to another. The study predicted that regardless of the present status of the NEPSE index, in the long run, the index will decrease with the highest probability, increase with a lower probability, and remain in the same state with the lowest probability. It was also observed that the index will remain increasing after three days when it starts to move from the increasing state. Jasinthan et al. (2015) developed a stochastic model to represent the price movement at various time intervals that have long been a nature of interest in the stock market, business processes, and others. The daily price data of vegetables at the Thirunelvelly market for 1704 days (Jan 2009-Sept 2013) have been collected from the Vallampuri paper corporation, Jaffna, Sri Lanka. The data were analysed to classify the price movement change on two successive days. The authors constructed the Markov chain models for the daily vegetable price movement in Jaffna. Two models were highlighted, where the price movement was considered as being in a state of gain or loss, large gain, small gain or loss, or large loss. Twelve different types of vegetables were considered, and models were used to analyse the price movement of each vegetable. These models obtained transitional probabilities, steady-state probabilities, and mean recurrence times. The results indicated that the pattern of the price movement of eggplant is similar to the price movements of other vegetables, in both models.

The Problem Statement: Perform the Price Evolution by using Markov Chains Monte Carlo. Design a simulation model to calculate the prediction. Apply What-If and Sensitivity Analysis to provide a comprehensive view of the probability of the outputs and quantify the sensitivity of the outputs based on the variability of the associated inputs including financial variables. This risk analysis helps management to decide on the prices of their business.

ELABORATION

The scenario presented in this chapter is hypothetical, using data published by Palisade™ Corporation.

Model Data Definition

The simulation model for the prediction of the Price Evolution with Markov Chain Monte Carlo is detailed in this section. The simulation is designed to perform the analysis.

The initial state at time zero given inputs are i) Initial State (*InitialState*), which could be one (1), two (2), or three (3); ii) Initial Price (*InitialPrice)*, which is $1,000.00; iii) One-Step Transition Probability Matrix (*TransitionProbabilityM(j,j)*) shown in Table 1; iv) Parameters of Price Changes in States including, Mean Vector (*Mean(j)*) and Standard Deviation Vector (*SDV(j)*) given in Table 2. The simulation variables are vectors of 45 values: i) Time Vector (*TimeV(i)*); ii) Simulate State Vector (*SimulateStateV(i)*); iii) Price Vector (*PriceV(i)*); where $i = 1, 2, \ldots, 45$.

The simulation output vectors of three values, i.e., one for each state, are: i) State Vector (*StateV(j)*); ii) First Visit Vector (*FirstVisitV(j)*); iii) Average 1st Visit Start 1 Vector (*Average1stVisitStart1V(j)*); iv) Average 1st Visit Start 2 Vector (*Average1stVisitStart2V(j)*); v) Average 1st Visit Start 3 Vector (*Average1stVisitStart3V(j)*); vi) Fraction Vector (*FractionV(j)*); vii) Average Fraction Start 1 Vector (*AverageFractionStart1V(j)*); viii) Average Fraction Start 2 Vector (*AverageFractionStart2V(j)*); ix) Average Fraction Start 3 Vector (*AverageFractionStart3V(j)*); where $j = 1, 2, 3$.

The simulation output variables are i) Average Price (*AveragePrice*); ii) Price @ Time 1 (*Price@ Time1*); iii) Price @ Time 45 (*Price@Time45*).

Calculations

Microsoft™ Excel®, Palisade™ @RISK®, and TopRank® are used for the calculations presented in this section. The Model Data Definition is given above. The calculations are the following.

Initial State

Initial State: *InitialState = RiskSimtable({1,2,3}) (1)*

Where *RiskSimtable* is @RISK function to run three simulations, one for each state, in the specified order.

Simulation Variables

Time Vector:

TimeV(i) = i (2)

Simulate State Vector:

SimulateStateV(i)=RiskDiscrete(StateV(j),IF(InitState=1, TransitionProbabilityM(1,j),IF(InitState=2, TransitionProbabilityM(2,j),TransitionProbabilityM(3,j)))) (3)

Price Vector:

PriceV(i)=RiskOutput(,Concatenate("Price",i))+InitialPrice* (1+RiskNormal(IF(SimulateStateV(i)=1,Mean(1), IF(SimulateStateV(i)=2, Mean(2),Mean(3))), IF(SimulateStateV(i)=1, SDV(1), IF(SimulateStateV(i)=2, SDV(2), SDV(3))))) (4)

State Vector:

StateV(j) = j (5)

First Visit Vector:

FirstVisitV(j)=RiskOutput(,"FirstVisit",j)+ MATCH(StateV(j),SimulateStateV(1):SimulateStateV(45),0) (6)

Average 1st Visit Start 1 Vector:

Average1stVisitStart1V(j) = RiskMean(FirstVisitV(j),1) (7)

Average 1st Visit Start 2 Vector:

Average1stVisitStart2V(j) = RiskMean(FirstVisitV(j),2) (8)

Average 1st Visit Start 3 Vector:

Average1stVisitStart3V(j) = RiskMean(FirstVisitV(j),3) (9)

Fraction Vector:

FractionV(j)=RiskOutput(,"Fraction",j)+ COUNTIF(SimulateStateV(1):SimulateStateV(45),StateV(j))/ COUNT(SimulateStateV(1):SimulateStateV(45)) (10)

Average Fraction Start 1 Vector:

AverageFractionStart1V(j) = RiskMean(FractionV(j),1) (11)

Average Fraction Start 2 Vector:

AverageFractionStart2V(j) = RiskMean(FractionV(j),2) (12)

Average Fraction Start 3 Vector:

AverageFractionStart3V(j) = RiskMean(FractionV(j),3) (13)

Average Price:

AveragePrice=RiskOutput("Average-Price-($)",, RiskSixSigma(690,2069,1379,1.5,3))+ AVERAGE(PriceV(1): PriceV(45)) (14)

Price @ Time 1:

Price@Time10 = RiskOutput("Price 10 ($)")+PriceV(1) (15)

Price @ Time 45:

Price@Time45 = RiskOutput("Price 45 ($)")+PriceV(45) (16)

Where items starting with "*Risk*" are @RISK functions; $i = 1, 2, \dots, 45$; $j = 1, 2, 3$; and the associated parameters are given in Table 1 and Table 2.

Measuring Simulations' Results

Simulation 1 Results

The Simulation 1 results of Price at Time 1, Price at Time 45, and Price Evolution are presented below. Simulation 1 probability distribution of Price at Time 1 is shown in Figure 1.

Figure 1. Simulation 1 price at time 1 distribution

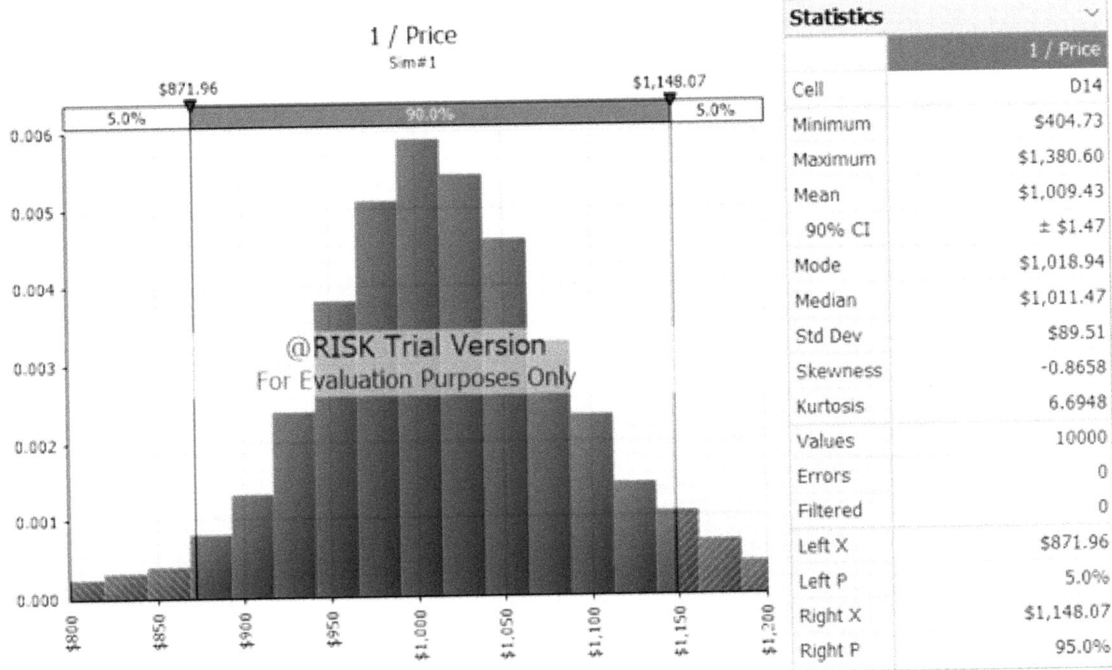

The Price at Time 1 *Mean* is $1,008.43 with a *Standard Deviation* of $89.51 (Figure 1). There is a 5.0% probability that the *Mean* will be below $871.96; a 90.0% probability that it will be in the range of $871.96 – $1,148.07; and a 5.0% probability that it will be above $1,148.07.

Simulation 1 probability distribution of Price at Time 45 is presented in Figure 2.

Price at Time 45 *Mean* is $1,882.96 with a *Standard Deviation* of $1,305.07. There is a 5.0% probability that the *Mean* will be below $473; a 90.0% probability that it will be in the range of $473 – $4,254; and a 5.0% probability that it will be above $4,254.

Figure 2. Simulation 1 price at time 45 distribution

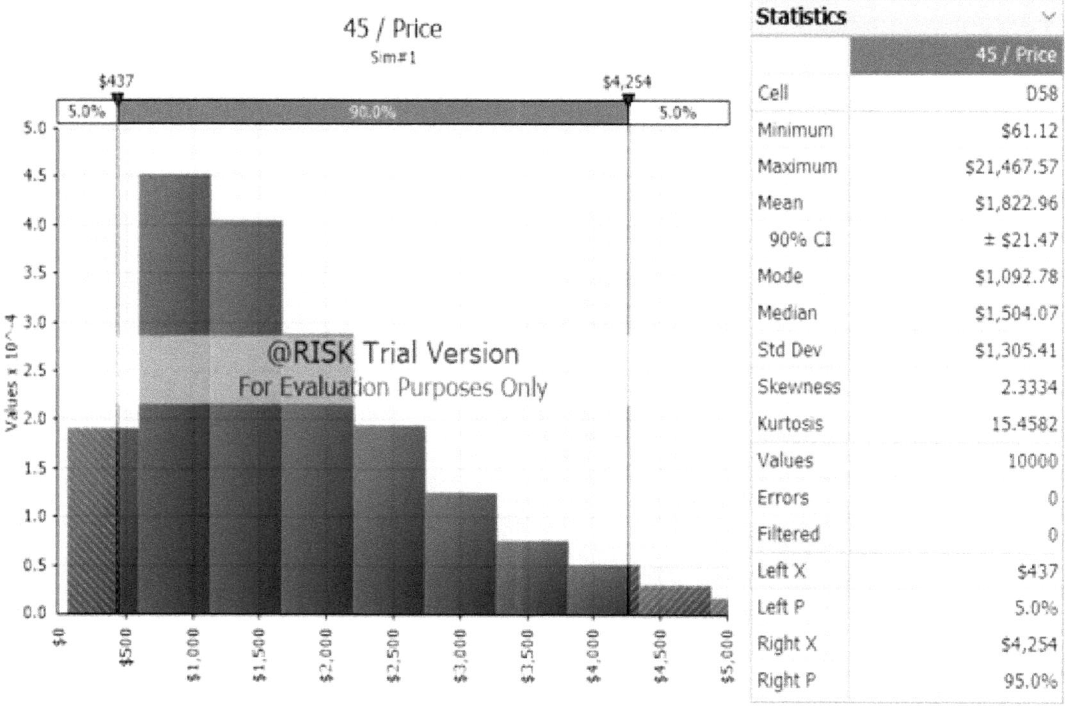

Simulation 1 Price Evolution Summary Trend is shown in Figure 3. The Simulation 1 Price Evolution starts with a Price *Mean* of $1,009.43 at Time 1, and then linearly increases reaching a Price *Mean* of $1,822.96 at Time 45.

Figure 3. Simulation 1 price evolution summary trend

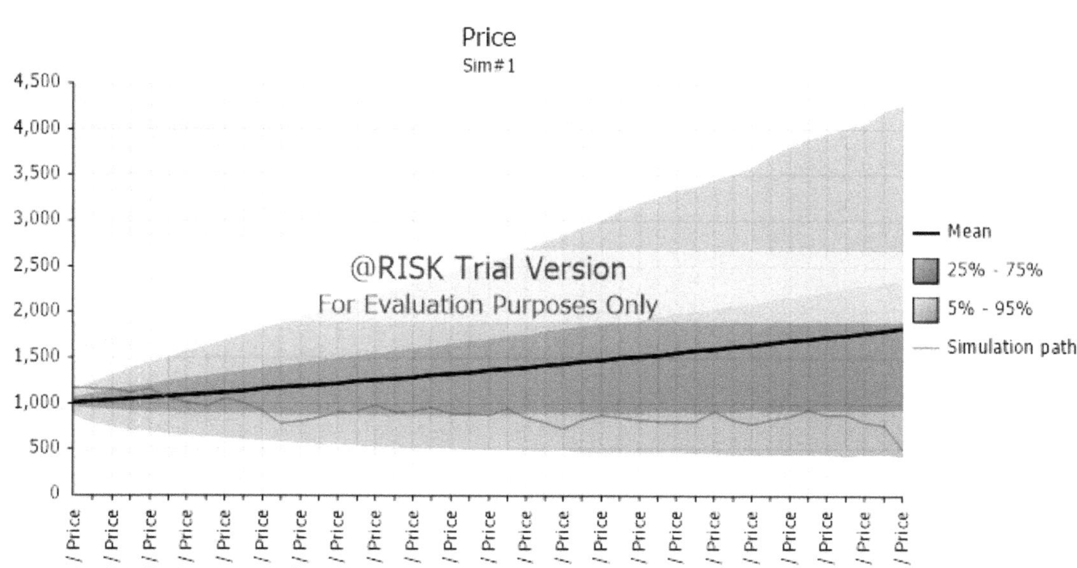

Simulation 2 Results

The Simulation 2 results of Price at Time 1, Price at Time 45, and Price Evolution are presented below. Simulation 2 probability distribution of Price at Time 1 is presented in Figure 4.

Figure 4. Simulation 2 price at time 1 distribution

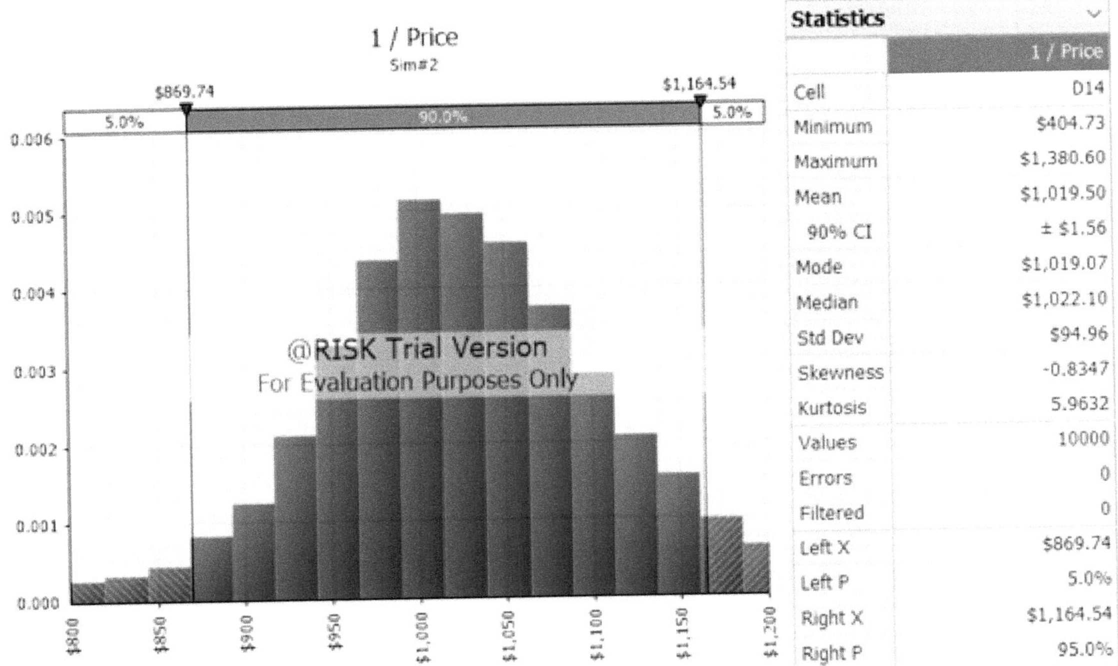

The Price at Time 1 *Mean* is $1,019.50 with a *Standard Deviation* of $94.96 (Figure 4). There is a 5.0% probability that the *Mean* will be below $869.74; a 90.0% probability that it will be in the range of $869.74 – $1,164.54; and a 5.0% probability that it will be above $1,164.54.

Simulation 2 probability distribution of Price at Time 45 is presented in Figure 5. The Price at Time 45 *Mean* is $1,846.94 with a *Standard Deviation* of $1,330.74. There is a 5.0% probability that the *Mean* will be below $440; a 90.0% probability that it will be in the range of $440 – $4,322; and a 5.0% probability that it will be above $4,322.

Figure 5. Simulation 1 price at time 45 distribution

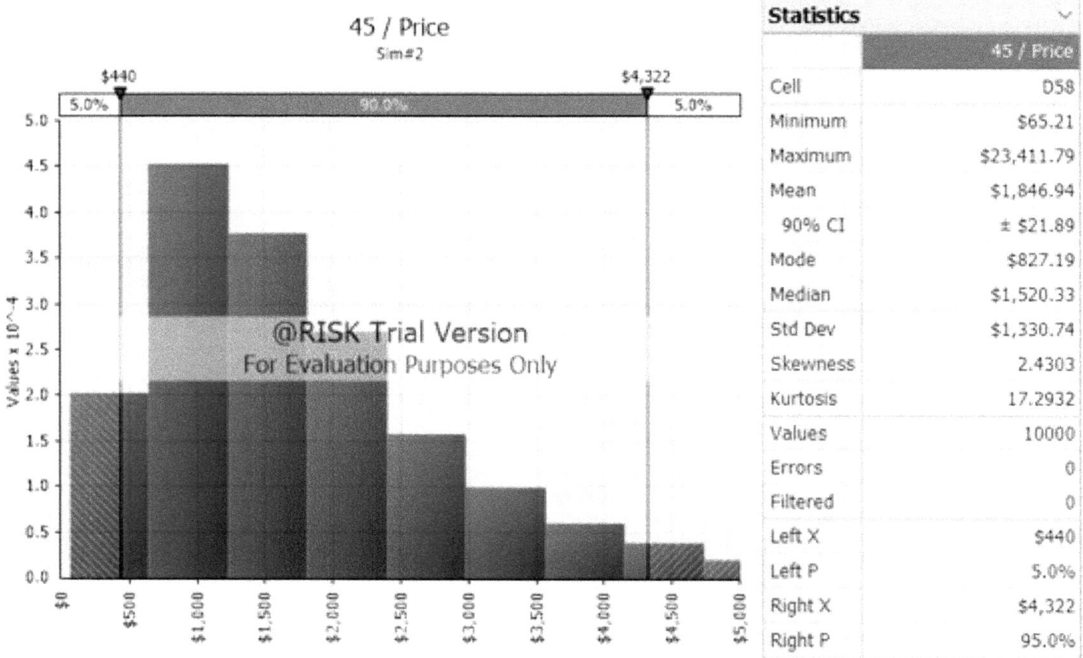

Simulation 2 Price Evolution Summary Trend is shown in Figure 6. The Evolution starts with a Price *Mean* of $1,019.50 at Time 1, and then linearly increases reaching a Price *Mean* of $1,846.94 at Time 45.

Figure 6. Simulation 2 price evolution summary trend

Simulation 3 Results

Simulation 3 probability distribution of Price at Time 1 is presented in Figure 7.

Figure 7. Simulation 3 price at time 1 distribution

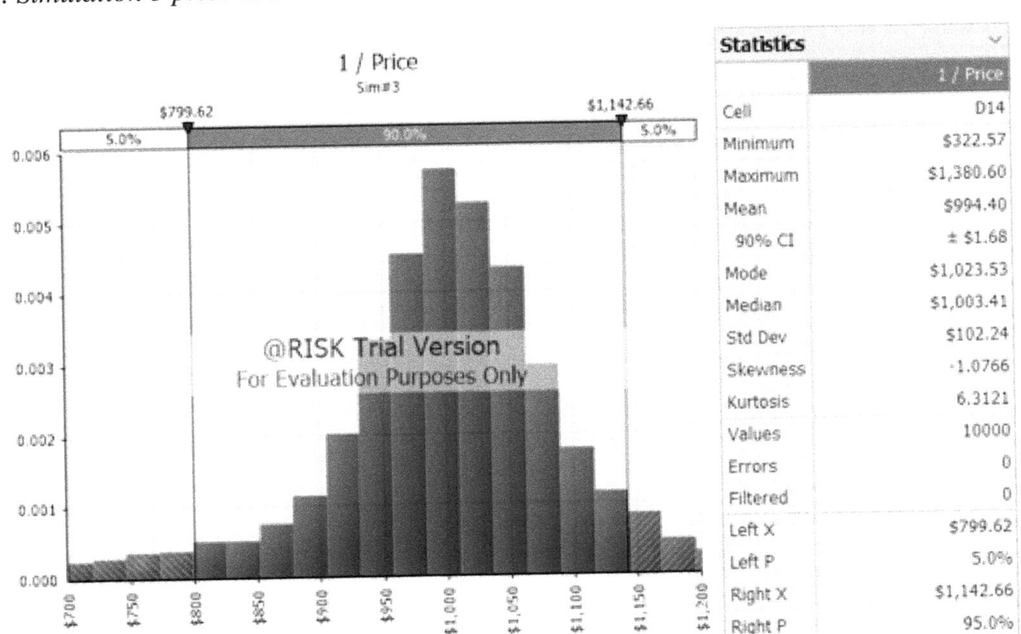

Statistics	1 / Price
Cell	D14
Minimum	$322.57
Maximum	$1,380.60
Mean	$994.40
90% CI	± $1.68
Mode	$1,023.53
Median	$1,003.41
Std Dev	$102.24
Skewness	-1.0766
Kurtosis	6.3121
Values	10000
Errors	0
Filtered	0
Left X	$799.62
Left P	5.0%
Right X	$1,142.66
Right P	95.0%

The Price at Time 1 *Mean* is \$994.40 with a *Standard Deviation* of \$102.24 (Figure 13.7). There is a 5.0% probability that the *Mean* will be below \$799.62; a 90.0% probability that it will be in the range of \$799.62 – \$1,142.66; and a 5.0% probability that it will be above \$1,142.66.

The Simulation 3 results of Price at Time 1, Price at Time 45, and Price Evolution are presented below. Simulation 3 probability distribution of Price at Time 45 is presented in Figure 8.

Figure 8. Simulation 1 price at time 45 distribution

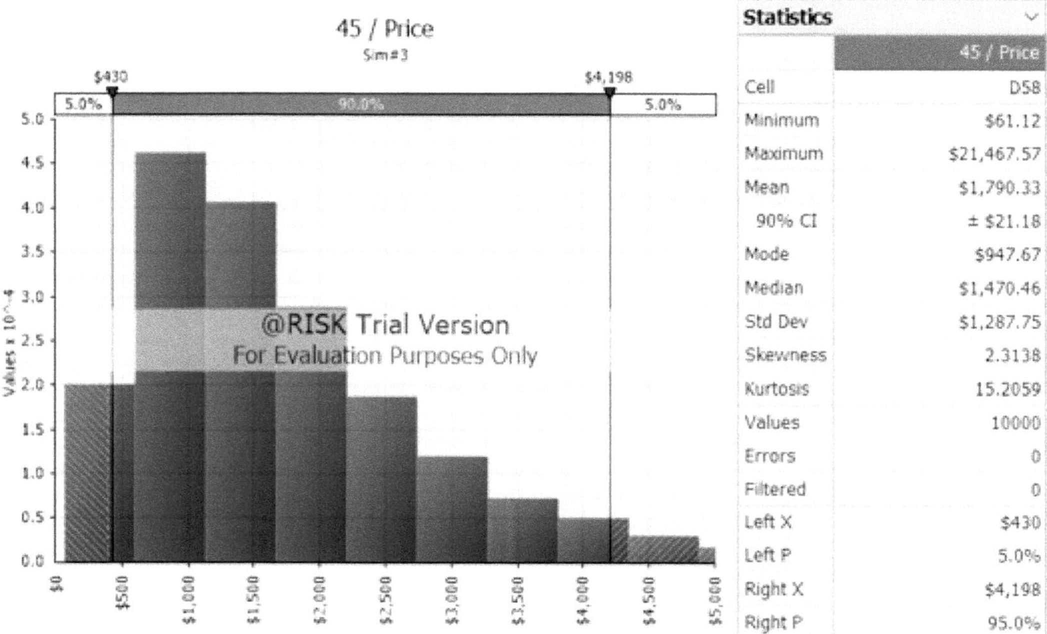

Figure 8 shows that the Price at Time 45 *Mean* is \$1,790.33 with a *Standard Deviation* of \$1,287.75. There is a 5.0% probability that the *Mean* will be below \$430; a 90.0% probability that it will be in the range of \$430 – \$4,198; and a 5.0% probability that it will be above \$4,198.

Simulation 3 Price Evolution Summary Trend is shown in Figure 9.

Figure 9. Simulation 3 price evolution summary trend

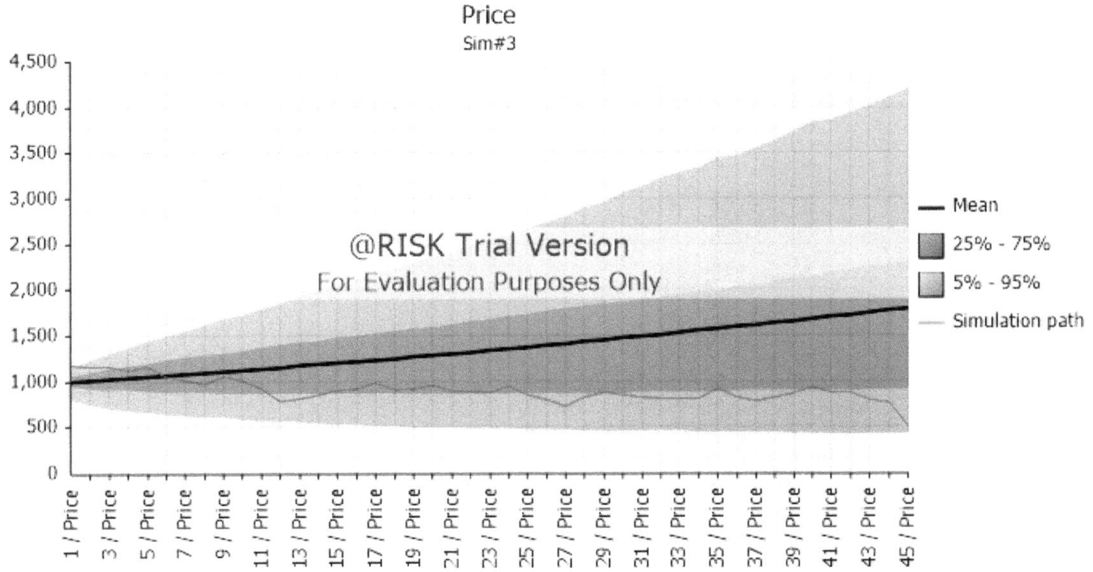

The Simulation 3 Price Evolution (Figure 9) starts with a Price *Mean* of $994.40 at Time 1, and then linearly increases reaching a Price *Mean* of $1,790.33 at Time 45 (Figure 9).

Results Evaluation, Sensitivity, and What-If Analysis

The results of the three simulations are presented below.

Simulation 1 Average Price Evaluation and Sensitivity Analysis

Simulation 1 Average Price Evaluation

The Average Price distribution is shown in Figure 10.

Figure 10. Simulation 1 average price distribution

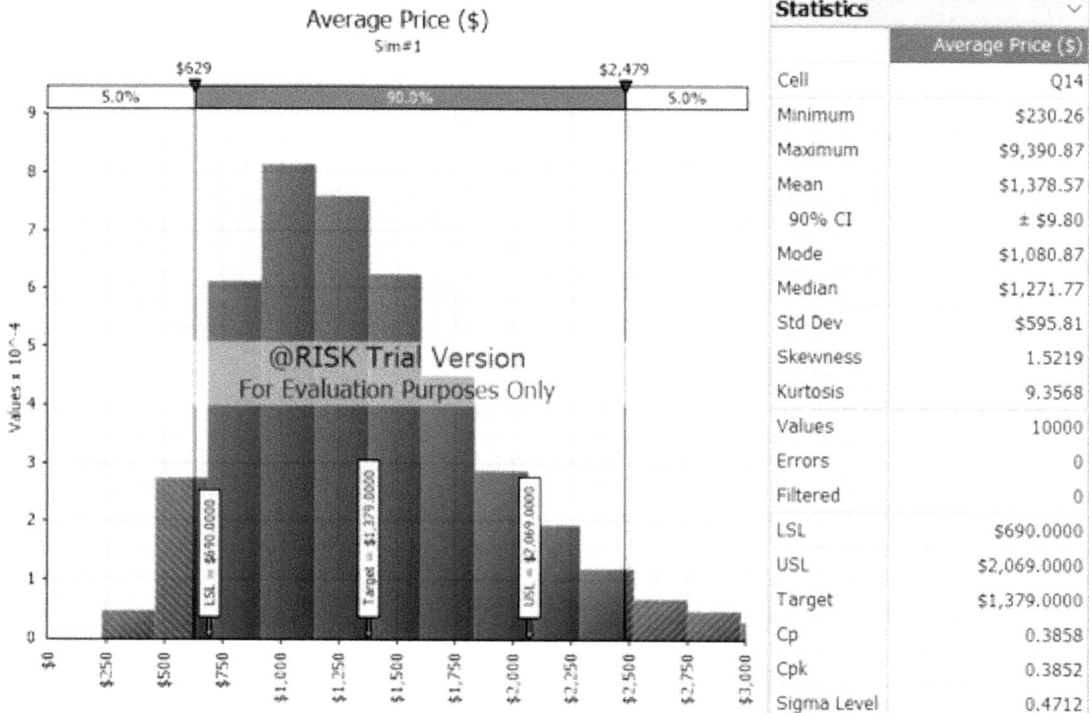

The Average Price *Mean* is $1,378.57 with a *Standard Deviation* of $595.81, i.e., 43.219%, which is an acceptable high risk (Figure 13.10). The Six Sigma target parameters are *TV* = $1,379.00; *LSL* = $690.00; and *USL* = $2,069.00. The Six Sigma process capability metrics are *Cp* = 0.3858; *Cpk* = 0.3852; and σ-*L* = 0.4712. There is a 5.0% probability that the Average Price *Mean* will be below $629; a 90.0% probability that it will be in the range of $629 – $2,470; and a 5.0% probability that it will be above $2,470.

Simulation 1 Average Price Sensitivity Analysis

Sensitivity analysis provides for identifying and quantifying the main contributors to variability and risk based on probability distribution.

The Inputs Ranked by Effect on Output Mean graph in Figure 11 illustrates that the effect of the top variable, Price at Time 2 (i.e., labelled as "2 / Price"), on the Average Price, is a change in the range of $1,120.20 to $1,625.97, which are respectively left and right from the Baseline of $1,378.57, which is marked on the graph. Other variables are less influential as their associated effects have smaller ranges.

Figure 11. Average price inputs ranked by effect on output mean

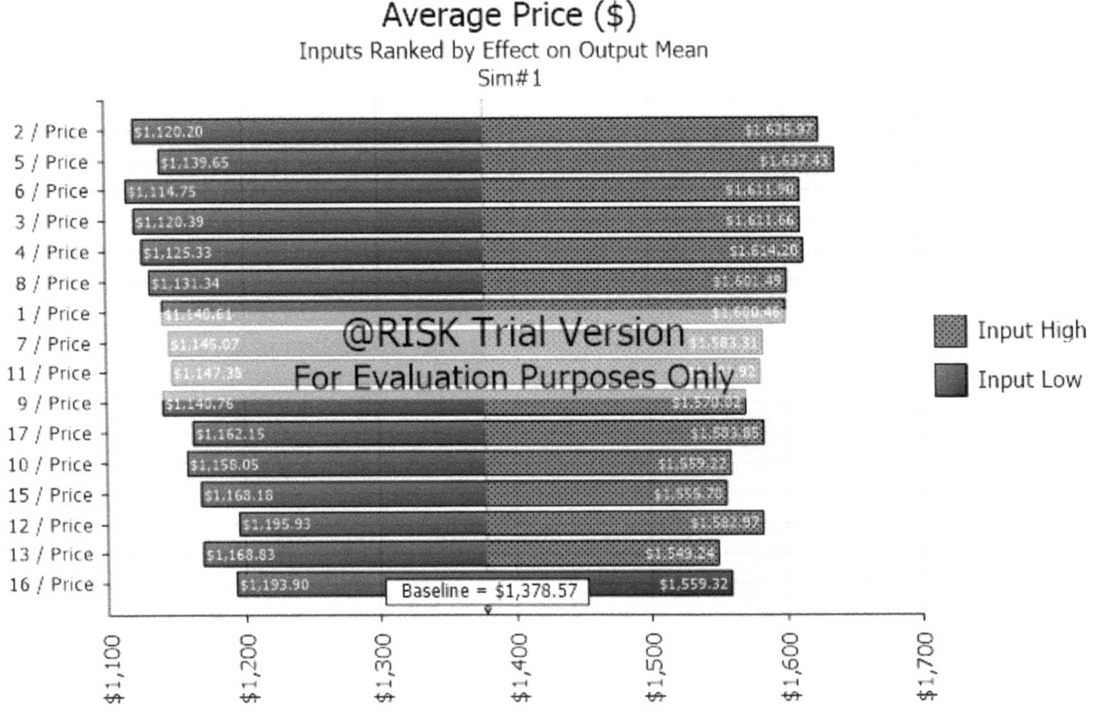

The Regression Coefficients graph is shown in Figure 12.

Figure 12 illustrates that if the top variable, Price at Time 2, with a regression coefficient of 0.21, changes by one Standard Deviation, the Average Price will change by 0.21 Standard Deviations. Other variables are less influential as their regression coefficients are in the range of 0.20 – 0.16 from top to bottom.

Figure 12. Average price regression coefficients

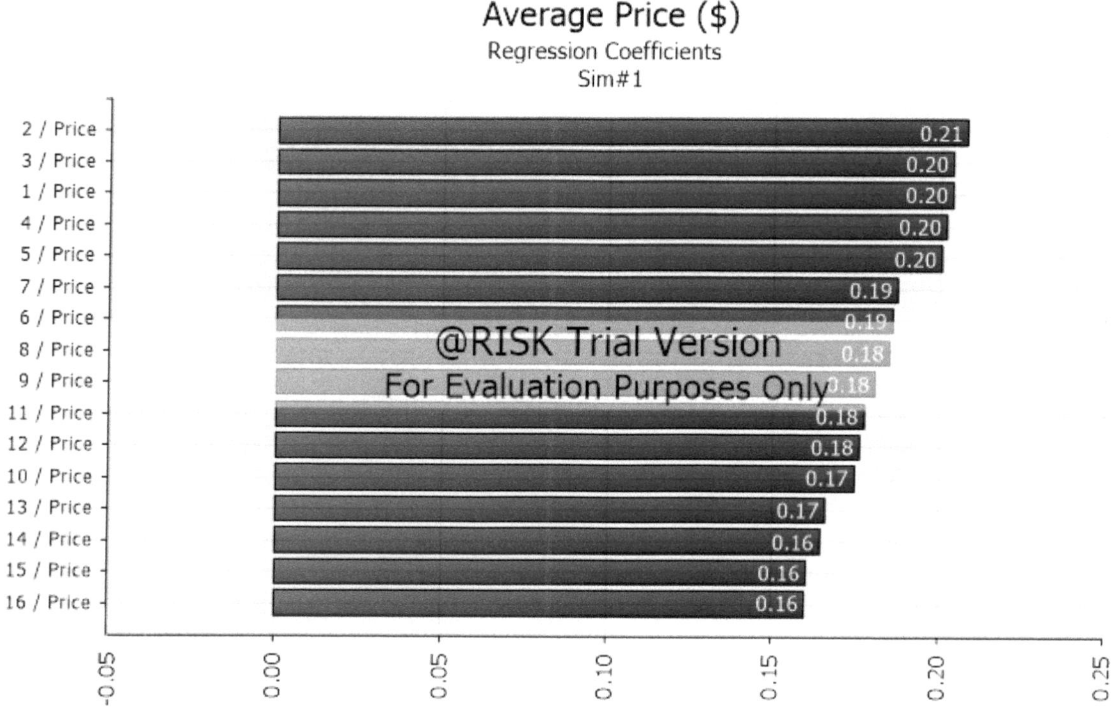

The Correlation Coefficients are presented in Figure 13.

Figure 13. Average price correlation coefficients

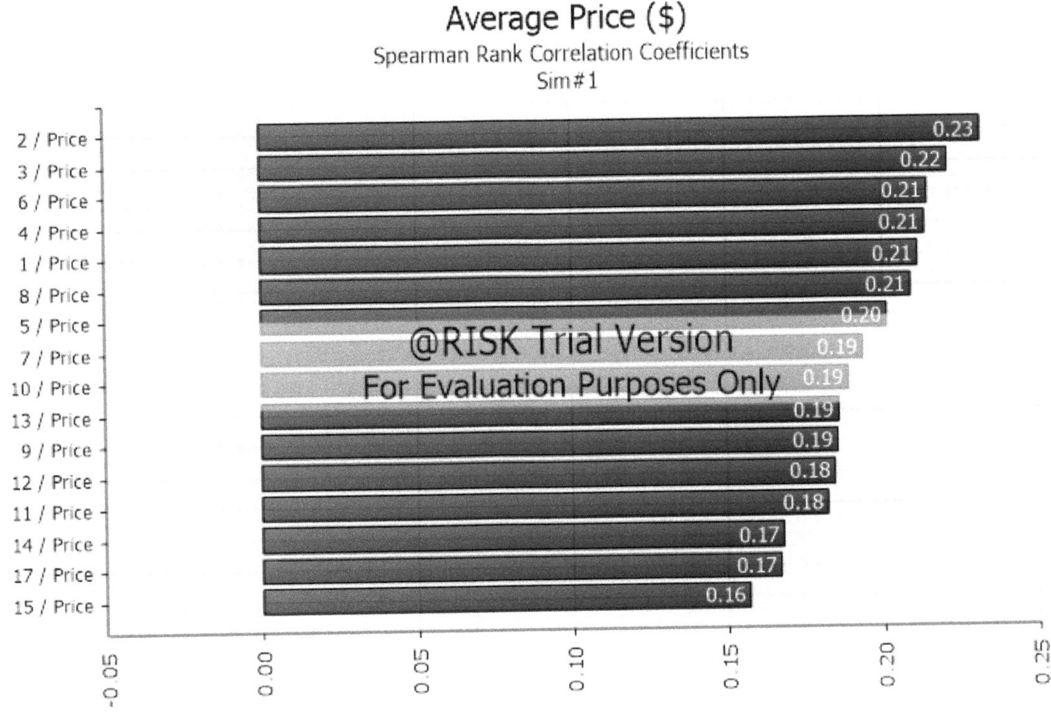

The graph shows (Figure 13) that if the top variable, Price at Time 2, with a correlation coefficient of 0.23, changes by one unit, the Average Price will change by 0.23 units. Other variables are less influential as their correlation coefficients are in the range of 0.22 to 0.16 from top to bottom.

The Contribution to Variance is presented in Figure 14.

Figure 14. Average price contribution to variance

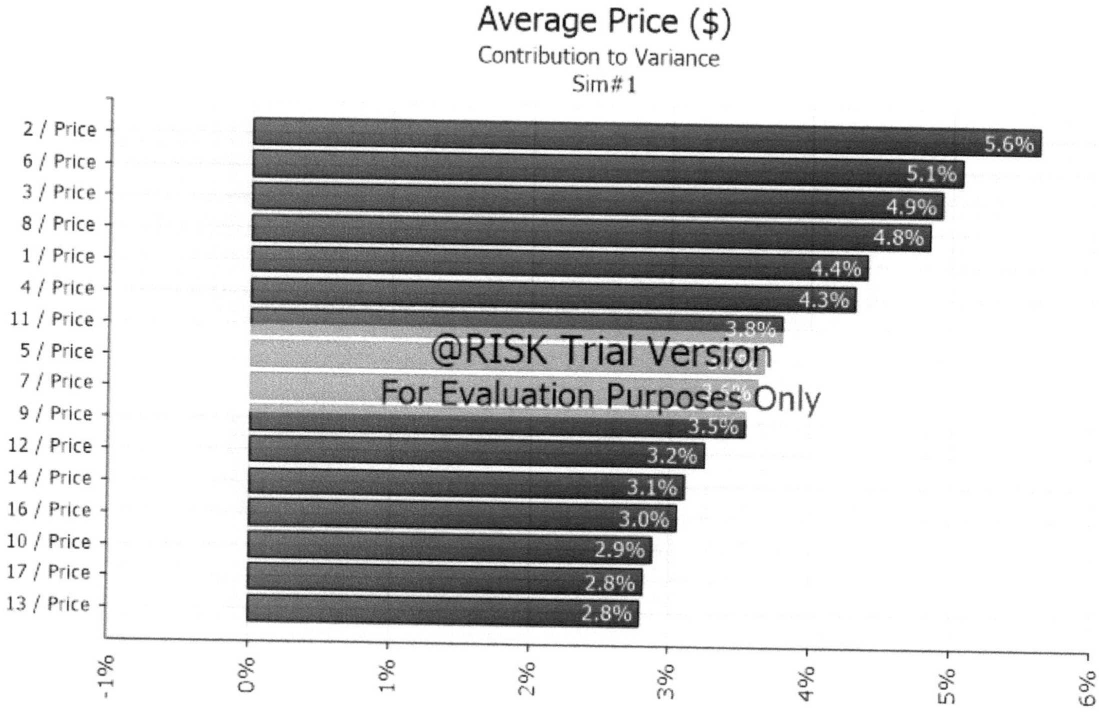

The graph (Figure 14) illustrates that the top variable, Price at Time 2, has a contribution of 5.6% to the variance of Average Price. Other variables are less influential as their contribution to variance is in the range of 5.1% – 2.8% from top to bottom.

Simulations 2 & 3 Average Price Evaluation

Simulation 2 Average Price Evaluation

The Average Price distribution is shown in Figure 15.

Figure 15. Simulation 2 average price distribution

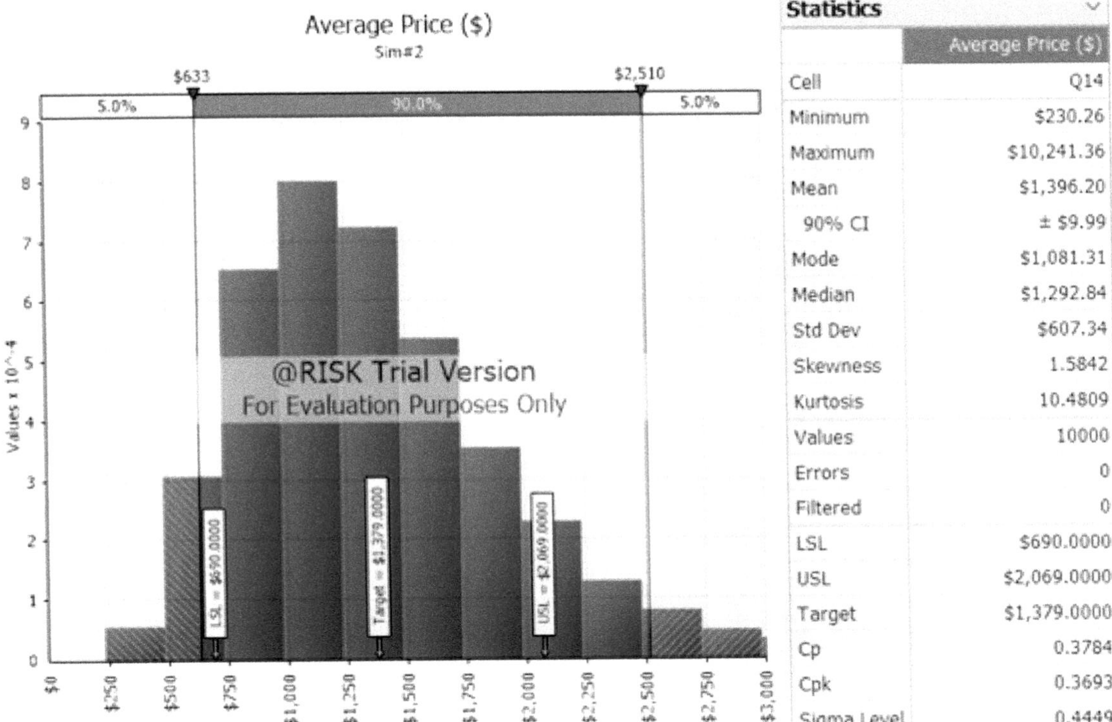

Statistics	Average Price ($)
Cell	Q14
Minimum	$230.26
Maximum	$10,241.36
Mean	$1,396.20
90% CI	± $9.99
Mode	$1,081.31
Median	$1,292.84
Std Dev	$607.34
Skewness	1.5842
Kurtosis	10.4809
Values	10000
Errors	0
Filtered	0
LSL	$690.0000
USL	$2,069.0000
Target	$1,379.0000
Cp	0.3784
Cpk	0.3693
Sigma Level	0.4449

The Average Price *Mean* is $1,396.20 with a *Standard Deviation* of $607.34, i.e., 43.499%, which is an acceptable high risk (Figure 13.15). The Six Sigma target parameters are *TV* = $1,379.00; *LSL* = $690.00; and *USL* = $2,069.00. The Six Sigma process capability metrics are *Cp* = 0.3784; *Cpk* = 0.3693; and σ-*L* = 0.4449. There is a 5.0% probability that the Average Price *Mean* will be below $633; a 90.0% probability that it will be in the range of $633 – $2,510; and a 5.0% probability that it will be above $2,510.

Simulation 3 Average Price Evaluation

The Average Price distribution is shown in Figure 16.

Figure 16. Simulation 3 average price distribution

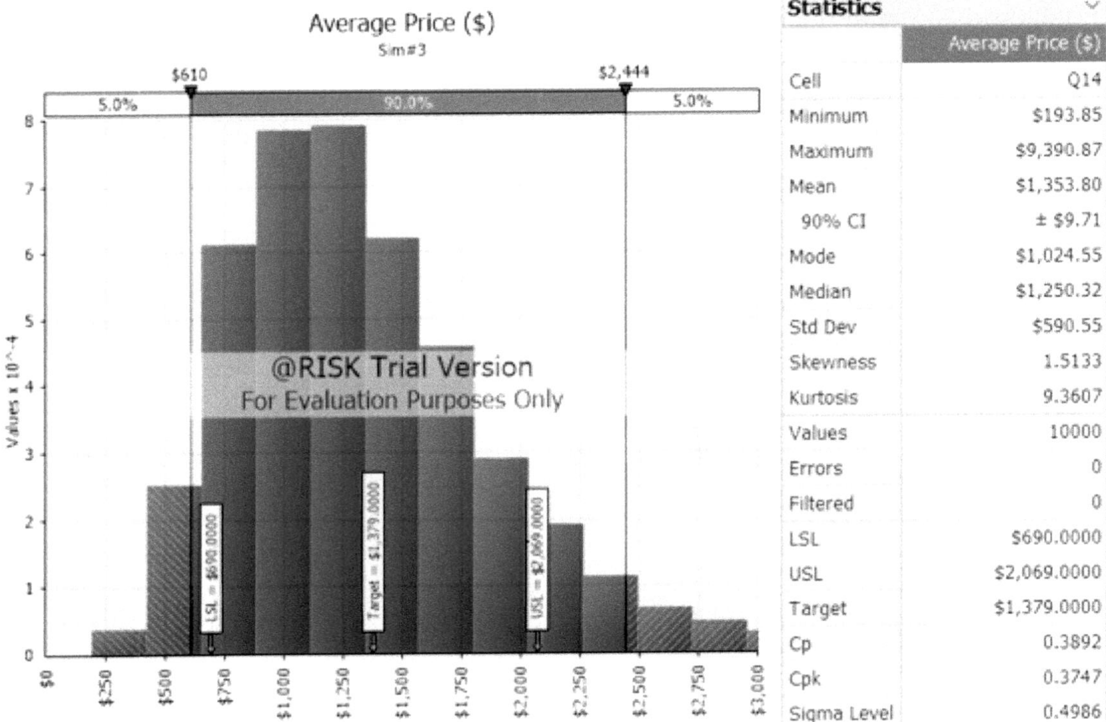

The Average Price *Mean* is $1,353.80 with a *Standard Deviation* of $590.55, i.e., 43.622%, which is an acceptable high risk (Figure 13.16). The Six Sigma target parameters are *TV* = $1,379.00; *LSL* = $690.00; and *USL* = $2,069.00. The Six Sigma process capability metrics are *Cp* = 0.3892; *Cpk* = 0.3747; and σ-*L* = 0.4986. There is a 5.0% probability that the Average Price *Mean* will be below $610; a 90.0% probability that it will be in the range of $610 – $2,444; and a 5.0% probability that it will be above $2,444.

Simulations 2 & 3 Average Price Sensitivity Analysis

Standard Deviation is a major risk factor. The Standard Deviation of the Average Price calculated above is i) 43.219% for Simulation 1; ii) 43.499% for Simulation 2; and iii) 43.622% for Simulation 3. Comparing the Standard Deviations, Simulation 1 has the smallest risk factor of 43.219%, so it is superior considering the risk factor. That is, the Simulation 1 results are the best considering the risk, for which Sensitivity Analysis is discussed above. Therefore, Sensitivity Analysis is not presented for Simulations 2 & 3 as they are inferior to Simulation 1 from the risk perspective.

Simulation 1 Average Price What-If Analysis

The What-If analysis provides for ranking the inputs by the variability of the output based on the calculation without a probability distribution. It also quantifies the minimum and maximum values and the change percentages of the output for the associated minimum and maximum values of the input, reporting the input base value. The Average Price tornado graph is given in Figure 17. The graph shows the Average Price values on the x-axis. The bars on the graph quantify the variability of the Average Price from every independent variable showing the Minimum and Maximum, which are respectively left and right from the Average Price calculated value.

Figure 17. Average price tornado graph

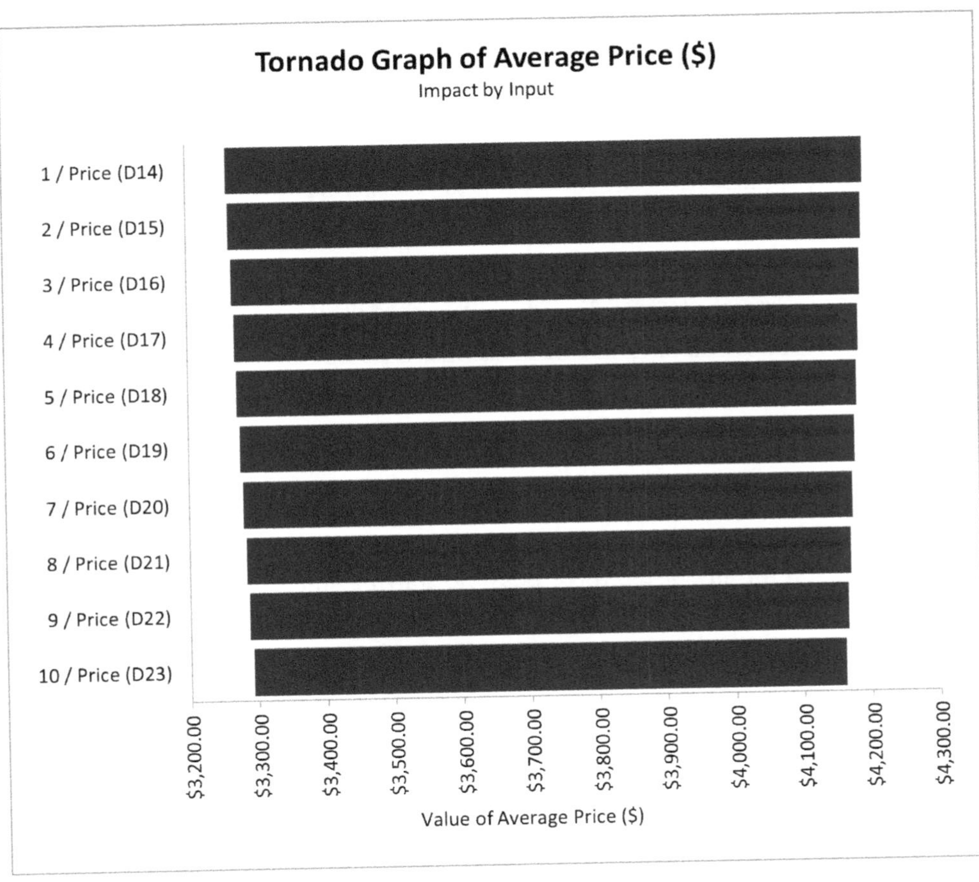

Figure 17 also shows that the ten most influential input variables are the Average Prices at Times 1, 2, …, 10. The other input variables are less influential.

The Average Price What-If Analysis Summary is presented in Table 3. The Summary table quantifies the minimum and maximum values and the change percentages of the output for the associated minimum and maximum values of the input, as well as the input base value.

For example, the top Rank 1 variable <u>Price at Time 1</u>: The input base value is -$0.10. The input minimum value is -$0.08, for which the Average Price has a minimum of $3,259.34, i.e., a change of 349.98% from the Average Price base Value. The input maximum value is $0.18, for which the Average Price has a maximum of $4,193.33, i.e., a change of 478.92% from the Average Price base Value; etc.

Table 3. What-if analysis summary for average price

What-If Analysis Summary for Output Average Price								
Top 10 Inputs Ranked by Change in Actual Value								
		Minimum			Maximum			Input
		Output		Input	Output		Input	Base
Rank	Input Name	Value $	Change %	Value $	Value $	Change %	Value $	Value $
1	1/Price	3,259.34	349.98	-0.08	4,193.33	478.92	0.18	-0.10
2	2/Price	3,262.27	350.38	-0.08	4,190.41	478.52	0.18	-0.10
3	3/Price	3,265.34	350.80	-0.08	4,187.34	478.09	0.18	-0.10
4	4/Price	3,268.56	351.25	-0.08	4,184.11	477.65	0.18	-0.10
5	5/Price	3,271.95	351.72	-0.08	4,180.73	477.18	0.18	-0.10
6	6/Price	3,275.50	352.21	-0.08	4,177.17	476.69	0.18	-0.10
7	7/Price	3,279.23	352.72	-0.08	4,173.44	476.17	0.18	-0.10
8	8/Price	3,283.15	353.26	-0.08	4,169.52	475.63	0.18	-0.10
9	9/Price	3,287.27	353.83	-0.08	4,165.41	475.07	0.18	-0.10
10	10/Price	3,291.59	354.43	-0.08	4,161.09	474.47	0.18	-0.10

CONCLUSION

This chapter presented a prediction of a Price Evolution with the Markov Chain Monte Carlo method.

Three simulations were applied to generate states and prices through time, starting with a given price, i.e., one simulation for any of the three possible starting states. The presented model is generic and applicable to all sorts of prices, including stock market prices, prices of goods in marketing, etc.

The initial state at time zero given inputs were i) State, which could be one (1), two (2), or three (3); ii) Initial Price, which is $1,000.00; iii) One-Step Transition Probability Matrix shown in Table 13.1; iv) Parameters of Price Changes in States incl. Mean and Standard Deviation (SD) are given in Table 13.2.

The simulation variables were vectors of 45 values: i) Time Vector; ii) Simulate State Vector; iii) Price Vector.

The simulation output vectors of three values, i.e., one for each state, were: i) State Vector; ii) First Visit Vector; iii) Average 1st Visit Start 1 Vector; iv) Average 1st Visit Start 2 Vector; v) Average 1st Visit Start 3 Vector; vi) Fraction Vector; vii) Average Fraction Start 1 Vector; viii) Average Fraction Start 2 Vector; ix) Average Fraction Start 3 Vector.

The simulation output variables were: i) Average Price; ii) Price @ Time 1; iii) Price @ Time 45.

A simulation model was designed and run to perform the Price Evolution prediction. Sensitivity and What-If Analysis were applied, which provided a comprehensive view of the probability of the outputs, and quantified the sensitivity of the outputs based on the variability of the associated inputs and financial variables.

Standard Deviation is a major risk factor. The Standard Deviation of the Average Price calculated above was: i) 43.219% for Simulation 1; ii) 43.499% for Simulation 2; and iii) 43.622% for Simulation 3. Comparing the Standard Deviations, Simulation 1 had the smallest risk factor of 43.219%, which is an acceptable high risk. Even though the Simulation 1 results were the best considering the risk, the technical conclusion is that management should consider all three simulation results. The management needs to decide on the prices based on their risk appetite.

Therefore, this risk analysis provided management with comprehensive decision support.

REFERENCES

Behrends, E. (2000). Introduction to Markov Chains: With Special Emphasis on Rapid Mixing. Springer Vieweg Verlag.

Bhusal, M. (2018, August). Application of the Markov Chain Model in the Stock Market Trend Analysis of Nepal. *International Journal of Scientific and Engineering Research*, *8*(10), 1733–1745. doi:10.14299/ijser.2017.10.008

Jasinthan, P., Laheetharan, A., & Satkunanathan, N. (2015). A Markov Chain Model for Vegetable Price Movement in Jaffna. *Sri Lankan Journal of Applied Statistics*, *16*(2), 93. doi:10.4038/sljastats.v16i2.7825

Revuz, D. (1984). *Markov Chains. North-Holland.*

Chapter 14
Risk Management Future Directions

ABSTRACT

This chapter outlines the future directions for risk management research. Eminent risk management scholars and practitioners are referenced considering the future direction for risk management in general across industries. Also, references to the future directions for specific industries, disciplines, and corporate businesses are provided including 1) financial risk management, 2) information systems security, 3) energy sector, 4) project management, 5) construction industry, 6) supply chain, 7) agriculture, and 8) Six Sigma.

AN OUTLINE

Continuous change is a universal principle. The universe is endlessly changing, and so is our world and everything in it. What was yesterday is not today, and what is today, won't be tomorrow. Consequently, the scenery of risk and risk management is rapidly changing as well. So, new strategies are constantly required to assess and control risk.

Albinson, Blau, and Chu (2016) published a generic report across industries about future risk management tendencies. They argue that organisations would respond to risk change by using cognitive technologies to supplement and, at times, even replace human decision-making. Also, they would deploy widespread controls as part of their operations to monitor and manage risk in real time. In addition, improvements in behavioural sciences would help to comprehend risk insights, influence risk behaviours, and improve risk decision-making. Moreover, organisations would realise that 100% risk prevention is impossible, so investment in detecting risk events as they happen as well as containing and reducing the impact of risk events would increase. Finally, risk transfer instruments would progressively be used to protect organisations from a wider range of risks, e.g., cyber-attacks, climate change, geopolitical risks, terrorism, business disruptions, etc.

The report also claims that risk change would influence changes within organisations. For example, the marketplace would reward organisations that take on strategic, high-risk inventions. Or, as risks

DOI: 10.4018/979-8-3693-3787-5.ch014

become more measurable and tangible, organisations would be more able to determine an accurate upside value of risk.

Lastly, as businesses engage more deeply with a large number of external stakeholders, they rely more heavily on them to identify, manage, and reduce risks together. The constant threat of disruption resulting from emerging technologies, business model transformations, and ecosystem changes, will force executives to make significant strategic choices to drive organisational success. To survive in a hyper-connected world, organisation leaders would proactively address the accelerated and amplified risks to their reputations.

Another generic study addressing future research directions in management control systems (MCS) was published by Chenhall (2003). This article presented a critical review of findings from contingency-based studies over the past 20 years, resulting in proposals for applying MCS to organisational frameworks. The author argues that recent developments, including strategic risk management, are only just beginning to be understood by researchers. Likewise, product life cycles place demands for new product initiatives and alter cost structures. So, decreasing life cycles increases operating risk and requires increased capital investment. Understanding how MCS innovations can assist management from these perspectives will probably become more and more important. Also, recent MCS research has recognized that managers have a 'strategic choice' to position their organizations in particular environments. For example, if the current product range is too uncertain, they may need to reformulate the product strategy in a more predictable market. This may limit potential opportunities and may require the organisation to study its approaches to the trade-off between potential returns and acceptable risk.

Alexander (2005) discussed the future aspects of Financial Risk Management. The author claimed that current research on financial risk management focuses on the truthful assessment of individual market and credit risks. So, there is comparatively little theoretical or applied econometric research on other types of risk, aggregation risk, data incompleteness, and optimal risk control. The paper discussed that the model risk originating from crude aggregation rules and insufficient data could lead to a new class of reduced-form Bayesian risk assessment models. Logically, these models should be set within a common factor framework that allows proper risk aggregation methods to be developed. The paper explained how such a framework could also provide the essential links between risk control, risk assessments, and the optimal allocation of resources.

A study of future directions in information systems security was published by Crossler et al (2013). This study claimed that although the major weaknesses of information security are the system users within an organisation, the emphasis of present security research is on technical matters. The study emphasised the future directions for "Behavioral InfoSec" research, arguing that this is a novel developing area. It presented the challenges currently faced, as well as the future directions that researchers should explore, for example, separating insider divergent behaviour from insider misbehaviour, approaches to understanding hackers, improving information security compliance, security cross-cultural research, and security data gathering and measurement matters.

Future directions in the energy sector were discussed by Edwards (2008). The article reviewed examples of Knowledge Management (KM) in the energy sector and identified key current issues. Important conclusions were made and future directions for research and implementation were identified. For example, in an uncertain future, enough diversity is required to successfully continue innovation, and organisations should retain the learning and knowledge. More specifically for the energy sector in the future, new sources of energy will require new processes as well as new technology, and perhaps differently trained and educated personnel. The theory should be further applied such as knowledge-based systems and the associated techniques of knowledge elicitation. Also, studying the wider theory of knowledge sharing and organisational learning would be required. For example, the movement of complexity theories into the mainstream and knowledge-based view of the organisation should be utilised.

Lyneis and Ford (2007) studied the application of system dynamics on projects, assessed project progress, and proposed directions for future development. Regarding future routes for risk management and project controls, the authors focus on several aspects of project management including i) project conditions required for project control decisions; ii) actions to take when a project is forecasted to miss performance targets; iii) amounts, durations, combinations, and order of application of measures to be applied to improve performance as much as is possible; iv) heuristics for managing project dynamics to improve performance; and v) qualitative and quantitative models required for these heuristics. They concluded that all these aspects should rigorously be studied using simulation models.

A study by Edwards and Bowen (1998) reviewed and analysed the works on construction and project risk management published from 1960 to 1997, to find practical and research tendencies and associated emphases. The objective was to identify variations in the knowledge and conduct of construction and project risk. The paper suggested that research on the categories of construction risk deserves greater attention. It also deemed that chronological aspects of risk and risk communication are key fields for investigation.

Packendorff (1995) published a theoretical paper discussing new research directions in project management (PM). This study identified three key limitations of PM theoretical research: i) PM is understood as a general theory in its own right; ii) research on PM is not adequately experiential, and iii) projects are perceived as utensils. It claimed that a diversity of theoretical perspectives should be employed in future research on "temporary organizations" aiming to create mid-range theories on different kinds of projects.

Future directions of Supply Chain Risk Management (SCRM) were studied by Singhal, Agarwal, and Mittal (20011). They claimed that organisations have implemented outsourcing, global partnerships, and lean strategies to improve their efficiency; however, these strategies made them vulnerable to market uncertainties, dependencies, and disruptions. Additionally, natural disasters and manufactured crises have negatively affected the strategic, operational, and tactical performance of organisations. These issues have initiated academic and corporate interest to consider risk as a major problem. The authors employ a multi-layered top-town taxonomy to classify and codify the literature and put forward probable dimensions for future research to capture the basic elements of diversified risk issues related to the supply chain. They also studied the SCRM literature concentrating on coordination and decision-making.

Idrees (2009) discussed the future research directions in agriculture considering the agribusiness supply chain. The author proposed a Total Risk Management Process model arguing that an agriculture sector-specific framework can be developed by implementing this model. Also, future research in this area can address food or country-specific issues. This approach can be applied to the non-organic food industry as well. Although only the crop sector of agriculture was covered, other agriculture areas can be explored to further gain the benefits of this research.

A structured review of Six Sigma and implications for future research were presented by Aboelmaged (2010). This study systematically analyzed the published work on Six Sigma from 417 referred journal articles in business and management disciplines, information systems and computer science, engineering, healthcare, etc. Conclusions from the analysis were that: i) Six Sigma research was rapidly growing, covering various disciplines and domains with a great focus on Six Sigma tools and techniques; ii) empirical research was dominant with more emphasis on a case study approach; and iii) the growing gap between manufacturing and service focused works confirmed the return of Six Sigma to manufacturing, i.e., its initial origin. Although a large volume of applications was published, Six Sigma is still under development and offers potential opportunities for future research and applications.

To date, however, Six Sigma has not been specifically applied to risk management on an ongoing basis. This book proposed a generic Six Sigma DMAIC structured approach to risk management. In conclusion, considering that Six Sigma is in expansion today and offers future opportunities for implementations (Aboelmaged 2010), the proposed approach has not only contemporary but prospects for utilisation across industries as well.

REFERENCES

Aboelmaged, M. G. (2010). Six Sigma quality: A structured review and implications for future research. *International Journal of Quality & Reliability Management*, *27*(3), 268–317. doi:10.1108/02656711011023294

Albinson, N., Blau, A. & Chu, Y. (2016). *The future of risk: New game, new rules*. Deloitte.

Alexander, C. (2005). The Present and Future of Financial Risk Management. *Journal of Financial Econometrics*, *3*(1), 3–25. doi:10.1093/jjfinec/nbi003

Chenhall, R.H. (2003). Management control systems design within its organizational context: findings from contingency-based research and directions for the future. *Accounting, Organizations and Society*, *28*, 127–168.

Crossler, R. E. (2013). *Future directions for behavioral information security research. In Computers & Security* (Vol. 32). Elsevier Ltd.

Edwards, J. S. (2008). Knowledge management in the energy sector: Review and future directions. *International Journal of Energy Sector Management*, *2*(2), 197–217. doi:10.1108/17506220810883216

Edwards, P.J., Bowen, P.A. (1998). Risk and risk management in construction: a review and future directions for research. *Engineering, Construction and Architectural Management*, *5*(4), 339 –349.

Idrees, F. (2009). Total Risk Management Process in Agrifood Supply Chain. *Symposium*.

Lyneis, J. M., & Ford, D. N. (2007). System Dynamics Applied to Project Management. System Dynamics Review, 23(2-3), 157–189.

Packendorff, J. (1995). Inquiring into the temporary organization: New directions for project management research. *Scandinavian Journal of Management*, *11*(4), 319–333.

Singhal, P., Agarwal, G., & Mittal, M. L. (2011). Supply chain risk management: Review, classification, and future research directions. *International Journal of Business Science and Applied Management*, *6*(3), 15–42.

Conclusion

Six Sigma is a standard means to accomplish process and quality improvements and increase customer satisfaction recognised across industries today. The financial industry has also accepted and successfully applied Six Sigma, but only to improve its operations and provide higher-quality services to its customers. Six Sigma introductory topics for financial professionals were published in 2003 (Stamatis 2003). Hayler and Nichols (2006) presented how American Express, Bank of America, and Wachovia have applied Six Sigma, Lean, and Process Management to their service-based operations. Tarantino and Cernauskas (2009) published an operational risk framework by using Six Sigma and Total Quality Management (TQM) in financial risk management. Bubevski (2017) published a new Six Sigma DMAIC generic approach to Risk Management in Finance, Oil and Gas, Research and Development, Software Engineering, Project Management, Agriculture, Production, and Retail.

Financial crises can expose underlying faults in the financial institution's systems and processes. The 2008 financial crisis exposed the failure of a prevalent laissez-faire economic and regulatory philosophy that financial institutions could and should manage their own risk with little outside interference. Now, many see the danger of fragile financial service networks bringing systemic risk to the real economy. So, financial organisations face increasing regulations such as Basel III for banks, and Solvency II for insurance. To meet the requirements of the increased and rigorous regulation, financial organisations are striving to improve their formal risk assessment and management processes, which is their ultimate objective.

This book presented applications of the Six Sigma DMAIC approach to Financial Risk Management offering improvements for Basel III and Solvency II to help financial institutions to achieve their ultimate objective and meet the regulators' requirements. In addition to conventional stochastic optimisation (Lee, C.F., Lee, A.C., and J. Lee 2010) and Monte Carlo simulation (Bratley & Schrage 1983, Rubinstein & Kroese 2008), the book tactically applied the DMAIC framework to Financial Risk Management. DMAIC and Financial Risk Management are generic, compatible, and complementary, so tactically merging them, resulted in a powerful synergetic tool.

The application of the approach to Financial Risk Management was presented in 12 chapters i) Six Sigma Quotation Process; ii) Six Sigma DMAIC Yield Analysis; iii) Six Sigma DMAIC Failure Rate; iv) Six Sigma DMAIC Failure Rate with RiskTheo Functions; v) Financial Statements Predictions; vi) New Products Profitability Analysis; vii) Banks' Credit Losses Analysis; viii) Discounted Cash Flow Projections; ix) Comprehensive Investment Risk Assessment; x) Risk Assessment in Investment Portfolio; xi) Estimating Loan Interest rates and Payments; xii) Bank Loan Portfolio Credit Risk Analysis; xiii) Price Evolution with Markov Chain Monte Carlo; and xiv) Financial Risk Management Future Directions.

In conclusion, Bernstein stated, "*The risk will always be there, so we must explore many interesting tools that can help us to control risks we cannot avoid taking*" (Bernstein and Damodaran 1998). Therefore, the presented approaches in this book are one such tool.

REFERENCES

Aboelmaged, M. G. (2010). Six Sigma quality: A structured review and implications for future research. *International Journal of Quality & Reliability Management*, *27*(3), 268–317. doi:10.1108/02656711011023294

Alexander, C. (2005). The Present and Future of Financial Risk Management. *Journal of Financial Econometrics*, *3*(1), 3–25. doi:10.1093/jjfinec/nbi003

Bernstein, P. L., & Damodaran, A. (1998). *Investment Management*. John Wiley & Sons.

Bratley, P., Fox, B. L., & Schrage, L. E. (1983). *A Guide to Simulation*. SpringerVerlag. doi:10.1007/978-1-4684-0167-7

Bubevski, V. (2017). *Novel Six Sigma Approaches to Risk Assessment and Management*. IGI Global.

Härle, P., Havas, A., & Samandari, H. (2016). The future of bank risk management. *McKinsey Working Papers on Risk*, 3.

Hayler, R., & Nichols, M. D. (2006). Six Sigma for Financial Services: How Leading Companies Are Driving Results Using Lean, Six Sigma, and Process Management. McGraw-Hill.

IRM. (2015). *Perspectives on the future of risk*. The Institute of Risk Management (IRM).

Koch, S., Schneider, R., Schneider, S., & Schröck, G. (2017). Bringing Basel IV into focus. *McKinsey Working Papers on Risk*, 4.

Li, S. (2003). Future trends and challenges of financial risk management in the digital economy. *Managerial Finance*, *29*(5/6), 111–125. doi:10.1108/03074350310768797

Rubinstein, R. Y., & Kroese, D. P. (2008). *Simulation and the Monte Carlo Method*. John Wiley & Sons.

Stamatis, D. H. (2003). *Six Sigma for Financial Professionals*. Wiley.

Tarantino, A., & Cernauskas, D. (2009). Risk Management in Finance: Six Sigma and Other Next-Generation Techniques. Wiley.

Glossary

Asset & Liability Management (ALM): The administration of policies and procedures that address financial risks associated with changing interest rates, foreign exchange rates, and other factors that can affect a company's liquidity.

Basel: Financial Regulator for banks including Basel I, Basel II, Basel III, and Basel IV accords.

Beta: A measure of the volatility of an investment portfolio related to the financial market.

Cp – Process Capability: Six Sigma process capability metric, which is the measure of what the process can deliver.

Cpk – Process Capability Index: Six Sigma process capability metric, which is the measure of what the process can deliver.

Credit Risk: Credit risk is the risk of losses due to borrowers' default or deterioration of credit standing.

DMAIC (Define, Measure, Analyse, Improve, Control): Six Sigma methodology comprising five phases: Define; Measure; Analyse; Improve; and Control.

Efficient Frontier: A set of the optimal portfolios in the range of expected returns.

Foreign Exchange Risk: Foreign exchange risk is the risk of incurring losses due to fluctuations in exchange rates.

Interest Rate Risk: The interest rate risk is the risk of declines of net interest income, or interest revenues minus interest cost, due to the movements of interest rates.

Investment Management: Discipline that quantitatively and qualitatively studies the investments in financial markets.

Liquidity Risk: Liquidity risk is broadly defined as the risk of not being able to raise cash when needed.

LSL – Lower Specified Limit: Six Sigma process capability metric which specifies the lower limit of the target range.

Market Risk: Market risk is the risk of losses due to adverse market movements depressing the values of the positions held by market players.

Markov Chain: A Markov chain is a Markov process with discrete time and discrete state space. So, a Markov chain is a discrete sequence of states, each drawn from a discrete state space (finite or not), and that follows the Markov property. The Markov property expresses the fact that at a given time step and knowing the current state, we won't get any additional information about the future by gathering information about the past.

Markov Chain Monte Carlo: Markov Chain Monte Carlo (MCMC) methods comprise a class of algorithms for sampling from a probability distribution. By constructing a Markov Chain that has the desired distribution as its equilibrium distribution, one can obtain a sample of the desired distribution by recording states from the chain. The more steps are included, the more closely the distribution of the sample matches the actual desired distribution.

Monte Carlo Simulation: A simulation in which random data are generated from a specified distribution and used as input in a deterministic model (e.g., a formula for calculating a dependent variable (y) from the values of the independent variables).

Neural Networks: A neural network is a series of algorithms that endeavours to recognise underlying relationships in a set of data through a process that mimics the way the human brain operates. In this sense, neural networks refer to systems of neurons, either organic or artificial. Neural networks can adapt to changing input; so, the network generates the best possible result without needing to redesign the output criteria.

Operations Research (OR): Operations research (OR) is an analytical method of problem-solving and decision-making that is useful in the management of organisations. In operations research, problems are broken down into basic components and then solved in defined steps by mathematical analysis. Analytical methods used in OR include mathematical logic, simulation, optimisation, stochastic optimisation, network analysis, queuing theory, and game theory.

Optimisation: Method to find the optimal value, i.e., minimum or maximum, of a dependent variable from the values of many independent variables.

Portfolio Analysis: 1. Commerce: An analysis of elements of a company's product mix to determine the optimum allocation of its resources. The two most common measures used in a portfolio analysis are market growth rate and relative market share. 2. Securities: An analysis of an investment portfolio relative to an idealised balance of holdings, used as means of optimizing allocation.

Risk: 1. Finance: A possibility of financial loss that is inseparable from the opportunity for financial gain. 2. Pure Risk: The possibility of suffering some form of loss or damage where there is no corresponding opportunity for gain.

Risk Management: Risk management is the process of identifying, assessing, and controlling threats to an organisation's capital and earnings. These threats, or risks, could stem from a wide variety of sources, including financial uncertainty, legal liabilities, strategic management errors, accidents, and natural disasters.

Sensitivity Analysis: Sensitivity analysis determines how different values of an independent variable affect a particular dependent variable under a given set of assumptions. In other words, sensitivity analyses study how various sources of uncertainty in a mathematical model contribute to the model's overall uncertainty. This technique is used within specific boundaries that depend on one or more input variables.

Sharpe Ratio: A risk-adjusted measure of the performance of a portfolio related to the Risk-Free Rate.

Sigma Level: Six Sigma process capability metric is defined as the distance in terms of standard deviations between the mean of the actual performance of the process and the expected performance limits, which is the measure of process performance, i.e., the higher the Sigma Level, the better the performance.

Solvency: Financial Regulator for insurance companies including Solvency I, Solvency II, and Solvency III accords.

Solvency Risk: Solvency risk is the risk of being unable to absorb losses with the available capital.

Standard Deviation: A measure of the dispersion of statistical data. It is a square root of Variance. The standard deviation of the returns from an investment is used as a measure of risk.

Stochastic Optimisation: Method to find the optimal value, i.e., minimum or maximum, of a dependent variable from the probability distributions of the values of many independent variables.

Target Value: Six Sigma process capability metric which specifies the desired target value for the process.

USL – Upper Specified Limit: Six Sigma process capability metric which specifies the upper limit of the target range.

Value at Risk (VAR): a) The level of losses over a particular period that will only be exceeded in a small percentage of cases; b) A cut-off value for portfolio gains and losses (e.g., the bottom 1% of outcomes; VAR is then measured relative to that cut-off value.

Variance: Statistical measure of the dispersion of the distribution of outcomes. It is the square of Standard Distribution.

What-If Analysis: A what-if analysis is a technique that is used to determine how projected performance is affected by changes in the assumptions that projections are based upon. What-if analysis is used to compare different scenarios and their potential outcomes based on fluctuating conditions.

Compilation of References

Abbott, J. C. (2012). The Executive Guide to Six Sigma. Robert Houston Smith Publishers.

Aboelmaged, M. G. (2010). Six Sigma quality: A structured review and implications for future research. *International Journal of Quality & Reliability Management*, *27*(3), 268–317. doi:10.1108/02656711011023294

Adam, A. (2007). *Handbook of Asset and Liability Management: From Models to Optimal Return Strategies*. John Wiley & Sons.

Albinson, N., Blau, A. & Chu, Y. (2016). *The future of risk: New game, new rules*. Deloitte.

Alexander, C. (1996). *The handbook of risk management and analysis*. John Wiley & Sons.

Alexander, C. (2005). The Present and Future of Financial Risk Management. *Journal of Financial Econometrics*, *3*(1), 3–25. doi:10.1093/jjfinec/nbi003

Anderson, R. (2020). *Money Management & Financial Budgeting*. Academic Press.

Atkinson P., & Blundell-Wignall A. (2010). Thinking beyond Basel III –Necessary solutions for capital and liquidity. *OECD Market Trends*, *98*(1).

Axson, D. J. A., & Rosander, K. (2014). *Measuring the True Profitability of Products, Services and Customers*. Accenture.

Barfield, R. (2011). *2011. A Practitioners Guide to Basel III and Beyond*. Sweet & Maxwell.

Basel Committee on Banking Supervision. (2014). *Consultative Document: Fundamental review of the trading book: A revised market risk framework*. Bank for International Settlements, Basel Committee on Banking.

Basel Committee on Banking Supervision. (2016). *Standards: Minimum capital requirements for market risk*. Bank for International Settlements, Basel Committee on Banking Supervision.

Baxter, R. (202)3. Lean Six Sigma DMAIC Workbook: for Instructor-Led Workshops. Value Generation Partners.

Baxter, R. (2023). Lean Six Sigma DMAIC Workbook: for Instructor-Led Workshops, Value Generation Partners.

Baxter, R. (2023). Lean Six Sigma DMAIC Workbook: for Instructor-Led Workshops. Value Generation Partners.

Behrends, E. (2000). Introduction to Markov Chains: With Special Emphasis on Rapid Mixing. Springer Vieweg Verlag.

Berger, A. N., & DeYoung, R. (1997). Problem loans and cost efficiency in commercial banks. *Journal of Banking & Finance*, *21*(6), 849–870. doi:10.1016/S0378-4266(97)00003-4

Bernstein, P. L., & Damodaran, A. (1998). *Investment Management*. John Wiley & Sons.

Bhalla, D. (2019). *A complete guide to credit risk modelling*. ListenData.

Bhusal, M. (2018, August). Application of the Markov Chain Model in the Stock Market Trend Analysis of Nepal. *International Journal of Scientific and Engineering Research*, *8*(10), 1733–1745. doi:10.14299/ijser.2017.10.008

BIS. (2011). *Basel III: Long-term impact on economic performance and fluctuations*. Working paper No 338, February 2011.

Bloomsbury. (2012). *Asset Liability Management for Financial Institutions: Balancing Financial Stability with Strategic Objectives*. Bloomsbury Information Ltd.

Bloomsbury. (2012). *Asset Liability Management for Financial Institutions: Balancing Financial Stability with Strategic Objectives*. Bloomsbury.

Borror, C. M. (2009). *The Certified Quality Engineer Handbook* (3rd ed.). ASQ Quality Press.

Bourdeau, M. (2009). Market Risk Measurement Under Solvency II. In M. Cruz (Ed.), *The Solvency II Handbook* (pp. 193–226). Risk Books–Incisive Media.

Bratley, P., Fox, B. L., & Schrage, L. E. (1983). *A Guide to Simulation*. SpringerVerlag. doi:10.1007/978-1-4684-0167-7

Brinson, G. P. (1998). Global Management and Asset Allocation. In P. L. Bernstein & A. Damodaran (Eds.), *Investment Management* (pp. 117–161). John Wiley & Sons.

Britten-Jones, M. (1998). *Fixed Income and Interest Rate Derivative*. Academic Press.

Brodersen, S., & Pysh, P. (2014). *Warren Buffett Accounting Book: Reading Financial Statements for Value*. Pylon Publishing.

Bubevski, V. (2016). *A Novel Approach to Investment Portfolio*. Academic Press.

Bubevski, V. (2016a). Solvency II Internal Models – An Alternative. Frontier in Finance. doi:10.14355/ff.2016.02.001

Bubevski, V. (2012). *A New Practical Approach to Asset Liability Management for Basel III and Solvency II*. European Modelling & Simulation.

Bubevski, V. (2016). Risk Management: A Novel Six Sigma Approach. In B. Darnel (Ed.), *Risk Management: Past Present and Future*. Nova Science Publishers.

Bubevski, V. (2017). *Novel Six Sigma Approaches to Risk Assessment and Management*. IGI Global.

Bubevski, V. (2018). Managing Credit Risk in Bank Loan Portfolio. In V. Bubevski (Ed.), *Six Sigma Improvements for Basel III and Solvency II in Financial Risk Management* (pp. 10–36). IGI Global.

Bubevski, V. (2018). *Six Sigma Improvements for Basel III and Solvency II in Financial Risk Management*. IGI Global.

Buffett, M., & Clark, D. (2011). Warren Buffett and the Interpretation of Financial Statements: The Search for the Company with a Durable Competitive Advantage. Simon & Schuster.

Busse, J. A., Goyal, A., & Wahal, S. (2010). Performance and Persistence in Institutional Investment Management. *The Journal of Finance*.

Busse, J. A., Goyal, A., & Wahal, S. (2010). Performance and Persistence in Institutional Investment Management. *The Journal of Finance*, *65*(2), 765–790. doi:10.1111/j.1540-6261.2009.01550.x

Cannata, F., & Quagliariello, M. (2011). *Basel III and Beyond*. Risk Books.

Carmona, R., & Tehranchi, M. R. (2007). *Interest Rate Models: An Infinite Dimensional Stochastic Analysis Perspective*. Springer.

Chatterjee, S. (2015). *Modelling credit risk*. Bank of England.

Chenhall, R.H. (2003). Management control systems design within its organizational context: findings from contingency-based research and directions for the future. *Accounting, Organizations and Society*, *28*, 127–168.

Christodoulakis, G. A., & Satchell, S. (Eds.). (2007). *The Analytics of Risk Model Validation, Elsevier Science & Technology*. Academic Press Inc. Ltd.

Christoffersen, P., Diebold, F. X., & Schuermann, T. (1998). Horizon Problems and Extreme Events in Financial Risk Management. Economic Policy Review, 4(3).

Clark, R. G. (1998a). Alternative Measures of Risk. In P. L. Bernstein & A. Damodaran (Eds.), *Investment Management* (pp. 81–98). John Wiley & Sons.

Clark, R. G. (1998b). Managing Portfolio Risk. In P. L. Bernstein & A. Damodaran (Eds.), *Investment Management* (pp. 274–326). John Wiley & Sons.

Cokins, G. (2017). *Strategic cost management for product*. Academic Press.

Comptroller of the Currency Administration. (2015). *Loan Portfolio Management: Comptroller's Handbook*. CreateSpace.

Cornyn, A. G. (1997). *Interest Rate Risk Models: Theory and Practice*. Global Professional Publishing.

Crossler, R. E. (2013). *Future directions for behavioral information security research. In Computers & Security* (Vol. 32). Elsevier Ltd.

Crouhya, M., Galaib, D., & Marka, R. (2000). A comparative analysis of current credit risk models. *Journal of Banking & Finance*, *24*(1-2), 59–117. doi:10.1016/S0378-4266(99)00053-9

Cruz, M. (2009). *The Solvency II Handbook*. Risk Books – Incisive Media.

Daly, J. L. (2001). Pricing for Profitability: Activity-Based Pricing for Competitive Advantage. John Wiley & Sons.

Damodaran, A. (1998a). Models of Risk. In P. L. Bernstein & A. Damodaran (Eds.), *Investment Management* (pp. 58–80). John Wiley & Sons.

Damodaran, A. (1998b). Asset Selection: Strategies and Evidence. In P. L. Bernstein & A. Damodaran (Eds.), *Investment Management* (pp. 185–229). John Wiley & Sons.

Damodaran, A. (1998c). The Hidden Costs of Trading. In P. L. Bernstein & A. Damodaran (Eds.), *Investment Management* (pp. 259–273). John Wiley & Sons.

Dash, R., Kremer, A., Nario, L., & Waldron, D. (2017). Risk analytics enters its prime. *McKinsey Working Papers on Risk*, 3.

De Feo, J.A. & Barnard, W.W. (2005). *JURAN Institute's Six Sigma Breakthrough and Beyond*. McGraw-Hill Education.

Diebold, F. X., Hahn, J., & Tay, A. S. (1999, November). Multivariate Density Forecast Evaluation and Calibration in Financial Risk Management: High-Frequency Returns on Foreign Exchange. *The Review of Economics and Statistics*, *81*(4), 661–673. doi:10.1162/003465399558526

ECB. (2007). *The use of portfolio credit risk models in central banks. European Central Bank (ECB).*

Edwards, P.J., & Bowen, P.A. (1998). Risk and risk management in construction: a review and future directions for research. *Engineering, Construction and Architectural Management*, *5*(4), 339 –349.

Edwards, P.J., Bowen, P.A. (1998). Risk and risk management in construction: a review and future directions for research. *Engineering, Construction and Architectural Management*, *5*(4), 339 –349.

Edwards, J. S. (2008). Knowledge management in the energy sector: Review and future directions. *International Journal of Energy Sector Management*, *2*(2), 197–217. doi:10.1108/17506220810883216

Engelmann, B., & Rauhmeier, R. (Eds.). (2006). *The Basel II Risk Parameters: Estimation, Validation, and Stress Testing*. Springer. doi:10.1007/3-540-33087-9

Fabozzi, F. J. (1998). *Bank Loans: Secondary Market and Portfolio Management, –(CFA Institute investment series)*. John Wiley & Sons.

Fabozzi, F. J. (Ed.). (1998). *Bank Loans: Secondary Market and Portfolio Management*. John Wiley & Sons.

Fight, A. (2005). Cash Flow Forecasting. Butterworth-Heinemann – Elsevier.

Fridson, M. S., & Alvarez, F. (2011). Financial Statement Analysis: A Practitioner's Guide. John Wiley & Sons.

Froot, K.A., & Stein, J. (1998). Risk management, capital budgeting, and capital structure policy for financial institutions: An integrated approach. *Journal of Financial Economics*, *47*(1), 55–82.

Froot, K.A., Scharfstein, D.S., & Stein, J.C. (1993). Risk Management: Coordinating Corporate Investment and Financing Policies. *The Journal of Finance*, *48*(5), 1629-1658.

Gamerman, D., & Lopes, H. F. (2006). Markov Chain Monte Carlo: Stochastic Simulation for Bayesian Inference. Chapman and Hall/CRC. doi:10.1201/9781482296426

GDV. (2005). *Discussion Paper for a Solvency II Compatible Standard Approach*. Gesamtverband der Deutschen Versicherungswirtschaft.

Gelman, A. (2013). Bayesian Data Analysis. Chapman and Hall/CRC. doi:10.1201/b16018

George, M. L. (2005). The Lean Six Sigma Pocket Tool-book: A Quick Reference Guide. McGraw-Hill.

Gilks, A. (1996). Markov Chain Monte Carlo in Practice. Chapman and Hall/CRC.

Glasserman, P. (2004). *Monte Carlo Methods in Financial Engineering*. Springer Science.

Gordy, M. B. (2003). A risk-factor model foundation for ratings-based bank capital rules. *Journal of Financial Intermediation*, *12*(3), 199–232. doi:10.1016/S1042-9573(03)00040-8

Guide for Business Leaders. (2011). John Wiley & Sons.

Gygi, C., & Williams, B. (2012). *Six Sigma for Dummies*. For Dummies.

Härle, P., Havas, A., & Samandari, H. (2016). The future of bank risk management. *McKinsey Working Papers on Risk*, 3.

Harris, T. S., Khan, U., & Nissim, D. (2018). The Expected Rate of Credit Losses on Banks' Loan Portfolios. *The Accounting Review*, *93*(5), 2018. doi:10.2308/accr-52012

Hasan, M. N., Kapadia, N., & Siddique, A. (2017, December). Issuer bias in corporate ratings toward financially constrained firms. *The Journal of Credit Risk*, *13*(4), 1–35. doi:10.21314/JCR.2017.226

Hayler, R., & Nichols, M. D. (2006). Six Sigma for Financial Services: How Leading Companies Are Driving Results Using Lean, Six Sigma, and Process Management. McGraw-Hill.

Hayler, R., & Nichols, M. D. (2006). *Six Sigma for Financial Services: How Leading Companies Are Driving Results Using Lean, Six Sigma, and Process Management*. McGraw-Hill.

Higson, C. (2006). Financial Statements: Economic Analysis and Interpretation. Rivington Publishing Ltd.

Homaifar, G. A. (2004). Managing Global Financial and Foreign Exchange Rate Risk. Wiley.

Homer, S., & Sylla, R. (2011). A History of Interest Rates. John Wiley & Sons.

Hsieh, D. A. (1993). Implications of Nonlinear Dynamics for Financial Risk Management. Journal of Financial and Quantitative Analysis.

Hünseler, M. (2013). *Credit Portfolio Management: A Practitioner's Guide to the Active Management of Credit Risks*. Springer. doi:10.1057/9780230391505

Idrees, F. (2009). *Total Risk Management Process in Agrifood Supply Chain*. Academic Press.

Idrees, F. (2009). Total Risk Management Process in Agrifood Supply Chain. *Symposium*.

IPOL - EGOV Briefing. (2016). *Upgrading the Basel standards: from Basel III to Basel IV*. European Parliament.

IRM. (2015). *Perspectives on the future of risk*. The Institute of Risk Management (IRM).

Ittelson, T. R. (2020). *Financial Statements: A Step-by-step Guide to Understanding and Creating Financial Reports*. New Page Books.

Jacob, N. L. (1998). Evaluating Investment Performance. In P. L. Bernstein & A. Damodaran (Eds.), *Investment Management* (pp. 329–371). John Wiley & Sons.

Jasinthan, P., Laheetharan, A., & Satkunanathan, N. (2015). A Markov Chain Model for Vegetable Price Movement in Jaffna. *Sri Lankan Journal of Applied Statistics*, *16*(2), 93. doi:10.4038/sljastats.v16i2.7825

Jeffrey, R. H. (1998a). Tax Considerations in Investing. In P. L. Bernstein & A. Damodaran (Eds.), *Investment Management* (pp. 99–111). John Wiley & Sons.

Jeffrey, R. H. (1998b). Taxes and Performance Evaluation. In P. L. Bernstein & A. Damodaran (Eds.), *Investment Management* (pp. 372–386). John Wiley & Sons.

Johnson, R. (2023). 100 DMAIC Tools: A Comprehensive Guide to Six Sigma Problem Solving. Academic Press.

Jorion, P. (2011). *Financial Risk Manager Handbook*. John Wiley & Sons.

Keller, P. (2011). *Six Sigma Demystified* (2nd ed.). McGraw-Hill Education.

Koch, S., Schneider, R., Schneider, S., & Schröck, G. (2017). Bringing Basel IV into focus. *McKinsey Working Papers on Risk*, 4.

Kritzman, M. (1998). Risk and Utility Basics. In P. L. Bernstein & A. Damodaran (Eds.), *Investment Management* (pp. 27–57). John Wiley & Sons.

Kubiak, T. M., & Benbow, D. W. (2017). The Certified Six Sigma Black Belt Handbook (3rd ed.). Academic Press.

Lawton, P., & Jankowski, T. (2009). Investment Performance Measurement: Evaluating and Presenting Results. CFA Institute.

Lawton, P., & Jankowski, T. (2009). *Investment Performance Measurement: Evaluating and Presenting Results*. CFA Institute.

Lee, C. F., Lee, A. C., & Lee, J. (Eds.). (2010). Handbook of Quantitative Finance and Risk Management. Springer. doi:10.1007/978-0-387-77117-5

Li, S. (2003). Future trends and challenges of financial risk management in the digital economy. *Managerial Finance*, *29*(5/6), 111–125. doi:10.1108/03074350310768797

Li, W., & McMahan, P. (2015, December). A case study on loan loss analysis of a community bank. *The Journal of Finance and Data Science*, *1*(1), 11–32. doi:10.1016/j.jfds.2015.07.001

Lütkebohmert, E. (2009). *Concentration Risk in Credit Portfolios*. Springer.

Lyneis, J. M., & Ford, D. N. (2007). System Dynamics Applied to Project Management. System Dynamics Review, 23(2-3), 157–189.

Macaulay, F. R. (1938). *Some Theoretical Problems Suggested by the Movements of Interest Rates*. National Bureau of Economic Research.

Maginn, J. P. (2007). Managing Investment Portfolios: A Dynamic Process (3rd ed.). John Wiley & Sons.

Markowitz, H. M. (1952). Portfolio Selection. *The Journal of Finance*, *7*, 77–91.

Markowitz, H. M. (1987). *Mean-Variance Analysis in Portfolio Choice and Capital Markets*. Basil Blackwell.

Meier, J. P. (2009). Investment Performance Appraisal. In Investment Performance Measurement: Evaluating and Presenting Results. CFA Institute.

Merton, R. C. (1974). On the Pricing of Corporate Debt: The Risk Structure of Interest Rates. *The Journal of Finance*, *29*(2), 449–470.

Miller, F. P., Vandome, A. F., & McBrewster, J. (2011). Net Present Value. VDM Publishing.

Miller, K.D. (1992). A Framework for Integrated Risk Management in International Business. *Journal of International Business Studies*, *23*(2), 311–331.

Mitra, G., & Schwaiger, K. (2011). *Asset and Liability Management Handbook*. Palgrave Macmillan.

Mitra, G., & Schwaiger, K. (2011). *Asset and Liability Management Handbook*. Palgrave Macmillan. doi:10.1057/9780230307230

Montgomery, D. C. (2004). *Introduction to Statistical Quality Control*. John Wiley & Sons, Inc.

Neef, D. (2003). Strategy and Risk Management: An Integrated Practical Approach. Taylor & Francis Ltd.

Nersesian, R. L. (2011). *RISK Bank Credit and Financial Analysis* (2nd ed.). Palisade Corporation.

Packendorff, J. (1995). Inquiring into the temporary organization: New directions for project management research. *Scandinavian Journal of Management*, *11*(4), 319–333.

Panneman, T., & Stemann, D. (2021). Six Sigma DMAIC: 8 Simple Steps for Successful Green Belt Projects. Academic Press.

Personal RePEc Archive (MPRA). (2007). MPRA Paper No 5048.

Peterson, P. P., & Fabozzi, F. J. (2002). Capital Budgeting. Wiley.

Plantinga, A. (2007). Performance Measurement and Evaluation. Academic Press.

Plantinga, A. (2007). *Performance Measurement and Evaluation*. Munich Personal RePEc Archive (MPRA), MPRA Paper No 5048.

Plantinga, A. (2007). *Performance Measurement and Evaluation*.

Pyzdek, T., & Keller, P. A. (202)3. The Six Sigma Handbook, Sixth Edition: A Complete Guide for Green Belts, Black Belts, and Managers at All Levels. McGraw Hill.

Pyzdek, T., & Keller, P. A. (2023). The Six Sigma Handbook, Sixth Edition: A Complete Guide for Green Belts, Black Belts, and Managers at All Levels. McGraw Hill.

Rael, R. (2017). Managing Corporation Reputation and Risk: A Strategic Approach Using Knowledge Management. John Wiley & Sons.

Ramirez, J. (2017). *Liquidity Management: Handbook of Basel III Capital: Enhancing Bank Capital in Practice*. John Wiley & Sons.

Redington, F. M. (1952). *Review of the Principles of Life Office Valuations*. Academic Press.

Redington, F. M. (1952). Review of the Principles of Life Office Valuations. *Journal of the Institute of Actuaries, 78*(3), 286-340.

Revuz, D. (1984). *Markov Chains. North-Holland.*

Rossia, S. P. S., Schwaigerc, M. S., & Winklerd, G. (2009). How loan portfolio diversification affects risk, efficiency and capitalization: A managerial behaviour model for Austrian banks. *Journal of Banking & Finance, 33*(12), 2218–2226. doi:10.1016/j.jbankfin.2009.05.022

Rubinstein, R. Y., & Kroese, D. P. (2008). *Simulation and the Monte Carlo Method*. John Wiley & Sons.

Savant, S. (2018). DMAIC: Project Execution Essentials Handbook. Independent Publisher.

Seal, K. (2016). *Market Risk, International Monetary Fund*. In 2016 Seminar for Senior Bank Supervisors, Washington, DC. Retrieved from http://pubdocs. worldbank.org/en/253431477065134529/4-Minimum-Capital-Requirements- for-Market-Risk.pdf

Sekhar, C. (2016). Capital Budgeting Decisions: PBP, DPBP, ARR, NPV, PI, IRR & MIRR (Theory & interpretation Book 1). Academic Press.

Sekhar, C. (2018). *Capital Budgeting Decision Methods*. Independently Published.

Shapiro, A. C. (2004). Capital Budgeting and Investment Analysis. Pearson.

Sigma and Other Next-Generation Techniques. (2009). Wiley.

Singhal, P., Agarwal, G., & Mittal, M. L. (2011). Supply chain risk management: Review, classification, and future research directions. *International Journal of Business Science and Applied Management, 6*(3), 15–42.

Siviy, J. M., Penn, L. M., & Stoddard, R. W. (2007). *CMMI® and Six Sigma: Partners in Process Improvement*. Addison-Wesley Professional.

Skonieczny, M. (2012). The Basics of Understanding Financial Statements: Learn how to Read Financial Statements by Understanding the Balance Sheet, the Income Statement, and the Cash Flow Statement. Investment Publishing.

Slywotzky, A. (2003). The Art of Profitability. Grand Central Publishing.

SST. (2004). *White Paper of the Swiss Solvency Test*. Swiss Federal Office of Private Insurance.

Stamatis, D. H. (2003). *Six Sigma for Financial Professionals*. Wiley.

Stulz, R. M. (1996). Rethinking Risk Management. Journal of Applied Corporate Finance.

Tarantino, A., & Cernauskas, D. (2009). Risk Management in Finance: Six Sigma and Other Next-Generation Techniques. Wiley.

Tham, J., & Velez-Pareja, I. (2004). Principles of Cash Flow Valuation. Academic Press – Elsevier.

The Basel Committee. (1999). *Principles for the Management of Credit Risk*. The Basel Committee.

U.S. Congress Committee on Government Operations, 1982. Small Business Administration's variable interest rate. (1982). U.S. Government Printing Office.

Wahidudin, A. N. (2011). *Interest Rates in Financial Analysis and Valuation*. Bookboon.

Wilson, T. C. (1998). Portfolio Credit Risk. *Economic Policy Review*, *4*(3).

Winston, W. L. (2001). *Decision Models Using Simulation and Optimization II*. Palisade Corporation.

Zagst, R. (2013). *Interest-Rate Management*. Springer.

Ziemba, W. T., & Vickson, S. W. (Eds.). (2006). Stochastic Optimization Models in Finance. World Scientific.

Ziemba, W. T., & Vickson, S. W. (Eds.). (2006). *Stochastic Optimization Models in Finance*. World Scientific. doi:10.1142/6101

About the Author

Vojo Bubevski comes from Berovo, Macedonia where he completed his primary and secondary education. He has a Degree in Computer Science and Informatics from the University of Zagreb, Croatia in 1977. He started his professional career in 1978 as an Analyst Programmer at Alkaloid Pharmaceuticals in Skopje, Macedonia. At Alkaloid, he worked on applying Operations Research methods to solve commercial and technological pharmaceutical problems from 1982 to 1986. For these applications, he developed his software for optimisation including Linear and Non-Linear Programming, Dual Algorithm, and Integer Programming. In this period, he was a part-time lecturer at the "Koco Racin" Open University in Skopje, for which he, as a co-author, published a couple of textbooks. In 1987 Vojo immigrated to Australia. He worked for IBM™ Australia from 1988 to 1997. For the first five years, he worked in IBM™ Australia Programming Centre developing systems software. The rest of his IBM™ career was spent working in IBM™ Core Banking Solution Centre. In 1997, he immigrated to the United Kingdom where his IT consulting career started. As an IT consultant, Vojo worked for Lloyds Bank in London, Svenska Handelsbanken in Stockholm, and Legal & General Insurance in London. In June 2008, he was engaged as a Senior Consultant by TATA Consultancy Services Ltd. He is a specialist in Business Systems Analysis & Design (Banking & Insurance) and has delivered major business solutions across several organisations. He retired in May 2018. Vojo has a very strong background in Mathematics, Operations Research, Modelling and Simulation, Risk & Decision Analysis, Six Sigma, and Software Engineering, and a proven track record of delivering solutions applying these methodologies in practice. He has received several formal awards. Since 2007, he has been doing practical research in applications of Stochastic Risk & Decision Analysis. His work evolved and resulted in a novel stochastic Six Sigma DMAIC method for Risk Management. Vojo published many written works in eminent international conferences and journals, featured as a guest speaker at several prominent conferences internationally, and published one chapter and 13 books applying his method (Ref. ORCID: 0000-0002-7181-4445). The author's distinguished book "Six Sigma Improvements for Basel III and Solvency II in Financial Risk Management", including the Six Sigma DMAIC methods for Risk Management, is recognised and currently ranked 91 with 4.03 stars in the "100 Best Financial Risk Management Books of All Time" by the BookAuthority (Ref.). Bernstein stated, "The risk will always be there, so we must explore many interesting tools that can help us to control risks we cannot avoid taking" (Bernstein & Damodaran 1998). The author's Six Sigma DMAIC Methods are one such tool.

Index

Q

R

S

T

Milton Keynes UK
Ingram Content Group UK Ltd.
UKHW050756230424
441593UK00007B/302